DATE DUE

E·P·DUTTON & CO.INC.

1852 1952

CELEBRATING 100 YEARS OF PUBLISHING

THE GREAT RETREAT

N. S. TIMASHEFF *has also written*

PROBATION

OFFENSES AGAINST RELIGION

THE LAW OF SOVIET RUSSIA

OUTLINES OF THE CONSTITUTIONAL LAW
OF SOVIET RUSSIA

AN INTRODUCTION TO THE SOCIOLOGY OF LAW

ONE HUNDRED YEARS OF PROBATION, 1841–1941

RELIGION IN SOVIET RUSSIA

THE
GREAT RETREAT

THE
GROWTH AND DECLINE
OF COMMUNISM IN
RUSSIA

BY

NICHOLAS S. TIMASHEFF
ASSOCIATE PROFESSOR OF SOCIOLOGY
FORDHAM UNIVERSITY

NEW YORK

E. P. DUTTON & COMPANY, INC.

FOREWORD

THE PURPOSE of this book is to show the Communist Revolution in Russia and its aftermath in its correct historical perspective, and in this way to build a solid foundation for the discussion of Russo-American relations so important for the maintenance of peace. To achieve this purpose I have made a study of the main social and cultural trends in Russian life before and after the Revolution. Sources are abundant and diversified on pre-Revolutionary Russia. But material is less abundant and no longer so diversified regarding Russia after the Communist Revolution, since only official or State controlled publications are permitted to appear there. Material of this character forms the main source of my investigation, supplemented by reliable reports of foreign observers, and for the earlier period by personal observations and contacts with people of different social levels, so important for the understanding of the real functioning of a social system.

In this study I have emphasized the last stage of the development, characterized by "The Great Retreat" from purely Communist positions, which started in 1934. There is much less known about The Great Retreat than about the Great Communist Experiment which preceded it, but it deserves the greatest attention, since the Russia of our day—the one with which the United States must co-operate—cannot be understood without a knowledge of the scope and meaning of The Great Retreat.

N. S. TIMASHEFF

September 1, 1945.

ACKNOWLEDGMENTS

I WISH to express my gratitude to the following editors and directors for their kind permission to reprint parts of this book which have appeared in their magazines:

Rev. Ralph Gallagher: "Cultural Order in Liberal, Communist, and Fascist Society," and "Inter-ethnic relations in the USSR," in the *American Catholic Sociological Review;*

Joseph A. Brandt: "Vertical Social Mobility in Soviet Russia," in *The American Journal of Sociology,* published by the Chicago University Press.

Professor Walter B. Kennedy: "The Schneiderman Case," in *Fordham Law Review;*

Professor Alison Reppy: "The Crisis in the Marxian Theory of Law," in *New York University Law Quarterly Review;*

Professor Waldemar Gurian: "On the Russian Revolution," in *Review of Politics,* published by the University of Notre Dame, Indiana;

Professor Dimitri von Mohrenschildt: "Overcoming Illiteracy," in *The Russian Review;*

Selzo C. Mayo: "Structural Changes in Soviet Russia," and "The Population of the Soviet Union," in *Rural Sociology;*

Rev. Gerald G. Walsh: "The Soviet Constitution," "Revolution and Competition for Power," and "Four Phases of Russian Internationalism," in *Thought;*

Louis Minsky: for use of releases published by *Religious News Service.*

My gratitude is also acknowledged to Pioneer Publishers for permission to use material from Leo Trotzky's *Revolution Betrayed;* to Houghton-Mifflin Company—from John Scott's *Duel for Europe,* to International Publishers—from Lenin's *State and Revolution,* and Sheed and Ward—from the present writer's *Religion in Soviet Russia.*

I am greatly indebted to Professor M. Karpovich, of Harvard University, for many valuable suggestions relating to the Selected Bibliography. My indebtedness is also acknowledged to Jay Du Bois for her invaluable assistance in preparing the manuscript for publication.

N. S. TIMASHEFF

CONTENTS

LIST OF CHARTS

THE GREAT RETREAT

Chapter I

THE RUSSIAN MIRACLE:

A Preview

THE RUSSIAN REVOLUTION is one of the major events in the history of the twentieth century. It is one of the turning points not only in the history of Russia, but also in universal history. Its result—the creation of a Communist society in Russia—has become a challenge to the Western world, as an invitation to imitation, and at the same time as a threat of forcible transformation.

For many long years the threat of forcible transformation through the International Communist Revolution was in the foreground. Gradually the threat withered away, but the invitation to imitation gained strength. In the early 'thirties the devastating effects of the world crisis were often compared with the marvelous achievements of the Five-Year-Plans in Russia. The conclusion seemed to be evident: that to overcome the disastrous situation of "poverty in conditions of virtual plenty," Western society would have to abandon "the anarchy of capitalist production" and shift to the principle of "planned economy" so brilliantly applied in that unknown country in the East.

Then came war, with Hitler's onslaught on Russia, and the indomitable will to resist displayed by the Russian nation despite initial military catastrophes. The ability of the nation to transform defeat into victory, expel the invader, and make a magnificent contribution to the victory of the anti-Fascist coalition was clearly shown. If this were compared with the tragic collapse of France, the most powerful and typical "capitalist" nation of the European continent, this conclusion could be drawn: that the people did fight for the New Order as embodied in Communist Russia, whereas they did not fight for the

Old Order in France. Does this not prove that the New Order is superior to the Old?

This conclusion can easily be refuted. The Germans have also fought admirably for their New Order; but the British and the Americans have fought with valor for their Old Order, and the Italians have not fought at all for their variety of the New Order. This proves:

1. That the point at issue is not the contrast between the Old and New Order, but perhaps the contrast between the people's acceptance or rejection of the order under which they have to live;

2. That the character of the New Order is not a determining factor, since the difference between the Communist Order in Russia and the National Socialist Order in Germany has not prevented the two nations from fighting equally well.

Has it been proven conclusively, then, that the Russians have fought valiantly for the New Order embodying the Communist ideal? If this is actually so, then we are compelled to admit that a miracle has happened in Russia. The possibility of completely transforming a society according to a preconceived plan and attaining good results has always been denied by sociologists and historians, who could show numerous examples whereby such attempts were doomed to failure. But, contrary to expectations, the complete transformation of a great national body according to a blueprint formulated in another country seventy-five years ago does seem to have taken place, and endowed the people in question with the will to fight to the death in order to protect their new society.

A miracle, in the sense of a departure from well-established laws of the social process, must be recognized; in consequence, our body of knowledge concerning the social process must be substantially reworked, if no other explanation is possible. But is there none?

The idea is sometimes expressed that the Russians (as well as the Germans) have fought so well because they were ordered to do so, and the order could be enforced. This, however, is a preposterous idea; no totalitarian organization, no iron discipline, no unlimited repression or terrorism can compel people to fight for months and years if they do not want to do so.

Another explanation could be this: that the Communist ideal was not at all opposed to but, on the contrary, was in conformity with the historical trends of the development of Russia. Those who are inclined to such an interpretation point to two facts. First, on the eve of the Revolution the majority of the Russian people lived in agrarian communities, the famous *mirs,*° in which, they say, conspicuous elements of socialism were present.[1] Second, the central theme of Russian philosophy and literature is social justice. Consequently, they continue, the Communist transfiguration of Russia was in accordance with major manifestations of the Russian national spirit. [2] This is an appealing hypothesis, but there are imperative reasons for rejecting it.

First of all, the *mir* structure was not at all socialist, since within a *mir,* land was tilled individually, and the producer was free to dispose of the harvest. Moreover, the reluctance of the peasants to accept socialist patterns was so great that the Communists had to wait twelve years before launching the "collectivization of homesteads" according to their ideal, and they had to overcome resistance which cost Russia millions of human lives. Finally, the social justice aspect of Russian philosophy and literature was closely connected with the religious background of Russian culture which was rejected by Communism. Therefore, after the victory of Communism, Russian philosophy and literature had to be crushed because it was a serious obstacle to the planned transformation.

A third explanation is the Communist one: old Russia was a hopelessly backward country, and her development was checked by international capital which was interested in maintaining in Russia a market for its industrial output.† This ex-

---

° A description of the *mir* structure is given in Chapter II.

[1] All numbered references, arranged according to chapters, will be found on pages 419 to 442.

† This has not been the only Communist explanation of their success in Russia.

planation, as will be shown in the next chapter, is entirely contradicted by facts.

Here is the real explanation of the Russian miracle:

(1) Pre-Revolutionary Russia was a highly dynamic society rapidly advancing towards democracy, industrialization, and universal education, displaying a great creative spirit in many phases of culture.

(2) The Communist Revolution was a shock inflicted on this rapidly advancing body; as in every shock, it caused deviation and disturbance, in some phases of a magnitude comparable with that of a geological catastrophe.

(3) All the later events can best be understood as a conflict between the group embodying the revolutionary impulsion, and the forces of national tradition.

(4) The restoration of national tradition was well advanced when Russia became involved in the Second World War.

(5) Russia's magnificent resistance and glorious contribution to common victory is due to the situation just described. In other words, the New Order for which the Russians have fought so well is not at all a New Order embodying the Communist ideal, but to a large extent a New Order combining the revolutionary impulsion with the reviving national tradition, with emphasis on the latter.

The reader does not necessarily have to agree with the above statements. There value lies in the presentation of a hypothesis. To verify this hypothesis, the specific procedure of empiric science will be offered: facts will be presented and discussed; corollaries will be drawn from the hypothesis and compared with the facts.

The relevant facts are the answers to these questions:

1. What was pre-Revolutionary Russia?

2. What was the place of the Communists and their doctrine in the framework of that society?

3. How did it happen that the Communists became the heirs of the Tsars?

If, on the basis of these answers, our shock-hypothesis is preliminarily verified, the subsequent events must be compared with two sets of expectations. One follows the taking over of the government of a country by persons who embody the objective needs, historical trends, and popular aspirations of that country. The other follows the ascent to power by persons whose vision of things to come is independent of historical trends, and who have nothing but contempt for the national tradition.

In the first case, these expectations are natural:

1. On the basis of the community of views between the rulers and the governed, the political structure is likely to advance very rapidly towards democracy, not necessarily in one of the forms already known to the civilized world, but perhaps in a new form more congenial with the mode of life of the particular nation.

2. The policy of the government is likely to be determined by plans shared both by the rulers and the majority of the governed; therefore, the social process must receive the shape of smooth and steady advance towards the realization of the common goal. Minor fluctuations can take place, as shown by the examples of the periods of great reforms in democracies, such as the New Deal in the United States. This is unavoidable, since social reforms are always carried out by trial and error, implying the recognition of errors, their undoing, and new efforts according to somewhat modified plans.

Quite different must be the development in a society where power has been acquired by Utopians. Then the new rulers have to choose; they must either carry out their plans through coercion, or renounce the materialization of their dreams. Since they usually believe in their doctrine and the plan of social transformation derived from it as firmly as good Christians believe in Christ, they are inevitably obliged to choose dictatorship. Moreover, instead of gradual, step-by-step realization of the program, post-Revolutionary events must present the feature of a series of convulsions, abrupt changes of policies, and announcements of unparalleled victories, followed by the recognition of abysmal defeats and catastrophes.

Why is it so? The attempt to realize a preconceived plan of

social transfiguration necessarily meets obstacles, mainly created by the very efforts aiming at its realization. These obstacles are perceived by the rulers as "resistance," which may appear in different forms. The most drastic is active resistance, culminating in armed insurrection. Next comes passive resistance, manifested in mass attempts to evade the law, such as failure to pay taxes, perform a duty (military or labor service) or to send children to school. Finally, the obstacle may receive the most depressing form of impersonal resistance tantamount to social disintegration: people almost stop breeding children; farmers stop producing food beyond their personal requirements; factories stop producing even that which is indispensable for the survival of an industrialized society; schools stop communicating even the most elementary knowledge to the younger generation. All these things may happen without any conspiracy among the persons involved, and almost without deliberate actions on their part. They happen when the invisible ties between the component parts of a complex culture are broken by the attempts of Utopians to impose an impossible social order.

The nature and origin of trouble is not easily recognized by those in power: they are unable to concede that the real cause is their stubborn insistence on arbitrarily chosen goals. Therefore, perceiving difficulties, they first give new impetus to the policy conducive, they think, to the realization of their plans. In this way difficulties increase and accumulate. If, under these conditions, the rulers persist, the total social order breaks down, and they are eliminated through a revolution giving power to some other group no longer obsessed by Utopia—at least not by the same Utopia. Or perhaps the weakened social body becomes an easy prey for a conqueror; then Utopia is replaced by an order imposed from the outside.

But not always do they insist. Being in power almost inevitably teaches some lessons and, as concerns Utopians, imperceptibly changes their view of the situation. Being in power gives to those involved such gratification as social prestige, money or its equivalent in kind, the ability to command, and the pleasure of being obeyed. When difficulties accumulate Utopia is not rejected, but may be relegated to the second plane, and then the difficulties are interpreted as manifestations of ignorance and ingratitude on the part of those whom the rulers tried to make happy. The idea naturally emerges that they, the Utopians, are entitled to retain power although they are no longer able to realize their plan.

Consequently, it may happen that before it is too late, the Utopians in power might recognize the danger and decide to do the necessary; namely, to abandon, at least partly, their Utopia. Then they may preserve power and even the opportunity to cultivate some part of their Utopian garden. But the price is that of directing the nation towards a situation which would have obtained if their Utopia would not have interrupted the organic development. This is the reason why, sooner or later, in one way or another, every revolution led by Utopians must partly undo what it did, or give way to another revolution, or to foreign power.

There is another consequence of the ascent of Utopians to power. Since the distance between their program and the objective needs of the nation is different in the various fields of social and cultural life, the particular policies of the government meet insuperable resistance now here, then there. In consequence, while the trend must reverse in specified fields, elsewhere efforts to realize the blueprint can be continued. Thus, very often the direction of change in the different fields appears to be opposite. Hence the conspicuous character of convulsive movements following the rise of situations corresponding to our shock-hypothesis.

Political dictatorship, convulsive movements in the various fields of social and cultural life, and finally either total disintegration or partial revival of the past—these are the necessary consequences of a shock situation. In this work the attempt will be made to prove that these consequences have actually obtained in Russia after the Communist Revolution.

Relating to the political phase of life, not only must the question be studied as to whether dictatorship emerged in the course of the Revolution, but also the question arises as to whether it has persisted throughout the later years. Contrariwise, one could assert that, though the initial situation was of the shock type, later development brought correction either by subsequent acceptance of the plans of the new rulers by the nation, or by the complete conversion of the new rulers to principles ingrained in national tradition.

Next must come the study of the movements which took place in the various fields of social and cultural life. It must be shown that they have not been of the type of the smooth unfolding of a plan, similar to the organic growth of a plant from a seed, but really of the convulsion type described above. Naturally, it must be established what the correlation of the individual reversals was and in what conditions these reversals have taken place.

Two plans are possible for the conduct of such a study. The study can be either primarily chronological, or bear the character of a dissection, going through economic, cultural, demographic, and social developments. Both plans are logically correct, but it seems to this writer that, because of the character of Russia's development since 1917, the latter could yield clearer results. But since the developments in these particular fields have been closely interrelated, the following preview is perhaps permissible—to be substantiated later on by evidence gained in the course of the analytical study.

The development to be studied has been the history of a tragic conflict which began in those foggy days of November, 1917, when to the amazement of the believers in the invincibility of democracy, a democratic-minded government was overthrown by a *coup d'état* performed by an infinitesimal minority. It was aggravated during the years of Civil War and War Communism (1917–21) characterized by the ardent belief of the new leaders in the possibility of promptly reorganizing society on the basis of this plan, first of all by persuasion and example, but if necessary by force; by their direct attack on the foundations of Russian society and culture; and by the complete lack of political, administrative, or business experience on the part of those who had to carry out the program of social transformation. The conflict was somewhat mitigated during the period which entered history under the name of the New Economic Policy (NEP, 1921–29) in the course of which large parts of the social and economic reforms of the previous period were undone. The conflict was brought to a climax in the course of the Second Socialist Offensive (1929–34) * which was conducted by the new leaders with much greater vigor than the first one, on the basis of experience acquired in the course of twelve years in power position. In 1934, the offensive broke down and a period began for which the term "The Great Retreat" seems to fit best. This term will be used throughout this work, though it is personal to this writer and could not be found in any official source. In many cases, this last phase will be opposed to all the three preceding ones. In such cases, the term Communist Experiment will be used to designate the three phases as a whole characterized by the dominance of the belief in the forthcoming realization of the initial goal.

Once more, this is only a preview. With the reconstruction of the main fluctuations according to the four phases pattern, the last or synthetic part of this work can begin. It must also comprise a study of the scope and meaning of The Great Retreat which, for obvious reasons, must receive a much more detailed treatment than the three phases of the Communist Experiment, the formulation of a final balance sheet of the Communist Revolution, and a tentative outlook into Russia's future, derived from the interpretation given to her development in the course of the Communist period of her history.

* This phase is often called the period of the Five-Year-Plans. This term is, however, misleading and can be used only by those who have no idea of the tremendous reversal of the trend which occurred in 1934. For one who knows, the term is impossible, and the term, "Second Socialist Offensive" naturally emerges. This offensive coincided with the First Five-Year-Plan and the first half of the Second, whereas the second half of the Second Plan and the Third one belong to the phase of The Great Retreat.

CHAPTER II

PRE-REVOLUTIONARY RUSSIA:

A Dynamic View

1

IT IS THE generally accepted opinion that pre-Revolutionary Russia was a backward and stagnant nation. There are many people who share the view that the Imperial government was reactionary and did what it could to keep the people in a state of patrimonial allegiance to the Tsar and the landlords, and to prevent them from acquiring the culture of advanced nations; that this situation was an indignity, and the awareness of this indignity produced a revolutionary movement which, using the opportunity of a poorly conducted war, overthrew the established order. That when, after a short period of trouble, the Communists gained power, they found the molding of Russia left to their unfettered discretion; that everything was to be rebuilt anew, so they used this opportunity to create an order giving the Russian people access to modern culture—naturally, in the framework of Communist principles.[1]

Are such judgments corroborated by facts? Was, or was not Imperial Russia a backward and stagnant nation?

In order to make our case clear, we must first of all stress the distinction between backwardness and stagnation. When speaking of the backwardness of a person or a social group, we use as a yardstick the development of other persons or groups. An individual is backward if he has not reached the level expected from the members of his class and age group; even an all-inclusive society such as a nation is backward if in some relevant aspects its institutions and culture are on a level which, in other groups or societies, prevailed in the past, but was replaced by better institutions or kinds of culture.

When speaking of stagnation, we compare the development of a person or social group at two dates sufficiently remote from one another. If we do not notice any significant difference, we say that the person or group is stagnant; if substantial differences are observable, we deny stagnation and state that there has been substantial change.

It is obvious that the evaluations of a given society in terms of backwardness and stagnation are independent of one another: a society may be (1) backward and stagnant; (2) backward but progressing; (3) advanced but stagnant; (4) advanced and progressing. Most preliterate societies are both backward and stagnant. In the 'seventies and 'eighties of the nineteenth century, Japan was backward but rapidly progressing. Between the two World Wars, at least up to 1936, France was an advanced but conspicuously stagnant society. During the same period this country was both advanced and progressing, the last statement being independent of one's like or dislike of the specific features of the boom of the late 'twenties and the advent of the New Deal.

2

Let us now apply these general statements to pre-Revolutionary Russia. It is undeniable that in many aspects pre-Revolutionary Russia was a backward society, especially if compared with England, France, Scandinavia, or this country. Backwardness was especially noticeable in the political field, since it was only a few years before the breakdown of 1917 that Russia had abandoned the autocratic form of government and accepted a constitutional regime, whereas the nations mentioned had already surpassed the level of constitutional monarchy and become democracies (parliamentary monarchies or republics). The backwardness was also very noticeable in the socioeconomic field, since in Russia the capitalist method of production and its symptom, industrialization, were only beginning, and survivals of the pre-capitalist, or quasi-feudal organization were much more numerous and significant than survivals of feudalism in the countries with which we chose to compare her. The standard of life of Russian peasants was substantially lower than that of British or German farmers. And, when compared with conditions in England or Germany, the state of the labor class was lamentable; wages were low, working hours long, quarters poor; up to 1906, the right of association in trade-unions was denied them, as well as the right to use the weapon of strike.

Russia was an illiterate country, to what extent will be discussed below. Nevertheless, it would be wrong to term pre-Revolutionary Russia a culturally backward country without qualifying this statement. The upper level of Russian society received an education similar to that given in Western Universities and high schools, and the standard of culture production was high. Beginning with the last decades of the nineteenth century, the Russian novel, Russian music, and the Russian theater, especially the Russian ballet, deeply influenced Western European art production; in the field of painting, changes in "schools" were synchronous with those in France, then the leader in that particular field, and sometimes even preceded them.[2]

We have chosen to compare Russia with England, France, Scandinavia, and this country. But quite obviously during the last centuries, these countries have been the leaders of progress. Compared with them, not only Russia was backward, but also a good number of other European countries. Germany and Austria-Hungary belonged to the same type of constitutional monarchy as Russia, and today we know how superficial was the political democracy of Spain, Portugal, Italy, and the Balkan States. Survivals of the feudal order, especially in the matter of land-distribution, were at least as strong as in Russia, in Ostelbien (i.e., Germany east of the Elbe river), in large parts of Austria-Hungary (namely in those parts which later on formed Czechoslovakia and Hungary proper) and in Rumania.

As regards the standard of living, purely chronological comparisons are unfair. To judge correctly the state of the labor class in Russia late in the nineteenth century, one should rather compare it with that in England in the early nineteenth century, when capitalism was in the state of infancy in that country. Any one who has read Engels' famous book [3] will hardly assert that the Russian government and the Russian industrialists oppressed the labor class more than their British counterparts.

Russia was an illiterate country, but also illiterate were the populations of Portugal,[4] large parts of Spain, southern Italy, the eastern part of the Austro-Hungarian monarchy, and the Balkan States. In any case, Russia was only one of the members of a respectable company of "backward European nations."

What were the causes of this backwardness? It is usual to link it with the reactionary character of the Imperial Government which, it is taken for granted, opposed any kind of progress. On the other hand, there are social philosophers who ascribe Russia's backwardness to the specific character of her national spirit—the laziness of "the Slavic soul."

The second explanation is actually no explanation at all: to explain something by the "national spirit" is simply to make the trivial statement that major trends in the life of nations depend at least partly on their history, which actually shapes and reshapes what is called "the national spirit."

As regards the first explanation, the following facts should be considered. On the eve of her history (especially in the first half of the eleventh century) Russia was a comparatively advanced country, due to her close connection with Byzantium, then the bearer of civilization.[5] But because of her geographical position, Russia had to be the bulwark of the European civilization against Asiatic nomads. In the middle of the thirteenth century, Russia was conquered by the Tartars and was dominated by them for two-and-a-half centuries. In contradistinction to the Arabs who conquered Spain, and who at about the time of the conquest belonged to the leaders of progress, the Tartars were barbarians, and their influence on Russia was purely negative. After the yoke had been broken (1480) a century more was needed for the reconquest of the Eastern part of the Russian plain. Thus, three-and-a-half centuries were lost for normal advance. Then a rapid "progressive" movement started; the advance became exceptionally quick under the reign of Peter the Great. During the eighteenth century and the first quarter of the nineteenth century, this advance was mainly the work of the autocracy which only later on, and then with interruptions, became an instrument of conservatism, sometimes of reaction. The impulse given by the court was closely followed by the upper level of Russian society, and much less by the other strata; later on this proved to be a source of great difficulty.

Summing up, it may be said that the backwardness of Russia, which was undeniable when Russia was compared with the most advanced nations, was not due to the intentional actions of the government or of the upper classes, but could very well be explained in terms of special conditions under which the Russian nation had to develop.

3

Let us now examine the idea that pre-Revolutionary Russia was a stagnant society, and divide this examination into three parts, paying successive attention to the political, socioeconomic, and cultural aspects of the total situation.

Regarding the political aspect, the examination can be carried out by comparing the political structure of Russia on the eve of the nineteenth century and immediately before the outbreak of World War I. On the eve of the nineteenth century, Russia was an autocracy of the unlimited type, or a despoty. In such circumstances, everything depended on the personality of the monarch: the despoty was "enlightened" under Catherine the Great (1762–1796) and malevolent under Paul (1796–1801).

The beginning of the nineteenth century was characterized

by the first period of "Great Reforms"; under Alexander I (1801–1825) a State Council was created which had to deliberate about drafted statutes; it was composed of the highest dignitaries of the Empire, appointed for life by the Emperor, and its decisions did not bind him. But through its creation the idea of the impersonal rule of law was introduced in Russia, the law meaning the body of rules approved by the Council and ratified by the Emperor. Twice during the reign the idea of granting Russia a Constitution based on elected bodies was considered; it could not be actualized so long as the largest class of the subjects of the Emperor, the peasants, were still in a state of serfdom.

A second period of Great Reforms took place under Alexander II (1856–1881). After the liberation of serfs (1861) a new system of judicial courts was created in which the English and French patterns were merged (1864). Elected justices of peace had to try the minor cases, both civil and criminal; trial by jury was introduced for major criminal cases; a Supreme Court, with the functions of the French *cour de cassation*, was placed at the top of the system. All judges above the level of the justices of peace began to be appointed for life and were granted independence of the wishes and suggestions of the Executive. This reform was a marked success, as well as the introduction of self-government in rural districts, towns, and provinces (1864–1870). Very fortunately for Russia, the large majority of persons elected justices of peace or members of the executive boards of the agencies of self-government (*Zemstovs*) were imbued with the spirit of social service, and not with that of group or class interest. After these reforms, the Russian autocracy ceased to be a despoty: in the large and important spheres of activity of the judicial courts and self-governmental bodies, decisions and actions no longer depended on the mood of the monarch.

Once more a Constitution based on the co-operation of elected bodies with the government was envisaged, and once more the idea was not realized, this time because Emperor Alexander II was killed by revolutionists (who hated the prospect of peaceful advancement) the very day he had signed a manifesto on the Constitution.

A third period of Great Reforms marked the second half of the reign of Emperor Nicholas II. Under the pressure of defeat by Japan, the Russian autocracy was forced to abdicate. This time a Chamber of Representatives (the State Duma) was created (1905–6) and no law could any longer be enacted without the consent of this body. Russia had not become a democracy: the franchise at the elections of the Duma was restricted and unequal, and the Emperor retained the right of veto. The new structure did not function smoothly, but the decisive, the most difficult step towards democracy was made, and a further advance, through expanded franchise and gradual approximation to the type of parliamentary monarchy seemed probable. Under the impact of the Constitutional Reform, the administrative system substantially improved. A new spirit was inculcated into quite a few governmental activities, especially those dealing with the agrarian reform; perhaps it was the same beneficial spirit of social service which had first appeared in the 'sixties of the nineteenth century.

In any case, the distance covered by Russia between 1801 and 1914 on the road of political development was a long one. There was significant advance, and not stagnation. Perhaps some more could have been and ought to have been achieved. But the events of 1917 have given experimental proof of the fact that Russia was not yet ready to become a democracy— overnight.

Socioeconomic advance began later than political advance, but proceeded with much greater velocity. The impulse was given by the liberation of serfs (1861). In contrast with what happened in other European countries, in Russia the liberated serfs, now free peasants, received not only personal freedom, but also a large part of the land which they had tilled under the landlord. They had to pay for this land, but the State immediately compensated the landlords, and the peasants had to pay the State in installments. These payments might have been too high. In 1906 the peasants were liberated from paying the balance. In opposition to ideas spread outside of Russia,[6] no juridical bonds whatsoever remained between the peasants and their former landlords.

It proves how wrong the frequently recurring assumption is that not until the Russian Revolution of 1917 had land been given to Russian peasants.[7] Already at the time of the Emancipation, they had received more than half of the arable soil of European Russia, namely 148 million hectares (*vs.* 89 million which remained the property of the landlords, and eight million which were the property of the State).

Half a century later, on the eve of World War I, the situation was quite different. Only 44 million hectares were still the property of landlords; the rest, as well as about six million hectares of State lands, had been bought by peasants. In 1916, the peasants owned 80 per cent of the arable soil of European Russia and rented from the owners half of the residue.[8]

The process of liquidating large estates took place with the help of the government, which in the years of 1882 and 1885 created special banks for that purpose. The speed of the process increased with every decade. During the last decade before World War I, the peasants' possessions expanded nearly as much as in all the preceding forty years. Twenty years more of peaceful development with the same trend, and the landlords in Russia might have become only a historical reminiscence.

Unfortunately, the Act of Emancipation did not give land, as individual property, to peasant families, but made it the property of agrarian communities, the so-called *mir*, composed of groups of homesteads.[9] This land was divided and, after a certain number of years, redistributed among the homesteads; every homestead received a portion of every field or of every subdivision of the field; land was allotted to the separate homesteads in the ratio of the number of family members or, in certain parts of Russia, of adult male workers in the homesteads. For the corresponding period the allotments had to be cultivated individually; but almost everywhere local custom imposed upon the homesteads the obligation of allowing the cattle of the village to be pastured on fallow ground until late in the summer; a definite rotation of crops was also imposed by the *mir*.

This structure was a very unfortunate one. On the one hand, it inhibited advance in agricultural technique. Could a peasant be expected to invest money, or even his labor, in land which by the next redistribution might be assigned to another homestead? Only improvements effected collectively, by the total community, were economically possible. But how could one persuade a community to depart from the ways of its fathers and forefathers, since it is the very nature of a community to maintain and enforce such ways?

On the other hand, since the size of the allotment granted to an individual homestead depended on the size of the family, it was economically advantageous to breed large families. It was well known in rural Russia that larger homesteads used to do better than small ones, even if both tilled the same number of acres *per capita*.

Thus, the structure favored an unlimited increase of the rural population without providing for additional means of subsistence. Moreover, the psychological effects of the *mir* structure should not be disregarded: having no land of their own, the Russian peasants could not develop that strong respect for property which characterizes Western farmers and makes (or at least made) them the foundation of social stability.

However, near the end of the period studied, the relation of peasants to their land was substantially changed. A provisional law of November 9, 1906—which on June 10, 1910, and May 29, 1911, was replaced by definitive ones—allowed the peasants to separate their allotments from the agrarian communities. They could become private owners of the allotments which they possessed in the common fields and, if they wished, have their portions united into one allotment and their houses and stalls rebuilt there with governmental help. This was the famous Stolypin °
reform which, once peacefully carried out, would have been

° Prime-Minister, 1906–1911.

one of the greatest agrarian revolutions known to history. The peasants seemed to have been won over by the sound doctrine that only increased production by means of improved tech-nique could help them, and that this was feasible only without agrarian communities. On January 1, 1916, 6.2 million home-steads (out of the total number of approximately 16 million) had made application to become separated in the near future.[10] Had the movement continued with the same speed, agrarian communities would no longer have existed by the year 1935.

Naturally, the reform was not a panacea. First of all, for many parts of Russia it came too late and was no longer suffi-cient. Secondly, using the opportunities of the Stolypin laws was an excellent solution of the problem for the rich and well-to-do peasants, but the poor ones lost even the possibility of survival on their dwarf farms after their more fortunate neigh-bors had forsaken the community. The chief trouble was that the fallow grounds at their disposal were no longer large enough for pasturing their cattle. Their homesteads would have to dis-appear, and they had either to go to the cities, where industry was rapidly advancing, or to be resettled on free land in the Asiatic part of the Empire.

Stolypin explicitly recognized that his program aimed at the stabilization of Russian society on the firm foundation of well-to-do farmers. To accelerate the migration movement to-wards Siberia, a large program of land reclamation was started there simultaneously with the agrarian reform.

Despite the handicaps inherent in the *mir* structure, which only began to be overcome when the First World War broke out, economic progress in the Russian countryside was undeni-able. From 1900 to 1913, the area sown with cereals increased by 8%. The use of fertilizers jumped from 0.2 million tons in 1908, to 0.5 million in 1913. Between 1896 and 1913, the net harvest increased by 38%.[11] There was also a substantial increase in cattle; the number of horses increased from 25.6 million in 1895, to 35.8 in 1916, and that of horned cattle from 31.6 mil-lion in 1895, to 60.6 million in 1916.[12]

No less important was the progress of industry. Witte and

Mendeleyev, a Minister of Finance (1893–1903) and a great scientist, understood that the future of Russia rested in a reasonable exploitation of the tremendous industrial possibilities of the country. Under the impulse of a well-conceived governmental policy, the number of industrial workers doubled from 1890 to 1913 (from one-and-a-half million to three million) and the production of large-scale industry increased four times (from one-and-a-half billion rubles to six billion). Especially important was the increase in the production of producers' goods. From 1888 to 1913, the output of coal increased from 5.3 to 29 million tons, or five-and-a-half times; that of cast iron from 0.7 to 4 million tons, or also five-and-a-half times; that of oil from 3.2 to 9 million tons, or 2.8 times. One might be tempted to explain these high indexes of increase by the exiguity of the absolute figures: when industry is in the age of infancy, the relative figures are always high. However, one would be wrong, since from 1863 to 1888, i.e., for an equal period of time as that just discussed, the output of cast iron had only doubled.[13]

The progress was spread through all the branches of industry. From 1910 to 1914, the output of the machine building plants doubled. The number of spindles operated by cotton mills increased from three-and-a-half million in 1890 to nine-and-a-quarter million in 1913; correspondingly, in 1913 Russia consumed three times as much raw cotton as in 1890. From 1890 to 1913, sugar production increased four times; from 1895 to 1910, the sugar consumption *per capita* increased by 120%.[14]

The obvious conclusion is that around 1890 a very important change took place in the economic structure and mentality of Russia: she ceased to consider herself as a purely agricultural nation and resolutely entered a period of industrialization.

If we acknowledge this to be true, we must stop expressing indignation about the lamentable conditions of the Russian labor class; instead we must give consideration to the fact that as early as the 'eighties, a protective labor legislation limiting the labor day, especially of women and children, and prohibiting female night work was enacted; that in 1906, strikes ceased to be a punishable offense; that in 1912, two decades earlier than in this country, the scheme of social security was inaugurated in Russia covering, in the beginning, the risks involved in industrial accidents and sickness.[15] Throughout the years of industrial advance, the labor day was shortened, wages increased, and the standard of living slowly but steadily improved.[16]

An additional symptom of economic advance is to be found in the development of the railways. The first line was built in Russia in 1837. But before the liberation of the serfs the progress was slow (1,400 miles in 1861). Later on, the velocity of the process became quite remarkable. The greatest achievement was the construction, in 1891–1905, of the Trans-Siberian railway (4,000 miles). In 1900, Russia possessed 36,000 miles of railways, and 49,000 on the eve of World War I. In this regard her place was second only to that of this country.

A very careful study of the movement of national income in Russia carried out by Professor S. N. Prokopowicz (a socialist, and therefore a person hardly inclined to overestimate the achievements of Imperial Russia), yielded the information that it jumped from 6.6 billion rubles in 1900 to 11.8 billion in 1913, an increase of 79.4%. Since the price index in 1913 was higher than in 1900, a net increase of 39.4% is left. The population having increased by 19.1%, the final result is that in the course of 13 years, the real *per capita* income increased by 17.1%, an achievement not often surpassed in the economic development of nations.[17]

Summarily, it may be said that only a deliberate distortion of facts or crass ignorance would permit one to speak of economic stagnation in pre-Revolutionary Russia.

The liberation of the serfs, the processes studied above relating to agriculture, the start of industrialization, and the expansion of railways gave tremendous impetus to the Russian nation, which responded by an extraordinarily rapid increase in population. The total population of Russia increased from 70 million at the time of the liberation of serfs, to 127 million in 1897 (date of the First Census) and to 167 million at the outbreak of World War I.[18] The average increase in population, without any immigration, was 16 per thousand a year, a ratio almost without precedent in a great country over a long period. In many cities the number of inhabitants increased four times or even more during half a century. The speed of the development was comparable with that of this country.

In regard to the intellectual phase of social life, up to the liberation of serfs and the creation of local self-government, the masses remained in a state of crass ignorance. Then, under the impulse of the liberal reforms of Emperor Alexander II, especially through the activity of the *Zemstvos,* a system of public education arose in Russia which progressed with increasing speed up to the outbreak of the First World War, and by that time had granted literacy to a large part of the younger generation. A law of May 3, 1908,[19] proclaimed the principle of making public education available to all children of the nation. A complicated system of State subsidies to the local bodies was introduced with the aim of creating an adequate school system in ten years. In the course of three years a number of *Zemstvos* carried out a third part of the program: erecting new buildings, repairing old ones, improving equipment, and raising the salaries of the teachers.[20] If the peaceful development had continued, from 1920 on all Russian children of school age would have had access to the primary school.

This statement so completely contradicts the common ideas about the state of public education in pre-Revolutionary Russia that they ought to be confirmed by figures. In 1880, the population of Russia was 98 million, and the number of pupils in elementary schools 1,141,000, or 1.16% of the total population. In 1915, the population of Russia was 165 million, and the number of pupils 8,147,000, or 4.93%.*

The figures are conclusive; the school population increased much quicker than the total population, as reflected in the fact that, in the course of thirty-five years, the index of education increased 4.2 times. This is an objective proof of the efforts made by Imperial Russia for the advance of popular education.

* For more details, see Table 6 in Appendix II.

What have been the results of these efforts? In this respect, reliable data may be found in the census of 1897.

Out of 90.3 million inhabitants above the age of ten, 25.8 million, or 27.8% were literate. Naturally, there were high differentials between men and women; between towns and the countryside; between the population of Russia proper, of the more advanced western provinces with a population of non-Russian origin, and the semicolonial territories (Caucasus, Siberia, Central Asia). In 1897, 38.5% of the men and 17.5% of the women were literate; likewise, 54% of the urban vs. 23% of the rural population; 89.5% of the population of the Baltic provinces, 41.2% of the population of the Polish provinces, 26.8% of the population of Russia proper, and only 13.3% of the population of the semicolonial territories.* Highly important, for our purposes, is the distribution of literacy among the age groups. In 1897, 34% of the Russians between the ages of 10 and 20 were literate. For the age groups 30 to 40, 50 to 60, and over 60, the percentages were respectively 27%, 19%, and 13%.

The meaning of these figures is clear: the younger the people, the greater was their literacy. In other words chronologically the later a group of Russian people reached school age, the greater was their chance of being given education.

What were the results of the educational efforts about 1914, on the eve of the First World War and the Revolution? Since, after 1897, no census was taken in Imperial Russia, no direct evidence is available. However, it is possible to make an estimate which yields the index of literacy as 40.2% for 1914.[21]

The progress of literacy may also be seen from these facts: Among army recruits (young men of 21) 21.4% were literate in 1874, 37.8% in 1894, 55.5% in 1904, and 67.8% in 1914. A census of industrial workers taken in 1918 showed that the index of literacy of workers between 14 and 20 years of age was 77.1%, while among those between 30 and 35, the index was 64.8%, and among those older than 50 it was 43.4%.[22]

---

* When comparing the state of education in Russia with that in Western countries, one must not forget that Russia contains a number of peoples whose cultural development corresponds to that of the population of the colonies of the Western powers.

The advance between 1897 and 1914 appears to have been remarkable, but the goal of overcoming illiteracy was still far ahead. It was very difficult to reach it because of the rapid increase of the population. Every year the agencies of public education substantially increased the number of pupils in elementary schools; but for many years (namely, 1898–1908) this increase was almost exactly equal to the increase of the number of children of school age, so that the absolute number of children who were not granted access to schooling remained unchanged.

Cultural advance was not limited to elementary education. From 1894 to 1914, the number of pupils in secondary schools increased from 225,000 to 820,000, and the number of students in universities and other institutions for higher education from 15,000 to 80,000.[23]

Once more, then, it can be noted: there was no cultural stagnation in pre-Revolutionary Russia, since the nation very rapidly advanced towards the goal of "universal elementary education," and at the same time made great efforts to promote secondary and higher education.

In the realm of art, the early twentieth century was most brilliant. This was a period when the best poems of A. Block appeared, the Russian poet commonly held second only to Pushkin; when the philosophically and religiously minded Merezhkovsky was contrasted with Gorki, the prophet of the coming revolution; when the magnificent circle *Mir Iskusstva* (The World of Art) brought Russian painting to its climax; when the Russian theater blossomed, headed by Stanislavski, the realist, and Meyerhold, the formalist; when the Russian ballet was unsurpassed; when Scriabin, Stravinsky, and Prokofieff showed new ways to music. These were the years when, through the vision and energy of Diaghilev, Russian art, especially music and ballet, made their appearance in Western Europe, were accepted as a revelation, and gained eminence. If this was stagnation, then what should a nation achieve to be dynamic?

4

On the basis of the evidence produced in the preceding section, one may safely assert that the Russian Revolution could not have been caused by stagnation since, in pre-Revolutionary Russia, there was nothing of the kind. In politics, economics, and culture pre-Revolutionary Russia was a rapidly advancing nation displaying tremendous efforts to overcome the retardation imposed on it by a chain of unfavorable historical circumstances. Change took place in the same direction as in more advanced Western societies, the institutions and techniques of which were often regarded by the Russians as ideals to be imitated, often on the basis of an erroneous, too optimistic interpretation of their significance and impact on human life.

Was everything, then, bright and promising in pre-Revolutionary Russia? Of course not. Advance took place in all major fields of social and cultural life, but so much was to be done that numerous remnants of the dark past continued to exist. Among the most conspicuous were the persecution of certain groups of religious dissenters, substantially mitigated in 1905, and the persecution of some national minorities, very unfortunately aggravated at the beginning of the 'eighties in the nineteenth century, when the policy of Russification superseded the earlier "Imperial" policy, or the tendency to treat all the ethnic groups of Russia as equal partners in the great cooperative effort of building up an Empire.[24]

Moreover, the rapid advance accumulated difficulties because it was unequally distributed, and such inequalities always produce social tensions analogous to those which originated in a mechanical system of weight united by elastic ties —if you move part of the weights to the capacity extension of the ties, other ones only a little, and the residue not at all. What were these tensions?

A tension was created by the discrepancy between the rapid increase of the rural population and the slow advance of agricultural technique. The agrarian problem, ingrained in the very nature of the *mir* structure, was a very serious one: on the eve of the twentieth century, there existed in the heart of Russia regions characterized by relative agrarian overpopulation, and a large percentage of peasants in these areas experienced a decrease in food supply, despite the improvement of the economic conditions in the countryside as a whole. As often happens, the objective situation was wrongly rationalized by those concerned. It was interpreted by peasants in terms of social injustice personified in the very existence of landlords. The confused doctrine that land was God's and should belong to those who tilled it appeared and formed the background for agrarian unrest and riots. Today we know that this reflection of objective facts was quite wrong: the wholesale redistribution of land under the Communist Revolution was not and could not have been of any good to peasants; the only way out of their difficulties was the improvement of technique, and one of the possible premises for such an improvement was created by the Stolypin agrarian reform. Despite all its shortcomings, it can be asserted that the first and basic tension in pre-Revolutionary Russia decreased during the last decade before the Revolution.

Another tension was created by the disharmony between the relatively slow and intermittent advance in political forms and the very quick advance in economic and cultural fields. The growth of industry was accomplished by the rise of a liberal bourgeoisie and of a turbulent proletariat. The growth of education resulted in the rise of a numerous *intelligentsia*—a special Russian term, now adopted also in English, to designate a group of intellectual workers considering it their duty to struggle for far-reaching social and political reforms. This discrepancy was the root of the revolutionary movement which persisted in Russia in the course of the last fifty years before the collapse of 1917, and was more or less openly supported by many liberals who, in the threat of a revolution, saw an excellent means to extort concessions from the government.

The conflict between the government and the rising social forces was a dangerous one. However, the difficulty was not insuperable, and early in the twentieth century began to decrease. It was the Constitutional Reform which mainly contributed to the mitigation of the tension; important groups among the bourgeoisie and the intellectuals considered that, after that reform, the revolutionary movement should no longer be supported.

The third tension was the result of the discrepancy between the rapid advance of education among the higher strata of Russian society, under the impulsion of the Petrinian reform, and the retardation of the advance of the lower strata, in conditions already studied. This discrepancy resulted in an estrangement between the cultural élite and the "people." This estrangement was a serious and dangerous problem, especially in a society where the additional tensions studied above were present. But, since the tension was largely due to the low cultural level of the masses, the rapid advance of education promised to put an end to this situation; but a certain lapse of time was still necessary for it.

Thus, all the important social tensions were on the decline at the beginning of the twentieth century, owing to the Constitutional Reform of 1905–6, the Stolypin agrarian reform, the laws on social security, and the rapid advance of education and industrialization which opened up new horizons to large groups of the population. This general line of development was well expressed in the curve of the revolutionary movement. This movement reached its first apex in 1881, when Emperor Alexander II, the liberator of serfs, was murdered. The second apex coincided with the Japanese war and resulted in the Constitutional Reform. The later years were characterized by a steady decline in the number of revolutionary acts and in governmental reprisals.*

On the basis of evidence so far produced, the following diagnosis of pre-Revolutionary Russia seems to be correct: pre-Revolutionary Russia was a backward but highly dynamic

---

* Before the revolution of 1905–6, the average number of capital executions in Russia (where only political offenses were punishable by death) was 15 per year.

society. Her dynamism was mainly caused by the apprehension of her backwardness and the desire to overcome it. This dynamism was disharmonious and produced dangerous social tensions. But since the beginning of the century, these tensions decreased. Pre-Revolutionary Russia needed a few decades more of peace to be transformed into a society no longer conspicuously backward as compared with the West, and no longer endowed with dangerous tensions.[25] Russia was well on the way towards entering the family of nations enjoying the advantages of modern civilization. Consequently, the Communist experiment to which she was submitted after 1917 could not have the significance of an introduction into that family, as assumed by those who wrongly think of pre-Revolutionary Russia as a hopeless wilderness.

Chapter III

THE COMMUNIST PARTY:

A Dark Horse

1

In the picture of pre-Revolutionary Russia just outlined, those to whom the role of Russia's rulers was assigned after the breakdown of the old order were not even mentioned by name. This is not an accidental omission: in pre-Revolutionary Russia the role of the Communists, who then were called Bolsheviks, was infinitesimal.

However, it is easy to locate them in the general picture. They formed a party of the Revolutionary Movement which, in its totality, was a substantial social force declining in its importance after the Constitutional Reform of 1905–6, and characterized by strong dissensions in its midst.

These dissensions did not prevent the movement from being unified in one significant aspect: it was mainly socialist, laying stress on the establishment of a new social order, and considering political change merely as a means towards the end of social revolution.[1] But right here the agreement stopped. As early as the 'eighties of the nineteenth century, the Russian socialists were divided into two main camps continuing two famous lines of Russian thought: the Slavophiles and the Westerners.[2]

Continuing the trend of the Slavophiles the Populists, later on called Socialist-Revolutionists, asserted that Russia ought to progress according to her own ways, different from those of Western Europe; particularly, that Russia could attain the happiness of Socialism without passing through the degradation of Capitalism. This was possible because of the predominantly agrarian character of the nation, and because of the preserva-

41

tion of the *mir* structure in which they perceived the elements of socialism already present. Their goal was a kind of agrarian socialism under which there would be neither landlords nor farmers, but only members of the All-Russian Commune, periodically redistributing land among those tilling it, in accordance with their needs and working capacity.

The Populists were opposed by the Social-Democrats, or socialists of the Marxian trend. They appeared in Russia in the 'eighties of the nineteenth century, as part of the great movement to import ideas from the West. They asserted that there were iron laws of social development applicable to every country, including Russia. These laws were derived by them from the famous "economic interpretation of history," the quintessence of Marxism. According to Marx, men enter into relations of production independent of their will, and the social organization of production forms the foundation of every society, whereas everything else—religion, philosophy, political organization, law, literature, art, and so on—forms a superstructure which is entirely determined by the substructure. Marx sometimes qualified this statement, admitting a secondary influence of the superstructure, or ideas, on the substructure, or economic organization, but such mitigations were usually neglected by his followers.

How does the economic substructure change? It changes by inner necessity, according to the dialectical scheme borrowed by Marx from Hegel. Everything first appears in a positive form (affirmation, thesis) then gradually evolves to negation (antithesis) and finally reaches the stage of a harmonious merger of the opposites (synthesis). Applied to the historical process as understood by Marx, the scheme yields the following interpretation: at certain stages of their evolution, men enter such relations of production which are favorable to production and the development of productive forces; this organization displays the tendency to persist despite changes in economic conditions (new inventions, the discovery of new markets, and the like); gradually the existing organization becomes a hindrance; this is the stage of negation. Every nega-

tion must be overcome and actually is overcome through a
revolution, which means the creation of a new order; this is
the synthesis. As a corollary of the propositions above, the
Marxists assume that in every society there are two, and only
two basic classes: one composed of persons interested in the
maintenance of the traditional order, and another interested in
its change. Struggle between the two is inevitable and forms
the essence of history. For Marxists, every historical study has
to explain what, during a certain period, were the classes opposed to each other, and what were the forms of their struggle.
There can be intermediary groups, but Marxist analysis always
permits their distribution among the two basic classes.

This general philosophy of history is applied by the Marxists
to the analysis of capitalist society. This society was built by
the bourgeoisie which in the preceding, feudal society represented the progressive class. In the beginning, capitalism was
the best possible organization of production, but gradually
the situation changed, and the bourgeoisie began to represent
the historical, already detrimental order of production, in opposition to the proletariat representing the future. The an-
tagonism of capital and labor under capitalism cannot be overcome by any means, since the interests of the two classes are
diametrically opposed. Capitalism has become universal and
international; the labor class must follow suit; hence the famous
slogan, "proletarians of all countries unite." To a German
worker, an English worker is closer than a German capitalist,
and to a British worker, a German worker is a brother, and a
British capitalist a foe. National antagonisms which distort
these basic relations are provoked and fostered by the bourgeoisie in order to conceal the natural community of interests
of workers throughout the world.

Advanced capitalism corresponds to the negative stage in
the capitalist cycle; it is manifested in the concentration of capital in the hands of a few and in the correlated impoverishment
of the masses. When both processes reach a certain point, "the
knell of the private capitalist property will be sounded," and
the expropriators will be expropriated. A new, classless so-

ciety will emerge. This will be the manifestation of the providential role of the proletariat. Its victory will mean the beginning of real history, a jump from the realm of necessity into that of liberty.

The Marxists were rather reticent about the structure of the new society they promised to establish. The fathers of Marxism explained their attitude in this way: that the new culture will be based upon an entirely new economic foundation, the productive system of classless society. So long as it has not yet been born, it is impossible to foresee the particular aspects of the new superstructure, for the ideas of men living in the new social order will be produced by that order.

However, a few guesses were made. In socialist society the means of production will belong to the collectivity; in consequence there will be no class division of society and no class struggle. The distribution of goods will take place, to begin with, according to the services rendered by the individuals to the collectivity, and later on, when plenty of goods are produced, according to one's needs.* The State being, in Communist doctrine, merely the organization of class dominance in class society, the transition to classless society means the beginning of the withering away of the State with all its attributes: no standing army, no bureaucracy, no courts of justice or prisons are expected to exist in the society of the future. However, for a transitional period, a specific political order called "the dictatorship of the proletariat" is foreseen. Together with the State, such "bourgeois" institutions as the Church and the family must go; in the society of the future, men will be free of "religious prejudice" and of the rigid bonds of bourgeois marriage molded, as the Communists hold, on the image of property.[3]

This complicated theory was accepted by the Russian Marxists without qualification. Applying it to the Russian condi-

---

* In Marx's terminology, the first stage is called Socialism and the second Communism. This terminology has been the source of great confusion, since later on, in Western Europe and America, the terms Socialism and Communism started being used to designate two trends within Marxism, approximately corresponding to Russian Menshevism and Bolshevism.

tions, they formulated the idea that Russia, as every country, had to pass from the feudal stage (which, in their opinion, was the state of Russia in their time) through the stage of capitalism, to the final stage of socialism. At first only a small minority among the Revolutionary Movement, they gained more and more followers since events seemed to verify their interpretation; the accelerated industrialization of the 'nineties and the rapid differentiation among the Russian peasants, despite the *mir* structure, were their chief arguments. They did not believe in the *mir* as a precursor of socialism, and assumed that the Russian peasant class had to go through the same process of proletarianization as in the older countries.

Anyone familiar with Russian literature of the late nineteenth and early twentieth centuries,[4] and the type of Russian political discussions of the time, is well aware of the fact that the focus of interest included the two expectations—that of the Populists and that of the Marxists. The Populists thought that it was an indignity to advocate or even applaud the advance of capitalism in Russia—which was what the Marxists did— and declared that the indignity of capitalism could be avoided. The Marxists laughed at the dilettantist predictions of their opponents and asserted that science—was not Marxism scientific socialism?—was on their side. Capitalism was an indignity, but an unavoidable one, and the only gateway to the paradise of socialism. To encourage capitalism signified the acceleration of the advent of socialism. The bourgeois had to do the dirty work, and then bow out. When? Nobody could tell exactly, but in the Marxist discussions decades—many decades—were usually understood to be necessary for the preparation of the felicity of socialism.

2

For what reasons did men choose between the Populists and the Marxists when joining the Revolutionary Movement? Obviously, much depended on accidental circumstances and contacts with members of one or the other trend. Naturally, the

Populists were more successful among the rural population to which the idea of land redistribution would appeal, and the Marxists among industrial workers, to whom they ascribed a providential role, always pleasant to believe in. But among the youngsters of the *intelligentsia* and the converts from among the ruling class or the bourgeoisie such a predetermination did not exist, so that the choice between the two trends took place mainly on the basis of the differential appeal of the two doctrines. What were the significant differences, besides those already studied?

One of the main differences was that Populism did not possess any definite and complete philosophy. Its leaders shared the Religion of Progress and Humanity [5] which, at about that time, dominated among intellectuals not only in Russia, but also in Western society. This religion did not necessarily involve negative attitudes against religion as taught by the historical Churches. While many leaders and rank-and-file members were atheists, others were not and tried to combine the two faiths, thus accentuating the ethical element in their socialist doctrine.

On the other hand, the Marxists possessed a complete philosophy of life based upon the principles of materialism and atheism. Matter and its motion, they thought, was all that existed; consciousness was determined by this material existence and was its product or modification. Religion, like every spiritual or idealistic explanation of the world and man, must be rejected as an invention of the dominating class, used by them as a means of exploiting the masses. "Religion is an opiate for the people," was one of the most frequently quoted sentences from Marx's collected works.

Another difference was connected with the problem of "the role of the personality in history." The Populists accepted the teaching of a group of Russian social philosophers headed by Lavrov-Mirtov (1823–1900)—the Populists always were inclined to accept Russian ideas *vs.* imported ones—and held that the role of "the critically minded personality" was paramount. Nothing happened by itself; if the socialists wanted socialism to be realized, they had to struggle for it actively, destroying the obstacles—first of all the existing political organization. It was in their midst that terrorist groups arose and carried out a number of political murders, among them that of Emperor Alexander II.

In opposition to them, the Russian Marxists were originally dominated by the implications of their necessitarian philosophy. Acts of terrorism were rejected by them as conducive to no good: socialism could not be introduced by murder or decree; it had to grow up naturally as the result of a necessary social process; the only sensible means of individual participation in the process was that of accelerating it by transforming the amorphous group of industrial and agricultural workers into a class-conscious organization. Patience was necessary, for many years had to pass before the realization of the goal.

But patience is not a virtue often found among revolutionists. In consequence, a tendency to revise the necessitarian feature of the Marxist philosophy arose and finally produced a schism among the Russian Marxists. In this way Bolshevism was born, and therefore this schism deserves some attention.

It was only late in the 'nineties that scattered groups of Russian Marxists united into a Social Democratic Party which, up to the Revolution of 1917, never was granted legal existence in the framework of the Russian State.* The unification was not complete since the leaders were already divided with regard to the troublesome problems of the role of the personality, and the related problem concerning the organization of the party. In 1903, at a conference held in London,† dissension among the leaders appeared to be so strong that unity could no longer be preserved. Two "fractions" were formed, one un-

* Prior to the Constitutional Reform of 1905–6, the mere fact of participation in a socialist group was considered as conspiracy against the existing social and political order and was treated accordingly. After the Reform, the indiscriminate persecution of socialism was mitigated, but the socialist parties never were registered by the courts, as required by the electoral law. Nevertheless, members of these parties were elected to the Duma and formed there a Social-Democratic and a Labor (Socialist Revolutionist) fraction.

† The conference gathered in London because of the situation described above.

der the leadership of Lenin, another under that of Martov. Lenin's group held that a resolute minority, strongly organized, had to assume the leadership of the Revolutionary Movement and use the first opportunity to overthrow the existing social and political order, thus at least substantially accelerating the advent of socialism. As a corollary, the Party had to assume the role of the vanguard of the proletariat and was to be organized according to a semimilitary pattern, involving strong discipline and concentrated leadership. The mere acceptance of the program, which suffices in political parties, was explicitly declared to be insufficient. Emphasis was laid on "professional revolutionists," men devoting their lives to the promotion of class struggle and the acceleration of the process leading towards the Social Revolution.[6]

The other group, headed by Martov, maintained the necessitarian doctrine of the formative years of Russian Marxism, the doctrine endorsed by the majority of the Social Democratic parties of Western Europe. Socialism was considered by them to be a self-realizing goal, to be achieved in democratic forms through persuasion of a sufficient number of persons, after the social evolution had advanced far enough to make this possible. The structure of the Party was to remain democratic, and also to be democratic was the form of the growth of the Party; anyone who declared his acceptance of the program was welcome.

Since at the conference the majority of the delegates shared Lenin's opinion, and only a minority that of Martov, the two groups received respectively the names of Bolsheviks and Mensheviks, both derived from the Russian words meaning "more" and "less." But since the Bolsheviks also required more from the members and were more radical, and the Mensheviks demanded less and were less radical, gradually a shift in the meaning ascribed to the terms by less educated people took place and this, incidentally, was of some advantage to the Bolsheviks; prospective revolutionists were eager to join a group which promised more than its opponents; later on quite a number of people voted for those who were more generous in their promises.

From where did Lenin's ideas come? Throughout his life he claimed to have been the most faithful of Marx's disciples, confirming his own doctrine by direct quotations from the writings of the Master. This would have been a sufficient argument in favor of Lenin's claim if another claim could not be opposed to it: the necessitarians were able to produce as good and convincing quotations from Marx and Engels to support their evolutionary doctrine. The puzzle has been solved by a great Russian scholar, Novgorodtseff, who has masterfully proved that the ideas of Marx and Engels on this controversial subject had fluctuated, the earliest and latest works being rather in favor of the Utopian-revolutionary interpretation, and those of the years of maturity in favor of the necessitarian-evolutionary interpretation.[7]

In consequence, we may take it for granted that Lenin's ideas about the necessity of active interference with the social process were actually borrowed by him from Marx. But this is not the whole story. Marx never gave any precision to his ideas about the forms of this interference and the organization necessary thereto. At this point, a specifically Russian trend of ideas must have influenced Lenin; namely, the same social philosophy which was at the basis of the doctrine of the Populists. It is, however, true that the particular doctrine of violence, or direct action embodied in Bakunin's anarchism and Lenin's professional revolutionism was not specifically Russian. Early Russian revolutionists, both in exile and within their country, diligently learned from Western revolutionists and imitated them. Among them a definite school of thought existed, from the days of the French revolutionist, Blanqui (1805–1881), up to the time when young Lenin was in exile. Incidentally, it was from this same school of thought that young Mussolini received his initiation in the Religion of Revolution and his ideas about the role of "resolute minorities."[8]

The teaching of the Bolsheviks (later on, Communists) on

violence was this: being Marxists, they agreed that a necessary evolution was going on in capitalist society preparing for
Socialism-Communism. But, they asserted, this evolution made
a social revolution only possible, not necessary. Without violent
action on the part of a resolute minority guided by determined
leaders, this revolution would never materialize. The task of
these leaders was, first of all, to prepare the striking group
for the decisive moment and, secondly, to determine this moment correctly. What this moment was in Marx's formula remained rather unclear. The basic statement was that there had
to be an obvious discrepancy between the development of
economic forces and the legal order, the latter becoming a
hindrance for the further development of the former. It is
considered by the Communists as one of Lenin's great contributions to Marxism that he gave a much more precise shape
to the time element: the discrepancy between the economic
forces and the legal order, giving rise to a "revolutionary situation," must be manifested in a crisis within the dominant
class, such as produced by military defeat. On this basis he
formulated the famous theorem of the transformation of "imperialistic wars" into "civil wars" conducive to the social revolution.[9]

The idea of salutary and necessary violence obsessed Lenin
throughout his life. One of his major works, *The State and the
Revolution,* written shortly before the major event of his life,
the October Revolution, is especially devoted to it. Throughout this work Lenin unequivocally maintained that upheaval,
violence, civil war, and oppression of the defeated bourgeoisie
were the only ways to the felicity of Communism:

> Democracy is of great importance for the working class in its
> struggle for freedom against the capitalists. But democracy is by no
> means a boundary that must not be overstepped . . . In capitalist
> society we have a democracy which is curtailed, wretched, false;
> a democracy only for the rich, for the minority.[10]

It is true that Marx said once that there were certain countries such as the United States and England in which the work-

ers may hope to secure their ends by peaceful means.[11] This is one of the points relating to which Lenin permitted himself to disagree with the great master. The relevant statement in *The State and the Revolution* reads as follows:

Today, in 1917, in the epoch of the first great imperialist war, this distinction of Marx's becomes unreal, and England and America, the greatest and last representatives of Anglo-Saxon "liberty," in the sense of the absence of militarism and bureaucracy, have today completely rolled down into the dirty, bloody morass of military-bureaucratic institutions common to all Europe, subordinating all else to themselves. Today, both in England and America, the preliminary condition of any real people's revolution is the breakup, the shattering of the available ready machinery of the State.[12]

Continuing the general discussion of violence, Lenin said:

Democracy for the vast majority of the people, and suppression by force, i.e., exclusion from the democracy, of the exploiters and oppressors of the people—this is the change democracy undergoes during the transition from capitalism to Communism. The dictatorship of the proletariat . . . will, for the first time, create democracy for the people, for the majority, in addition to the necessary suppression of the minority. . . . [The bourgeois State] cannot be superseded by the proletarian State (the dictatorship of the proletariat) in the process of the "withering away"; as a general rule, this can happen only by means of a violent revolution. The panegyric Engels sang in its honor, and which fully corresponds to Marx's repeated declarations, is by no means a mere impulse, a mere declamation or a polemic sally . . . The necessity of systematically imbuing the masses with this and precisely this view of violent revolution lies at the root of the whole of Marx's and Engels' doctrine. The betrayal of their doctrine by the now predominant social-chauvinist Kautskyan trends is brought out in striking relief by the neglect of such propaganda and agitation by both of these trends.[13]

Three points ought to be stressed in these declarations:

1. The necessity of a violent revolution was professed after Russia had overthrown the autocracy of the Tsars and was ruled by democrats preparing democratic elections to a Constituent Assembly; in other words, violence against democracy was advocated.

2. As if foreseeing what could be said in order to minimize the significance of such statements, Lenin emphasized that his masters and himself meant business when speaking of violent revolution.

3. Not only in the course of the violent struggle for power, but after having gained victory, the Communists must "suppress" a whole class of the population, excluding them from democracy.

The emphasis on violence as a substantial part of Lenin's political doctrine should not be interpreted as implying that Lenin was a "Blanquist," a man holding to the idea that direct action against the existing order ought to be carried out at any time. Lenin always denied that he was a Blanquist and was right when doing so. The difference between him and the Blanquists was that he stressed the necessity of analyzing every social situation to find out whether it was revolutionary or not. His ideas on the subject may be summarized as follows:

1. The transition from capitalist society to socialist society cannot be effected simply on the basis of the desire to do so. Certain indispensable conditions are required; in the first place, the proletariat must be firmly united around its "vanguard," the Communist Party, and disorder must reign in the ranks of the enemy, based on an irreparable discrepancy between the exigencies of economics and the legal order.

2. When the conditions just mentioned are present, the labor class can and must overthrow the existing social and political order. This can be done only if there exists resolute and class-conscious leadership. To provide the labor class with this leadership is the very reason for the existence of the Communist parties in capitalist society.

3. The overthrow of the social and political order of capitalist society cannot take place otherwise than through direct action, i.e., struggle on the street, armed insurrection, and civil war.

4. The immediate effect of victory is the complete annihilation of the political apparatus of the bourgeois state and the creation of a new political order, that of the Soviet State. In

the Soviet State, the dictatorship of the proletariat is manifested. The Soviet State aims at oppressing the defeated bourgeoisie and giving satisfaction to the economic needs of the formerly oppressed classes, in forms dictated by the leadership. Seeing their interests satisfied, the masses will appreciate the Communist leadership and start supporting them, thus giving them the solid foundation of recognition by the majority.[14]

5. This recognition by the majority can take place only after the event, never before it.

In 1917, Lenin correctly defined the state of Russia; a revolutionary situation was present, and a resolute minority could seize power. This does not prove the validity of the procedure in general: Lenin was mistaken when expecting, on the basis of class analysis, the immediate outbreak of the International Socialist Revolution in 1919–20, first in Germany and then elsewhere. But, as we shall see, the correct diagnosis of 1917 tremendously enhanced Lenin's authority.

3

His authority had been great many years before that correct diagnosis, but only within a very small circle. Today it seems almost incredible, but the fact is that one year before Lenin became the master of Russia, his name was almost unknown outside the group of his followers, the other professional revolutionists who opposed him, and a few specialists interested in the gamut of political doctrines. The author of a few rather dull books, he was usually by-passed in academic discussions. The leader of a negligibly small revolutionary group, he was regarded with contempt by the leaders of more numerous revolutionary groups and of the legal political parties. The Imperial police thought it expedient to help him clandestinely in the competition with other revolutionary groups, believing that the absurdity of his program would direct the Revolutionary Movement into a blind alley.

Nobody besides his followers took him seriously. Nobody ever imagined that he could become the heir of the Tsars. The liberals were sure that victory would be theirs, either by means of an evolution transforming Russia into a parliamentary monarchy of the English style, or by means of a short revolutionary shock, making Russia a democratic republic. The Mensheviks shared this opinion, and considered that a period of capitalism was ahead in Russia under the leadership of the liberals reflecting "the capitalist mode of production." The Socialist Revolutionists were divided, some of them sharing the ideas of the liberals and the Mensheviks, others expecting a social revolution under Socialist Revolutionary leadership. To all of them the idea of a revolution under the banner of the dictatorship of the proletariat advocated by Lenin seemed inconceivable in a predominantly agrarian country, with industry still in the stage of infancy.

Before the outbreak of the World War of 1914, Lenin and his Party did nothing more to make them any more brilliant on the political horizon.[15] In the course of the abortive revolution of 1904–6, Lenin returned from his exile to Russia. But he found almost nothing to do, the situation being not yet ripe for direct action, and soon left the country once more. Acute polemics of the Bolsheviks against their political neighbors were not very convincing and were commonly judged to be erecting new obstacles for the cause of the Revolution. Moreover, in the course of the years between the close of the Revolution of 1904–6 and the outbreak of the World War I, Lenin spent the greater part of his energy in combating attempts to rejuvenate the Marxist creed by taking into account the philosophical and scientific achievements of the decades which had elapsed since that creed had been formulated; in consequence, to many he appeared as a reactionary doctrinaire. The endorsement of the practice of "expropriation" to adduct some money into the meager Party treasury induced many people to reflect that the Bolsheviks had degraded themselves to the rank of brigands. The discovery of quite a few *agents provocateurs* among persons whom Lenin trusted made the Party ridiculous.[16]

No wonder that early in 1917, at the outbreak of the Revolution, the number of Bolsheviks was only approximately 30,000, including many members who had just joined the Party fairly recently, when Russia was already in the period of turmoil which preceded the Revolution. The quantitative weakness was by no means made up by quality. While workers affiliated with the Bolshevik Party were neither better nor worse than those who joined the Mensheviks or, in exceptional cases, the Socialist Revolutionists, the intellectual element of the Bolshevik group, except Lenin's inner circle, was definitely inferior. In conditions which prevailed in Russia on the eve of the First World War, joining the Bolshevik group testified to a lack of sound judgment; it opened no immediate political opportunity and made adjustment to the existing social order very difficult in any form except that of a professional revolutionist. This naturally resulted in directing rather dull men towards the Party, who were unable to analyze the situation in its complexity, fanatics of the poorest kind, and in addition, social outcasts: lawyers without clients, doctors without patients, Faculty instructors with no expectation of promotion— all embittered against the existing social order, hating it and its representative members, and seeing their only chance in a cataclysm turning society upside down.

Under these conditions, only a miracle could give power to the Bolsheviks.

CHAPTER IV

THE COMMUNIST REVOLUTION:

The Dark Horse Wins

1

YET STILL THIS miracle occurred. How was it possible? There are different ways to answer this. One is to narrate the sequence of events giving, when necessary, portraits of the principal actors of the historical tragedy. Another is to apply to a particular situation a set of general ideas derived from the study of a number of similar situations. In this case the ideas to be applied, naturally, must concern the causation of revolutions and the mechanism determining the particular shape received by them.[1]

In opposition to the commonly accepted idea that revolutions are caused by stagnation, many societies such as the Egyptian, Chinese, or Hindu were stagnant for long centuries and were still not subject to revolutions. On the contrary, revolutions are relatively frequent in periods of rapid social change especially if, between the individual phases of social and cultural life, differences in speed have appeared and caused significant social tensions.[2] The accumulation of tensions makes a society plastic; in other words, two or three directions of further development become objectively possible.

To understand what plasticity means, it is well to contrast it with the stable or "solid" society of days of normalcy. When society is "solid," almost everybody can foresee what will take place tomorrow. Slight changes are probable, but we know that fundamentally, society will continue as it is. On this basis of expectation depend such common activities as investing, insuring, and providing for the higher education of children.

In a plastic society, expectations are quite different; nobody knows what tomorrow will bring; everybody knows that tomorrow will be different from today. Some worry, fearful that the coming change will weaken their social status and that of their group and even of the nation as a whole. Others exult because of bright expectations for themselves, their group, and the nation. If plasticity develops to this degree, revolution is near.

Even under such conditions, however, revolution is not a necessity. In addition to revolution other possible outcomes are "reaction" (or the restoration of equilibrium on one of the previously reached levels) * and "reform" (the peaceful and orderly creation of equilibrium on a new level).

Pre-Revolutionary Russia showed examples of different possibilities: the liberal reforms of Emperor Alexander II were consciously carried out in order to prevent threatening revolution. The social tensions which accumulated on the eve of the twentieth century were treated by a combination of reaction and liberal reforms; this combination was Stolypin's master plan of preventing a revolution. In America a high degree of plasticity was reached in the early 'thirties. Further deflation on the basis of orthodox economic theory would have meant "reaction." The lack of action might have produced a revolutionary outbreak, and this virtual revolution might have taken a Communist, Fascist, or some other form. Fortunately, the way of reform was chosen; but it must be noted that the New Deal was only one of the possibilities that might have been tried.

Objective possibilities ingrained in a plastic society are not merely mental constructs. They are embodied in groups or individuals assuming the role of leadership; the government, the army, the bureaucracy, a faction within one of these, a legally existing party, or the revolutionary movement (if it is unified) or factions within this movement. Such groups may be in competition for power even in "solid" society; but in

---

* "Return to normalcy" after the First World War is one of the most conspicuous examples of "reaction" in the meaning used in this work.

"plastic" society, their competition is intensified through awareness of the fact that the general outcome of the crisis depends
on the outcome of this competition. Victory for one or the other
of the competitors decides whether the outcome will be reaction, reform, or revolution, and eventually what form will be
given to reaction, reform, or revolution.

Usually, in conditions of plasticity, society is first directed
towards reaction or reform. Such efforts may be successful, and
the balance restored. But they are not always strong enough
or carried out in the right direction; sometimes they come too
late. If what is done is of the too-little-and-too-late variety, the
social order is broken. This is revolution. It appears that revolution is a residual phenomenon occurring when the leaders are
neither strong enough to impose reaction, nor clever enough
to carry out the necessary reforms.

2

Let us apply these general ideas to the particular situation
which existed in Russia directly before the outbreak of World
War I and the 1917 Revolution. As has been demonstrated in
Chapter II, there were great social tensions present, but during the last few years before the catastrophe they were declining. This made a revolutionary outcome less and less probable; think the war away, and you can very easily see Russia
peacefully advancing according to her historical lines.[3]

The general trend away from revolution towards peaceful
evolution was reversed by the war of 1914 which, from the
standpoint of the internal development of Russia, was an accident depending on her location in the Great Society of Humanity, and on processes which occurred therein. This statement may be objected to by those who consider that Russia's
participation in the war can be derived from some particular
feature of Russian society on the eve of the war.[4] But, in actuality, there was no War Party in Russia—in other words, no influential group of military men, statesmen, or politicians who
would have been eager to seize the opportunity of involving

their country in a military adventure—and there was no expansionist tendency among the intellectuals. The undeniable revival of Slavophile tendencies in Russia was by no means aggressive. The Slavophiles thought that Russia had to act as the natural protector of Slavs when their existence was threatened or their natural development checked by other nations. But nobody in Russia thought of attacking any country; especially in governmental circles, everybody was aware of the necessity of quite a few decades of peace for the further advancement of such important social processes as industrialization, the agrarian reform, and universal education, which made Russia stronger with every passing year.

However, like every great nation, Russia had a few vital interests of a negative character.* Without aiming at the acquisition of the Straits or of any portion of the Balkans, Russia could not permit any other great power to acquire a dominating position there. Unfortunately for Russia, a development independent of the Russian one actualized this negative interest; this was the German *Drang nach Osten*. Reacting to this development, Russia armed, strengthened her alliances and friendships with the other nations opposed to Germany, and entered the war. At the beginning, no positive ends could be formulated. Only gradually were they found to be the final unification of Russia through the acquisition of Eastern Galicia; the unification of Poles into an autonomous State under the Russian Emperor; and the realization of the old dream of the restoration of the Cross on the cathedral of St. Sophia in Constantinople. But it is certain that without the actualization of the threat to the "key to the Russian house," as the Straits were called in Imperial Russia, Russia would not have accepted the challenge of a major war.

War is always a test of a nation's internal unity; for Russia it was a very dangerous test because of the existence, though already in mitigated form, of the social tensions described above, and because it is quite usual, after a short time when

---

* Such, for instance, is the principle of British policy not to permit any great power to acquire the Lowlands.

difficulties seem to have been alleviated, that a war would increase them.

It was the second of the three tensions which was directly affected by the war, the tension based on the lag of the political behind the economic and cultural advance of the nation. To win a great war in 1914, national unity was necessary. In existing conditions, this unity could have been effected only by introducing into the government representative leaders of the liberal bourgeoisie and the *intelligentsia*. But war, as confirmed once again by the development of political institutions in our day, favors the concentration of political power, but not its dispersion. Thus, the trend of the political development was reversed and autocracy almost completely restored, with all the dangers involved in such a restoration.[5] Once more, everything depended on the personality of the monarch, and it was Russia's evil fate to be headed by a narrow-minded and ill-informed man at one of the most critical periods of her history. The *intelligentsia* and the bourgeoisie violently resented this retrogressive movement. The better part of the higher bureaucracy shared these sentiments, and was ousted by the Emperor. In consequence, the bureaucratic machinery rapidly deteriorated, and the problems posed by a war of unprecedented magnitude did not receive sensible solutions.[6]

This was particularly dangerous because of the existence of the other two tensions. The cultural distance between the higher and lower levels of Russian society made it very difficult to explain to the people why Russia had to enter the war and continue fighting. The people were irritated by the hardships imposed on them—partly by necessity, since such is the impact of modern wars—but partly because of the inefficiency of the governmental machine. In such circumstances, the Revolutionary Movement could revive. It naturally used the particular mentality of the rural masses, shaped by the first of the three tensions: namely, their belief in the injustice of the existing agrarian order, whereas the industrial workers could be inculcated with the idea that this war was not their war, since it was waged by a coalition of capitalists against another coalition of capitalists for the supremacy on the world market.

The rapid intensification of the tensions and of their reflection on the minds of the people created a revolutionary situation. It was by no means produced by military defeat, as is sometimes asserted.[7] On the eve of the Revolution, the military situation of Russia was far from being desperate. The great defeats took place in 1915, but they did not destroy the Russian army. The campaign of 1916 culminated in the famous Brussilov offensive which almost knocked out Austria-Hungary. Early in 1917, the stock of munitions was as high as it had ever been; the Russian military leaders were confident of their ability to carry out another, perhaps decisive offensive, and the German military leaders considered that their situation was very serious.[8]

The Revolution was finally brought about by the unfavorable turn of events in the internal development of Russia. Under the impact of war the tensions became at least as strong as they had been on the eve of the century, but still the revolution was not "inevitable" in that it could have been averted by appropriate measures.[9] However, this time capable leadership lacked, or perhaps was not permitted to exert its creative abilities. The existence of high social tensions and the absence either of "reaction," which at that time probably was impossible, or of adequate reforms forced the social process to choose the destructive form of revolution.

This revolution was not a response to stagnation, since Russia was a rapidly advancing nation. It was the response of a rapidly but disharmoniously advancing society to a challenge of History which remained uncomprehended by those in responsible positions.

3

Thus far we have tried to understand why a revolution did occur in Russia, despite the fact that after 1905–6 the probability of a revolution rapidly decreased. Now we must study another very complicated problem: how did it happen that the

Russian Revolution finally received the Communist shape, despite the fact that the Communists (Bolsheviks) were a negligible quantity in the field of forces which was Russia?

It is natural to begin by discussing the official Marxist explanation. The situation is embarrassing for them. Before the war of 1914, orthodox Marxists did not believe in the possibility of launching the International Communist Revolution in Russia. According to their doctrine, Communist Revolution had to emerge from the overmaturity of Capitalism. The symptoms of the forthcoming revolution were described as the concentration of capital and the impoverishment of the masses, and it is obvious that in the general context of the doctrine, these symptomatic phenomena could occur only in highly industrialized countries with the industrial proletariat as the largest social group. However, when the revolution broke out in Russia, scarcely five per cent of the population belonged to that group.

Lenin, and later on Bukharin, gave a quite superficial explanation of the discrepancy between Marxist expectations and reality. They pointed to the fact that in Russia the average number of workers in an industrial plant was larger than in any Western country, and concluded that the process of concentration of industry was more advanced in Russia than elsewhere. And the precapitalist poverty of the masses was equalized by them with the impoverishment expected by Marx as a corollary of the advance of capitalism.[10]

Facts do not confirm Lenin's and Bukharin's interpretation. In Western society, capitalism was imposed on a precapitalist industrial society, and the remnants of that society—that is, the small shops operated by artisans—statistically decreased the average number of workers. In Russia capitalism was superimposed on an agrarian society in the midst of which many industrial commodities had been produced by the *kustari* (rural artisans) during their seasonal idleness due to the severity of the Russian climate. To compare the situation in Russia with that in Western society, one has to use one of these procedures: (1) either to take into consideration merely capitalistic plants, excluding the artisans in the West and the *kustari* in Russia; or (2) contrariwise, to include the artisans in the West and the *kustari* in Russia. In both cases, Lenin's and Bukharin's thesis is invalidated.[11]

Trotsky, the heretic among Communists, gives another explanation. In his book, *The Revolution Betrayed,* he states:

> In conditions of capitalist decline, backward countries are unable to attain that level which the old countries attained. Russia took the way of proletarian revolution not because she was ripe for a socialist change—she was the weakest link in the capitalist chain—but because she could not develop further on a capitalist basis. The law of combined development for backward countries, uniting bourgeois and socialist revolutions . . . was displayed in Russia. The democratic tasks of pre-Revolutionary Russia (the liquidation of monarchy and the half-feudal slavery of peasants) could be achieved only through the dictatorship of the proletariat; but the proletariat could not stop at the achievement of these democratic tasks.[12]

This analysis is obviously not in accordance with facts. The rapid development of Russian economics proves that "the international capital" was either unwilling or unable to stop Russia's advance, and that there was no such thing as "the half-feudal slavery of peasants," a redundant phrase addressed by an experienced propagandist to a public which, he supposed, was unable to check his assertions.

As shown in an earlier part of this work, equally wrong is the explanation of the Communist shape assumed by the Russian Revolution by the affinity between Communism and the Russian national spirit. No other explanations, however, are known to exist.

4

To solve the problem correctly, let us continue the discussion of the revolutionary process (section 2). It was stated there that in revolutionary situations, when society is highly plastic, the different possibilities are embodied in groups and leaders, and that the decision takes place in the form of the victory of one of them in the competition for power. Supposing that a revolutionary situation develops towards actual revolution, what gives victory to one of the competitors as opposed to the others?

Success obviously depends on the selection of one of the simultaneous offers made by the competitors, akin to the selection by a purchaser of one of the offers simultaneously made by different sellers. But who makes the choice? Obviously a human mass strong enough to impose its selection on the nation of one of the objective possibilities and, consequently, of one of the competitors for power. What human mass is to play the decisive role in a specified revolutionary situation depends on the degree and character of the disintegration obtaining in it. For the sake of brevity, we shall call such a human mass "the revolutionary mass."

If the process of disintegration is in its initial stage, the ascendancy of the sociocultural *élite* is not yet shaken: the nation continues to follow the leadership of those who form its "upper level" by reason of birth, wealth, education, personal achievement, or the like. The disintegration, then, consists in tensions within the sociocultural *élite* itself, especially between those in power and those out of power. If a revolution takes place under such conditions, the crisis is solved by the *élite*. The rest of the nation obediently follows suit.

If the process of disintegration has advanced beyond the initial stage, the exclusive authority of the sociocultural *élite* to make decisions for the nation is no longer recognized by those who do not belong to it, but the *élite* is not yet excluded from the number of the determinants of the social process: this is a situation where the decisive role belongs to the nation, perhaps minus the former government.

In later stages of disintegration, the role of choosing the center of reconstruction belongs to the "people," that is, to the nation minus the sociocultural *élite*. This situation obtains in so-called "great revolutions" of the French and Russian type. Its symptom is the loss of self-confidence among the sociocultural *élite*, especially the loss of the belief, so firm in times of normalcy, that the role of leadership naturally belongs to it.

At all times human masses are imbued with more or less specified ideas concerning the adequacy or inadequacy, justice or injustice, of the existing social institutions and the desirability of changing them. The range of such ideas depends partly on "objective interests," both material and nonmaterial (for example, social prestige) of the revolutionary mass, but mainly on its "culture history." In times of crisis, frustrations which perhaps already existed in times of normalcy are accentuated, and dominance is easily gained by systems of ideas focused on the basic frustrations. On the other hand, the conditions of plasticity resulting in the crisis are sometimes caused not so much by actual frustrations as by the conversion of large masses to a new creed, religious, political, or social. Then, the range of ideas expecting re-enforcement and systematization is based on these new creeds. To programs reflecting such ideas, the masses are highly responsive, whereas no "great man" was ever able simply to impose his program on them. To designate a set of ideas to which "the revolutionary mass" is readily responsive, the term "natural program" will be used.

Both the objective situation and the ideas circulating in the masses are reflected in the minds of the competitors for power and give rise to their individual programs, expressing their views of the situation, possible outcomes, and the desirable solution of the crisis. In each program, first of all, the author's "definition of the social situation" is expressed, especially his diagnosis of the human mass to play the decisive role.

On the other hand, the program of each potential leader, in its original form, not yet accommodated to the competitive situation, reflects the life history of the authors and the culture history of the group to which they belong: Lenin's program was determined by his early conversion to Marxism; in Mussolini's original program the school of George Sorel was conspicuous; in Hitler's program the drill of the German army, the fantasy of George Feder, the anti-Semitic climate of Vienna, re-enforced by certain ideas imported from Russia by Alfred Rosenberg were easily recognizable.

Almost necessarily, each competitor compares his original program with the natural program of the "revolutionary mass" as defined by him. This comparison yields either conformity or discrepancy. If it is conformity, the situation is most favorable for the competitor in question. The natural course is to organize propaganda according to the competitor's original program.

If discrepancy is established, a problem both technical and ethical is posited: the potential leader has to decide whether he is willing and able to conceal the discrepancy and to pretend to have a program that conforms to the expectations of "the revolutionary mass." In revolutionary situations, sensible and decent men cannot promise much more than "sweat and tears"; on the other hand, "the revolutionary mass" is inclined to accept optimistic interpretations of the situation and to welcome superficial views about remedies. This explains why it is rare that truly decent leaders gain power in "great" revolutions.

An additional condition of the success of a competitor's program is its adjustment to the level of intelligence and knowledge of the addressees; the lower the level, the simpler the offer must be. Since the level of the masses is lower than that of the sociocultural *élite,* situations where the decisive role belongs to "the people" are favorable to the victory of extremists, right or left, for their plans are naturally of the simplest kind, such as "expropriate the expropriators," or "kill the Jews."

It may be taken for granted that, in a revolutionary situation, the human mass playing the decisive role in the contest for power is shapeless. Gradually, the particular dominance-submission relationship is established between it and one of the competitors for power. The initial relationship, however, is rather precarious. Cases are known where the incipient power structure has broken down. To make final the crystallization around a specified competitor, the incipient relationship must be re-enforced by adequate actions. Since the simplest aspect of a power structure is physical dominance of man by man, the demonstration of the ability to break resistance is one of the most important requirements. This ability must be demonstrated in numerous face-to-face situations finally integrated into a new social structure transcending such situations.

There is, however, another element involved—appeal to the higher capacities of men. Experience shows that, for the re-enforcement of incipient power structures, nothing is more important than correct prediction, on the part of the leader, of the outcome of his actions, especially if his plans are controversial. It is very probable that a sequence of correct predictions is the very basis for the establishment of the so-called charismatic leadership.* The ascendancy of a prophet is a primary fact so thoroughly understandable that it does not need any further explanation.

Finally, it is obvious that for the establishment of the specific *rapport* forming the power structure between an individual competitor for power and the revolutionary mass, an efficient organization of propaganda is necessary, securing the systematic recurrence of the "offer" whenever possible. Consequently, to gain victory in the revolutionary competition for power, a virtual power center must comprise a sufficient number of persons knowing the great art of placing the right man in the right job.

The preceding analysis permits us to formulate these propositions:

1. Other things being equal, among the competitors for power in a highly disintegrated society, those men possess a greater chance to gain victory and receive the authority for reconstruction who offer a program (a) nearest to the expectations of "the revolutionary mass" and (b) best adjusted to its cultural level.

2. Other things being equal, among the groups competing for power, those groups possess a greater chance of victory which are comprised of persons endowed with the highest capacity for revolutionary leadership, specified as follows: (a) ability to organize effective propaganda, through selection and indoctrination of suitable individuals; (b) ability to define the social

---

* In Max Weber's terminology.

situation correctly, especially to detect the actual "revolutionary mass" and its "natural program"; (c) ability to enforce decisions and to break resistance; and (d) ability in correct prediction.

It is by no means predetermined that the same competitor for power would be simultaneously endowed with all the properties suitable for victory. If, in a concrete case, one group has a more appealing program to offer, but another has better leadership, a long and complicated struggle ensues. If the two sets of advantages are present in the same group, its victory is easy.

Unfortunately, the two sets are often combined in groups consisting of fanatics. This does not imply that the advantageous situation is present *only* in groups consisting of fanatics; nor that *every* group of fanatics would possess those advantages. Fanatics are characterized by subnormal inhibitions: they do not see anything but their own ideas and their projection into reality and are blind to other ideas and expectations. This lack of inhibitions permits them, on the one hand, to offer "the people" the most radical, that is, the simplest program, and on the other hand, to break resistance by brute force. They are the most probable victors in competition for power in conditions of high disintegration, but only in such conditions.

5

Let us now apply this lengthy theoretical digression to the situation which obtained in Russia in 1917. After the "February Revolution," i.e., the overthrow of the old order and the establishment of the Provisional Government composed of Liberals and moderate Socialists, only the Communists correctly defined the situation, understanding that in the given state of cultural development and social disintegration which obtained in 1917, the role of the revolutionary mass belonged to the nation minus the cultural *élite*.

To this revolutionary aggregate they offered the most appealing slogans; while the liberal and moderate socialist parties spoke of such abstract things as democracy and international pacification, the Communists concentrated their propaganda on four points:

1. Peace, i.e., the immediate cessation of a war whose ends were never sufficiently understood by the masses;

2. Land, i.e., the immediate gratification of the peasants' longing to have the landlords' estates divided among them;

3. Bread, i.e., the immediate alleviation of the food crisis in the major cities, and

4. "All power to the Soviets," which was interpreted as the abolition of bureaucracy, direct rule by the masses, and the likelihood of the cessation of taxation and compulsory military service.[13]

They were reticent on quite a few features of their program —for instance, on its antireligious phase. The program they used in competition was not their genuine, or esoteric one, but an accommodated, or exoteric one.

Moreover, leadership was more efficient in the Communist Party than elsewhere. This party had evolved according to a pattern of semimilitary subordination to the leader and of blind acceptance of the Party doctrine; the leader himself possessed a genius for diagnosing concrete situations correctly and for drawing realistic conclusions from his premises; many excellent organizers and able propagandists (among them Trotsky) assisted him. The structure of the other parties was democratic; none was headed by a person whose ascendancy was beyond question, and none of them had that intuitive understanding of reality which was so eminent in Lenin. They concentrated all attention upon squabbling among themselves and fighting off the imaginary bugbear of monarchial restoration; they completely overlooked the possibility of a Communist *coup d'état*. They possessed brilliant speakers, but their propaganda was addressed to fictitious "revolutionary masses" which, according to their books, ought to have existed. They had no eyes for the living men and women who, if they had been sensibly approached, might have become their supporters.[14]

It was not pure accident that within the Communist Party efficient leadership and adequate propaganda were united. Their propaganda was adequate in the particular situation of high social disintegration within a society where the cultural distance between the higher and lower level was large, and only in this situation. It was the propaganda of radical Utopians reckless enough to adjust their overt program to the expectations of the embittered masses unable to discern its fallacies and reticences. And their leadership also was of the kind natural among radical Utopians. Its outstanding ability to deal with the particular situation which obtained in Russia after the breakdown of the Old Order was due to the very fact that, prior to that disintegration, their chance had been so slight. This leadership was outstanding only in that particular situation. Had an adequate response to the challenge of war been found by the cultural *élite* (of which the government was a part) Lenin would probably have died outside of Russia as an obscure Marxist theoretician, just one item more on the roster of revolutionary dreamers.

Bolsheviks, or Communists gained power in Russia, already in a state of revolutionary disintegration, not because their real program would have conformed with the objective needs of the Russian people or even with their expectation, but because a revolution in Russia, before the final elimination of the cultural distance between the *élite* and the masses, was to be a great revolution; [15] and because, with regard to such a revolution, they possessed decisive advantages in comparison with the other competitors for power.

We have explained:

1. The fact of the Russian Revolution by the sudden intensification of social tensions ingrained in Russian society, to which no adequate response was found by the cultural *élite*, and,

2. The fact of the final victory of the Communists by the combination, in their midst, of efficient leadership and adequate propaganda, efficient and adequate with regard to a particular set of conditions. This is not a simple explanation, but the very complex fact of a revolution cannot be explained

simply. This explanation preliminarily confirms the thesis that the Communist Revolution was a shock inflicted on a rapidly advancing society and compelling it to depart from its historical ways; and that the Communist Experiment was not the continuation of the organic developments but, on the contrary, a violent disruption of continuity, a conflict between a Utopian idea and historical tradition. In consequence, an instrument for the imposition of the Utopia on the national body had to be created, and it actually appeared in the form of a strongly organized dictatorship.

CHAPTER V

THE DICTATORSHIP:

A Necessary Instrument of Communist Transfiguration

1

WHEN, ON NOVEMBER 7, 1917, the Communists gained power over Russia, they found themselves in a paradoxical situation. They had to choose between Communist transfiguration through dictatorship, or no Communist transfiguration at all, since without dictatorship Russia would have evolved towards a variety of the liberal State. They chose dictatorship.

But they had gained power in the name of the Marxist creed, according to which the State had to wither away after the Communist Revolution. Moreover, they had received the support of large masses of the people through the slogan, "all power to the Soviets," which means the transfer of real power to these masses. Their solution of the challenging problem was the only possible one: they created a dictatorship under the screen of democracy. To this fake-democracy they gave a peculiar form, the so-called Soviet structure.

The term "Soviet" seems to have received some mystical connotation. In the Russian language, it means merely "council." But a specific revolutionary nimbus had been acquired by the term since the abortive revolution of 1904–6. Then it was used to designate short-lived committees to which revolutionary workers of St. Petersburg and other big industrial centers sent their delegates. In 1917, after the overthrow of the Imperial government, the radical elements among the revolutionists were dissatisfied with the relatively moderate Provisional Government and revived the revolutionary form of political organization.

It was a masterpiece of statesmanship that, having over-thrown the Provisional Government, the Communists did not assume power in their own name, but ascribed it to the Soviets in whose name they started to rule. Their leaders formed a Council of the People's Commissars which was supposed to be responsible to the All-Russian Congress of the Soviets of the Workers' and Peasants' Deputies.

To the newly-born political structure, a peculiar meaning was ascribed. In the official doctrine of those days, the Soviet system was the bourgeois State turned upside down; naturally, not the real bourgeois State, i.e., the State of the liberal society, but the bourgeois State as interpreted by the Communist doctrine. In this interpretation, the bourgeois State was the instrument of the dominance of the exploiting bourgeoisie over the exploited proletariat. The Soviet State was, then, the instrument of the dominance of the victorious proletariat over the conquered bourgeoisie. Thus, the existence of dictatorship was not denied, but was given a meaning acceptable to the masses that was *their* dictatorship over their former exploiters. And the flattering of the masses was continued by statements that while in the bourgeois State supremacy belonged to the central bodies necessarily remote from the people, the Soviet system gave direct dominance to the masses of toilers. The miracle of an immediate democracy of the toilers was performed in this way: workers of every factory sent a delegate or delegates to a body called a Soviet, rural or urban. Peasants residing in a village, soldiers of a military unit, teachers and adult pupils of a school, officers of an administrative body did the same. The Soviet was considered to be the "supreme power" in its territory.°

If such bodies had ever actually taken shape, Russia would have been divided into some 65,000 small communal republics. It was to prevent this that agencies for co-ordination were created under the name of Soviet Congresses. The Soviets elected delegates to a District Congress, which in its turn sent delegates

° The political structure of the Soviet State is shown on Chart I.

THE PARTY SYSTEM

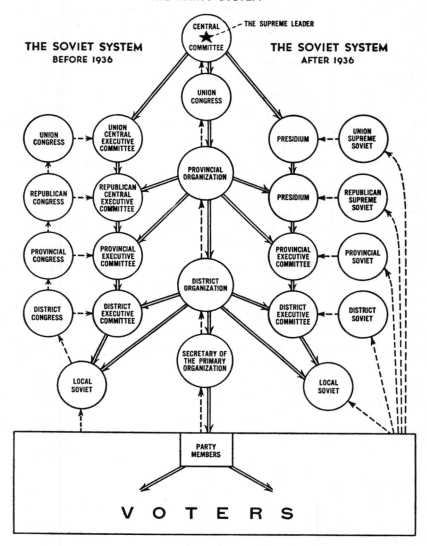

I. THE POLITICAL ORGANIZATION
Double lines show the direction of political pressure. Dotted lines show the direction of electoral procedures.

to the Provincial Congress.* A District Congress had the function of co-ordinating the activity of the Soviets, to find out
their common will. So, too, in earlier Constitutions and laws,
provisions had been included to ensure that the activity of
the delegates corresponded with the desires of their electors.
The same process occurred at the Provincial, Republican,† and
Federal (Union) levels.

According to the very principle of the Soviet State, elections
did not imply universal suffrage. A category of the disfran-
chised was created in 1918. To this category belonged both
the "bourgeoisie" (people who gained or had previously gained
profits by hiring workers or possessing estates) and also the
"helpers of the bourgeoisie," above all the clergy. Elections
were also unequal because urban Soviets were granted more
delegates *per capita* in the Soviet Congresses than the rural
ones. The elections to the Congresses were also indirect because of the "pyramidal" structure of the system. Thus, the
Union Congress of the Soviets consisted of persons separated
from the voters by four sets of elections. As to the secrecy of
the ballot, the practice fluctuated, with the tendency to make
the ballot open.

It is well known that the ability of an electoral system to
express the will of the people adequately depends on the
amount of freedom available to the citizens. If we take at face
value the constitutional texts, beginning with the First Soviet
Constitution of July 10, 1918, ‡ everything seems to be all right.
This Constitution, reproduced almost *verbatim* by subsequent
Constitutions, comprised the following articles:

Art. 14. In order to secure to the laboring masses genuine freedom
of expressing **their** opinion, the RSFSR annuls the dependency of
the press upon **capital** and hands over to the working class and the

* Since 1917, the territorial division of the country has been changed more
than once; the text is adapted to the structure now in force.

† The term "Republican" is used to designate the Federal Republics.

‡ This was the Constitution of the Russian Socialist Federated Soviet Re-
public (RSFSR) which in 1923 became the nucleus of the Soviet Union. The
Constitution of 1918 was imitated in all other Soviet Republics (Ukraina,
Belorussia, Georgia, etc.).

poor peasants all the technical and material resources necessary for the publication of newspapers, pamphlets, books, and all other printed matter, and guarantees their free circulation throughout the country.

Art. 15. In order to guarantee to the laboring masses complete freedom of assembly, the RSFSR, recognizing the right of the citizens of the Soviet Republic freely to organize meetings, processions, etc., places at the disposal of the workers and of the poor peasantry all premises fit for public gathering together with their furniture, lighting, and heating.

Now, according to an official theory to be discussed later on, the Labor class is represented by its vanguard, the Communist Party. Under such a theory, the transferring of instruments of printing, etc., from Capital to Labor means placing them at the disposal of the vanguard party, that is, of the ruling Communist Party, but not to freely formed groups of toilers who would apply for reasonable amounts of the material requisites of printing with the intention of starting the publication of books, pamphlets, or papers expressing their opinion.

The cited articles of the Soviet Constitution have always been strictly observed in that a monopoly of the instruments of forming and influencing public opinion has been created in favor of the Communist Party; and that is what freedom of the press, officially, means in the Soviet State. On the other hand, freedom of speech, of the press, of assembly, and the like as interpreted in democratic countries has been debunked; this, they claim, is merely an emanation of the bourgeois spirit, a manifestation of the class structure of society.[1]

A political group which possesses the monopoly on the means of propaganda necessarily wins every election. And the Communist Party has actually won every election in that it was able (1) to introduce into the rural Soviets all the Communists available in the countryside [2] and (2) to gain a majority in all urban Soviets and all the Soviet Congresses. To give an idea of the technique used, let us quote an official document describing an election in Moscow:

The electoral meeting was convoked for four P.M. and opened at five. A representative of the center made a short speech about foreign affairs. Then a representative of the District Party Organization offered a list of candidates and asked those present to nominate additional candidates. This actually was done. Then the Secretary of the Communist cell began to discuss the official list, saying with regard to each man on it, "You know him; he is a good man; acclaim him." Nobody was appointed to count the votes, carried out by the raising of hands. Among 400 persons present, only 200 to 300 actually voted. The official candidates were proclaimed "unanimously elected," and no voting was permitted with regard to the additional candidates, since the required number of delegates had already been elected.[3]

In such conditions the outcome of elections may be predicted in advance, and the elections are merely ceremonial actions void of any political significance. Gradually becoming aware of the real situation, the voters lost interest in them. Elections which in the beginning had to take place every three months became less and less frequent: once in two years in 1927, once in four years in 1931. Also less and less frequent became the meetings of the Soviets: instead of being in almost permanent session, they assumed the practice of gathering for only a few days a year.[4] The meetings lost all political significance. Nobody could expect to find in the records anything but lengthy speeches of the leaders, local or central, and much shorter speeches of the delegates, either praising the achievements of the leaders, expressing small local grievances, or offering minor suggestions as to improvement.

The Soviets and the Congresses could have disappeared at any time, and no change whatsoever in the administration of local or central affairs would have materialized. But simultaneously with the decline of the "representative bodies" of the Soviet system, executive agencies belonging to it grew in importance. This was the process:

When the enthusiasm of the first days after the Revolution had passed, direct administration by the Soviets and their Congresses proved to be impossible. Some persons had to be permanently present at headquarters to take care of current affairs. Thus, within the Soviets and the Congresses, Executive

Committees were created, officially elected by them. In the intermission between the sessions of the Soviets and the Congresses, these Committees were granted "supreme power" primarily belonging to the main bodies. Gradually, even the Executive Committees appeared to be too large and cumbersome; therefore, they were permitted to appoint Bureaus and, in the intermission between the sessions of the Committees, the Bureaus were declared to possess that "supreme power" which originally belonged to the Soviets and their Congresses. In this way, a cluster of "supreme powers" was established for each area. Naturally, none could be really supreme.

But neither the Executive Committees nor the Bureaus could really perform the tasks of the State machinery, which meanwhile were tremendously expanded through the Communist Experiment. Agencies of the familiar bureaucratic type very soon appeared, called "sections" of the Soviet or of the Executive Committee. And it just happened that the heads of these bureaucratic agencies became the members of the Bureaus. And it also happened that the bureaucrats acting on the lower levels displayed the readiness to obey the orders of those acting on the higher levels. Thus, the exertion of political power was transferred to a newly born bureaucracy.

2

But what was the moving spring behind the pyramid of Soviet bureaucracy? The Soviets and their Congresses could not play this part since, as we know, they were transformed into ceremonial institutions. To get insight into reality, one must look through the holes in the screen of the Soviets. And what one sees behind the screen is the dictatorship of "the vanguard of the proletariat," i.e., of the Communist Party.

Lenin, the Utopian and realist rolled into one, knew that after the Communist Revolution dictatorship would obtain. In *The State and Revolution* he acknowledged that after the revolution, increased coercion would be necessary, to assume the form of the dictatorship of the proletariat. Under this transitory structure, he said, men would be compelled to act in accordance with the patterns of Communist society. Gradually, such behavior patterns would evolve into habits which, as everybody knows, induce men to act in a specified manner without thinking about it and without external coercion. When the large majority of the people would have acquired such habits, inducing them automatically to act as fitting in Communist society, external coercion would become superfluous and could be gradually abandoned.[5]

The latter part of Lenin's prediction failed to materialize. But the first part did. Today, no Soviet authority would deny the fact that dictatorship exists. However, during the first few years of the regime, dictatorship was ascribed to the Soviets, and it was considered a criminal offense to say that power actually belonged to the Party. Later on, the existence of the Soviet and Party dualism was officially recognized and justified by an often repeated theory: in November, 1917, the working class of Russia overthrew the power of the landowners and capitalists. These classes were vanquished, but not totally destroyed; they had not lost the hope of revenging their defeat and would have liked to exploit the political inexperience of the working class. Therefore, in the struggle to maintain power, the working class needed a strong organization, the class leadership of its intelligent elements. The organization of this enlightened part, the "vanguard of the working class," was the Communist Party. The Party had to be at the head of the struggle for the true interests of the class: if possible, in conformity with the will of the whole class, but if necessary, in opposition to this will, lest it be led astray by the skillful propaganda of the exploiting class. Therefore, the dictatorship of the vanguard party was indispensable until the definitive creation of a classless society throughout the world.[6]

Still later, the idiom "the Soviets and the Party" was invented and officially introduced. Quite a few laws have been signed since 1931 by Stalin in the name of the Party, and Molotov (or Kalinin) in the name of the Soviets.

Before the Communist Revolution, the Communist Party was

a party competing for power with quite a few other parties. After the Revolution, it was transformed into *the* Party, a social group endowed with the monopoly of political activity. No legal enactment could be pointed to in which the change would have been manifested. But, early in 1918, many persons were imprisoned because they *had belonged* to the Constitutional Democratic (Liberal) Party or to one of the moderate Socialist parties. For a certain time, Left Wing Socialist Revolutionists were tolerated, since a few among them had joined the Communists in forming the Soviet Government. In July, 1918, they were accused of having conspired against the Communists and were outlawed. In 1922, Lenin said:

We shall detain Mensheviks and Social Revolutionists in prisons.

Later on, he even accentuated this threat:

For public manifestations of Menshevism our judges must condemn the culprits to death.

In 1923, Zinovyev unambiguously defined what the dictatorship of the proletariat meant:

We have the monopoly of legality. We do not grant our opponents political freedom. We do not give the possibility of legal existence to those who pretend to compete with us.[7]

The Communist leaders could more easily establish and enforce dictatorship, as they were believers in power: in other words, they assumed that every order could be enforced and every resistance broken provided that those in power were not effeminate persons holding humanitarian ideals, shunning bloodshed, and considering persuasion the only permissible way of social action. This characterized their antagonists, they said, but not themselves.

Very significantly, the official bearer of the "dictatorship of the proletariat" was organized on the same pattern as the Soviets. A primary organization (up to quite recently called "cell") unites the Party members working together in a factory (or in a shop, if the factory is big) in a village, in a governmental board, in a school, or in a military unit. This organization elects a Secretary and sends delegates to the District Conference of the Party. This conference discusses the Party affairs of the district, elects a committee which designates a Secretary, and sends delegates to the Provincial conference. The same happens on the Provincial level which sends delegates to the Union Congress of the Party. This Congress, which in the earlier years of the regime gathered yearly, but after 1934 had to convene only every four years,* elects a Central Committee, now composed of seventy members and approximately as many deputies. The Central Committee elects three executive bodies: The Political Bureau, the Organization Bureau, and the Secretariat; one of the men composing the last body is given the title of the Secretary General, now the First Secretary of the Central Committee.

Obviously, the idea behind this organization is that power belongs to the mass of the Party members. However, it is emphasized that the will of the members cannot be formulated otherwise than through the official agencies (the conferences, committees, and so on). Once the corporate will of the Party has been formulated all discussion stops, and every Party member is supposed to obey strictly. This is called "the principle of democratic centralism." The creation of factions, or of organized groups within the Party, but outside the official organization, is strictly forbidden.

The principle of democratic centralism, it is explained, is necessary in order to secure "the monolithic structure of the Party," essential for its role in a dictatorially ruled State. This principle could hardly be enforced without a number of additional institutions.

First of all, the Party is surrounded by a high barrier. Holding to the principles set down by Lenin in 1903, the Party does not open its door to everyone who wants to join it; on the contrary, access to the Party is difficult. Before joining it, one has to pass through the preliminary stages of an aspirant and a

---

* According to the revised statute of 1939, it is due every three years.

candidate; in every stage, the future Party member must spend a certain number of months or years displaying understanding of the doctrine and readiness to obey. To advance from stage to stage, up to that of a Party member, he must be recommended by a determined number of Party members having behind them a specified number of years of Party membership. Up to 1939, conditions governing entrance into the Party were differentiated according to the class or party origin of the candidate; they were made easiest for industrial workers and most difficult for former members of other political parties. Obviously, men with previous political experience could not be so easily assimilated as freshmen in politics.

In all cases, the promotion of an aspirant or candidate depended on the Party Committee. These Committees were directed to limit the number of new members accepted in the course of a year to a figure determined for each organization by the central agencies of the Party, in accordance with the general plan of the recruitment of Party members. The reason is obvious; complete assimilation of new party members is possible only if their relative number is small. Never was the Party permitted to grow very large. At the last Party Congress (February, 1939) they numbered 1,600,000.[8] In the course of the war, an increase up to three or even five million has been reported.

Secondly, a new Party member has to go through "Party education." The Party doctrine must be inculcated into him, since every Party member is expected to be well acquainted with Marxism-Leninism-Stalinism.

Thirdly, all Party members are subject to severe discipline. The first clause of the Party statute defines as a Communist a man who accepts the Marxist doctrine and obeys the orders of the Party leaders. The last clause enumerates the punishments which may be inflicted on the violators of Party discipline; they begin with reprimand and culminate in expulsion from the Party. In a society of the Communist type, an ex-Party member becomes an outcast.

Finally, there is the purge. The purge may be individual or

general. In the former case, special agencies scrutinize the conduct of those Party members who are suspected of having violated the statute, or the directions of their superiors, or Party ethics. In the latter case, every Party member is required to prove that he has made positive contributions to the welfare of the Party. General purges may last for many months and sometimes result in expelling about half the members from the Party. The last purge, that of 1936–38, victimized 580,000 members.

Thus, the attitude of obedience is firmly inculcated into Party members. Comprised of men endowed with this attitude, the Party is actually close to the ideal of the monolithic structure. On the other hand, it is obvious that under such conditions Party democracy could never materialize, in spite of periodic orders to bring about this state. Cells, conferences, and congresses have always elected committees and secretaries nominated by members on top. Men were ousted from the Party in accordance with directions coming from Moscow. Never was an officially recommended "resolution" rejected by any Party agency, and never did any original idea emerge on any level but the highest.

The docility of the Party organization is comparable with that of the Soviets and their Congresses. Within the Party, elections and discussions have also been transformed into ceremonial actions void of any political significance. As within the Soviet system, the executive agencies have prevailed over the representative bodies and merged into a strongly centralized bureaucratic system, directed from above. Nevertheless, the functions of the Party are important.

First, the Party is the reservoir from which men are selected to be granted dignities and power. Though membership, as such, does not confer any authority on the individual member, nor endow him with any material or honorary advantage, the expectation of a Party member to be appointed to a position conferring authority, honors, and money is much greater than that of a non-Party man. All higher positions in the administration, including business administration and the management of culture are reserved exclusively for Party members. In intermediary and minor positions, the Communists' share is much larger than that of the outsider.

Secondly, the Party is the mechanism through which the dictatorship is exerted. To perform this function, Party members are distributed according to plan, as are military forces eventually.

Thirdly, the Party is an agency of supervision.[9] Inasmuch as non-Party men of necessity are called upon to carry out socially relevant functions, Party members are present to ensure that their actions conform with the directions of the Party leaders. This is the idea behind the Political Commissars in the Army, and the appointment of Communists to high positions in technical agencies.

These three functions are not and could not have been carried out by the Party in the framework of its democratic statute.[10] These real functions by their nature point to something behind the official structure. Once more, this official structure appears to be merely a screen.

3

Now let us remove this second screen and look at the ultimate reality. Since 1917, there exists in Russia a person (which may be replaced by a Triumvirate) who exerts political power in its entirety. This fact is not officially acknowledged, and the person involved does not bear any particular title. But his actual power is independent of positions and titles; it is clearly of the "charismatic" type, or based on the assumption that a specified man is endowed with almost supernatural gifts as to political leadership.[11] Since 1929, more and more often, this man has been called the Leader. To him all possible perfections are ascribed. He is the Wise, the Good, the Almighty. He is the Father of the Peoples of the Soviet Union, the Head of the World Proletariat, the Generalissimo of Humanity. He is the first specialist in every branch of knowledge. Before his appearance, no historian knew how to write history. He is the Great

Philosopher having given the final shape to Marxism. He is the great strategist having actually won all the battles ever gained by the Red Army. He is a prophet. Time and again articles appear in the Soviet press emphasizing this gift, such as this:

> Our great Stalin has given examples of ingenious prevision of events. Already in 1917 he said: "It is not impossible that Russia will show the world the way to Communism." Now Russia is turning Communist. In 1933 he predicted that the Trotskyites, counterrevolutionists, and bourgeois nationalists would create trouble. And they did. He who knows the laws of social development may foresee the future and possesses the best possible tool for the transformation of the world.[12]

A man endowed with such properties is almost a deity. And as a deity he is almost invisible. With the exception of a few months in 1935–6, he has seldom appeared in public. But his influence is felt day and night in everything.

His actual power is limited by nothing. He is the legislator. Nothing could become the law which did not conform with his views; on the other hand, his will, if expressed in a generalized form, is the law. No law in force limits his power: without repealing it, he can transgress it or order that it be transgressed by others. A doctrine of "revolutionary expediency" has been established directing all State agencies to act without regard to the law if a certain line of action is indicated by "the policy of the Soviet government," which in actuality is the policy of the Supreme Leader.

All the officers of the State depend upon him. He appoints them or allows them to be appointed by his henchmen, shifts them from one position to another, or dismisses them. In so doing he can disregard the decisions or desires of any corporate body or any specified personality. He has around him a few advisory bodies. But the members of these bodies depend entirely on him; moreover, he is not obliged to ask them for advice; he can take advice from anyone he wants to consult, or from nobody; he is free to act in accordance with the advice received, or to ignore it.

It is obvious that the power of the Leader goes much farther than that of a Russian Emperor, even before the Constitutional Reform of 1905–6. The Emperor could make and repeal laws, but so long as a law was in force, he was considered bound by it. After 1864, the courts of law were independent in democracies. And in reality the power of the Emperor was limited by the bureaucracy, the services of which he could not avoid using. The last Russian Emperor whose power was comparable with that of the Leader in Communist Russia was Paul I (1796–1801).

Let us emphasize the fact that the omnipotence of the Leader does not appear in any Constitutional act. He usually occupies a high position within the Soviet or the Party system, but still one which would not confer unlimited power on its holder. Lenin, the first among the Supreme Leaders, was merely the Chairman of the Council of the People's Commissars; as such, he was constitutionally responsible to quite a few "representative" bodies of the Soviet system. During the period of interregnum (1924–27) the three members of the Triumvirate—Kamenev, Zinovyev, and Stalin—occupied a number of high positions within the two systems which once more made them, on paper, responsible to different assemblies. Stalin, the Supreme Leader since 1927, was for many years satisfied with the rank of Secretary General (later on, First Secretary) of the Central Committee of the Communist Party, to which he added some modest positions within the Soviet system. It was only in 1941, well after the termination of the Communist Experiment that, resuming Lenin's practice, he appointed himself to the rank of Chairman of the Council of the People's Commissars. In the course of the war Stalin was elevated to the rank of Marshal and immediately after victory in Europe—to the newly created rank of Generalissimo.

All power belongs to the One. But he is obviously unable personally to exert it in totality. A vast network of auxiliary agencies surround him, and in these auxiliary agencies we may well recognize quite a few bodies which possess high status in the Soviet and Party systems.

For many years there was among these agencies one which was often considered "the real government of Russia." This was the Political Bureau. Created by Lenin a fortnight before the upheaval which gave him power, it was primarily an unofficial council around the Leader, without regular sessions or jurisdiction. During Lenin's last sickness and the interregnum, the Political Bureau was the arena where the combat was fought first between Trotsky and the Triumvirate, then between Stalin and the other Triumvirs. After Stalin's victory, its importance diminished; it became a counterpart of the President's Cabinet in this country. In the Political Bureau, the Supreme Leader used to meet the chiefs of the main branches of the administration. It was, so to speak, the organization of "the inner circle" which necessarily exists within every complicated political machinery. In later years, the influence of the Political Bureau has steadily declined. At the outbreak of the war it was the Party Secretariat, consisting of four men, among them Stalin, which played the part of the Cabinet.

Below the Political Bureau and the Secretariat, highly complicated central and local agencies are in operation. Among them, the first place belongs to the secretaries of the Republican and Provincial Party Committees. Actually they play the part of governors-general or viceroys. Within the limit of his province the provincial leader, appointed "for the good pleasure" of the Supreme Leader, is as omnipotent as the latter in Moscow, naturally within the "area of freedom" left to him by the Leader, an area which is never well determined and always subject to fluctuation. The Provincial Secretary is assisted by an advisory Council, a counterpart of the Political Bureau; this is the Bureau of the Republican or Provincial Party Committee. Officially, it ought to be elected by the respective Committees; in actuality, its members are appointed by the Supreme Leader on recommendation of the provincial leader. Commonly, membership is granted to the heads of the chief administrative agencies of the province.

A similar organization with simplifications exists on the lower levels, i.e., in the districts, cities, towns, and villages. On the lowest level, the Secretary of the Primary Party Organization represents the most remote ramification of the dictatorial system.

On different levels, large and small assemblies are attached to this complicated pyramid of bureaucratic agencies which officially belong to the Soviet or Party system, or to the system of the Trade Unions. All these assemblies, called congresses, conferences, committees, Soviets, and the like do not actually participate in power. They are there not to command, but to obey; they convene to receive information about the policy chosen, for the time being, by the top of the dictatorial system and to convey it to those who are supposed to elect them. Except for this function, they are nothing but ceremonial institutions, shadows of the ideal systems of the Soviets, the Party, and the Trade Unions.

On the other hand, the individual levels of the bureaucratic pyramid are both supported and supervised by the many-branched system of the Secret Police. It was first known as "the Extraordinary Commission to Combat Counter-Revolution and Speculation"; in 1922, it received the name of the State Political Office (GPU); on July 10, 1934, already under The Great Retreat, it became the Division of Public Security within the Commissariat of the Interior; in 1941, it became a special Commissariat for Public Security. Actually, the nature of the machine never changed.

If a political machine is to be evaluated on the basis of its capacity to convey strictly and quickly to all who are concerned the impulsions originating in the center, and to transform these impulsions into actions, then the machine just described is close to perfection. There is perhaps one weak point in the structure: that is the lack of any regulation concerning the succession in supreme power. The shift from Lenin's leadership to that of the Triumvirate has been smoothed down by the fact that during the two years of Lenin's last sickness, the Triumvirate ruled in his name, as a kind of Regency. After his death (1924) it tried to rule as if he were alive, quoting sentences from his writs to justify every step and produce the impression that the deceased would have followed the same course. However, they had to fight against Trotsky, who considered himself Lenin's natural heir; they were able to defeat him, but immediately a struggle arose between Stalin and the other members of the Triumvirate. Finally, victory was Stalin's, and it is well known what the results were: Trotsky was exiled and, later on, murdered in Mexico; Kamenev and Zinovyev were deprived of all their positions, suffered all kinds of humiliation, and were finally executed, ten years after having lost the game. After 1927, apparently a few minor attempts were made to challenge Stalin's omnipotence, but all efforts were easily crushed by the machine, so that the problem of succession never was posed.

Succession, it appears, is determined by victory in struggle. There are rumors that Stalin has nominated his successor, but it is doubtful whether charismatic power may be transferred in this way. From the events of the earlier years, the following rule seems to emerge: succession in the line of the Supreme Leaders belongs to the most astute of the predecessor's immediate aids, but the virtual successor has to prove the validity of his claim by victory in combat. The pattern is approximately the same as that used in claiming and defending the champion's title in major sports: the individual's valor is decisive and no other title may be opposed to it.

4

Two complicated social systems, the Soviet democracy and the Party oligarchy, have been used both as screens and as material for the construction of the formidable fortress of the dictatorship of the One. Two problems are thus posed: how can the dictatorship within the Party be explained? And how can the existence of the corporate dictatorship of the Party over the Soviets be explained? To answer these questions, one must realize that no political structure, perhaps no social structure in general can be explained on the basis of present conditions and relationships only; past conditions and relationships are equally important because of the existence of social inertia, or of the tendency of social relations and structures to persist and become petrified.

Applying this principle to the first problem, we must take into consideration that when gaining power, the Party was not a party in the meaning used in democratic society; it was a semi-military organization uniting persons sharing a common faith, blindly obeying their leader, and bound by strong discipline. Two exceptionally good predictions of Lenin made his position invulnerable. Against the common belief of the secondary leaders, he asserted that in the fall of 1917 an upheaval would be successful; and, against the opinion of the majority of the secondary leaders, he asserted that the Brest-Litovsk peace treaty with its tremendous concessions to Germany would not be in force for more than one year. The second Leader, Stalin, gained final ascendancy within the inner circle of the Party when it was proven that he had been correct in predicting that the resistance of the peasants against collectivization could be crushed.

The leaders who gained power for the Party used it to take measures which would secure dominance "forever." These measures we already know: careful selection of applicants to the Party; Party education; enforcement of discipline; systematic purge. Stalin, the second Leader, added to these measures that of the planned selection of the personnel of the main Party officers, especially of the provincial and district secretaries. To do this, he used his position of Secretary General of the Party, being backed first by Lenin, who appointed him to this position, and then by the Triumvirate of which he was a member. When it came to a showdown with the other members of the Triumvirate, it appeared that all "commanding positions" were firmly in Stalin's hands.

But why do the others obey? The power of the One does not preclude high advantages for the many, especially for those located on higher levels. Having to obey blindly the orders of the One, the secondary and tertiary leaders still possess an "area of freedom" where they may display power; thus, one of the basic urges of man is gratified. High honors are awarded to them, and the ambition of many can be satisfied through gradual advance within the system. Material advantages, in kind or money, also await those who behave in accordance with expectations. Certainly, in the One's lifetime, none from among the secondary leaders can hope to be promoted to the highest rank. But why should anyone be so ambitious as to aspire to it?

How can the second problem, that of explaining the dictatorship of the Party over the Soviets be solved? The key may easily be found by pointing out that in 1917, power was actually gained by the Party and not by the Soviets, so that the Party was able to place men in whom they had confidence in all commanding positions. Only Communists were granted membership in the Council of the People's Commissars.* Only Communists were granted chairmanship in the numerous "Revolutionary Committees" formed in the big cities to impose and enforce the new order. The control of these commanding positions permitted the Communists to obtain the political monopoly discussed above. With such an instrument in their hands, they had nothing to fear from the elections: Communist majorities could be easily secured.

When this advantage was gained, an ingenious mechanism was invented to consolidate it. It was known as "the rule through Communist fractions" and was based on the principle that every Communist fraction, or the totality of Communists within a specified body, is subordinate to the corresponding Party organization. For example, the Communist fraction of a District Congress of the Soviets has to obey the orders of the District Party Committee. Every question to be officially discussed in a Soviet or a Congress has first to be decided by the Party organization, according to directions coming from the top. The decision is conveyed to the individual members of the fraction by the Party Secretary, and they have to vote unanimously in accordance with the directions received, under

---

* In the very beginning, a few left Socialist Revolutionists were permitted to join. They never had a share in real power.

threat of expulsion. Since the Communist fraction always possesses a majority, the system predetermines the outcome of the vote, though it appears that the decision is made by the Soviet or the Congress. Naturally, the same procedure is used with respect to elections: candidates are nominated by the Party organization and necessarily receive the votes of all the members of the Communist fraction.

It must be emphasized that the same system is used in regard to all human groupings permitted to exist in the Soviet State, especially to Trade Unions, the co-operative societies, and the so-called "voluntary societies," such as the Militant Atheist League, the League for the Combat against Illiteracy, the Union for Aerial and Chemical Defense, etc. Everywhere, Communist fractions determine the actions of the bodies which, at face value, should be independent.

It is obvious that the system is self-perpetuating; those in power are able to manage the elections in such a manner that the returns are always in their favor. A question arises at this point. If the dictatorial system and its policies were not supported by the nation at large, why did the nation not revolt? Actually, the people did revolt, but not as a nation: one day a group opposed intolerable blasphemy in one township; the next day in some other place another group fought the collectivization of their homesteads or the confiscation of food necessary for their survival. But modern technique gives to centralized power a decisive advantage against local revolts; and the use, by centralized power, of reckless means to check the crystallization of hostile forces prevented the agglomeration of partial revolts from evolving into a revolution aiming at the overthrow of the tyranny. Revolts have been frequent, but all were pitilessly crushed. This taught the Russian people the lesson that an attempt to overthrow the dictatorial order would have been as foolish, say, as the opening of the Second Front before the accumulation of forces which would determine victory. They had to wait. They waited—until circumstances imposed The Great Retreat on the government, which brought with it the realization of many of their demands, though not in the realm of politics.

5

However, has not The Great Retreat modified the political structure given to Russia under the Communist Experiment? This question must be raised since, in the midst of this retreat, one of the most conspicuous reforms of the whole period was carried out. The Soviet Union was granted a new Constitution, the famous Stalin Constitution of December 5, 1936.

When the Draft Constitution was published, Sidney Webb called it "a document which has astonished the Western World." [13] The general impression abroad was that dictatorship would be curtailed, democracy introduced, and political freedom established.

There are, however, very good reasons to oppose such an interpretation of the change. First of all, the circumstances in which the new Constitution was first announced showed a complete lack of regard for the institutions in which, according to earlier constitutional ideas, "Soviet democracy" was embodied. The announcement was made at one of the last meetings of the Seventh Union Congress of the Soviets by Molotov, Chairman of the Council of the People's Commissars, in the name of the Central Committee of the Communist Party. [14] This, as was frequently the case, had been convoked for a parallel session. The Union Congress tamely applauded a decision which in a genuinely democratic Soviet State could have originated only in the Congress itself. A Constitutional Committee was elected by the Union Central Executive Committee, with Stalin, First Secretary of the Communist Party, as Chairman. On June 12, 1936, a Draft Constitution was published, and an "informal discussion" was inaugurated. In order to help the discussion, fifteen million copies of the Draft Constitution were published, and there were frequent broadcasts. [15] The discussion consisted of making speeches at meetings of "toilers," publishing letters to the editors of Soviet papers, and so forth. No less than 43,000 proposals for changes in the Draft were made.

On November 25, 1936, the Union Soviet Congress met in a special session. No elections took place; local Soviets, elected in 1934–5, before the announcement of the constitutional reform, sent delegates to the Congress. The Draft encountered no opposition. A certain number of minor changes were retained and, on December 5, a unanimous vote gave Russia a new Constitution which has been in force since January 1, 1937.

Secondly, the Soviet leaders themselves have unanimously asserted that no major change in the political setup was considered. During the "informal discussion" Kalinin, Chairman of the Union Central Executive Committee, stated that the new Constitution was a legal document which established formally legal relations already existing.[16] About the same time one could read in *Pravda:* "The Constitution is not a program, because it simply registers firmly and indisputably what the Soviet Nation has achieved."[17] It was especially emphasized that the salient features of the political structure of new Russia —dictatorship and the one-party system—were to be preserved. At the Soviet Congress, Krylenko, then the People's Commissar for Justice, said:

> Inasmuch as we are still surrounded by capitalist countries, our Constitution is not only a declaration of the rights of the people, but also provides for the extermination of the enemies of the people. The revolutionary dictatorship was, is, and will remain the only form of our Soviet government.[18]
>
> As regards political parties [said Stalin], several parties can exist where there are antagonistic classes. In the USSR there is no soil for several parties. There is soil for only one party, which can only be the Communist Party.[19]

Out of the real changes, the most important one was this: The New Constitution replaced the original Soviet structure by a structure purporting to imitate that of Western democracies. Voters elect directly both the local, district, and provincial Soviets, and also the Supreme Soviets of the republics and of the Union. Contact between the political bodies of different levels has been definitively broken. In this way the "pyramidal" or "peripheral" structure of the original Soviets has been replaced by the normal "centralized" structure.

For many years the specific "pyramidal" structure of the Soviet State was declared to be the "true" democracy in opposition to the "pseudo democracies" of the Western countries.[20] The constitutional reform means, therefore, either replacing a better and more democratic structure by a worse and less democratic one, or repudiating the idea that the original Soviet structure was a "new word" in political organization.[21]

Closely related to structural changes were changes in the mode of election. First of all, the principle of general franchise was adopted. During the "popular discussion" of the new Constitution, the idea of giving priests the right to vote and be elected was opposed.[22] The decision was finally taken to abolish all discriminations. Under former Constitutions, elections were indirect. The structural reform of the Soviet pyramid resulted in introducing direct elections. Moreover, earlier elections were unequal. In 1936, after an almost wholesale collectivization of peasants which transformed them from individual producers to members of collective enterprises, all votes were given the same force.[23] Finally, before 1936, elections were generally open. The new Constitution ordered that elections should be secret.

General, direct, equal, and secret elections, in a country which had not had them since 1917,* may seem to be a great victory for the democratic ideal. The examples of Italy and Germany, as well as older examples—for instance, that of the second French Empire—have shown that a dictatorship may allow "general elections," provided that freedom of electioneering and of nominating candidates is controlled. Such is the case

---

* In 1917, elections to the Constituent Assembly took place; but this Assembly was disbanded by the Communists after its first meeting on January 18, 1918.

in the Soviet Union, and the new Constitution does not change anything in this respect. In what concerns the nomination of candidates, the situation is clearly defined by Clauses 126 and 141 of the Constitution:

The most active and politically conscious citizens from among the working class, and of the other strata of the toilers unite in the Communist Party of the USSR, which is the vanguard of the toilers in the struggle to strengthen and develop the socialist system and which represents the leading core of all organizations of the toilers . . .

Candidates are nominated for elections according to electoral districts. The right to nominate candidates is granted to public organizations and societies of toilers: Communist Party organization, trade-unions, co-operative, youth organizations, and cultural societies.

These clauses may seem to be innovations in the new Constitution. As a matter of fact, they correspond to the practice established from the very beginning. It is the meaning of the clauses which is significant. The voters elect delegates directly and secretly to Soviets of all levels, but they have to choose exclusively among candidates nominated directly by the Communist Party or by organizations controlled by the Party. If two or more candidates are nominated by the appropriate organizations for an electoral district, personal preferences [24] of the voters may decide whether the candidate presented by the Party is to be elected, or the one nominated by the Trade Union controlled by the Party. But there is clearly no political difference between the two cases, and if the appropriate organizations agree on one candidate, the voters have absolutely no choice. They would have to abstain from voting in order to show their disapproval of the political system or of the governmental policy; but abstaining might be noticed on special lists, and would not be completely safe in any dictatorial State. On the other hand, only a free press or free opposition parties would be able to induce larger groups of voters to protest by means of abstention; and there is neither a free press nor any legal party outside of the "ruling" one in Soviet Russia.

Consequently, the new electoral system is of a kind which determines in advance the "victory" of the government. Russian dictatorship has clearly nothing to fear from elections.

But are these statements correct? Is not the freedom of press and assembly guaranteed by Clause 125 of the new Constitution:

The citizens of the USSR are guaranteed freedom of speech, of the press, of assembly, and of holding mass-meetings, street processions, and demonstrations. These rights of the citizens are insured by placing at the disposal of the toilers and their organizations printing presses, supplies of paper, public buildings, the streets, means of communication, and other material prerequisites for the exercise of these rights.

Sidney Webb has professed to see in this clause a "unique and unprecedented conception of public freedom." [25] It might perhaps have been so had Clause 125 been something more than a curtailed repetition of Clauses 5 and 6 of the Constitution of the RSFSR of May 11, 1925, which in their turn were merely a repetition of Clauses 14 and 15 of the Constitution of the same Republic of July 10, 1918, discussed above. For one who has compared the texts, there can be no doubt here. The freedom proclaimed by the new Constitution is the same as that proclaimed by the Constitutions of 1918, 1923, and 1925.

There are several other provisions concerning political freedom. The much-debated Clause 125 guarantees "freedom of religious worship and of antireligious propaganda." But this is merely an echo of Clause 4 of the Constitution of the RSFSR of 1925, modified in an important point in May, 1929.

Clause 127 of the new Constitution may seem to introduce into the Soviet law freedom from unauthorized arrest and imprisonment. Its text is as follows:

The citizens of the USSR are guaranteed the inviolability of person. No person may be placed under arrest except by decision of a court or with the sanction of a State attorney.

In reality, this Habeas Corpus is not new in Soviet law. The code of Criminal Procedure of February 15, 1923 (still in force), includes the Clause (5):

No person may be placed under arrest except of cases indicated by law and in forms foreseen by law.

Unfortunately, the existence of such a statement has done little to prevent measures highly incompatible with the Habeas Corpus principle.

That the reformed Soviet system functions just as the original one did may be proved by a survey of the practical application of the Constitution. An electoral law was published on July 9, 1937. It seemed to be more liberal than the Constitution, for it granted the right to nominate candidates (in addition to the bodies mentioned in the Constitution) to the general assemblies of workers and employees in factories, of peasants in collective farms, and of soldiers in military units.[26] If applied at face value, the electoral law could have created great technical difficulties, for hundreds of candidates could have been nominated in every electoral district by the numerous "general assemblies." The leadership solved the difficulty in the following manner. A Coalition of the Communists and the Non-Party Citizens was proclaimed,[27] and the task was imposed on it to secure, in every electoral district, the unanimous election of the candidate of the coalition. In order to designate this candidate, a "guiding staff" was appointed by the Party organization, and this staff decided both which general assembly (or general assemblies) should be granted the privilege of nominating the candidate, and also who this candidate would be.

The technique of the nomination in these assemblies has been described in the following words: "Someone on the floor would suggest a candidate . . . and he would be nominated by a show of hands. Anyone failing to vote for the designated candidate would be known." [28] Thus the practice of the open ballot was revived in regard to the preliminary, but actually decisive act of the nomination of the candidate. Almost without exception, of course, only one candidate was nominated in each district.

The elections (held on December 12, 1937) proved to be as unanimous and, accordingly, as devoid of political significance as those in the Fascist States: 96.8% of the voters took part in the election; the candidates of the coalition received 98.6% of the votes in the elections for the Union Council and 97.8% in the elections for the Council of Nationalities.[29] The residue represented invalid ballots. The result was that 855 of the 1,143 members of the Supreme Soviet were Communists;[30] the "Communist fraction" formed 81% of the Union Council and 71% of the Council of Nationalities.* It is noteworthy that in the last Union Congress of the Soviets, the seventh (which met in February, 1935), the Communists fraction formed 73.8% of the house, the figures for the two preceding congresses having been 72.8% and 73.0%. Thus the new Constitution resulted in an increase in the strength of the dictatorial organization in the highest constitutional body.

The forms of the activity of the Supreme Soviet proved to be no different in any respect from those of its predecessors. Just as under the old Constitution the sessions of the Union Congress of the Soviets and of its Central Executive Committee were rare, short, and uneventful, so have been the sessions of the Supreme Council. Up to Hitler's attack on Russia, it had only eight active periods (an average of 2.5 periods a year). The periods have lasted, respectively, 8, 12, 7, 4, 3, 8, 7, and 5 days (an average of 6.75 days). The earlier sessions had to ratify a few bills introduced by the government and selected almost at random among those which were ready, whereas other bills of equal or greater importance were ratified in other manners. Only one bill, that concerning the ratification of international conventions, was introduced by one of the Committees of the Council of Nationalities.[31] The activity of later sessions was restricted to the ratification of changes in the Constitution,[32] the examination and ratification of the

---

* The two Councils form the Supreme Soviet of the Soviet Union; they correspond roughly to the House of Representatives and the Senate.

Union budget, and the ratification of the "*Ukazes*" of the Bureau of the Supreme Council.

During the sessions, no one has dared to disagree with government drafts. Government speakers have occupied the chair for a much longer time than private members. Private members have had nothing to say but to report the glorious achievements of Communism in their respective areas. American correspondents frequently found nothing to wire except that "the debate . . . revealed nothing of particular interest." [33]

Every time the Commissioner for Foreign Affairs has made a declaration, the Supreme Council has unanimously decided to abstain from debate; when this happened in regard to the tremendous shift from the policy of collective security to that of friendship with Hitler, the Supreme Council renounced discussion, "because of the clarity and consistency of the foreign policy of the Soviet government." [34]

Moreover, the Supreme Soviet did not become the unique or even the main legislative body of the Soviet State, as might have been expected from statements made when the Constitution was drafted. Just as in earlier years, the Central Committee of the Communist Party was convoked to session simultaneously with the Supreme Council, and it was the Committee, not the Soviet, which decided problems of major importance. [35]

Finally, the Bureau of the Supreme Soviet continued the practice of the Bureau of the Union Central Executive Committee, and between the active periods of the Supreme Soviet (that is, almost throughout the year) functioned instead of the Soviet, introducing changes [36] in laws and even in the Constitution, and appointing and dismissing the people's commissars. An innovation occurred only in regard to words: an act of the new Bureau is designated as a *Ukaz*, a term which in Imperial Russia was used to designate nonlegislative acts of the Emperor and certain acts of the highest administrative and judicial bodies. With great docility and without asking for any explanation, the Supreme Soviet, at the end of every active period, ratified long lists of such changes and appointments.

6

We have seen that Stalin's Constitution did not produce
any reversal in the trend of political development: political
things remained where they had been before its promulgation.
Neither has there been any substantial change in the Party
system, despite declarations regarding its reorganization in the
spirit of democracy. A few months after the new Constitution
was ratified, the Central Committee of the Communist Party
published a "resolution" about the preparation of the Party
for the elections. The Central Committee declared that the
dictatorship of the Proletariat was to become "more flexible
and therefore more powerful." In order to attain this, the
democratic structure within the Party was to be re-established.
This meant re-establishing elections (in place of co-optation)
as the means of creating Party Committees, using the secret
ballot in these elections, and restoring the right of Party members to criticize candidates.[37] In practice, the introduction of
Party democracy has resulted in nothing more than in the
ratification, by the eighteenth Party Congress, of a new Party
statute submitted by the leadership, and quite insignificant
from the standpoint of the development of democracy.[38]

The chief change was that, in conformity with the tendencies of the new Constitution, the class differentials concerning the admission of new Party members were abolished. New
members were no longer required to know the Party program
in detail, but had only to accept it in general. The Party
agencies carrying out the purges have been brought under the
direct authority of the Supreme Leader, while previous to the
reform they were given some semblance of independence.
General purges have been abolished since, during the last one,
the authors of a large part of the persecution were later on
found to be "enemies of the people." Despite redundant declarations, Party elections continued being managed as they always had been.[39]

The major fact is, however, that the Constitutional Reform
coincided with the Great Terror which began after the assas-

sination, by a Communist, of Stalin's best aid, Kirov (December 1, 1934). A decree was immediately promulgated entitling the courts, in political trials, to sentence the defendants to death without having heard them or their counsels. Mass executions started immediately. The climax was reached in the famous Moscow trials (1936–8) which resulted in the conviction and execution of the Old Guard of Bolshevism, i.e., of nearly all men who had co-operated with Lenin and remembered well that there had been a time when Stalin was not a Great Man within the Party.[40] The meaning of the executions is clear to anyone who understands the general trend of the political development, uninterrupted by The Great Retreat. The purge eliminated virtually all persons who, in case of trouble, could have become Stalin's rivals for supreme leadership; the list naturally was comprised of all those who, in the course of the twenty years prior to the trials, had competed with Stalin or opposed his policies. After the purge, no man was left in Russia whose political rank and prestige was not derived from Stalin's favor.[41]

The execution of Stalin's rivals was preceded by the "self-liquidation" of a few bodies in which a slight vestige of self-government within the inner circle was expressed; these were the Association of the Old Bolsheviks and the Association of the Political Prisoners of Imperial Russia.[42] The Great Terror was accompanied by a general purge of the Party which resulted in the expulsion of 580,000 members.

The wave of terror reached far beyond the scope of the Party. The Habeas Corpus clauses of the new Constitution did not prevent the execution of the leaders of the Red Army (June, 1937). The restatement of "religious freedom" did not prevent a revival of religious persecutions under the pretext of possible interference of religious organizations in the electoral campaign. Unbelievable numbers of Soviet officials, in high or humble positions, were accused of counterrevolution, wreckage, espionage, affiliation with Trotsky, and other crimes; for these crimes, after trial or without trial, they were jailed, exiled, deported, or executed.

Most symptomatic of the persistence of political tension is, however, the fact that the practice of detaining large numbers of dissenters has not been abandoned or mitigated. The extent to which this practice is applied is unknown. But it must be tremendous. Quite a few recent visitors to Russia have, more or less accidentally, taken notice of it.[43]

No dictator, however cruel, would detain millions of men in prisons or prison camps simply for the pleasure of inflicting pain on them. Consequently, there must be millions of men whom Stalin and his henchmen consider dangerous to the regime. This means that they oppose the dictatorship, either because they dislike dictatorship as such, or because they disagree with its policies. This shows that the basic situation which made dictatorship necessary has not changed. Were the dictatorial pressure lifted, new men and new ideas would at least have started competing with the present-day leaders. The leaders know this and follow the natural path of all governments ruling without the consent of the governed.

7

Our findings may be summarized as follows:

1. Political dictatorship has been one of the most salient features of the Communist regime from its birth up to the present day.

2. With time, dictatorship has become more concentrated and more ostentatious; while in the beginning dictatorial power was officially ascribed to the Soviets, today the concentration of power in the hands of the One is no longer concealed.

3. In the denial of personal freedom and self-government, this dictatorship is incomparably more emphatic than the Russian autocracy was before the Constitutional Reform of 1905–6, not to speak of the years of Constitutional Monarchy. Politically, Russia has been brought back to the end of the eighteenth century.

4. The Constitutional Reform of 1936 has not materially changed the situation.

On this basis, the following preliminary conclusions may be drawn:

1. The inner necessity to rule the country on the basis of dictatorship is a strong argument in favor of the shock-hypothesis as formulated in this work.

2. The persistence of dictatorship proves that the shock situation which obtained in 1917 has not yet been completely liquidated.

3. The liquidation of dictatorship would be tantamount to the final liquidation of the shock situation—in other words, to the termination of the attempts to impose policies contrary to the will of the governed. Vice versa, the termination of such attempts would eliminate the very reason for the existence of the dictatorial system.

CHAPTER VI

THE ECONOMIC TRANSFIGURATION:

The Goal Was Just Around the Corner

1

DICTATORSHIP WAS NOT the ultimate end of those who created it, operated it, and profited from it. The ultimate end of the Communist leaders was the creation, through dictatorship, of a new society on the basis of the Marxist doctrine. Since the Marxists held that the social organization of production is the very foundation of every society, and that all other phases of social and cultural life depend on that organization, they thought that the economic transfiguration of Russia was paramount. In capitalist society the means of production, i.e., land, factories, raw material, money, belong to a few who form the masters' class. In socialist society the private ownership of the means of production must be abolished, and the collective property of these means established. In this way the division of society in classes is destroyed, and with it the very source of inequality.

The attempts to realize this program inevitably met strong resistance. In Russia the typical "masters," in the Marxist interpretation of this term, i.e., the landlords and businessmen, were not numerous and could be easily crushed. But the majority of the Russian people consisted of peasants, "little masters" in Lenin's terminology, strongly imbued with the "bourgeois" spirit. In their actions they were determined by economic self-interest and had no stronger desire than to acquire more land, not for the collectivity, but for themselves— if necessary, at the expense of their neighbors. The hostility to Marxist plans of the little masters from the countryside was so

implacable, and they were so numerous and so obviously irre-
placeable as food producers, that a basic distinction had to be
made from the start—namely, between urban and rural areas.
Only the former could be submitted to speedy social and economic transformation; in the latter case, the "little masters"
were to be given satisfaction. To that end the First Agrarian
Revolution * was launched and carried out by the Soviet government with the support of the rural population, but in direct
contradiction to the Communist doctrine.

The Russian Communists were orthodox Marxists. According
to their opinion, only concentrated production could be efficient; therefore, land should be expropriated in totality and
large estates created and managed by representatives of the
victorious proletariat in the same way as factories. This was
obviously inacceptable for the village. Therefore, the land-
decree of November 8, 1917 (enacted the day after the successful upheaval) was inspired not by the Communist, but
by the Populist program.[1] Land (landlords' as well as peasants') was nationalized without any indemnity. The landowners' estates disappeared. The principal tension which existed
in rural Russia before the revolution, that between landlords
and peasants, ceased to exist. Those lands which, in the years
1861–1917, had been bought by peasants were united with the
mirs. Richer peasants lost their land-surpluses; but they remained members of agrarian communities and were therefore
not entirely despoiled. The new farms created by the Stolypin
reform were also subjected to the process of equalization; frequently they were simply reincluded in the agrarian communities, and their owners became *mir* peasants. According to
the Populist program, hiring agricultural workers and leasing
land was forbidden; every family was to cultivate its allotment by its own means. If these means were insufficient, the
land was to be partitioned anew.

It cannot be sufficiently emphasized that the First Agrarian
Revolution did not engender rural socialism: after the reform,
the head of the homestead remained a "little master," individ-

* The Second Agrarian Revolution took place in 1929–30.

ually tilling his allotment and selling the surplus on the market. Therefore, he continued being motivated in his acts by the prerevolutionary principle of self-interest.

Except for a few State and collective farms retained as springboards for a later offensive,* the agrarian revolution in the Populist style was carried out throughout the country. The increase of the surface of land tilled by peasants was not and could not be substantial since, as we already know, in 1917 the landed estates did not comprise much arable land and, moreover, almost half of such land was leased to the peasants. Therefore, the increase in the area tilled by the peasants did not exceed eight per cent; for an additional eight per cent, the peasants no longer had to pay rent. The exiguity of the increase was a great disappointment to the peasants, who were used to comparing their small allotments with the big estates and expected wonders from "the black partition" (wholesale equalization of land holdings) forgetting how numerous they were and how small the number of the estates.

Moreover, the Populist ideal of achieving complete equality throughout rural Russia—perhaps of transforming her into one gigantic *mir*—was not reached. Landlords' estates were distributed throughout the country in an irregular way. They were more numerous and larger in districts where the villages were relatively not overcrowded, and less numerous and smaller in districts where agrarian overpopulation existed. According to the Populist program, such inequality was to have been corrected by redistributing the population through the country. But there was civil war, and the Soviet government did not care for such plans. It left the peasants free to arrange their affairs as they liked. The intensity of equalization was quite different in various districts; in general, the section composed of central and eastern Russia was submitted to this principle with more rigor than the northern, western and southern provinces.

* State farms were tilled by workers hired by State agencies. Collective farms of that period were "agrarian communes" on which farm hands were settled with the instruction to till land corporately and to share the output in a brotherly manner.

On the other hand, the so-called "black partition" was not a sudden act, but lasted through the whole period; land redistribution took place again and again, depriving the peasants of the feeling of security, and making the situation in villages a chaotic one.[2]

The wholesale return to the *mir* system signified the destruction of the germs of agricultural progress which had accumulated since the Stolypin reform, and the inhibition of all incentives for technical improvement and investment. Naturally, the crops fell below their previous, already low level. This meant a substantial deterioration of the situation, more than compensating for the insignificant gain from the acquisition of the landed estates.

In the countryside, the Utopia of the Populists was tried and refuted by experience. In urban areas, the same occurred with the Marxist Utopia. In the very beginning, the new rulers did not destroy the private ownership of industrial and commercial enterprises and were satisfied with placing them under "the workers' control," i.e., making the owner dependent on the decision of a workers' committee. The final solution was, however, "collective ownership" of the means of production, completely eliminating the "bourgeoisie," but also eliminating the claims of the individual groups of workers on the factories where they worked.

Two aspects were involved in the realization of the program: nationalization or the breakdown of legal ties between the economic units and their former owners, and the reorganization of industry and commerce on the basis of subservience to collective needs.

Nationalization was an easy task, since the owners were not in a position to resist. This task was carried out by a series of decrees, part of which directly nationalized specified groups of enterprises, whereas others conferred on specified agencies the right to nationalize those economic units which they considered fit.[3] On the basis of these decrees, almost the totality of industrial and commercial enterprises, as well as almost all the "dwelling space" in towns and cities were taken over from their former owners and incorporated into the collective domain of the nation, to speak in the style of the epoch.

After having nationalized the majority of economic units, the new rulers had to organize them into a system which would operate at least as well as the capitalist one had. At this point, extremely difficult problems arose. First, in capitalist society the economic process goes on as the result of the activity of an indeterminate number of economic agents motivated by economic self-interest. This interest was to be replaced by something else. According to the Doctrine, the incentive of social service had to emerge. Very soon it appeared that this was not the case. The second difficulty was that of replacing by a workable scheme the automatic price mechanism existing in capitalist society and depending on the free market. By whom and how were the prices to be determined? Or perhaps ought money to be abolished in order to evade the problem? But, then, what device could replace it? The third difficulty was that of securing smooth adjustment between socialist economics in urban areas and individualistic economics in the countryside.

To face such problems, the new rulers had no plans whatsoever. Very probably they did not even suspect that such problems would emerge. Lenin had in mind only the vague idea of "the unique factory" unifying all branches of production under a single direction, approximately as Ford unifies all particular processes which converge in the production of automobiles.

Since no original idea was present in the minds of the new rulers, and the situation demanded an immediate solution, imitation of an already experienced pattern was the natural response. Such a pattern was found in the structure improperly called German War Communism. The new rulers were well acquainted with it through a series of brilliant articles published, under the Imperial regime, by the Communist, Lurie-Larin, in one of the most respectable, liberal, but by no means socialist journals of Russia.

However, the pattern was imitated with a substantial change.

In Germany, the councils of the semipublic corporations which, in the course of the war, regulated the economic life comprised a large number of businessmen. Early in 1918, Russian industrialists offered Lenin a plan of the same kind. After deliberation, he rejected the offer; according to his doctrine, former owners necessarily would be guided by their class-consciousness and therefore act in opposition to the interests of the Communist Revolution.

Therefore, "the single factory" was organized according to an entirely bureaucratic pattern. Every nationalized enterprise was placed under the orders of a director whose selection depended upon his loyalty, with complete lack of regard for his business experience. If the enterprise was big, he was aided by a staff of men of the same type. Above the director a cluster of co-ordinating agencies was created, both on territorial and functional bases, with vaguely delimited and usually overlapping jurisdiction. The structure was crowned by a number of "Central Boards," such as that of the Textile or the Coal Industry, which in their turn were headed by the Supreme Council of National Economy consisting of numerous departments and sections, always in flux. The chairman of the Council had the rank of a People's Commissar; in his person, the system was incorporated into the total system of the new Soviet bureaucracy.

The rulers expected that the new directors would act approximately as the old-style managers did and thus keep the process of production and exchange going on. But they did not and could not do so. First of all, the degree of their preparedness for the assigned tasks was very low.[4] Secondly, they were not stimulated as economic agents in capitalist society are: they received their monthly salary independently of the economic results of their activity, and held their positions so long as their loyalty remained above suspicion. Thirdly, the structure being entirely bureaucratic, the responsibility of the managers of individual enterprises was restricted to technical matters. The entire commercial side of their work, which formerly was made up a series of operations of free economic agents, was henceforth to be a part of the complex system of operations effected by State agencies. Requests for raw material, fuel, and so on were sent from below upwards, while orders to manufacture certain commodities and distribute them traveled in the opposite direction. The principle of unity required almost all requests to travel the full length of the administrative channel to the central organization, and every order to make the return journey to the local enterprise. The number of questions that had thus to be settled in Moscow was beyond imagining.

The situation was further complicated by the equalitarian trend involved in Communist mentality, especially as understood on the lower levels of the new society. It is true that the leaders never ordered the equalization of all wages and salaries. But the general tendency was to decrease social distances, and to pay technicians and skilled labor only a little more than unskilled labor. With the advance of inflation, which had started before the Revolution but gained momentum after it, monetary remuneration became more symbolic than real, and the remuneration in kind, on the basis of ration books, depended not on an individual's skill and efficiency, but on his membership in a more or less privileged class. In this way, the most powerful incentive for efficient work was lost: good work, poor work, or no work at all—the material situation of an individual was not affected.

The inefficiency of the system was acknowledged hundreds of times by those who created and operated it—after they had shifted to another, better system. For many years the specter of an eventual return to War Communism terrified all minds. The situation was aggravated through the fact that the system was operated in the course of a Civil War demanding the highest efficiency to maintain tolerable conditions of life.

There exists no means to determine whether the inefficiency of the economic system or the Civil War contributed more to the disaster. But the magnitude of the catastrophe may be measured. Regarding industry, it is expressed in the fact that, in 1920, the industrial output was approximately 18 per cent of that of 1913.* The collapse of industry became the starting point for further disastrous developments. Since the government rightly considered that the cities were its strongholds, the curtailed industrial output was almost entirely distributed among the urban population. For the countryside, nothing was left. The peasants were at that time individual producers. Their response to the new situation was the natural response of such producers. They decreased the cultivated area and the number of cattle in order to have no more surpluses, which had become useless. This signified starvation for the towns, industrial districts, and the army. The new government could not allow it. Bread and other products of agriculture could no longer be bought in villages; consequently, they had to be taken away by force. A general obligation of supplying the State with products of agriculture was imposed.[5] In many cases, the requisition did not leave enough food for the survival of the rural population and their cattle. The resistance of peasants was broken by military expeditions. The civil war between Reds and Whites was complicated by a civil war between towns and villages.

Rationing had to be introduced in cities, and the class principle was applied to its organization: manual workers came first, intellectual workers came second, and the members of the former upper classes received nothing. The rations were quite unsatisfactory even at face value and, in practice, still less was distributed. To survive, the urban population, including the bureaucracy and the Party members, had to use the services of "bag-bearers" or "speculators," i.e., of illegal traders who, under tremendous hardships and always exposed to prosecution and even execution, performed a kind of barter trade between city dwellers who gave away all durable goods they possessed (such as plates, dishes, watches, clothes) and the peasants who were eager to acquire some real things for part of their production.

* The basic figures as to the output of industry and agriculture in the course of the Communist period of Russian history are collected in Appendix II, tables 2 and 4; see also Charts II and III.

Russia has never been a rich country; the socioeconomic degradation of the years 1917–21 made her no longer self-sufficient. When in 1921 the climatic conditions were exceptionally bad, this resulted in famine.

2

The first attempt to endow Russia with socialist economics was defeated by famine, peasants' upheavals, industrial catastrophe, and the return to primitive barter. Lenin ordered a retreat which lasted eight years and is known as the New Economic Policy (NEP). Retreat is not always a symptom of final defeat; it may be carried out the better to prepare an offensive. Such was the meaning of the NEP; in its course, forces for a new socialist offensive had to be accumulated. Hence, the basic structural pattern of the period, "the two sectors economics." This was an invention of the leaders of the Russian Communist Party, one of the surprisingly few social inventions made by them.

The two sectors were the collective and the private ones. The collective sector consisted of "key positions" retained by the State; the rest was returned to private enterprise, to be organized on capitalist principles. The key positions were defined by Lenin as follows: (1) basic industry; (2) banking; (3) means of communication and transportation, and (4) foreign trade. In its turn, basic industry was defined as large-scale industry plus industry producing means of further production. The conspicuous failure of the "single factory" pattern demanded reorganization of State industry according to some new pattern which would guarantee efficiency. This new pattern was not invented by Lenin, but borrowed by him from the practice of Western society. Two systems of organization appeared best fitted for imitation in the regime which was rising from the ruins of the Communist Experiment of the years 1917–21. The first was "the municipal corporation," according to which public utilities, such as electrical power plants, street cars, and the like, though owned by cities, counties, or prov-

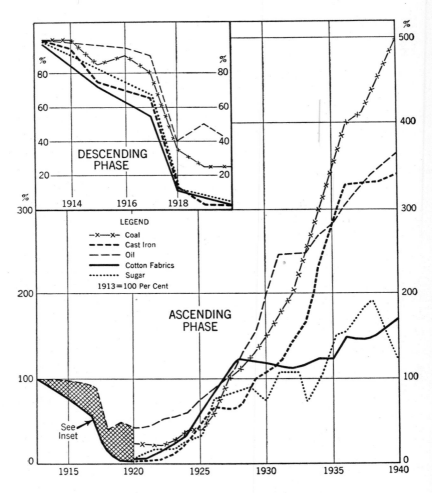

II. INDUSTRIAL OUTPUT, 1913–1940

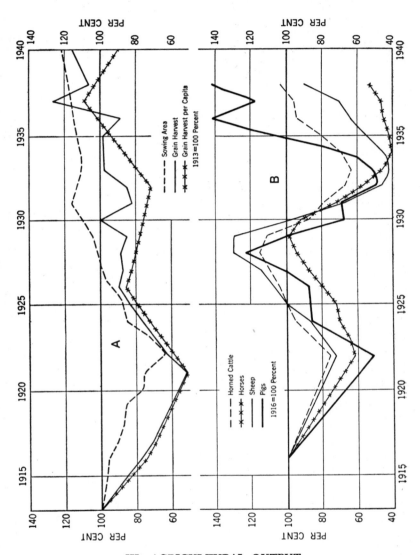

III. AGRICULTURAL OUTPUT

inces, were separated from the political domain and managed as if they were private enterprises, the owner giving to the manager only very general directions and refraining from interference with business details. The second was the "trust" formed by the grouping of several independent undertakings under one management. The combination of these two forms gave rise to a peculiar system of organization. Henceforth, State industry no longer took the form of a single vast enterprise, and instead of "the single factory," a network of relatively independent units (trusts) made their appearance (approximately 500 in basic industry).

Starting from the idea that the restoration of capitalist forms would enable the ruined industry to revive, the decree of April 10, 1923, gave the trusts a structure that in many respects resembled that of joint stock companies in capitalist society. They had an administrative board, a managing director, managers of the individual enterprises, and an auditing committee, and the statutes regulating the rights and duties of these agencies were exact counterparts of the articles of association of a company. But the general assembly of shareholders was replaced by the State authority to which the trust was attached; more often than not this was the Supreme Council of National Economy. This authority had to draw up the general plan of work, supervise its execution, sanction specified operations, and appoint and dismiss the higher staff. In the framework of these directions, the managers were given the right to make decisions as freely as private owners or executives do: they could hire and fire workers, buy raw material and machinery, and sell the output. In other words, their acts ceased to be administrative acts and became free acts of economic agents, as they are in capitalist society. Naturally, their decisions were limited by the labor legislation and the general directions of the Supreme Council. In the beginning, these directions were rather vague; often they were reduced to the formula that the manager earn a profit for the State, as managers in capitalist society do for their masters. Furthermore, the basic economic incentive of capitalist society was restored in its operation: the managers were given substantial shares in the profits (bonuses) and the workers resumed being paid according to skill and efficiency, often under the principle of piece work. To gain profits, the managers had to use the same technique as in capitalist society: the free market was restored, and even such "bourgeois" institutions as the stock exchange.

In pure form, the structure described above existed only during the first few years of the period. Gradually, two substantial changes were introduced. First, wholesale home trade was incorporated into the collective sector. Secondly, the State, as the owner of the trusts, increased its interference with business; above the trusts, "syndicates" and later on, even "central boards" dealing with the main branches of economic activity were created, which were entrusted with such functions as the fixation of prices, the elaboration of norms of production, the division of markets, etc.

In the private sector, two subsectors were distinguished, one formed by the residue of industry, home trade, and housing, and the other by the rural homesteads. In the urban subsector, change was drastic. The principle of denationalization was applied: work done during the period of War Communism was undone, and former owners and managers invited to take over their enterprises; if they could not be found (many had died, others had emigrated) or if they refused the honor, other persons were granted property or lease of the enterprise.[6] If nobody was willing to operate the economic unit, its operation was discontinued; in no case did the State continue operating it. The owners of the denationalized and leased enterprises were assumed to act on the basis of economic self-interest. Naturally their acts were to be guided by situations prevailing on the free market. Legal forms were essential for the smooth functioning of the system, and they were granted by the Civil Code of October 31, 1922, a somewhat hasty compilation of legal rules borrowed from the most progressive legislative acts of mature liberal society.[7] This Code recognized the "bourgeois" institution of inheritance. In the beginning, the size of the estate which could be inherited was limited, but in 1926 such restrictions were dropped. Moreover, the monetary system was restored and put on the solid basis of the gold standard. The reform was drafted by outstanding Russian economists of the "bourgeois" school. For quite a few years, the price level was close to stability.

In the rural subsector change was not so drastic, since there, even under War Communism, "capitalistic relations" had been preserved. However, under the NEP these relations were stabilized and liberated from the inhibitions introduced because of the acceptance of the Populist Utopia. A series of special decrees, which were later included in the Agrarian Code enacted October 30, 1922, restored order in regard to the using of the land. The Code maintained the principle of nationalization; but, according to clause 11, the land was leased in perpetuity to the peasants or peasant groups who cultivated it.° The *mir* structure was once more reinforced with regard to almost all of the arable soil. But disorderly and too frequent land partitions were prohibited. Land tenure was regulated in the same way as it had been before the Revolution.[8]

The same Agrarian Code allowed the peasants (with certain exceptions) to hire workers and lease land. Corn levies were replaced by taxes in kind, later on by taxes in the regular monetary form. Private trade with corn and other agricultural products was re-established; peasants were enabled to sell their surpluses on the free market at prices determined by the law of supply and demand. Since industrial commodities were again available on the market, the principal incentive towards increasing rural production again existed.

The NEP was greeted by the population as "return to normalcy"—still more, as liberation from a nightmare. Very rapidly, the economic machinery resumed working and satisfying the needs of the people. Seven years after Lenin's recantation, the industrial output returned to the prewar level. This was a great achievement as compared with the destructive years of War

---

° Less than eight years later this promise was broken by the policy of wholesale collectivization.

Communism. However, one must not forget that in 1928 the level of 1913 was just regained, whereas in the years preceding war and revolution, industrial production rapidly advanced. Thus, fifteen years were lost for economic progress.

In the countryside, towards the end of the period, the cultivated area was nearly the same as before the Revolution, but the crops were smaller. But with regard to cattle, the year 1928 reached a maximum attained neither before nor since. However, this advance was not yet sufficient to restore the old economic level, for the population rapidly increased. This resulted in curtailing the average food supply. Very accurate investigations of the question have shown that from 0.49 metric ton per inhabitant before the Revolution, the crops had decreased to 0.45 towards the end of the NEP period.[9]

This was one of the unfavorable aspects of the situation, but from the viewpoint of the Soviet government there was another, which was considered much more important. The new agrarian structure resulted in a very rapid differentiation within the Russian village. The rise of the *kulak* group made the government dependent on its good will with regard to the food supply of towns and industrial districts. According to official data, out of the 10.5 million metric tons of grain sold on the free market during the later years of the NEP, 2.8 million, or 20 per cent, were of *kulak* production.[10] The *kulaks* were able to retain their corn if dissatisfied with prices; this actually happened in the fall of 1927 and again in the fall of 1928.

During the later years of the NEP, the government tried various means to induce peasants to sell their crops to governmental agents and, when their failure had become obvious, reintroduced compulsion; Clause 107 of the Criminal Code, prohibiting the artificial raising of prices, was applied against rich peasants who had refused to sell their corn. In accordance with this law, their crops were confiscated. The experience of War Communism was repeated: compulsion applied to individual producers resulted in decreasing the output. A total change had to take place in order to save the situation.

3

The attitude of the *kulaks* was only one of the causes of the abandonment of the NEP. The main cause was obviously not economic, since economically the NEP had been a marked success; it was political and social, and will be studied at another place. However, the decision to abandon the NEP and to proceed to a Second Socialist Offensive was greatly facilitated by the gradual evaporation of the dark reminiscences of War Communism. When a war is over, people are ready to swear that never again will they fight; a generation passes, and they find themselves fighting another war. However, in order to overcome the terror inspired by a previous war, the new generation must be persuaded that meanwhile a new weapon has become available, or a new situation has emerged making victory easy and certain.

Similar processes take place in regard to costly social experiments. In 1928–9, the memory of War Communism was no longer as vivid as in 1922–3; and, additionally, a new idea had appeared on the horizon and could be used to overcome hesitation. This was the idea of planned economy. War Communism collapsed, they said, because the idea was not yet known; this time, Communism could gain victory without imposing sacrifice on the people.

In an abstract form, the idea of planned economy was present in the older socialist doctrine. But it was only in 1919 that two "bourgeois" economists gave the necessary precision to it. One was Walter Rathenau, a great German businessman and statesman; another was the Russian Professor Grinevetsky, who published an illuminating study on the reconstruction of Russia after the catastrophe of War, Revolution, and Civil War.[11] Both were hostile to Communism; Grinevetsky's book was even published under the protection of the White Army in Kiev. But Lenin was very interested and ordered Rathenau's book to be translated and Grinevetsky's to be reprinted in Moscow. Already in 1920, a State Planning Commission was created. In 1921, it was given the modest task of elaborating directions for the guidance of the managers of the trusts, informing them of the general economic situation and of probable developments. In 1925, the commission published the first one-year-plan; it was nothing but a set of recommendations. Meanwhile the idea of long range planning emerged; different terms were discussed, and the term of five years was finally chosen. Later on, the term "five-year-plan" received some mystical connotation; but in the beginning there was no special emphasis on the figure five. More important was another change: the plan idea was proclaimed to be the salvation, permitting an attempt at the second Communist Experiment without returning to the blunders and miseries of the first. By that time the plan was no longer a recommendation, but a binding order of a very complex nature, similar to the budget.

Thus, the plan idea became the instrumentality for the resumption of the attempts to realize the Communist blueprint. The rulers succeeded in making this idea an article of faith and in persuading many people that the fulfillment of the plan would signify the emergence of paradise on earth. In this way a kind of socialist enthusiasm was temporarily created among technicians and part of the younger workers. The plan as such did not involve any particular sacrifice and was the more gladly accepted. But later on, after its sublimation to the level of a dogma, sacrifices on its altar could be demanded.

The First Five-Year-Plan was elaborated by the State Planning Committee with the co-operation of the best economists of Russia. It represents a sincere effort to trace the line of development conducive to rapid industrialization without sacrificing any aspect of economic or cultural activity. Two sets of figures were elaborated; the normal and the optimal plan, the latter to be realized only in exceptionally favorable conditions. The highest Party authorities ratified only the optimal plan. Officially, the plan had to be executed from October 1, 1928, to September 30, 1933. But it was ratified by the supreme Party agencies only in April, 1929, and consequently could not start being executed before the fall of 1929. During its execution, the ridiculous idea of a "five-year-plan in four years" arose;

when the idea appeared to be unreal, an additional trimester was added, and the plan was declared terminated on December 31, 1932. But the policy involved in this plan continued well into the Second Five-Year-Plan period; a radical change took place in the midst of the latter.

The plan foresaw the transformation of Russia from an agricultural into a mixed society, one that was both agricultural and industrial. To achieve this, the output of industry had to be increased by 150%, that of agriculture only by 50%.[12] Such increase necessitated great investment of capital. A financial plan was elaborated by Party authorities. At its basis was the Marxist theorem that, other things being equal, large-scale production is more efficient and therefore cheaper than small-scale production. It was decided to invest in industry all the profits gained by the existing industrial system; these investments were to be used to create industrial giants, larger than the biggest plants in this country. The giants had to be constructed in a very short time and very cheaply. As soon as they started production they would yield big profits, since production costs would be low, and the prices would be maintained on the initial level. These profits would once more be invested. In this way, a self-perpetuating and accelerating process would start running and permit the increase of production with vertiginous speed.

Optimistic computations yielded the heartening result that a yearly increase of production by 30% was in the range of possibility. If Marxist theorems and optimistic computations were correct, a material paradise would have emerged in Russia about 1932. The vision of a future paradise was made the incentive for work in socialist society, instead of the economic self-interest of capitalist society.

Instead of paradise, Russia got hell. Why?

4

Before attempting to answer this question let us establish that, to carry out the new offensive, the industrial organization of the country was submitted to partial change. Semi-independent trusts, unified by syndicates, continued to exist; they were given no concrete orders, as was the case under War Communism, but the abstract order to achieve the Plan.[13] But from the start private industry and trade, restored under the NEP, were once more nationalized. This time no decrees were issued, and the nationalization was carried out by concrete orders, often under the pretext of the nonpayment of taxes, or of alleged counterrevolutionary activity of the owner, etc. Naturally, no compensation was paid, and the nationalized units were either incorporated into the existing trusts or combined into new trusts.

However, the existing enterprises were not in the foreground. According to the Plan, a large number of new plants and mills of large size started being constructed, often with the aid of foreign specialists. But their construction proved to be much more costly and lengthy than foreseen by the Plan. On the basis of reports published by some of the experts, the causes of the departure from expectation were these: first, the experts never were permitted to act freely; ignorant heads of departments and the like introduced changes in their plans, calculations, and orders. Secondly, definite plans almost never existed; plans were changed many times after the execution had started; in some cases half-finished buildings were torn down and rebuilt according to new plans. Thirdly, there was a great shortage of skilled labor and well-trained engineers. Fourthly, the quality of material was so poor that much larger quantities were required than expected.

The difficulties were aggravated because the government, meeting the "impersonal resistance" of the whole economic system, responded by accelerating the program of industrialization. Every year, sometimes every three months, new orders were addressed to the leaders of industry, breaking the harmony of the Plan. All efforts were concentrated on heavy industry. But light industry, on which the satisfaction of human needs depends directly, as well as the railways lagged behind. New railways foreseen by the Plan were not built and the exist-

ing lines were permitted to deteriorate so badly that extraordinary measures became necessary. The most resolute and reckless
among the secondary leaders were successively appointed commissars of the railways, but could not achieve anything of importance. About the end of the period, Stalin acknowledged
that the state of the railways was one of the darkest points in
the picture.

Redundant statements were time and again made asserting
that victory was certain, later on that it was gained. Outside of
Russia, a large literature emerged around the question as to
whether the Plan was a success or a failure. In this general
form, the discussion is fruitless. Here are the facts.

Since the production of new plants entered the scene much
later than anticipated and at much higher cost, the financial
plan did not materialize. The rulers had to choose: either to
abandon the whole enterprise, or to find other ways of financ-
ing it. Naturally, they chose the second alternative. The real
sources of investment were: (1) expropriation, almost without
compensation, of the riches accumulated in the countryside;
(2) decrease of real wages to starvation level, and (3) depre-
ciation of currency, so painstakingly avoided under the NEP.
It must be emphasized that none of these measures was foreseen by the Plan. The second means, the reduction of wages,
was imposed on the government by unfavorable developments
in agriculture, as the result of the first measure. The food supply dropped sharply, and the reaction of the government was
the same as under War Communism: ration cards for everybody, with differentiation according to class membership and,
in actuality, still less food than the meager rations permitted
one to expect.

In addition to the failure of the financial plan and the necessity of using the unpleasant substitutes, there were other
reasons for disappointment. The Plan foresaw increasing efficiency of labor. In actuality, its efficiency decreased, owing to
the undernourishment of workers, the equalization of wages,
and the necessity to introduce into the labor class millions of
peasants without any technical training. All these reasons of

deterioration appeared on the scene because of the Utopian character of the Plan as remolded by the Party and the foolish idea of its acceleration.

To combat decreasing efficiency, the government tried a few devices which then seemed very ingenious. These were "socialist emulation" and "uninterrupted work." Socialist emulation was based on the premise that enthusiasm was the dominant attitude of labor. The names of the most efficient persons and groups were placed on the "red board" and those of the least efficient on the "black board." Uninterrupted work meant that machines were operated day and night, by three or more shifts of workers; every individual worker had to work five days and have a rest on the sixth, but these days did not coincide, and factory work never stopped. The two devices proved to be failures. Socialist emulation did not work because socialist enthusiasm very soon faded,[14] and uninterrupted work resulted in dangerous deterioration of machinery and in the undermining of the vital force of the labor class.

The hopeless decrease of efficiency was accompanied by another unfavorable departure from expectation. The obsession with the Plan idea made underproduction a crime without excuse. Therefore, plant managers, when unable really to carry out the Plan, still tried to produce the required quantity, but of poorer quality. The press of the period is full of reports about rails which had to be replaced after six months of use, of galoshes which lasted only three days, etc. This meant waste of raw material and human energy.

The greatest disappointment of the leaders was probably the unspeakable chaos which emerged throughout the economic system, a worthy counterpart of "the capitalist anarchy of production" vilified by the Marxists. Nevertheless, no industrial catastrophe in the style of 1920 appeared. About the end of the period studied, Russia was actually endowed with heavy industry, approximately according to plan. In this regard, the claims of the Communist rulers of having fulfilled the Plan were justified. But light industry produced no more than in 1928, and what it produced was incredibly poor. The means of transportation was close to breakdown. This, however, was nothing in comparison with the catastrophe in agriculture.

This catastrophe was caused by the Second Agrarian Revolution aiming at the collectivization of the countryside. This revolution was a centrally initiated action in contrast to the first one, which had been initiated on the periphery of the nation. The First Agrarian Revolution had been a concession of the Soviet government to the peasants, a compromise with the Populist program. The Second Agrarian Revolution was an attempt to give Russia an agrarian structure entirely in keeping with the Communist doctrine.

Collectivization means a complete realization of the Communist doctrine with regard to rural structure; not only land-use, but also agricultural production becomes collective. During the years 1929–33, great efforts were made to realize this structural idea as completely as possible. Later on the efforts weakened, and a new compromise structure got the upper hand. But let us begin by explaining how the idea of complete collectivization was born, for it did not exist in the Communist mentality of earlier years.

Already during the period of War Communism some landlord estates were not submitted to partitioning among peasants but remained State farms; they were to become models of agricultural progress. Very seldom were such attempts successful, and in general the agricultural technique of State farms was very poor.

Among the exceptions was the State farm "Shevchenko" in the Ukraine.[15] Here two favorable conditions were combined: (1) an exceptionally able manager, Markevich, headed the farm; (2) the farm was endowed with much more machinery than could be used on its fields. This was an accidental result of a very inadequate distribution of instruments of production, for the majority of State farms were badly handicapped by lack of machinery of any kind. The surrounding villages were suffering from land shortage and backward techniques (the three-field system, the custom of common pasturage, poor machinery). Markevich proposed to the peasants that they combine all their possessions in one large organization. A six-year rotation of crops would be introduced and all the fields cultivated with the improved machinery of the State farm; the peasants would help, with their horses, on days indicated by Markevich. On five out of the six fields all jobs would be accomplished in this way; the sixth, to be used for potatoes and beets, would be separated into allotments corresponding to homesteads and, after the "collective" plowing, peasants would cultivate their portions individually. As remuneration for the use of the machinery, the State farm would receive a certain percentage (25% to 30%) of the grain; the rest, as well as the straw and the crop of the sixth field, would remain the property of the peasants.

After some hesitation, the peasants of twenty-six villages agreed. The plan was put into effect in 1928 over an area of 24,000 hectares and was a great success. Markevich's farm gained high profits, and the economic conditions of the villages which became copartners improved remarkably. Markevich described his experiment in a book entitled *Inter-Village Tractor Stations*, in which he warned against imitating him in the absence of the necessary conditions.

The idea of collectivization was included in the first Five-Year-Plan. According to the plan, collectivization was to advance slowly, in close correspondence with changes in peasant mentality, i.e., with the degree of their free acceptance of the idea and with the amount of available machinery. Therefore, the plan provided that by its close, January 1, 1933, only fifteen per cent of all peasant homesteads were to have lost their independence. But the government was in a hurry. The moderate plan of collectivization was transformed into a plan of wholesale collectivization when the failure of the financial aspect of the general plan became obvious. The village was the only place where some riches were accumulated and could be grabbed in order to replace the mythical profits from State industry. In order to carry out this modified plan, collectivization was combined with "the wholesale liquidation of the *kulak* class."

On December 27, 1929, Stalin declared that the Communist government had decided to put an end to the very existence of the *kulak* class. On January 6 and February 1, 1930, corresponding decrees were enacted. According to them, the *kulaks* were to be expropriated without compensation and their belongings transferred to the groups of the poorest peasants provided that they joined the *kolhozes* (collective farms). In this way, the solidarity of rural communities was destroyed and a conflict situation created. By that time, one of the most terrible periods of the Russian Revolution began. For no other reason than that they had cleverly profited by the opportunities of the NEP period, the *kulaks* were expelled from their homesteads, with their families, with nothing but the clothes they had on at the moment of the expropriation. If they showed the smallest tendency to resist, they were deported to labor camps in the far north, where the majority of them perished from cold and starvation. Their fields, cattle, and machinery, as well as their homes, became the property of the *kolhozes*. The middle-class and poorer peasants were more favorably treated. But they had to abdicate their economic freedom and become members of the *kolhozes*.[16] Many among them were reluctant; but commissars were sent to the countryside to explain that collectivization was Stalin's desire and that those who did not agree would be considered counterrevolutionists and deported to Northern Siberia. In the majority of cases, after such explanations, the peasants "unanimously approved" the plan. On March 1, 1930, 55% of the homesteads (14.3 million) were already collectivized.° The intensity of the process was also very great; by March 1, 1930, 78% of the cattle of collectivized homesteads had already been made collective property.

The attitude of the peasants became more and more threatening. Practically no preparations were made to sow the fields. Slaughtering cattle in order to prevent collectivization became a kind of epidemic. Stalin realized the danger. On March 2, 1930, he published an article in which he accused the local authorities of having misunderstood his instructions and of

° For more details, see Table 3 in Appendix II.

having created many *kolhozes* on paper only. The fictitious "compulsory" *kolhozes* were to be disbanded. Peasants who were unwilling to become *kolhoz*-members and could not be persuaded were to be left alone. Very soon Stalin's article was followed by corresponding decrees (of which that of March 15, 1930, was the principal one). The wave of collectivization relaxed: on May 15, only 24% of the homesteads remained collectivized; this proves that the first attempt had been a compulsory one.

This was only a temporary retreat. By different means, among which an excessive taxation of individual (noncollective) homesteads played a large part, the government succeeded in bringing forward the whole enterprise. Towards the middle of the year 1931, the Russian peasantry was separated into two nearly equal classes: that of *kolhoz*-members and that of "individual" (in actuality *mir*) peasants. Later on the process gradually advanced towards the entire elimination of the second class, which had been a remnant of the old, prerevolutionary agrarian structure.

The new structure given to the Russian village through collectivization is complicated. *Kolhozes* have not become technically and economically self-sufficient units. Tractors and heavy machinery have been concentrated in governmental "machine and tractor stations." The co-operation of such stations is almost unavoidable for the majority of *kolhozes*, as had been the case in Markevich's experiment; but the stations enjoy the position of monopolists and use it to exert pressure on the *kolhozes* just as monopolists do in capitalist society.

The rest of the capital, namely land, cattle, and tools of minor importance belong to the individual *kolhozes*, but not to the individual farmers. The management decides how many workers, male and female, every homestead should place at its disposal every day and what the corresponding persons should do. The management, if the *kolhoz* statute is taken at face value, is democratic: the chairman and the other officers are elected by the general assembly of the members; however, the general pattern of elections previously studied (Chapter

V) is applied, and actually those persons become officers who have been thus designated by political leadership. It is symptomatic that, in 1929–30, twenty-five thousand Communists were delegated from cities to rural districts to direct an activity about which they had not the least elementary notion. Labor became half-compulsory; the system of remuneration was entirely inadequate. The profits were distributed in equal parts among the members (the old *mir* idea); this resulted in a total lack of any interest in good work. Since light industry was in a state of stagnation or even of regress, the peasants were again unable to buy anything when selling their surpluses; the most important incentive for large agricultural production was gone.

Decreased agricultural production and the cessation of rural-urban exchange resulted in a new rural-urban tension, which repeated that of War Communism. Peasants had to submit to large levies in kind (corn, potatoes, butter, linen, cotton, etc.). The reaction of the peasants to the loss of economic independence and the unbearable levies was that of despair. Many of them preferred killing their cattle and eating more meat than ever before to surrendering cattle to the *kolhozes*, where they died in large numbers. Figures show the amazing magnitude of the destruction produced partly by voluntary acts of the peasants, and partly by the crass ignorance and carelessness of the managers.* Additionally, many peasants destroyed their machinery and sold it as scrap iron. Very soon they stopped really working in the *kolhoz* fields. Reporters of Moscow papers visiting the countryside were unable to see anybody working in the fields before nine A.M., and among workers they saw more children and old people than persons of working age, since the latter preferred tilling their little orchards or doing some minor industrial work to increasing their miserable incomes.

In Markevich's case, collectivization was a splendid success. Applied on a large scale, without regard to the availability of improved machinery or the attitude of the peasants, collectivization was a signal failure. Crops decreased, cattle was

* Compare the figures for 1928 and 1932 on Table 2 in Appendix II.

decimated. Famine once more took a heavy toll from Russia's population. But through the liquidation of the *kulaks* some riches could be immediately grabbed and distributed among the workers, to promote industrialization. Later on, the new agrarian structure permitted the rulers to collect large quantities of food in a much simpler manner than had been the case under War Communism. Once more, this food was used to promote industrialization. Industrialization advanced, but Russian agriculture was ruined. This fact should never be forgotten when discussing the success or failure of the Five-Year-Plans.

There were two ways to help agriculture out of the terrible deadlock caused by too hasty collectivization—reinforcing the pressure or making concessions. During the years 1932-33, the government hesitated. Concessions, but insufficient ones, were made, and simultaneously the pressure was reinforced.

The policy of concessions was started on March 26, 1932, when the Central Committee of the Communist Party declared that the practice of collectivizing all the cows, sheep, pigs, and poultry had nothing in common with the policy of the Party and ought to be stopped immediately. The declaration was a lie: up to March 26, wholesale collectivization was the policy of the Party; on that day it ceased to be. The decree, according to the Soviet press, provoked general enthusiasm; in many places, the peasants started claiming all collectivized cattle, including that which had been confiscated from "liquidated" *kulaks* or bred in collective farms. About the same time, the collectivized peasants were permitted to sell their "surpluses" on the market. But they had to accept the official price, which was so low that nobody seized the new opportunity. Then on May 6, permission to sell surpluses without price limitation was granted, but only as of January 15, 1933. A fortnight later, the date of January 15 was dropped and permission was made effective immediately. This sequence of events is typical of a situation where one is hard-pressed by circumstances and tries to meet pressure by gradually increasing concessions.

The peasants saw in these concessions not so much a series of benevolent actions of the Supreme Leader, as the proof of their strength. They started struggling for rights which the leaders did not want to grant them, namely, for a larger part of the harvest and for actual freedom of trade. This, in a dictatorship, was intolerable. Stalin retaliated quickly and resolutely: On August 7, 1932, the death penalty was introduced for stealing *kolhoz*-goods, and many peasants were shot for having harvested grain on collective fields for their own use. In January, 1933, "rural political sections" were created; they were closely related to the GPU and were invested with much power in order to help actualize completely the new rural structure, in spite of the passive resistance of the peasants. Never before had the formidable machinery of the secret police come so close to the peasants. The program of the Communist Experiment was to be enforced by the most drastic measures. Does this not prove once more that the Russian people did not want it?

5

Neither chaotic conditions in industry nor famine could have compelled the Communist leaders to abandon their Plan, the realization of which seemed just around the corner. A counter-revolution on the part of the *kulaks* no longer threatened. And still they were forced to retreat.

Granted that early in 1934 the Communist rulers of Russia foresaw war with a formidable enemy and simultaneously realized the dissatisfaction of the population with the existing social and economic order and the inefficacy of the economic system they had created, what policy had they to choose? Once more, as in 1921, they had to reverse the trend, and instead of continuing to advance towards pure Communism in economics, they had to proceed to a retreat and give up a part of the strong points already gained. However, neither the return to capitalism nor the inauguration of another NEP was possible: after the brutal liquidation of the NEP in the late 'twenties, nobody would take any promises at face value that another NEP would be durable and serious; moreover, a large part of the NEP personnel perished together with their short-lived enterprises and could hardly be replaced.

In consequence, the retreat had to be conducted towards new positions. Appeal to self-interest was indicated, as well as the relaxation of the strict control of consumption, if economic efficacy was to be restored and the dissatisfication of the population dissipated. But the State—more exactly—the Party control of the means of production was not to be abandoned. How far the retreat had to go and what the individual measures had to be could be determined only by trial and error. The following measures were tested and integrated into a new system which could be designated as Mitigated Communist Economy.

1. Under The Great Retreat, the goal continued to be speedy industrialization of the State, with emphasis on heavy industry. In anticipation of war, this was only natural. Still, an important change took place. The initial scheme of the Five-Year-Plans, the continuous increase of production in geometrical ratio, was mitigated. In the course of The Great Retreat the yearly percentages of increase had gradually diminished. This slowing down had been especially conspicuous after 1937.[17] Despite the slowing down of the tempo, the increase of industrial production, expressed in absolute figures, had been very high: smaller percentages, when applied to high absolute figures, still yielded high results. Beginning with 1937, observers have reported a slow but steady improvement of the standard of life in urban areas.

The new directions given to industry permitted the withering away of the "plan obsession" of the previous period. The plant managers could take more care of the quality of their products, which the consumers were now free to reject, as will be shown later. Moreover, they had won a much higher degree of independence than they ever had since the abolition of the NEP. In their work, they were no longer checked by the Trade Unions, which in 1935 lost the right of collective bargaining. They were able substantially to decrease the number of auxiliary workers, though in many cases it was still five times larger than in similar American plants.[18]

In the course of World War II, rationalization of the labor processes and the conveyor method of production have been imposed on industry, with the particular end in view of producing more, though employing a smaller number of men.[19]

2. The system of State monopoly and centralized planning was not abandoned, but important exceptions were permitted to materialize. Without any general announcement, artisans reappeared on the scene. The majority were organized into "co-operatives" managed by the Party; these were given certain privileges as to taxation and access to raw material. Some of them were granted "concessions" on small enterprises such as brick kilns, saw mills, smithies, and potteries. Permissions were granted them to open little shops producing felt shoes, homespun clothing, carts, and furniture.[20] A minority of artisans remained "individual," a counterpart to the individual homesteads untouched by collectivization. These were very definite departures from the Communist blueprint, and very definitely departures which could not but please large sections of the population.

Of equal importance was the decentralization of local industry through the decree of January 9, 1941. This decree reversed a policy which the government chose in the very beginning of The Great Retreat. Namely, on August 10, 1934, a decree was issued creating "commissariats for local industry." In this way the management of small enterprises was transferred from local Soviets to Republican centers. But in 1941, these enterprises were exempted from central planning and placed under the authority of local Soviets which could plan their production, acquire raw materials, and sell the finished goods on the market.

According to a well-established practice, the reform of 1941 was preceded by a number of "revelations" concerning the plight of the population, and by semiofficial suggestions as to possible measures for its alleviation. Already in the summer of 1939, *Pravda* wrote:

The population suffers because of the lack of shoes, hats, and furniture. Without a reorganization of local industry, Soviet trade cannot be put in order.

Early in 1940, the Trade Commissar of the RSFSR urged some decentralization of industry; this would, in his opinion, encourage local industry to cover at least one-third of the local food consumption, such as smoked fish, processed cheese, canned berries, and mushrooms. About the same time, *Pravda* gave the following information:

> In the township of Bronnitsy, there used to exist fifteen blacksmiths' and wheelers' shops. At present there is not one shop of this kind left in the township, though the district provides every opportunity for large-scale production of carts, sleighs, and harnesses. There is only one way to remedy the situation—to grant the local authorities the right to organize small trade and industry.[21]

The government continued insisting on the revival of local industry even during the war.[22] In 1943, one could read: "It would be highly detrimental to centralize the supply of all kinds of goods to the population completely. The local Soviets must organize production from local resources." Early in 1944, the vice-commissar of local industry scolded his subordinates for neglecting the production of carts, sleighs, cords, and similar commodities. One of the difficulties involved was revealed in the reply of a local official: ceiling prices for these commodities were so low that it was not worth while producing them. This fact gives insight into the arduous problem of mutual adjustment between centralized and local planning, which probably will be of great importance in the reconstruction process after the war.

However, from statements reported above it may be concluded that the reform of January 9, 1941, was a response to the unanimous desire of the population to see small industry in the hands of local men. In The Great Retreat, the two reforms just studied, therefore, form a substantial item.

3. Still more important was the solution of the problem of labor efficiency through an ingenious device which had been recorded in the annals as the Stakhanov movement. The spirit

of The Great Retreat has been embodied in it more clearly than in anything else.

In the spring of 1934, a new wage system was enacted by the government, known as the progressive piece work. Relating to every type of work, both piece remuneration and daily norms of production were fixed, but the piece remuneration was made flexible and significantly increased if a worker's output exceeded the norm.

This was an invitation to work better and earn more. But this invitation was not directly accepted by labor. Under the Second Socialist Offensive they were taught that a higher income, and in consequence a higher standard of life was, for the individual, a departure from Communist purity; anyone who tried it was commonly viewed as a petty bourgeois individualist, almost a counterrevolutionist. This mentality survived the Second Socialist Offensive and became an unexpected obstacle to the realization of the aims of The Great Retreat.

Then in August, 1935, a dramatized demonstration of the seriousness of the government's invitation took place. An obscure Donets miner, a non-Party man—that he was a non-Party man was often emphasized in later discussions—after consultation with his foreman, a Communist of good reputation, decided to show the world that in Communist society a worker could outproduce any worker in Capitalist society. It was claimed that he had produced many times more coal than expected according to the norm. In the course of the next month he repeated his deed time and again, and in consequence his payroll was about twelve times higher than it used to be. The deed was reported to the Moscow papers and received great approbation from the highest authorities. Very soon, an imitation movement began. The first follower was a certain Bussygin, a worker in the Gorki automobile plant; there followed a girl from a textile mill, then scores of others in various branches of industry, transportation, and agriculture; "combiners" boasted of having harvested three or four times more hectares than expected, engineers of having pushed their trains at double speed, dairy girls of having milked many more cows than foreseen in regulations, other *kolhoz* girls of having collected incredible quantities of beets or potatoes. In all cases, magnificent remuneration was awarded to those concerned, and their splendid performances were praised in local and central papers.

About the end of the year, three thousand prominent Stakhanovites were invited to come to Moscow. At a big meeting in the Kremlin, Stalin addressed them and then asked them a few questions: how did they perform their deeds and what had they done with their earnings? As to the latter question, it appeared that the men had acquired phonographs and records, sometimes cows for the homesteads of their relatives, or little houses in the countryside or suburbs. The girls spoke of nice dresses and silk stockings. Stalin fully endorsed them and declared that in Soviet society, the workers should be given the opportunity to enjoy life as they never could do in bourgeois society. One hundred and twenty among those gathered around Stalin were granted the order of Lenin, or that of the Red Banner. Later on, quite a few Stakhanovites were given privileges as to rooms in rest houses; some of them were given private lessons in science and foreign languages; still others were promoted to "commanding positions" in the administration. On the other hand, they could only occasionally repeat their performances, the rest of the time being spent for propaganda activity.

In this way the suspicions of the workers regarding the sincerity of the governmental invitation to work better and earn more were dissipated. The movement progressed with increasing speed. Thousands, tens of thousands, hundreds of thousands of workers declared their intention to join. The majority had to be refused since, as will be shown, it did not enter into the plans of the government to transform all workers into Stakhanovites; on the contrary, this would have been a sheer impossibility.

Why? The study of the speeches of the individual workers at the Moscow meetings and of numerous reports published in Soviet papers show that the miracle of the Stakhanovites consisted of two items: first, they rediscovered some elementary principles of the rational organization of labor, such as the division of functions. Many of them boasted that they no longer changed their tools every minute, but concentrated on some special operation. Secondly, their superiors organized a kind of friendly conspiracy around them. Typical is the following story concerning Bussygin:

That night all the thousands of workers knew that Bussygin would be working. All these thousands were united in the desire that their factory gain an honorable place in the great movement. Everything changed. Usually tools were lacking; this time, all were in place. Usually no parts for repairs were available; this time, they were abundant. The director and the chief engineer of the shop did not sleep that night: they were present and did all they could to secure success.

From such descriptions it appears that the deeds of the Stakhanovites were rather a kind of theatrical performance, and that in actuality scores of men took part in the production officially ascribed to the selected heroes.

But what was the gain of the government, i.e., of the monopolistic owner of all industrial plants? It was disclosed when, a few months later, decrees began to be issued increasing the norm without lifting the remuneration per piece. To some of them, preambles were attached praising the heroic deeds of the Stakhanovites which had shown the possibility of efficiently exploiting the riches embodied in the national factories and farms. The workers were given a choice: either to maintain the "speed" to which they were accustomed under the Second Socialist Offensive, and which was ridiculously lower than that of their brothers working in conditions of "capitalist exploitation," and then to receive substantially less than they did; or to accelerate their production and maintain their earnings, or accelerate their work further and increase their earnings. Naturally they chose the latter. In this way the hard problem of improving efficiency was solved, after all attempts to do it on the basis of "socialist emulation" and the like had failed. It must be emphasized that the solution was definitely contrary to the spirit of the Doctrine and to its earlier interpretation. The new system was therefore a substantial part of The Great Retreat.

The system has not been applied to workers only. The employees, especially the engineers, were given full part in the virtual benefits thus created. Depending on the increased production of the workers under their orders, they saw their earnings doubled or trebled, sometimes more than that, and this gave them an increased status in the changing society.

With the approach of war, many additional measures were taken to improve the efficiency of industrial work. On June 26, 1940, the six-day week introduced in 1929 was abandoned and the usual seven-day week restored; this meant nine more days' work a year. Moreover, the labor day was lifted from seven to eight hours, without any increase in earnings. The decree of December 29, 1938, provided punishment for truancy and tardiness and dismissal for absentees. This had to be changed, since in a country without unemployment dismissed workers immediately found other jobs; from June 26, 1940, on, they were punished by a 25% deduction from their wages. The decree of October 19, 1940, permitted the government to transfer engineers and workers compulsorily from one enterprise to another. Since war was already raging in the West and threatened to spread to Russia, all these measures were willingly accepted by a population permeated by patriotic sentiment.

4. The Stakhanov movement opened a way to the workers to acquire higher purchasing power. This would not have affected their attitudes and conduct if the system of standardized consumption typical of the former period had been maintained. It was therefore mandatory to create conditions in which the prospect of higher earnings would fully exert its stimulating force. A few months before the Stakhanov movement was launched, a sweeping reform took place in the system of distribution. On December 1, 1934, bread ration cards were abolished. In 1935, the same took place relating to other kinds of food and clothing. Now everybody was able to buy every commodity available, either in State or co-operative shops or on the market, paying a certain sum of money, independent of

his class position and occupation. Actually, this was a complete retreat, since the system introduced was identical with that used in capitalist society, except for the fact that the shops were mainly State agencies. Prices in these shops were now substantially higher than those paid before the reform when redeeming ration cards, but substantially lower than those which had prevailed on the free market. Some groups gained, others lost by this move, and there is reason to assume that the gainers were persons with higher incomes and the losers those with lower incomes; in any case, some readjustment of the wages of the latter took place to compensate them partly for that. But in general everybody was pleased, because after the reform one of the basic freedoms was returned to the population—the liberty of consumption, or the ability to choose freely the way of spending one's income. When the Stakhanov movement began, the new purchasing mentality, which was nothing but the "capitalist" one, had already been inculcated into the minds of the Soviet citizens. In consequence, when joining the Stakhanov movement and making more money, a worker or employee knew that he could spend his additional income as he pleased.

5. The restoration of the freedom of consumption was a conspicuous item in The Great Retreat. This freedom could certainly not have been granted if, simultaneously, the great *kolhoz* reform had not taken place.

Collectivization was not abandoned; on the contrary, it was insisted upon. In 1938, 94% of the homesteads were collectivized, instead of 73% in 1934. But the very meaning of collectivization changed. It was no longer paramount to the complete destruction of the economic independence of the homesteads. In the framework of mitigated Communism, a peasant was both a member of a collective (indirectly, State) enterprise, and an independent producer.

To prepare the reform, a convention of "prominent collective farmers" was convoked in Moscow (March, 1935). Stalin appeared at this convention and made a speech of which the following passages are essential:

If the collective farm cannot supply all the needs of the members and their families, then it is better to acknowledge frankly that a certain kind of work must be public and another kind individual. It is better to acknowledge that along with the large-scale form of collective agriculture there must be a system of small and individual farming to satisfy the individual needs of the *kolhoz* members. To harmonize the individual interests of the *kolhoz* members with the collective interest of the *kolhoz*—there lies the secret of how to strengthen the collective farm.[23]

In accordance with these statements, the new *kolhoz*-statute [24] allowed the peasants to possess small individual allotments within the collective farms (0.25 to 2 hectares, varying in different parts of the country). In addition to this, *kolhoz*-members were allowed to possess cows, sheep, and pigs (no horses) individually; the number of "individual cattle" was limited, but the *kolhoz*-management was ordered to help members in buying and feeding individual cows, and in other similar ways. This was not entirely new. Already in March, 1932, every *kolhoz*-member was allowed to possess a cow, and it has never been officially stated that he was not allowed to possess a garden or an orchard "individually"; but until 1934, the tendency was towards restricting individual economic activity within the *kolhozes*. The new tendency, on the contrary, was that of stimulating such activity.

The peasants were eager to seize the opportunity. They started tilling their allotments with the greatest care. Usually they could not use improved machinery, but with shovels and other hand tools they performed miracles. They used all the manure at their disposal on their allotments.[25] One year after the reform, the individual allotments covered four million hectares, more than the area cultivated by the still existing "individual" homesteads. Still more important was the restoration of individual cattle breeding. From 1934 to 1939, cattle of all kinds but horses rapidly increased in Russia, and the bulk of this increase was due to individual cattle breeding within the *kolhozes*.[26] It is noteworthy that no parallel increase took place as to horses; they remained taboo to the peasants since, in the government's opinion, a collectivized peasant could become too independent when he owned a horse.

Not only did the peasants seize the opportunity offered them by the new statute; as in many other cases, they went far beyond the legal limit. In 1939, the government checked the application of the statute and established that the individual allotments occupied an area much larger than foreseen by the law.[27] Moreover, the peasants did not display much interest in collective work and preferred to concentrate their efforts on their individual allotments and cattle. How little they did care for collective work is apparent from the decree of May 27, 1939, which imposed on members of collective farms the minimum obligation to work eighty days a year for the collective farm.[28] It is easy to draw the conclusion from this decree that prior to it the peasants worked less than eighty days a year for the *kolhoz*. The same decree ordered the local authorities to reduce the size of the individual allotments to the legal limit; this was to be carried out by November 15.

The decree of May 27 was a departure from the main trend of the retreat, an attempt to stop a movement driving the whole system too far away from the goal fixed in the blueprint. Events did not permit this backward movement to materialize fully; after the outbreak of war in the West, it was decided not to continue the reduction of individual allotments.[29] As to the imposition of compulsory labor on the *kolhoz* members, the latter found a simple means to evade it. In the summer of 1939, people visiting collective farms were startled by seeing line-ups before cashiers' windows; there, farmers bought "workdays" from the chairman.[30] The price is reported to have been three to five rubles a day; this signifies that they expected to earn substantially more working on their allotments.

What, however, are the workdays? They appeared on the scene as another aspect of the great *kolhoz* reform through which the remuneration of *kolhoz*-members has been entirely reformed and is now more or less adapted to the efforts displayed by every family in collective farming.[31] Every kind of labor is now evaluated in conventional units (called workdays); for instance, plowing one hectare of arable soil with a two-horse plow is equal to one unit; plowing one hectare of sandy soil with a one-horse plow, three-fourths of one unit; feeding cattle, one-half unit; working with a tractor and attaining the "norm," two units; conducting a column of tractors, three units, etc. There are complicated rules allowing the kolhoz-management to increase or decrease the statutory number of workdays depending upon the quality of the labor. Every week the number of units gained by a homestead is noted in special books. When the yearly account of a kolhoz has been approved, the net income is divided among the homesteads (in kind or in money) in ratio to the number of units they have gained during the agricultural year.* Moreover, one must keep in mind that the Stakhanov movement was not limited to industry, but appeared in agriculture as well, permitting ambitious members of the kolhozes to improve their earnings significantly.

The new kolhoz statute (1935) comprised another important reform.[32] Taken at face value, it provided for the shifting of the collective farms from the bureaucratic to the democratic type of organization. A general assembly of the adult members of a kolhoz had to elect and recall the officers, especially the chairman and members of the board of directors, and to ratify their plans and general directions. This democratic reform remained, however, on paper. Years after its proclamation the Soviet press was full of reports of brutal dismissals of kolhoz chairmen by local Party and Soviet agencies, resulting in a state of continuous flux of these essential economic agents. The same sources bring to our knowledge the fact that the general assemblies are not permitted to discuss the economic problems of the kolhozes and have to listen to political reports of the leaders.[33] It could not have been otherwise. The dictatorial and authoritarian structure of the State was maintained, and within that structure there was no room for local self-government.

* The distribution takes place after heavy deductions. On the average, out of a crop of 100 tons, 35 must be ceded to the machine and tractor station, and 23 sold to the State for a nominal price.

This is a situation which, in the course of The Great Retreat, has often recurred. To satisfy the people, the government had to make verbal concessions, but could not permit them to materialize.

On the other hand, the great *kolhoz* reform was not limited to the granting of individual allotments and to the differentiation of earnings of individual members through the ingenious device of the workdays. Once more (as during the NEP) natural levies were replaced by definite taxes in kind. In 1935 and 1936, they were greatly decreased and gradually modified in order to stimulate higher production. This complicated matter has been very well explained by John Scott:

> Previously grain delivery norms were fixed in proportion to the crop. Then in order to increase production Soviet authorities introduced the criterion of the sown area. The collective farms were obliged to contribute to the State a certain percentage not of the crop, but of the harvest which they theoretically should have received from their sown area. In this way, the collective farms were forced to struggle for a good yield per acre, or they might not have enough bread to last them through the winter. Since the spring of 1940, however, the process had gone one step further. The collective farms were required to contribute a certain percentage of the theoretical harvest from all arable land at their disposal. It thus became the duty of the president of the collective farm to see that all his arable land was sown if he wanted to have enough bread to last through the winter. Decrees of this nature have been published applying to grain, meats, dairy products, hemp, flax, wool, fruits, and truck products.[34]

Since 1934, peasants have been allowed to sell their surpluses direct to consumers (not to professional traders, who are still prohibited).[35] The market is free in the sense that prices are not regulated. The government influences them, of course, for ninety per cent of the commercial operations in the country are carried out by governmental shops and stores; but the policy of the authorities is that of holding prices on a level which should leave the peasants sufficient profits.

On December 28, 1939, a sweeping reform liberated the

kolhozes from a substantial part of centralized tutelage. State agencies were prohibited from imposing on the *kolhozes* detailed plans dictating what crops, when, and how they should be sown, and limited them to giving general directions, while concrete plans had to be elaborated by the *kolhoz* boards of directors. The yearly plan had to be submitted to the district Soviet six weeks before the start of spring labor; it had to be ratified in the course of a week, if necessary, with amendments. Speaking before an assembly of Ukrainian collective farmers Scherbakov, a member of the Politbureau, said some very sensible things; however, they were hardly in accordance with the Plan dogma:

Why should we decide that the *kolhoz* must sow so much oats, barley, and wheat, when the *kolhoz*-members know their soil better and may make better decisions? On the other hand, often specified kinds of seed are imposed on the *kolhozes,* though they do not appeal to the population. Now they are permitted to decide of their own free will. The government expects that because of this change the harvest will increase by seven million tons. From now on, the Soviet population will have enough shoes, clothes, and furs. The Ukraine will again be proud of her orchards, which today are unreasonably sown with wheat or millet.[36]

As often happens when speaking of bright expectations, the Soviet dignitary divulged a number of miseries in the past owing to the obsession of the rulers by the Plan dogma. The reform is well in line with the general trend of The Great Retreat. Its importance should not, however, be exaggerated because the decisions of the *kolhozes* are actually decisions of their executive Loards and these, despite the principles proclaimed in the model statute of 1935, consist of State employees, usually Party members. Through them plans designed by higher authorities still may be imposed on the collective farms. Nevertheless, there is now the possibility that the voice of local men may be heard when deciding how the *kolhoz* land could best be used. Once more, the desire of the peasants to have much more autonomy in their collective farms has pierced through the crust of official enthusiasm.

Finally, the rural "political sections" were abolished in December, 1934; now special vice-directors of "machinery stations" supervised, in a milder way, the political attitude of collectivized peasants and *kolhoz*-leaders.

The combined effect of these measures has been a weakening of the rural-urban tension and an increase in agricultural production, not so pronounced as in industry, but still sufficient to cover the elementary needs of the population. It is true that the average crop of cereals has not substantially increased and that the fluctuation between good and poor years has remained very large, a symptom of relatively primitive agricultural technique. But the increase in the production of fodder, potatoes, and cotton has been substantial and has created a solid foundation for dairy farming, the production of alcohol, and synthetic rubber, and for the independence of Russian textile mills from import. The growing herds permitted the supplying of cities with more meat and dairy products than they had seen since the termination of the NEP. These were significant improvements, and still greater ones seemed to be ahead when war put an abrupt end to rosy expectations.

6. The edifice of The Great Retreat has been crowned by the "commercialization of the Revolution," one of its least known aspects and one of the few social inventions made under the Communist regime.

Reporting to the 17th Party Congress (February, 1934) Mikoyan, the Commissar for Inner Trade, naïvely told the story of this invention. Once, he said, he had a talk with Stalin. The subject was combating "speculation," i.e., the irresistible tendency of adventurous individuals to gain high profits by breaking through the official prohibition of commerce. Supplying commodities which could not be found in sufficient quantities on the official market, they made several hundred per cent profit. Suddenly Stalin got an inspiration: if such profits were possible, why should they be gained by private individuals and not by the State treasury? Mikoyan applauded, and very soon a system was put into force which now forms the backbone of Soviet trade and finance. To this system the term "commercialization of the Revolution" seems to be adequate, though it never could be found in official sources.

Not every Revolution could be commercialized, but the Communist one in Russia could be. The State, as the only producer of industrial commodities and the overlord of agricultural productions, establishes how many commodities of every kind will be released on the market. As the monopolistic tradesman, it fixes the prices and holds them on a high level. It has to acquire part of the raw material it needs from collective farms and uses the combined strength of sovereignty and monopoly to accomplish this at ridiculously low prices. As the monopolistic employer, the State fixes the wages and once more holds them on a low level. Thus the State, as the only businessman of the country, is able to earn very high profits and at the same time secures the stability of currency and the budget.

To make things clearer, let us use the example of bread. Collecting grain from the farmers, the State pays them .09 ruble for a kilogram, but the State bakeries sell a kilo of bread for .60-1.50 rubles, depending on the quality and locality.[37] Assuming that the cost of production, besides the cost of grain, is once more .09 ruble, and without considering that one kilo grain yields more than one kilo bread, for .18 ruble spent, the State receives on the average of 1.15 rubles, making a profit of nearly 500%. The difference between the price of the finished goods and the cost of production is officially called the "turnover tax," [38] and the yield of this tax forms more than two-thirds of the entire State revenue.

Stalin's hunch has materialized: the Soviet State makes profits from its trade of which no "capitalist exploiter" could even dream. Naturally, this high profit is not simply distributed among those who hold power. The State revenue serves to pay both the current State expenses and the cost of "socialist construction," or of the expansion of the industrial equipment of the country, in accordance with the principle of the Five-Year-Plans. In these expenses, the wages and salaries form the bulk, and among the salaries the high remuneration of the ruling *élite* and of their fellow travelers is a significant item. Since the ruling *élite* exerts unlimited power, it actually determines what percentage of the national income will be retained by it.

However, the mechanism is rather subtle and is hardly grasped by the large majority of the workers and employees. On the other hand, it actually guarantees the smooth functioning of the system, cushioning the numerous shocks which it continues to receive from foolish planning and lax actualization of the plans. Moreover, it has made possible the payment of high wages to the Stakhanovites and other favorite sons of the regime and thus has permitted the reintroduction into Soviet economics of the mighty stimulus of competition for the attainment of a higer status.

6

The conclusion to be drawn from the preceding survey is obvious. In the field of economic activity, the retreat has been substantial, but still it has not gone far enough to substitute an entirely new pattern for that created under the Communist Experiment. The economic order created by The Great Retreat is a conspicuous compromise. The State has in principle maintained its monopolistic position; nevertheless, the monopoly is partly broken through the individual husbandry on the plots of the *kolhoz* members, as well as through the activity of individual artisans. The State economy is still centralized and centrally planned, but there is local planning as to the work of the *kolhozes* and of local industry. The State is the only employer and therefore it can dictate the wages to the millions of workers and employees. But, contrary to the Doctrine, the State had to recognize the necessity of differentiating the wages and salaries, making them dependent on individual achievement, thus creating the opportunity for competition between individuals for better pay. The State is the only merchant and therefore it can dictate the prices; but it had to abandon the idea of directly regulating consumption.

No basic principles can be found behind the concessions granted in the course of the retreat. The situation which has obtained can well be compared with a battle front after a military retreat: in one place the line has been thrown far back; in another almost no ground has been yielded; some strongholds are present which may be well defended, and other positions are weak and further retreat is likely. The only criterion of the concessions forming the retreat has been expediency; the Communist rulers have retreated as far as was proven to be necessary through trial and error, and have carefully checked their acts by the observation of results. It is undeniable that in general the results have been favorable. Once more, as under the NEP, the departure from Communist purity has been rewarded by increased production and satisfaction of human needs.

The final judgment about the economic system of the period of The Great Retreat is this: it is more efficient and in better conformity with the wishes of the people than that of the preceding period. The infernal tempo of the economic transfiguration of the country was abandoned and Soviet citizens witnessed something similar to the "return to normalcy," as was the shift from War Communism to the NEP. The policy of sacrificing the present for the future was mitigated, and the slogan of "wealthy and happy life for Soviet citizens" was proclaimed. Under the new system a gradual improvement took place, but at the moment when war interrupted it, a great deal remained to be done to give the Russian people conditions of life comparable with those prevailing in advanced countries of Western, i.e., capitalist, society.

The complicated economic processes which took place in Russia after the Communist Revolution may be summarized as follows:

1. From the standpoint of the Communist blueprint, the curve representing change in the economic structure consists of four sections, two ascending and two descending, corresponding, respectively, to (a) War Communism and the Second Socialist Offensive and (b) the NEP and The Great Retreat.

2. From the standpoint of the satisfaction of human needs, the economic curve also consists of four sections, two descending and two ascending: War Communism and the Second Socialist Offensive were characterized by deterioration, the NEP and The Great Retreat by amelioration.

3. A very definite correlation emerges from the comparison of the two curves; in Russia, in 1917 and after, the efficacy of the economic system has fluctuated in inverse ratio to the intensity of the application of Communist methods. Extreme Communist methods have produced economic disaster, while their mitigation permitted the economic system to recover and improve.

4. The major waves mentioned above (Nos. 1 and 2) have been disturbed by minor fluctuations. In the course of the NEP, central interference with industry was at a minimum in 1923 and later on increased; the amount of economic liberty left to the peasants was at a maximum in 1925–6 and was smaller both earlier and later. The great pressure of Communist methods corresponding to the Second Socialist Offensive was temporarily interrupted in March, 1930, and early in 1932. In the course of The Great Retreat, increasing pressure on agriculture was displayed in the spring of 1939. As to economic results, secondary fluctuations have obtained depending on good or poor harvests, which proves that despite speedy industrialization, Russia still depends largely on agriculture.

CHAPTER VII

WORLD REVOLUTION OR RUSSIA:
Fatherland Forgotten and Reconquered

1

WHEN THE COMMUNISTS won control over Russia, their main preoccupation was to submit that country to a complete social and economic transformation on the basis of their doctrine. But this was not their only aim. According to the very Doctrine, the new rulers of Russia had to destroy national States throughout the world and organize Humanity into a Universal Proletarian Society. The means to that end was International Communist Revolution.

This end was not independent of the transformation of society on the Marxist pattern but, on the contrary, closely related to it. More exactly, according to the Doctrine, one end could not be achieved without the other. Capitalism, said the founding fathers of Marxism, is international by its very nature. To resist international capital and, later on, to defeat it, the proletarians must unite and create a universal proletarian front. Though the proletarians may like individual products of bourgeois culture, they ought not to care for the national cultures as wholes. The national differentiation of cultures is, in Marxist doctrine, one of the tools used by the capitalists to preserve their domination. Pointing to the differences of individual cultures and emphasizing the nations as entities, the capitalists divert the interest of the proletarians from the only significant social process—class struggle—to a number of nonsensical processes, among them the struggle between the nations and their cultures. Gaining power, the proletarians may preserve some elements of national, bourgeois cultures but, once victorious throughout the world, they must create a new world culture in the framework of Universal Proletarian Society.

These ideas were fully shared by the group which gained power in Russia as the result of "the October victory." Looking around them, they defined the situation in these terms: all the world, except Russia, is under the power of capitalists. These capitalists are fully aware of their class interest and therefore they cannot permit the defeat of Russian capitalism to become final. If they did, the victorious proletariat of Russia would become a center of crystallization around which the forces of the international proletariat would gather to give the death blow to capitalism. Merciless war between world capitalism and the First Socialist State, Russia, seemed then unavoidable.

Measuring the forces of the two camps, the new leaders were not over-optimistic. In the course of the first few months, perhaps years, they were fully prepared for a crushing defeat. The only chance of survival, they thought, was the tremendous disturbance produced in the ranks of the capitalists by the World War. Could not the Communists profit from this circumstance to enlarge the fissure in the capitalist building? Was not this the only means to preserve power in Russia, and perhaps to gain it throughout the world?

International imperialism disposing of the might of capital cannot coexist with the Soviet Republic. Conflict is unavoidable, and here is the greatest difficulty of the Russian Revolution, its greatest historical task, that of provoking the International Revolution.[1]

Thus spoke Lenin at the Seventh Congress of the Communist Party of Russia which had to decide the problem of peace with Germany (March, 1918). For long years to come, these words were repeated with slight variations. "We are the Party of the World Revolution, not of the Russian Revolution," said Zinovyev in 1925.[2] One year later, Stalin said: "The Revolution in the USSR is only part of the World Revolution, its beginning and the base for its successful advance."[3]

In consequence, for many years after the Revolution the main purpose of the foreign policy of the First Socialist State was to foster Communist Revolution throughout the world. In the light of the Doctrine, this was not merely proselytism, but rather a measure of self-preservation.

"Socialism in one country is impossible." This was Lenin's thesis explaining the aggressive character of the internationalism of the Russian Communists during the first decade of their rule. To the challenge of the inevitable attack of the capitalist coalition, the creation of the Third, or Communist International (Comintern) was the adequate response. It was informally found in 1918, in Moscow, using the presence of numerous foreigners, especially of prisoners of war. Indoctrinated foreigners were united into "foreign groups" from among which, later on, "hundreds of thousands" were sent abroad to play the part of "the bacilli of Bolshevism." Members of these groups formed also the bulk of a gathering held in Moscow in March, 1919. This gathering, re-enforced by a few persons especially invited from foreign countries, resulted in the formal foundation of the Comintern and was reckoned as its First World Congress.[4]

Statutes were elaborated. Taken at face value, they meant a drastic change in the Russian situation: the Communist Party of Russia, like every other Communist Party, became a "section" of the new world organization; supreme power seemed to have been shifted to it from the Russian leaders. The first president of the International was Zinovyev, and Lenin seemed to have become one of his subordinates.

In reality, from the start the inequality of the partners was obvious. The Russian Communist Party had at its disposal the means of one of the largest States in the world. The other parties represented minorities of the labor movement in different countries, sometimes maintaining an illegal existence, always penniless. Consequently, the Russian Party—more exactly, its leaders—were able to dominate the organization which, in fact, became merely a branch of the new Russian bureaucracy. Zinovyev was never Lenin's superior. For a certain time, he was Lenin's foreign minister since, up to the late 'twenties, the actual foreign policy of the Soviet State was carried out through the Comintern and not through the Commissariat of Foreign Affairs.

According to the directions given by the leaders, the activity of the Comintern was concentrated on two closely related ends: (1) provoking and fostering revolutionary movements, wherever possible, but especially in Germany, which was held to be most responsive to Communist propaganda,° and in the colonies and dependencies of the great powers, and (2) struggling against the "social traitors," or the socialist parties adhering to the Second International; these parties were obviously the most dangerous competitors of the Communists in the struggle for leadership in the Labor class.

The creation of the Communist International was apprehended by the "bourgeois" society with the same indeterminate fear as, half a century earlier, the creation of the First one had been. This fear seemed to have been justified by such events as the Bavarian and the Hungarian Communist Revolutions and numerous Communist upheavals in Europe, China, and the colonies. But nothing of decisive importance followed; the World Revolution, that supreme hope of the Communists, the point of orientation of their eschatology, failed to materialize.

Nevertheless, the obsession by the Doctrine made the rulers blind to reality and especially to the particular interests of Russia. When in July, 1920, the Red Army seemed to be near victory over Poland, Lord Curzon offered the Soviets a demarcation line giving Russia western Belorussia and western Ukraine. The Soviet government declined the offer and declared that it could give Poland a much more favorable frontier provided that a "workers' and peasants' government" be established in Warsaw. A virtual success of the World Revolution proved to weigh heavier than the real interest of Russia in the acquisition of two provinces. No workers' and peasants' govern-

° On the basis of collective frustration caused by defeat and the treatment by the victors.

ment emerged in Poland, the Red Army was beaten, and the Soviet government had to sign the peace treaty of Riga (1921).

Despite the uninterrupted series of failures and disappointments, up to 1927 internationalism entirely dominated the policy of Russia's rulers. Then, step by step, departures from the original setup began, first only slight, but gradually increasing in significance so that, later on, the entire structure collapsed.

But let us begin with the earliest phases of the process. The weakness of the support granted by the Western capitalists to the White Movement in Russia which the Communists interpreted as the vanguard of international capitalism; the complete cessation of support in 1921; the tendency of the capitalist States to start "trading with cannibals" (Lloyd George); the competition between capitalist States as to who would be first to recognize the Soviet government and to sign with it advantageous commercial treaties—all these facts were heartening. Did they not prove that capitalism was decaying and that the International Revolution was just around the corner? But there were other facts showing that the development had followed other ways than those foreseen by Marx and Lenin. Communist regimes in Bavaria (1918) and Hungary (1919) were shortlived. The revolutionary situation which obtained in Germany in 1923 was dissipated without revolutionary outbreak. And in 1922, in Italy, a revolution opposite to Marxist expectation, a preventive revolution against the Communist danger occurred making Italy almost invulnerable to Communist propaganda.

The real fact was this: the process of senescence was going on within liberal capitalism, but not within capitalism as such. A large-scale transformation of capitalist society was taking place, manifested partly in Fascist revolutions, partly in grand-style social reforms of which the American New Deal is typical. Among the Communist leaders, the real process gave rise to two divergent schools of thought. Trotsky and his followers drew the conclusion that the attack on capitalism should be strengthened to the limit of possibility. Stalin was the first to formulate the opposite theory of "Socialism in one country." In 1925, he said:

The Soviet regime possesses all the requisites for the upbuilding of a fully socialized society provided it can overcome its internal difficulties. We are witnessing a temporary stabilization of capitalism and the stabilization of the Soviet regime. A temporary equilibrium has been established between the two stabilizations. This compromise is the basic feature of the present situation.[5]

The actual meaning of the struggle between Trotsky (seconded by Zinovyev and Kamenev) and Stalin was the conflict of the old idea of the impossibility of socialism in one country and the new idea of its possibility. In this struggle Stalin gained the upper hand, and the effect was a complete change in the corresponding chapter of the Doctrine; before Stalin's victory, the idea of preserving socialism in Russia without socialist revolution throughout the world was held a heresy. After the victory, the main heresy was seen in the idea that international revolution was a necessary condition of the survival of the First Socialist State. Before Stalin's victory, anyone who believed in socialism in one country only was demoted or exiled; after his victory, those were demoted and exiled who did *not* believe in socialism in one country only.

In this way, the internationalism of the Communists received a new shape. Stalin and his associates did not renounce the International Socialist Revolution. But that revolution ceased to obsess them. If this revolution materialized, well and good; but if it did not, ruling over one-sixth of the earth remained an interesting possibility. After 1928, the internationalism of the Russian Communists was no longer as it had been; perhaps it could be termed "ambivalent." *

The change in the official system of values was reflected in these facts. Up to 1928, the head of the Comintern (Zinovyev, then Bukharin) were members of the Politbureau. After 1928,

* This is a term borrowed from psychoanalysis; it might be used to designate situations when predictions as to the response of a person or group is ambiguous, the respective chances being 50-50.

its heads (Manuilsky, then Dimitrov) had to stay outside of it. In other words, the Ministry of International Revolution, or the Comintern, was demoted to the rank of a secondary ministry whose head does not participate in the private council of the supreme leader. Another symptom was the factual discontinuation of the Congresses of the Comintern: after the Sixth Congress (1928) seven years passed before the Seventh and last was held.

In the late 'twenties and early 'thirties, that is, during the period of ambivalent internationalism, the Communist leaders interpreted the situation in this way: Socialism was victorious in one country only. The other nations had not adhered to the gospel of Marxism because of the inertness of the masses, the nefarious activity of the social traitors, and the protective measures of the class-conscious bourgeois. Therefore, the environment was hostile and, for the USSR, the horizon was cloudy. The capitalists had not yet attacked the "only socialist country," but the attack was only postponed, not altogether abandoned. There were no means of guessing in what form the forthcoming "capitalist coalition" would materialize; but most probably the attack would come on the part of the "imperialists" of France and England. This expectation was symbolized in "the four empty chairs" which, in one of the political trials, were destined for Poincaré, Sir Austin Chamberlain, Sir Henry Deterding, and a Russian "White Guardist," formerly a rich industrialist.* The League of Nations continued to be considered as an association of warmongers, a disguise of the coming capitalist coalition against Russia. Its leaders were ridiculed and assailed, time and again burned in effigy, together with the Pope and a few businessmen, first of all the same Sir Henry Deterding.

But since the capitalist environment of the "only socialist State" was there, some form of adjustment was necessary. The signing of the Briand-Kellogg pact (August 31, 1928) was one

---

* This trial took place in 1934. Unfortunately for the prosecution, the Russian industrialist in question died many years before his alleged participation in the international plot directed against the Soviet Union.

of the earliest manifestations of the rising theory that, between the capitalist and the Communist worlds, peaceful coexistence was temporarily possible. There followed nonaggression pacts with Russia's neighbors—not very strong, but still needing to be eliminated from the forthcoming anti-Soviet Coalition.[6]

But despite the pacts, the activity of the Comintern continued. The Sixth Congress (1928) ratified a militant program which, among other things, demanded that the Communists be defeatists with respect to their own countries. As to the "social traitors," in 1929 Molotov said, "Today more than ever any coalition between revolutionists (Communists) and reformists (Socialists) is harmful and inadmissible."[7] Lozovsky added: "Antagonizing workers against the Social Democrats is the most important task of the Comintern."[8] Fruits of his senseless policy matured a few years later, in Hitler's ascent to power.

Duality represented in the nonaggression pacts and in the subversive activity of the Comintern was characteristic of the period of ambivalent internationalism. Events outside of Russia, especially Hitler's rise to power and the German-Polish pact (January, 1934), compelled the Communists once more to revise their position. From 1934 on, internationalism was in the stage of self-defense, and the new position was clearly expressed in the subordination of the activity of the Comintern to the official foreign policy of the Soviets.

In the latter, changes were drastic. Overnight, the League of Nations became the bulwark of peace-loving nations against virtual aggressors. Its leaders were declared to be exponents of that sensible trend within capitalism which realized the possibility of peaceful coexistence with the First Socialist State. Joining the League which, a few months earlier, had been considered a sheer impossibility, a mortal sin against the Doctrine, now became the purest expression of Communism. In consequence, the First Socialist State applied for membership and when this was granted (September 18, 1934) it was praised as an important victory. Litvinov, the foreign commissar at that time, became one of the greatest champions of the League;

nobody was more eager than he to promote the idea of collective security.

Collective security did not, however, become an article of faith in place of the original article which demanded that the Communists help overthrow any bourgeois government and undermine any bourgeois army. Collective security was chosen as the best device available, given certain circumstances, to prevent destruction through successful Fascist aggression. Therefore, if circumstances changed, departure from the principle of collective security was possible without real change in the new setup of Soviet foreign policy.

Such a departure was indicated when events proved that the system of collective security was but an illusion, not a real guarantee. The appeasement policy of France and Great Britain which reached its climax at Munich (September, 1938) imposed a reversal of the policy of the Soviet State. From collective security, it shifted to something akin to "splendid isolation." This was, however, no longer the "self-blockade" of the 'twenties, when the Soviet State disdained to keep company with other States since it was alone a righteous State based on the Doctrine, whereas the others were sinners doomed to destruction through the cataclysm of the inevitable International Revolution. No, this was isolationism of the "bourgeois" type to which a State recurs when its leaders, rightly or wrongly, consider that this policy best subserves its interest. From Munich to the outbreak of the Russo-German war, the Communists considered the capitalist world as consisting of two equally bad camps, one looking for the best moment to attack the Soviet Union, the other untrustworthy, ready to sacrifice the Soviet Union in the name of appeasement.

The best policy in this situation seemed to be provocation of an armed conflict between the two camps, with the intention of remaining neutral as long as possible and of intervening at the last moment, in the hope of gaining some advantages, especially security in a world shaken by a long and exhaustive conflict. This was the policy of the Soviet State between 1938 and 1941, comparable with the policy of many "bourgeois" governments. Did not, for instance, Napoleon III expect a long and exhaustive war between Prussia and Austria and hope for aggrandizement for France as the price for mediation, provided that she were able to preserve her military strength while the others fought?

In concrete circumstances, strict neutrality would probably have delayed, if not prevented, war between Fascism and Democracy. The outbreak of the conflict was to be precipitated, and this could be reached by assuming the position of benevolent neutrality in favor of the presumably weaker, that is, the Fascist camp. Litvinov, the protagonist of collective security and the League of Nations policy, was ostentatiously dismissed and replaced by Molotov, a yes-man not identified with any definite policy (May, 1939). Parallel negotiations with the two camps made it possible to check the correctness of the diagnosis; partnership with Democracy headed by the appeasers was of no good; partnership with Fascism was the lesser evil. Finally, the choice was made, the friendship pact with Hitler signed (August 23, 1939), the signal for the Second World War given.

This is not the place to judge the moral aspect or expediency of the Soviet policy of the years 1938–41. What matters in this context is that this policy was by no means determined by the Doctrine. The Communist Doctrine shaped by Lenin and applied about the end of the First World War was violent defeatist propaganda in the two camps, in the hope of transforming the Imperialist War into Civil War and of launching the International Revolution. In 1938, subversive Communist propaganda was resumed, but only within one of the camps, that of Democracy. Moreover, officially, even ostentatiously, help was granted to the camp of Fascism so that, from 1939 to 1941, the Soviet Union could be considered a non-belligerent partner of the Axis. This situation was so obvious that, early in 1940, in influential French and British circles, the question was debated whether the democracies should not declare war on the Soviet Union.

From the policy of benevolent neutrality towards the Axis,

the Soviet Union was removed against its will. Circumstances made it an ally of the democracies. This change was performed reluctantly, only because no other choice was left. For at least two years the Soviet Union waged a kind of *guerra nostra,* a war parallel with that of the United Nations, but not identical with it. Quite a few lessons had to be learned by the Soviet leaders before they finally chose to become one of the senior partners in the great coalition. But their reluctance was not based on Communist principles. The question of whether a Communist State might help Capitalist States win a war was not discussed.* Their reluctance was based on unpleasant reminiscences of the co-operation attempt in 1934–8, and on the alleged possibility of being delivered as spoils to the Fascists in the course of a new access of appeasement.

Once more, no moral judgment or utilitarian evaluation of this reluctance should be attempted at this point. What is important is that the policy was no longer dictated by the Communist Doctrine. In new conditions, there was simply no use for it.

A parallel development took place in the management of the activities of the foreign Communist parties through the Comintern. Very symptomatically, an open acknowledgment of failure took place, similar to Lenin's acknowledgment of failure in 1921, but quite exceptional under Stalin's rule. The failure was recognized at the seventh and last Congress of the Comintern held in Moscow in the summer of 1935. The recognition of failure was accompanied by the elaboration of a new policy. This was the strategy of the Popular or Common Front. Radical bourgeois parties were no longer implacable class enemies, social democrats no longer social traitors. Suddenly, they became valuable allies in the struggle against Fascism, recognized to be the aggressive branch of capitalism, whereas Democracy was assigned the role of a good neighbor. Since Democracy and Socialism were threatened at the same time as Communism, alliance was offered them. If other groups, like

---

* The analogous question whether a Christian and democratic State may help an atheist State was much discussed in this country before Pearl Harbor.

the Catholics, appeared to be hostile to Fascism and eager to fight it, all the better; alliance should be offered to them also. Now, the Comintern had to adapt the Communist movement of each country to the particular role assigned to it in the general plan of the Moscow leaders. If a particular country was a prospective enemy, old tactics could be maintained. If it was a prospective ally, the Communists of the country had to become fervent patriots especially interested in the valor and efficacy of the army. In 1935, Stalin declared that a strong French army was a great asset to the Soviet Union. What a blow this was to the French Communists who for fifteen years had displayed every imaginable subversive technique to undermine the army! But, for the Communists, an order from Moscow was beyond discussion. Overnight, the French Communists became fervent patriots and great admirers of the army—only to resume anti-militaristic propaganda once more in 1939.

The shift of internationalism from the ambivalent to the ancillary phase produced real consternation among orthodox Communists of foreign parties. Up to 1935, anyone was guilty of heresy who preached alliance with social traitors and bourgeois governments. Now, he was a heretic if he denied the soundness of such a policy.

Nevertheless, even in the course of this period, the basic doctrine as modified in 1927 was not completely abandoned. Very conclusive is this statement made by Stalin in 1938:

The victory of socialism in Russia is not complete because the danger of intervention from capitalist countries continues. The problem can be solved only by uniting the serious efforts of the international proletariat with the still more serious efforts of the entire Soviet people.[9]

The foreign Communist parties were curbed, but not disbanded—and for good reasons. First, the existence of these well-disciplined agencies was very convenient in negotiations with foreign powers; the promise to muzzle them was a valuable item to be given only for a substantial counterpart. Secondly, a reversal in the international situation was not out of the question, and in new conditions the foreign Communists could be used once more.

The official policy of the period of ancillary internationalism contained, however, an element which proved fatal to the former instrument of aggressive internationalism, the Comintern. This policy implied frequent changes in the directions to the Communist parties abroad, and the final effect of these variations was the wholesale discredit of Communist movements everywhere. The leaders of the individual parties who, in reality, were salaried officers of a particular branch of the Soviet bureaucracy did not mind obeying, provided that they continued being paid. But the followers, that is, the prospective soldiers of the army of the Communist revolution could not be persuaded so easily to change their minds every few months. Especially detrimental, for the cohesion of the Communist Brotherhood, was the shift from collective security to cobelligerency with the Axis, and the forcible change of sides effected through the German attack.

Though the complete degradation of the Comintern was an obvious fact, still its dissolution on May 22, 1943, was received throughout the world as a surprise. In reality, this was much more the recognition of a fact than a positive action: the Comintern was dead and could not be revived. Nevertheless, the declaration of dissolution was an adroit gesture. It appeased, at least partly, the fears of those groups in the allied countries who were afraid that, in helping the Soviets wage war against Germany, their countries were eventually helping the forthcoming World Revolution. It prevented secessions and revolts in the ranks of the foreign Communist parties, the leaders of which could no longer distribute subsidies.* It satisfied the Russians who were eager to fight for their national interests, but not for the sake of the International Revolution.

---

* In 1940, the Communist Party of America withdrew from the Comintern to avoid the necessity of registering according to the Registration Act, but continued to follow the zigzags of the Moscow policy.

It brought the entire foreign policy of the Soviets into conformity with the internal development characterized by an overwhelming outburst of nationalism and hostility to internationalism, the *idée force* of the Comintern.

The Comintern died of a long, painful sickness which began almost immediately after its birth, since it was never permitted to develop according to its nature and was always forced to live as a prisoner of the new rulers of Russia. The sickness was aggravated in 1935, when the leaders had to quit the paths traced in accordance with the Doctrine. When the Comintern died, nobody in the world mourned the decease of this monstrous being. Perhaps Hitler and Mussolini were a little worried about the disappearance of one of the most vulnerable targets of their propaganda.

The dissolution of the Comintern terminated that phase of internationalism which may be called ancillary. If, in the hearts of the Communist leaders, hope of the International Communist Revolution persists, it is no longer manifested in outward actions or embodied in institutions. Internationalism is now in the esoteric phase. The leaders, including Stalin, probably continue to believe that capitalism is doomed to collapse and that the future belongs to Communism which, sooner or later, must become the universal pattern of social and economic organization. The possibility of overcoming the present-day shortcomings of capitalism without accepting Communist or Fascist recipes probably escapes their minds.

But in the course of their long career these leaders were taught the lesson that Lenin's theorem as to the transformation of imperialistic wars into civil wars conducive to Communist revolution was not verified by facts. The First World War resulted in the establishment of Communism in Russia, but nowhere else. In the course of the Second World War, the tremendous vitality of the great Anglo-Saxon democracies was displayed. Progressive capitalism is now officially treated as the second best form of economic organization, the Communist one being the best and, more or less explicitly, a long period of coexistence with progressive capitalism is assumed to be ahead.

2

The logical counterpart to the program of World Revolution was an antinational program within Russia. In the course of the first few years after the Revolution, the famous sentence from the Communist Manifesto, "proletarians have no fatherland," was repeated as often as possible, and such words as fatherland and patriotism disappeared from the vocabulary. The Russian national sentiment, both the moving spring in the building of the Empire and the product of its successful expansion, was called "chauvinism," and denied the right to exist. In teaching and in official speeches, membership in the First Socialist State was emphasized just because of the socialist character of that community, not because of its national individuality. Members of that community were invited to become citizens of the World Republic of the Proletariat, no longer citizens and patriots of an historically given State.

In 1923, Lunacharski, the people's commissar for education, said:

The teaching of history which would stimulate the children's national pride, their nationalistic feeling, and the like must be banned, as well as such teaching of the subject which would point at stimulating examples in the past for imitation in the present. For I do not know what kind of thing is a healthy love for one's fatherland. Let us look at things objectively and recognize that we need internationalistic, all-human education.

In accordance with such ideas, the teaching of Russian history and of the history of Russian literature was discontinued. The official thesis was that up to Lenin's birth and the rise of the labor movement, Russian history had been all chaos, darkness, and oppression and not worth being memorized. The pre-Revolutionary culture was rejected to the limit of possibility, since this was a typically bourgeois culture. Perhaps a few bright spots could be found in the darkness, pointing to the Revolution to come. Symptomatic was the treatment of Pushkin: a few poems, mainly written when the author was young and in which he praised liberty and insurrection against tyranny, or professed superficial atheism in the style of the French Encyclopedists, were selected for study and imitation. The others, the great works which made him the national poet of Russia, were ignored.

In 1922–3, the designation of the First Socialist State as Russia was officially discontinued and replaced by the impersonal term, "Union of Socialist Soviet Republics." * Around 1930, the idea of abandoning the Cyrillic alphabet and shifting to the Latin one was seriously pondered upon.

It is remarkable that for a long time the departure of foreign policy from the initial direction had almost no influence on the situation within Russia. The Communist leaders ascribed great value to their dominance over Russia, but for them, Russia was still primarily an excellent springboard for the forthcoming International Revolution, and not a value in itself.

Then, in 1934, in conditions mentioned above, the trend suddenly changed, giving place to one of the most conspicuous phases of The Great Retreat, which in the course of a few years transformed Russia into a country with much more fervent nationalism than she ever had before the attempt of international transfiguration. The process started this way.

In June, 1934, "treason against the nation" was made a capital offense; actually it always had been one, but this time it was emphasized that the greatest villain was one who helped the enemies of the nation, not one who was the enemy of socialism. In July, an editorial published in *Izvestia* startled quite a few readers: it was stated that every Soviet citizen ought to love his fatherland. A little later on, the leader of the Young Communist League declared that one of the League's duties was to foster the love of their motherland among the youth so that they would consider it an honor to die for it.[10]

In 1936, Levin's play, *Fatherland,* was highly applauded by officials. When interviewed by representatives of Moscow papers, the author remarked: "The theme is immense; if I have succeeded in developing one-tenth of it, I am very happy." A

* The term Russian (Socialist Soviet) Republic continued designating the senior partner of the Union.

few days later, a group of engineers condemned in 1934 and later pardoned wrote a letter to the editor of *Pravda* in which they said that they were proud to belong to their "happy fatherland" and were willing to apply all their strength to serve it. Later in the year, a film entitled, *We, the Russians,* was produced.[11] A few months earlier, the title would have been considered impossible by the Kremlin authorities. In 1937, these statements by high authorities could be found:

> The word "fatherland" has become a fundamental political concept . . . The most important condition [of success] is the fighting patriotism of our nation, its unlimited faithfulness to the mother country . . .[12]

First of all, Russia's past was rediscovered by Russia. More exactly, after many years of denial of any value inherent in the past, Russia's people were given a spiritual vision of one thousand years of glory and national achievements surpassing those of any other nation. History, which for many years had been taught only in terms of mass activity, reappeared as a sequence of magnificent deeds performed by Russia's national heroes, no longer the few rebels such as Pugachev and later on Lenin, but the princes of Kiev, the Tsars of Moscow, the dignitaries of the Church, the generals and admirals of the Empire.

Naturally, Peter the Great was one of the first among the national heroes of Russia to be restored in their dignity—the indomitable reformer, considered by many as a precursor of Bolshevism, and also a great and victorious military leader. As great masters in the art of propaganda, the Communists asserted that Peter was being worshiped by the class which, according to the Doctrine, is infallible. They said:

> The workers of the Putilov factory (Leningrad) display great interest in the past of our fatherland. They are especially interested in the epoch of Peter the Great, in his war with Sweden, and in the great deed which was the creation of the Russian navy.[13]

After Peter the Great, the founders of the Moscow State, out of which the Russian Empire evolved, were reintroduced into the gallery of national heroes, especially Alexander Nevsky, the victor over the Swedes and Germans, and Dmitri Donskoy, the victor over the Tartars. Later on, even Prince Vladimir the Saint, under whom Russia had been Christianized, was added. The famous film, *Alexander Nevsky,* was first shown on the eve of the twenty-first anniversary of the Communist revolution (November 6, 1938). The next day the following words appeared in one of the leading papers of Moscow:

The youth, especially the members of the Young Communist League, enthusiastically applauded the deeds of the great Russian leader who lived 700 years ago. They did it because the Russian nation is imbued with flaming patriotism and had been imbued with it throughout her history.[14]

As to Dmitri Donskoy, the paper of the Red Army inserted the following comment:

The victory at the Kulikovo Pole opened the way for the growth of the national Russian State. The Russian people realize that only unity gives strength and secures a glorious future to the fatherland.[15]

It is noteworthy that all the leaders just mentioned had been canonized by the Russian Orthodox Church. A few years earlier, expressing reverence to one of them would have been judged almost a symptom of counterrevolution. Now it was explicitly stated that:

Despite the fact that Alexander Nevsky is considered a saint by the Orthodox Church and that many churches and monasteries have been dedicated to him, atheists have to avoid any defamation of his memory; they must remember that he is a beloved hero of the people and that he merited the gratitude of later generations by his patriotism and military prowess. The Church canonized him in consideration of the love of the people; the Militant Atheists League has failed to pursue an equally wise policy.[16]

Somewhat earlier a comic opera in the best style of the early 'thirties, ridiculing Prince Vladimir, was withdrawn from the repertoire, and the significance of the action was emphasized in a declaration of one of the highest governmental agencies:

It is well known that the Christianization of Russia was one of the principal factors in the rapprochement of the backward Russian people with the people of Byzantium and later with the peoples of the West, namely with peoples of higher culture. It is also well known what a big part clergymen, particularly Greek clergymen, played in promoting literacy in the Russia of the Kiev period; thus, from a historical standpoint Byedny's libretto is an example not only of an anti-Marxist, but also of a frivolous attitude towards history and a cheapening of the history of our people.[17]

Then came the turn of the great generals of the heroic epoch of Catherine the Great and Alexander I. Suvorov was honored in a film which, according to the paper of the Red Army, was enthusiastically received by the audience. The following order was directed to the Red Commanders: "You must fully understand the aggressive strategy of such remarkable Russian generals as Suvorov and his pupil Kutuzov." [18]

Professor Tarle, a great historian exiled in the course of the Socialist Offensive, was invited to glorify Kutuzov and the magnificent performance of the Russian nation in 1812. He did this in two brilliant books and, among other things, refuted the derogatory statements of Clausewitz about Kutuzov. It is noteworthy that Clausewitz had been one of the few authorities recognized by Lenin, so that a departure from Clausewitz was necessarily a departure from Lenin. Said *Pravda:*

In the hearts of the Russian people the memory of Kutuzov will live forever, as the head of a victorious army which liberated the beloved fatherland from foreign invaders.

Once more, to make the departure from previous evaluations as inconspicuous as possible, the government used a spokesman, this time a military man. He was directed to say:

It is incorrect that in 1812 Napoleon was defeated by cold and hunger. The Russian armies operated correctly, in full accordance with the situation. The Russian soldier has always displayed unsurpassed stubbornness and aggressiveness and a number of Russian military leaders (Bagration, Rayevsky, and others) showed great courage and skill. They had behind them the experience of the great wars of the late eighteenth and early nineteenth centuries, an experience second to none, even to that of the French marshals.

To strengthen the impression, unnamed professors of the Military Academy were scolded for their inability to describe correctly the patriotism of the Russian Nation in the course of the War of 1812.[19] In this way, a whole series of military heroes were given a place in the Communistic Pantheon. Among them Prince Bagration, another disciple of Suvorov, an army commander killed in the great battle of Borodino, was selected for special worship.

"It is time to rehabilitate the memory of Bagration," said *Krasnaya Zvezda*, "and to recognize in him a national hero, beloved by the army and having sacrificed his life to the independence of his fatherland." [20]

Then came the time to glorify the military leaders of Russia on the eve of the Revolution. This was the more surprising, as one of the justifications of the Revolution had been the alleged corruption and incompetence of the Russian generals in the course of the First World War. Now one could read:

"The Warsaw-Ivangorod operation (October, 1914) showed the world that the Russian army was as good as the German. Once more it displayed the courage and endurance of the Russian soldier." [21]

Up to that time all reforms enforced by the Imperial government were interpreted as dupery; thus, the Emancipation Act of 1861 which abolished slavery in Russia had been "unveiled" as "no reform at all," maintaining slavery in disguise. "This interpretation must be abandoned," declared the Commissariat of Education in its official paper: "the reform of 1861 actually was the beginning of a new epoch, that of bourgeois Russia." [22]

Another feature of Russian history to be reinterpreted was the Popular Army of 1611–13 which put an end to the Time of Trouble, liberated Moscow from the Poles, and opened the way to the election of the first Tsar of the Romanov dynasty. "A book by Professor Lubomirov on the Popular Army had been suppressed for many years," wrote one of the Soviet papers. "Now, it must be rehabilitated; the Popular Army was not at all a creature of the landed gentry and the merchants, but actually a popular army." [23] In the course of the war the names of the leaders of that army, Minin and Pozharsky, were often invoked as symbols of the traditional unity of the Russian nation in the face of foreign aggression.

Much later came the rehabilitation of the memory of Ivan the Terrible. Alexis Tolstoy, the most acclaimed of the then living Russian authors, was granted the honor of performing this deed. In an interview he said: "Ivan the Terrible was one of the most remarkable figures in Russian history. He represents Russia in all his grandiose ambitions, his fervid will, and his inexhaustible possibilities and power." [24]

In the course of the war quite a few figures were added to the neo-Communist Pantheon, among them Admiral Kornilov, a hero of the Crimean war, and Prince Gorchakov, foreign minister under Alexander II. On both occasions Tarle served as the government's spokesman.

The choice of the heroes and deeds was not chronological. Russia's past has been revealed to the Russian nation neither by looking backward, nor by looking forward. By trial and error, personalities and events were picked here and there which would appeal to the Russians of the 'thirties and 'forties of the twentieth century and which, in addition to this, could well symbolize the traditional attachment of the Russians to their soil, and their willingness to sacrifice everything for its protection. Finally, an almost uninterrupted series of heroes and heroic deeds emerged, beginning with Russia's Christianization and finishing with Russia's participation in the First World War.

Three heroes were selected during that time to receive the highest rank. These were Alexander Nevsky, Suvorov, and Kutuzov. Orders of military merit were created bearing their names. In 1943, schools were opened in which children of the heroes of this war were to be prepared for the glorious career of a Red Army officer; they were given the name of "Suvorov schools." Early in 1944, the first pupils of these schools wrote letters to Soviet papers: their central theme was: "We want to be like Suvorov."[25]

The rehabilitation of Russian history met some resistance in Stalin's inner circle, as shown by the following story. On January 27, 1936, Bukharin, then editor of *Izvestia,* said that laziness was the most universal trait of the Russian nation and that Oblomov, a famous "hero" from Goncharov's novel, was its chief symbol. On February 1, *Pravda,* without mentioning Bukharin, assailed those who asserted that Russia had been organized by foreigners, especially Germans, and enumerated the reasons why the Russians ought to be proud of their past. Bukharin did not understand the seriousness of his blunder and the next day published an article in which he obstinately defended his position. On February 10, a philippic against Bukharin appeared in *Pravda* in which, by numerous citations, it was "proved" that the slanderous distortion of the Russian past had nothing to do with Marxism. Now Bukharin had to apologize:

> The theory making Russian history a lasting darkness is historically wrong and politically harmful. Russian history knew periods of great progress and tremendous displays of energy. Russian science has given a number of brilliant names, Russian literature is entitled to occupy one of the first places in universal literature. I never shared that erroneous theory, but having made the unfortunate reference to Oblomov, I unwillingly deceived many. I am sorry that I have done so.

Official statements inducing the Russians to worship their past were insufficient. It was necessary to inculcate the new ideas, and still more the associated sentiments, into the minds of the younger generation. The study of Russian history was restored in schools of all levels. Great difficulties arose. First of all, no appropriate textbook was available. Naturally, when the government made it clear that it wanted a textbook on Russian history written from the standpoint of reviving nationalism, quite a few authors tried to do it. But it appeared that the competitors did not realize the magnitude of the swing of the pendulum. The first drafts introduced into an official committee, headed by Stalin himself, proved to be too "sociological," in other words, written according to the rejected pattern of "mass activity" and not emphasizing enough the positive value of such facts as the unification of Russia by the Grand Dukes of Moscow, the reforms of Peter the Great, and the emancipation of the serfs. Finally, a revised version of one of the drafts was selected and permitted to become the official textbook. The author, Professor Shestakov, has probably received tremendous royalties, and the students have received a rather dull textbook, lacking in any scientific value but well adapted to the new program.

Many years must pass before the young generation of the period of The Great Retreat reaches that age which gives access to high positions and honors. But the change in mentality, the reorientation of the nation towards national values was urgent. Therefore, all the means of mass adult indoctrination, this time with nationalism, were used. Thus, for instance, a series of pamphlets on the national heroes of Russia was published and distributed among the soldiers of the Red Army.[26] Naturally, the film and the radio were amply used. Those on Suvorov and Alexander Nevsky have already been mentioned; there have been others, such as on Peter the Great and Pushkin. The theater was also used. In this field, an almost incredible performance is worthwhile mentioning: the remodeling of Glinka's opera, *The Life for the Tsar*, which under the old regime was used to re-enforce monarchical sentiments. In the original opera the hero, Ivan Sussanin, saves the young Tsar Michael from capture by Poles. It was first planned to make him save Minin, the head of the Popular Army, but this was rejected as contrary to history. Finally, he was made to save Moscow. The final hymn (addressed to the Tsar) was re-worded to celebrate the glory of Russian arms, the might and indomitable character of the Russian nation.[27]

As a further means to re-enforce the national sentiment, historical exhibitions were organized. In 1936, Kutuzov's and

Napoleon's carriages were exhibited. In 1938, the Naval Academy organized an exhibition of Russian naval victories under Peter the Great and Catherine the Great, as well as the exploits of the Russian navy in the course of the Japanese war and the First World War. In 1939, an exhibition of Russian historical paintings was opened in Moscow. This exhibition was visited daily by thousands of people. It was on this occasion that *Pravda* began to rehabilitate the memory of Ivan the Terrible. *Pravda* wrote:

> The interpretation of some periods of Russian history, namely, of the time of Ivan the Terrible, is wrong. Only a few painters and sculptors, among them Antokolsky, have been able to grasp his greatness.

About the same time, in Kiev, an exhibition to celebrate the half-millennium of Russian artillery was organized. Wrote the paper of the Red Army:

> The exhibition shows that a number of inventions wrongly attributed to Western nations were made in Russia. Among other things, the exhibition shows the skill of the Russian artillery in the course of the Napoleonic wars, especially at the battle of Borodino.

In the cathedral of St. Basil in Moscow, an exhibition of the history of the Red Square (on which the cathedral is located) was opened. From 500 to 1,000 visitors were registered daily.[28]

It is well known that monuments of the past are of high symbolic value in re-enforcing the national sentiment. Such a device could not be neglected by the masters in the art of managing public opinion. Naturally, the great battlefields came first, such as Poltava (Peter's victory over the Swedes, 1709) and Borodino (glorious resistance of Russian armies against Napoleon, 1812). The government had to insist on this new tool, so entirely different from the practice of the previous years. Thus, one of the Moscow papers triumphantly reported that the monuments on the battlefield of Borodino had been completely restored. However, a few days later another paper asserted that in actuality nothing had been done, and on this occasion revealed the evil deeds of the previous years. In 1932, the monument to Bagration was sold as scrap iron. Reliefs on the monument to Kutuzov were destroyed. The church on the battlefield was demolished. On the wall of a former monastery, a board was placed with the following inscription: "We need not take care of the remnants of the accursed past." *Pravda* naturally explained these evil deeds by intrigues of the "enemies of the people," who knew that they hurt the dignity of a great nation and provoked hostility towards the Party and the Soviet government.[29] This, by the way, is an acknowledgment of tremendous importance: the destructions were carried out in complete accordance with the antinational policy of the first seventeen years of the Revolution, under the sponsorship of the high leaders. Their activity had provoked hostility to the regime; or, to put it in still other words: so long as the Communist rulers insisted on their antinational policy, they were considered as enemies by the people.

Among other items in the historical heritage of Russia restored under The Great Retreat were: the monument on the Kulikovo Pole where Dmitri Donskoy defeated the Tartars; the famous Trotsko-Sergyevsky cloister, the center of resistance against the Poles in the seventeenth century; the residences of the Moscow Tsars; the Petrinian Academy of Sciences in Leningrad; the Peterhof palaces; the Kutuzov hut where the famous general made the historical decision to surrender Moscow and thus preserve the army, as the instrument of coming victory; Yasnaya Polyana, the seat of Leo Tolstoy.[30] In addition to this, the government fostered the discovery of some monuments of Russian culture which had been forgotten or even unknown under the Imperial regime. The following story is interesting:

For more than half a year, work has been done on the restoration of Bazhenov's model for the reconstruction of the Moscow Kremlin. This was a gigantic project, transforming the whole Kremlin with its churches and palaces into one uniform architectural ensemble. If it were realized, the Kremlin would have surpassed the splendor of all known creations in the realm of architecture. It is difficult to convey to the reader the enthusiasm of all the participants in the attempt to restore the ingenious creation of a great Russian architect of the eighteenth century and to give an unsurpassed model to the country.[31]

Not only were monuments restored and exhibitions organized, but pilgramages to them fostered. Names already mentioned recurred on the list: Poltava, Borodino, Kulikovo Pole, Yasnaya Polyana and, in addition to this, a score of places where Pushkin lived or worked.[32]

On some occasions, the political purpose behind the rediscovery of Russia's past comes to the fore. Thus, for instance, a keen observer reports:

> On a poster which I can observe from my room there appears underneath a portrait of Kutuzov a quotation from Stalin in flaming letters reading: "Let the daring spirit of our ancestors inspire you in this war." [33]

What a contrast with the inscription of the Borodino monument executed in 1932!

A colorful feature of the historical tradition was restored relating to the Cossacks. For centuries they had formed semimilitary communities on the frontier and served the Tsars well against foreign and internal foes. For the latter they were hated by the revolutionists, and under the Communist regime their communities were disbanded. Then, later in 1935, letters from Don and Kuban Cossacks to Voroshilov (then war commissar) appeared in Soviet papers in which they declared their ardent desire to serve the fatherland as their fathers had done. Very soon, Cossack regiments were formed and quite a few special usages were permitted to revive. Thus, fathers resumed transmitting hereditary swords to their sons and this was done in ceremonies performed before big audiences. Young men returning from service in the Red Army resumed being received by similar assemblies. Cossack choirs were restored and invited to come to Moscow and perform before Stalin in their colorful folk costumes.[34]

The rediscovery of Russia's past was supplemented by the

rediscovery of the cultural heritage accumulated by generations but, because of its incompatibility with the Doctrine, ignored for many years. This is a subject to be treated in another chapter (IX). But one event must be mentioned in this context: Pushkin's centennial (1937) was used to organize a kind of Festival of Russian Culture. A special Committee was created, and on this occasion Pushkin was called "the great Russian poet, the creator of the literary language, and the originator of our great Russian literature." A few months later it was noteworthy that the country of the Soviets had rediscovered Pushkin.

We have dropped the silly attempts to make of Pushkin a revolutionist, a precursor of Bolshevism. But we declare war on those who dare to say that Pushkin's poetry does not mean anything for the proletarian. Pushkin is a genius who discovered the music of the mother tongue. He is the guiding star of Russian poetry. He is alive in the people's hearts.[35]

Never were the leaders closer to the truth than when making these statements.

The places where Pushkin had lived and worked were restored and opened for pilgrimage. Tens of thousands used this opportunity to display their deep attachment to the man who had given its highest expression to Russian culture.[36] His works were published in millions of copies, and a few days after their appearance in individual cities all the copies available were sold out, in contrast with Marx and Lenin, whose works stood in solid masses on the shelves of the bookstores or were used to wrap herrings. One of the slogans of the centennial days was: "Russia is a great nation because she gave Pushkin and Lenin to the world."

The Russian language, Pushkin's instrument, became a special object of worship. While the tendency under the Communist Experiment was to contaminate the language with slang, foreign words, and cacophonic abbreviations of official terms, the tendency under The Great Retreat turned towards its purification. A famous writer, Chukovsky, acknowledged that twenty years earlier it had been necessary to shake everything, even the language, but that since then things had changed, and it was not desirable to get rid of the awkward forms prevailing in literature, especially in poetry.[37]

A few years later this proud statement could be read in a Soviet paper:

> The Russian language has resisted the strain of the revolutionary years very well. The tendency to use official abbreviations has disappeared; as of September 1, 1938, the post offices have been forbidden to distribute mail if the addressee is designated by abbreviation. The number of foreign words in use is now smaller than before the Revolution. For many words of this type Russian counterparts have been found and accepted by everybody. The Russian language is more Russian than ever.[38]

It was only natural that, in the course of the war, efforts were made to link the present with the glorious past. "Stalingrad reminds us of Kulikovo Pole," one could read a few weeks after the decisive victory of the Red Army. When the battlefield of Borodino was liberated from the enemy, this statement was made: "The Russians think of Borodino as a prophetic symbol of this war." The restoration of the monuments on the battlefield torn down by the Germans was immediately ordered. A letter to Stalin from a group of peasants was given great publicity; in this letter the peasants said that they were proud of their sons, who were worthy great-grandsons of men who, in 1812, had valiantly fought under the banner of Kutuzov.[39]

In an article entitled *The Russian Soldier* these qualities are ascribed to him: greatness of soul, strength of will, clearness of mind.[40] To confirm such statements, the authors have always gone far back into history; Russia has obviously proven to be more solid ground than Communist Utopia.

As to culture in general, statements like these are typical of the war period: "The Russians look with pride on their past and with hope on their future";[41] "The Russian people has been granted the highest gifts. It has created a rich culture, it possesses a rich heritage in art and science, it has given birth to two of the greatest military men known to history, Peter the Great and Suvorov." Apropos Derzhavin's bicentennial, the role of Russian literature in the formation of Russia's national spirit was stressed. This literature, it was said, always reflected the heroic deeds of the Russian people correctly and brilliantly.

"We are proud of our science, literature, musiç, and painting," exclaimed Shostakovich, the leading Russian composer of our day. In the course of a special conference held at the University of Moscow, it was resolved that the great achievement of Russian,science had not yet been fully recognized and that all textbooks minimizing these achievements should be rewritten.[42]

In summing up, it can be said that in all realms of cultural activity, great achievements of the past have been shown to the peoples of the Soviet Union, young and old, advanced and backward. All the strength of the propaganda machine was now used to reawaken the national sentiment, the same machine which for seventeen years had been used to uproot this sentiment. The results have been quite different. In the earlier period, the propaganda machine worked against the natural aspirations of human beings and their cultural tradition. The result was not very edifying. Perhaps the tradition was weakened, but nothing did replace it in the hearts of the Russians. Enthusiasts of the International Proletarian culture could be found in books only, not in actuality.

Since 1934, the propaganda machine worked in the same direction as the national aspirations and culture tradition. No wonder that this time the effect was striking: not only was the national sentiment reawakened, but it grew overwhelming, perhaps stronger than desired by those in power.

For large portions of the Russian population, the return to the past meant the discovery of unsuspected treasures. Their reaction was similar to that of someone who has been told that he was a foundling, but suddenly discovers that he has very respectable parents. Their sentiment in regard to national culture became more violent than that of people who grew up in the knowledge that they belonged to a nation and a tradition. The sudden discovery of a glorious parentage by those who knew nothing but the misery of the Communist environment imbued them with the fighting spirit characteristic of neophytes. The character of this new nationalism is apparent in these statements:

The Russians can be exterminated up to the last man, but they cannot be conquered . . . In this struggle we ought to be inspired by the images of our glorious ancestors, Alexander Nevsky, Dmitri Donskoy, Minin, and Pozharsky, Suvorov, Kutuzov, and by the victorious banner of Lenin . . . The readiness of the present generation to give everything to protect the Russian country from invaders and struggle for its independence has deep historical roots. It began with the Tartar invasion and Alexander Nevsky and continued through Dmitri Donskoy, Minin, and Pozharsky, the battle of Poltava, and the Patriotic War of 1812. Soviet patriotism is national and historical. Also historical and national is the Russian Revolution which continues the tradition of the Russian nation. National consciousness is in the air of our time. The cosmopolitanism of the nineteenth century is a thing of the past, the dreamers who were patriots of time and space have died out. Love for one's own village has been resurrected. But this is not a reversion. Can one love mankind without loving one's own people? We have not lost faith in the brotherhood of nations, but love of our motherland has made it a living faith . . . Patriotism is love of one's country. What is one's country? My mountains, my trees, my history, the history of my people, my brothers and sisters, my beloved ones . . . Our love of the motherland has conquered all other sentiments. Human faces, human eyes, human language—this is our Russia, and we are their guardians in this age of calamity. Motherland: this is a stream of people from the remote past to the future in which we believe and which one builds up for himself and the next generation. In some remote future, these individual streams will combine into Humanity. But for our age this is a dream. Our age is an age of struggle for freedom, independence, and the right to construct society according to a nation's own laws . . . We love Russia not because other lands are less admirable, but because Russia is our country . . . We are proud of our people, and there is no purer sentiment in the world. The value of Russia has stood the test. We look at this value with calm and firmness. We have become the greatest nation in the world, because our ideals are human ideals.[43]

The definitions of patriotism just reproduced already belong to the war period. In the light of such definitions, it is understandable that the annexation of eastern Poland (September, 1939) was officially motivated by historical and racial reasons, as a kind of reunion of estranged brothers, and that no word was said about the fraternity of all toilers throughout the world, which certainly would have been mentioned if the annexation had taken place in 1920, in the course of the Russo-Polish war. It is also understandable that war propaganda has been entirely national; people have fought for their motherland, for the Russian soil which from time immemorial was tilled by their ancestors, and not for the realization of the initial blueprint of the Revolution.

In this line of development the climax was reached when on December 20, 1943, the government decided to drop the "International" as the national anthem and chose a new national anthem, which better than anything else expresses the compromise structure of the new society created under The Great Retreat. The Soviet Union and the great Russian country are used as interchangeable terms; Lenin and Stalin appear as heroes of the glorious fatherland which, in 1917, they hoped to see disappearing in the framework of the anonymous World Society of Toilers.

3

At the same time as the foreign policy of the Communist leaders was determined by the Utopia of internationalism and, within the country, antinational policy was paramount, the leaders had to solve the very difficult problem of organizing relations between the various ethnic groups ruled by them. This was a very complicated problem indeed, since the area under the Soviets is inhabited by 140 ethnic groups, one of which, the Russian, forms the absolute majority, whereas there are other groups with less than one thousand members. The cultural level of the different groups varies from primitive nomadism to industrial civilization of the Western type.

The Doctrine demanded complete lack of regard to the particularities of the ethnic groups. Before the war, both in

Russia and Austria-Hungary—the two great multinational States —the Social Democrats, though in violent opposition to their respective governments, strongly supported them on the issue of centralization; they emphatically denied the value of federation, especially of a federation of nationalities since, in their opinion, the national movements were tools used by the "bourgeois" to dupe the workers and come to terms with the "bourgeois" of other states, to the detriment of the workers, and because federation meant a decentralization which was unfavorable to the smooth functioning of planned economy.

But after having conquered power over Russia, the Communists proclaimed the program of transforming her into a federation of nationalities. The Communists' acceptance and realization of a program which, before their ascent to power, they strongly opposed can be explained by two reasons. First, they wished to attract and appease the "semicolonial peoples" of the former Russian Empire among whom autonomist and separatist movements existed. Secondly, they probably found, in their domination of an agglomeration of national republics, a compensation for their frustrated dream of a world-wide International Workers Republic.

Once accepted, the idea was vigorously carried out. The territory of Russia was divided into a complicated network of national republics and territories, on the basis of these three principles: (1) to every ethnic group a political unit must correspond; (2) only one political unit should correspond to every ethnic group so that a central agency for each culture would exist; (3) all these units must be united, not on the basis of an alleged ethnic or cultural affinity, but on that of the acceptance of the Socialist Soviet pattern.

The structure corresponding to these principles could not but be very complicated because of the greatly complicated ethnic relations involved.

The difficult architectonic problem has been solved on the basis of a classification of the ethnic groups and of a corresponding differentiation of their statuses.*

* The federal structure of the USSR is shown on Chart IV.

The Union consists of federal republics [44] which correspond to ethnic groups of the first class. Certain parts of the territory of several federal republics are segregated into autonomous republics which correspond to ethnic groups of the second class. Certain parts of the territory of federal republics not

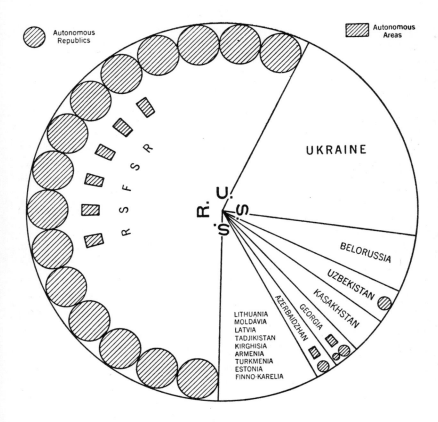

IV. THE STRUCTURE OF THE U.S.S.R. (1941)

The circle corresponding to the U.S.S.R. is divided into sectors proportionate to the population of the constituent republics; however, the nine minor republics are represented by one common sector. Within the sectors the number of autonomous republics and areas included in them is shown by symbols, with no regard to the size of their population.

entering into autonomous republics and certain parts of the territory of the autonomous republics are segregated into autonomous territories or national districts, which correspond to ethnic groups of the third and fourth classes. The status of the four classes differs in relation to the right of segregation, to participation in the federal government, and to the extent of autonomy.

As to separation, ethnic groups of the first class have the constitutionally recognized right of secession, and groups of the second class the constitutionally recognized right to be organized into autonomous units, whereas groups of the third and fourth classes have no specific rights at all.

In regard to participation in the federal government, the size of the representation in the Council of the Nationalities * varies according to the class.

The ethnic groups of the various classes are given different scopes of legislative and administrative autonomy. This gradation is expressed in an ingenious organization of the people's commissariats which roughly correspond to the ministries in "bourgeois" countries. These commissariats are divided into three levels: Union, Union-republican, and Republican. The first and third levels roughly correspond to Federal and State administration in this country; the second is peculiar to the Soviet Union. Such commissariats exist both on the federal and the republican (State) level, and the corresponding administrative activities are carried out by the federal commissariats *through* the republican ones. Thus, for instance, general directions concerning public health are given by the federal commissariat of health, but the real administration belongs, in each republic, to the republican commissariat of health. The latter is in the state of "double submission," since it is responsible both to the federal commissariat and the council of the people's commissars of the individual republic.

In contradistinction to the ethnic groups of the first and

* This roughly corresponds to the American Senate in that its members are elected by the people of the political units forming the Soviet Union. It is a part of the Supreme Soviet.

second classes those of the third and fourth do not possess any legislative or administrative autonomy; in their territory, the functions of the State are carried out by local agencies of the federal or autonomous republics.

Up to this place, the structure was described by taking the Constitution at face value. In practice, local liberties cannot develop since the actual power belongs to the Communist Party, and this Party is organized on a pattern of centralization and strong discipline. No reflection of the federal structure of the Soviet State is to be found in the structure of the Party. This is manifested in the fact that in the centers of the federal and autonomous republics, "provincial" committees of the Party function just as well as in all big centers scattered throughout the country.

The meaning of this Party structure for the actual amount of autonomy in the Soviet State may best be explained in the example of the status of a commissar heading a republican commissariat of the autonomous type. According to the Constitution, he should be freely elected by the Supreme Soviet of the national republic and be responsible to nobody but the Council of the People's Commissars of that republic. In actuality, the candidate is nominated by the Organization Bureau of the Central Committee of the Communist Party in Moscow, and "elected" by the Communist majority in the Supreme Council of the republic. Being a Party man, he has to obey strictly all orders which he may receive from the higher agencies of the Party. They may dismiss him at their pleasure, and a vote of the Supreme Soviet of the republic will give an official form to this dismissal.

Politically, no local liberties have arisen. But from the cultural standpoint the reform resulted in a substantial transformation of the life conditions of the ethnic groups forming Russia. Within the national republics and territories, the language of the corresponding ethnic group became the official language used in courts and administrative offices. It became the language of education, especially in primary and secondary schools.[45] Newspapers and magazines started appearing in the official languages of the republics and territories, and these languages gained dominance in the theater, whenever possible, also in movies and broadcasting. Cities, towns, streets, and the like previously known by Russian names received names in these languages. For part of them, literary languages were artificially elaborated by Russian scholars; in some cases the Russian, in others the Latin alphabet was adapted to embody them. Special measures were taken to train civil officers from among the backward groups.

In some cases, the policy of transforming Russia into a miniature International was obviously exaggerated. Efforts were made to increase the difference between kindred cultures. This was particularly the case with the Ukraine. Before the Communist Revolution, the Ukrainians in Russia did not possess a commonly accepted literary language, whereas those living in Galicia, under Austrian rule, could elaborate one. Because of great variations among the Ukrainian dialects, this Galician language was almost incomprehensible to the Eastern branch of the Ukrainians. Nevertheless, scientists and authors were invited from Galicia to help make the Ukrainian language as distinct from the Russian as possible, since the Galician dialect is a kind of transition to the Polish and Czech languages. What they produced was foreign to the majority of the Ukrainians, too.

The tendency soon evolved to impose the official language of the individual republics on all the groups living within their boundaries. Already in 1925, Larin-Lurie made a series of sensational speeches in which he told the story of the persecution of Russians by the Ukrainian administration, which went so far as to return without consideration all applications written in Russian, prohibited the import of papers published in Russian, closed Russian theaters, and denied to the Russian children the opportunity of being instructed in their language.[46]

Since, from the political standpoint, the transformation of Russia into a "national federation" remained on paper, no particular ideas could be elaborated within the individual ethnic groups. According to the official slogan, the culture of the USSR was to be "uniform in content" (socialist) but multiform as to expression (in the individual languages)." But the ethnic groups responded favorably to the opportunity of developing their cultures in their own languages. Thus, the opportunist reasoning of Lenin and Stalin proved to be correct and was conducive to the great success of consolidating the unity of the peoples inhabiting the Soviet State. However, let us not forget that this success was due not to the application of the Communist ideal, but to a drastic departure from it.

It was only natural that the change in the international policy of the Soviets and the reversal of the trend from internationalism to nationalism within the Soviet Union was accompanied by a significant reversal of the trend in the interethnic policy. The change has been twofold.

First of all, the scope of autonomy granted to the "national republics" was curtailed. The Constitution of 1923 provided autonomous commissariats for agriculture, interior (local administration and police), justice, public education (including art, theater, movies, newspapers, radio, etc.), public health, security. But in 1929 a federal commissariat of agriculture was created and superimposed on the commissariats of agriculture of the individual republics. In 1930 a specified structure of local government was imposed on the individual republics by a federal law. In 1934 a federal commissariat for internal affairs was organized. In 1936, newly organized federal councils for higher education and art curbed the autonomy of the national republics in the corresponding field. On July 20, 1936, a decree anticipating the Constitution of December 5, 1936, created federal commissariats for justice and public health. In 1943, only public education (excluding higher education and art), local industry, local transportation, local public utilities, and social security were carried out by republican commissariats of the autonomous type.

Early in 1944, a change took place which has aroused much attention outside of Russia; the federal republics (but not the autonomous ones) were granted the right to organize republican commissariats for foreign affairs and defense, to enter into direct relations with foreign powers, and to raise their own armies. This reform signified a departure from the general trend of The Great Retreat in inter-ethnic relations, but it was by no means as drastic as assumed by many. There is no question of independent diplomatic systems or armies. Actually, the new diplomacies and armies have been added to the federal diplomacy and army and put under strict control of federal agencies. This follows from the very text of the decrees. Moreover, one should not forget that only Soviet institutions have been involved, and not the Party system, which has not been touched by the reform and remains as centralized as it was.[47]

Secondly, the trend reversed regarding the policy of increasing the distances between the cultures of the Soviet peoples. It was declared that the peoples of the Soviet Union recognized their brotherhood and desired more unity, and that these peoples were full of sacred awe, indestructible love, and gratitude to the great Russian people.[48] It was especially said that the majority of the Ukrainians were unable to understand the books and papers published in the official language of the Ukrainian Republic, and that they demanded the return to more sensible speech. The reversal was so sudden that in 1933 Skrypnik, the Ukrainian commissar of education, committed suicide. Four years later Lubchenko, chairman of the Council of the People's Commissars of the Ukrainian Republic, did the same. He was accused of having protected the Galician scholars and stimulated animosity between Russian and Ukrainian musicians. The dictionaries and grammars published up to 1932 were put out of circulation. Another set of scholars were now entrusted with the task of preparing a dictionary and grammar which would be understandable to those concerned and emphasize the kinship of the Russians and Ukrainians. Similar events took place in Belorussia.

Oriental peoples inhabiting the Soviet Union could not be endowed with languages similar to the Russian, since they were of different root. But, reversing the trend of the early 'thirties, the tendency to create separate languages for each little group was discontinued, and languages started being elaborated for clusters of related dialects. The Russian alphabet was now used for the publication of books in languages for which the Latin had previously been chosen. Thus, the members of these peoples would at least learn the Russian script from their very childhood, and in this way the study of the Russian language would be facilitated. The study of Russian in "national schools" has been strengthened. For those pupils whose progress in Russian was slow, additional periods in Russian were introduced, at the expense of their mother tongue. The study of Russian has become one of the major subjects for the non-Russian members of the Red Army. At the outbreak of the war they received four lessons a week, the Russian soldiers serving as monitors.[49]

Naturally, the persecution of Russians in "national republics" was stopped. The Russian theaters in Kiev were reopened. The new policy reached its climax in a number of judicial trials, in which separatist tendencies in the "national republics" were severely repressed, despite the constitutional recognition of the right of secession.

Nevertheless, the peoples of the Soviet Union have not been denied the right previously granted them to cultivate their individual cultures. But now they are told that they are great peoples—under the leadership of the Russian people—which has organized them into a political body, given them participation in one of the greatest cultures known to history, and shown them the way of socialism.[50] Recently it has been stated that in the schools of the non-Russian republics, the Russian language is the preferred subject of study; that all the pupils do their best to get complete command of it; that in general everybody wants to speak Russian in order to understand anybody else in the Union.[51]

The local nationalisms have not been destroyed, but molded in a manner fitting them into a kind of corporate nationalism of the peoples of the Soviet Union. This is clearly a return to the "Imperial Policy" which prevailed in Russia up to the last quarter of the nineteenth century, a policy which em-

phasized that all the subjects of the Emperor were at home
in Russia, and that racial origin could not hinder anybody from
climbing to the very summits of society.

4

We have followed the strange fluctuations of the policies
of the Communist rulers of Russia depending on their international creed. Here are the relevant facts:

1. Immediately after the Revolution, the Doctrine was applied to the foreign policy of the new government and manifested in the antinational policy which prevailed regarding
Russian culture; but simultaneously, an opportunist departure
from the Doctrine was allowed to materialize in the realm of
inter-ethnic relations.

2. The Doctrine suffered its earliest defeat in the realm of
foreign policy; there the retreat started in 1927–8 and was accentuated in 1934–5 and in later years.

3. As to the antinational policy, the Doctrine remained intact up to 1934, when it was entirely rejected and replaced
by its very opposite, making flaming patriotism one of the basic
virtues.

4. Thus, the retreat from antinationalism has lagged behind
the retreat from internationalism, probably because in foreign policy the hand of the Communists was forced by developments beyond their control, whereas within Russia they
were thought to be absolute masters.

5. Two years before the decisive breakdown of internationalism and antinationalism, a reversal took place in the policy
molding inter-ethnic relations; the new trend brought the situation nearer the blueprint than it had been in 1932. But, very
significantly, in this particular regard the blueprint did not
depart manifestly from Russia's historical trend.

The final judgment may be this: The past few years have
witnessed a complete elimination of the achievements of the
first seventeen years of the new regime directed towards the
creation of a society of internationally minded proletarians.

Nationalism, i.e., the love of one's own country, is stronger than ever. But it is neither imperialism, i.e., the tendency to conquer peoples which do not belong to the historically delimited territory of the nation, nor racial exclusivism, since it is combined with a structure which, with some qualification, could be termed "inter-ethnic democracy." In any case, in Russian conditions the state reached at the outbreak of the war was the best possible background for the organization of resistance and victory. The natural desire of the rulers to gain victory in a war which they anticipated was the determining reason of their policy directed towards the revival of nationalism and the reintegration of ethnic groups into a coherent whole. But revival was possible only on the basis of survival. In turning nationalist once more, Russia proved that in the very depths of her national soul she never had abandoned her historical way, which on the surface seemed lost in 1917.

CHAPTER VIII

THE FAMILY, THE SCHOOL, THE CHURCH:

The Pillars of Society Shaken and Re-enforced

1

IN THEIR ATTEMPTS to create a new culture, the revolutionists always meet resistance. This resistance is displayed by individuals, but they resist because they have been molded by mighty institutions through which social structure and culture are perpetuated. In modern society these pillars of society are the family, the school, and the Church. From the standpoint of the revolutionists two of them, the family and the Church, are hopeless, for it is their very nature to preserve tradition. But the school might perhaps be transformed into an instrument of cultural revolution.

Hence, for those who are eager to endow a nation with a new culture, a definite program of action follows: they must loosen the family ties; they must destroy or at least weaken the Church; and they must transform the school into an accelerator of cultural revolution. This was the natural program of the Communists while they performed their Great Experiment.

With respect to the family, the destructive attitude is sometimes denied by pro-Communist writers outside of Russia.[1] The reason is obvious; the value of the family is beyond question, say, in this country, and a regime which is hostile to it cannot count on many sympathizers. But in 1919, an authoritative representative of the regime said: "The family has ceased to be a necessity, both for its members and for the State." A few years later, another high dignitary declared that the Communists had to undermine the family, "this formidable

192

stronghold of all the turpitudes of the old regime." [2] And acts were still more conclusive than words.

The family, which was to be destroyed, was of the patriarchal type. In old Russia, marriage was a religious institution. Only religious marriage and divorce were recognized, so that the rules of the corresponding religious communities were exclusively applied. The superiority of the husband over the wife was legally recognized, but there was no joint property of the consorts.[3] The wife received the husband's last name, but the Russians emphasized that, in contradistinction to the West, their women never were addressed as "Mrs. John Doe"; their first names had to be used. Parental authority was strong; up to the age of twenty-one, children needed parental consent for marriage and quite a few other significant acts. Naturally, the institution of inheritance existed. Thus, the strong family structure prevailed; this was especially the case among the peasants and the lower middle class, whereas among the upper classes, the intellectuals, and the workers there was a well-expressed tendency to weaken the family ties.

This stronghold of the old order, this instrument of culture tradition was attacked by the Communists from the very start of their rule.[4] The general tendency was to destroy the stable character of marital relations and make marriage as easily soluble as possible. Naturally, marriage was liberated from all bonds with religion: after a certain date, church weddings ceased to be accorded any legal effect. Instead of going to church, the prospective consorts had to apply for "registration" of their marriage to local boards established for that purpose. Measures were taken to deprive the registration of the character of an impressive ceremony. The boards were usually located in some dark and abject room of an office building, and no words about the significance of marriage were uttered by the officials.

The most drastic change concerned divorce: in contradistinction to the old law which made it so difficult, the decrees of December 17 and 18, 1917, permitted every consort to declare that he wanted his marriage to be canceled. No reasons were to be given to the board. Receiving the application, it had to grant the cancellation immediately if there was mutual consent; if this was not the case, divorce was to be granted by the court, but this was a meaningless formality, since the court had to do it at the request of each consort, even if the other one opposed it. If one of the consorts was absent, he or she was notified by a postcard.

In addition to this, incest, bigamy, and adultery were dropped from the list of criminal offenses. Abortion was explicitly permitted by the decree of November 20, 1920, provided that it was performed by an approved physician in a State hospital. Under these conditions the physician had to accede to requests for abortion even if no valid reasons could be established. Under War Communism, inheritance ceased to exist.

When marriage can be canceled by means of a postcard, when there is no distinction between legitimacy and illegitimacy, when inheritance is unknown, parental authority is naturally weakened, and this effect was one of the purposes of the measures described. In official propaganda the idea was persistently emphasized that children had to obey their parents only insofar as the parents complied loyally with the directions of those in power. This signified, among other things, that unless they wanted to risk placing themselves in a dangerous position, parents could not oppose the propaganda of the Marxist doctrine, including atheism, to which the children were exposed at school. There they were taught to do their best to re-educate their parents in the Communist spirit and denounce them to the authorities if they displayed a marked counterrevolutionary attitude. Numerous family tragedies evolved on that basis, the State backing the children against the parents. Time and again the idea was publicly discussed as to whether family education ought not to be abolished and replaced by education in State institutions. Reluctantly, the idea was rejected as impractical, at least for the period of transition.

During the NEP, a partial restoration of the family could

be expected, if the Marxist doctrine were correct and monogamy and the strong family were the counterpart of the individualistic manner of production. There was actually one almost unavoidable concession; this was the restoration of inheritance. But in contrast with the Marxist scheme, the attack on the family was rather strengthened. A new Family Code was prepared in 1925, and the draft was submitted to an informal discussion. Voices from the countryside were unfavorable, but this did not stop the government, and the new Code was enacted as of January 1, 1927. The main innovation was the introduction of the institution of "the nonregistered marriage," legally equal to the registered one. This meant that courts and boards were obliged to consider every union of a man and woman as marriage provided that at least one of the following conditions were present: (1) durable cohabitation; (2) common menage; (3) declaration of the relationship before third persons, or (4) mutual support and common education of the children. The unforeseen effect was the legalization of bigamy: applying the new law, the Supreme Court prescribed the division of the estate of a deceased man between his registered and nonregistered wife.[5]

The period of the Second Socialist Offensive was characterized by additional efforts to uproot the traditional structure of the family. The labor law of the period made it obligatory to accept any job imposed on the individual, and often husband and wife were assigned work in different towns. To the complaint of a teacher that she was artificially separated from her husband, the Labor Board replied that divorce was easy and that she probably could find another husband in the place of her occupation. In Stalingrad it was decided to create "socialist suburbs" consisting of houses without apartments for family life, replaced by single rooms, refectories, and nurseries. The plan fell through because nobody but bachelors agreed to live in such suburbs.

The antifamily policy was crowned by partial success: around 1930, on the average, family ties were substantially weaker than they had been before the revolution. But this partial success was more than balanced by a number of detrimental effects unforeseen by the promoters of the Communist Experiment. About 1934, these detrimental effects were found to endanger the very stability of the new society and its capacity to stand the test of war. Let us review these effects.

1. The abuse of the freedom of divorce and abortion resulted in an ominous decrease of the birth rate. No natality figures have ever been published for the crucial years, but in 1937, the population proved to be 13 million behind expectation, so that around 1934, the deficit must already have been large. To what extent this was due to the freedoms just mentioned cannot be established. But the following figures speak for themselves: in 1934, in the medical institutions of the city of Moscow, 57 thousand children were born, but 154 thousand abortions were performed; in 1935, already under changing conditions, the figures were 70 thousand, and 155 thousand. As to divorce, the frequency of which also pushes down the birth rate, the following figures were reported from Moscow: in 1934, in 100 marriages there were 37 divorces, and in the first half of 1935, there were 38.3 divorces.[6]

2. The dissolution of family ties, especially of the parent-child relations, threatened to produce a wholesale dissolution of community ties, with rapidly increasing juvenile delinquency as the main symptom. In 1935, the Soviet papers were full of information and indignation about the rise of hooliganism, i.e., of crimes in which the sadistic joy of inflicting pain on somebody or destroying something of value was paramount. Everywhere, wrote the papers, gangs invaded workingmen's dwellings, ransacked them, and destroyed or spoiled what they did not take away; if somebody dared to resist, he was mercilessly killed. In trains, the hooligans sang obscene songs; to prolong the fun, they did not permit travelers to alight at their destinations if they had not finished singing. Sometimes the schools were besieged by neglected children; other times gangs beat the teachers and attacked women, or regularly fought against one another.

3. Finally, the magnificent slogans of the liberation of sex

and the emancipation of women proved to have worked in favor of the strong and reckless, and against the weak and shy. Millions of girls saw their lives ruined by Don Juans in Communist garb, and millions of children had never known parental homes.

2

The disintegration of the family did not disturb the Communists, since this was precisely what they wanted to achieve, but they were disturbed by quite a few collateral effects of the disorganization. The unfavorable trend of the population figures threatened to undermine both the labor supply and the strength of the nation at arms—for wars to be waged by the next generation. In the specific circumstances of 1934, the waste of human energy in juvenile delinquency, the combat against it, and love affairs, and the accumulation of unfavorable attitudes among the victims of the new family order—or perhaps disorder is the correct word?—could no longer be tolerated: they undermined the strength of the nation for the war which was straight ahead. The unfavorable development had to be stopped, and to achieve this the government had no other choice but to re-enforce that pillar of society which is the family. These were the main lines of development:

1. Contrary to the teachings of the previous years, young people were instructed to consider marriage "as the most serious affair in life," since in principle it should be a union for life. Statements such as follow, which never could have appeared in the course of the Communist Experiment, now daily adorned the Soviet papers and magazines: "There are people who dare to assert that the Revolution destroys the family; this is entirely wrong: the family is an especially important phase of social relations in socialist society . . . One of the basic rules of Communist morals is that of strengthening the family . . . The right to divorce is not a right to sexual laxity. A poor husband and father cannot be a good citizen. People who abuse the freedom of divorce should be punished." And actually, in 1935 the Soviet government started to prosecute

men for rape who "changed their wives as gloves," registering a marriage one day and divorce the next. *Pravda* told the following story:

Engineer P. seduced a girl by promising to marry her. When symptoms of pregnancy appeared, the girl reminded him of his promise. His reply was: "Look, dear, you are the seventh girl in my life to whom the same unpleasant thing has occurred. Here is a letter from another woman who is also bearing a child of mine. Could I marry her, too?" The girl insisted, but the engineer terminated the discussion by saying: "Forget about marriage. Do as you like. Here is money to pay for an abortion." Having told the story, the paper added: "This man should be tried, and his trial ought to be a 'demonstrative trial.' " [7]

In the official journal of the Commissariat of Justice these amazing statements may be found:

The State cannot exist without the family. Marriage is a positive value for the Socialist Soviet State only if the partners see in it a lifelong union. So-called free love is a bourgeois invention and has nothing in common with the principles of conduct of a Soviet citizen. Moreover, marriage receives its full value for the State only if there is progeny, and the consorts experience the highest happiness of parenthood.[8]

To inculcate the rediscovered value of marriage into the minds of the younger generation, not only the negative method of deterrence by trials and producing indignation by well-chosen stories was used, but also the positive method of glorifying marriage by well-staged ceremonies; perhaps one could speak of "demonstrative marriage." Here is a story from *Izvestia*. The people involved are a *kolhoz* brigadier, V., and the first parachutist among *kolhoz* girls, B. The scene is Northern Caucasus, one of Russia's granaries.

The romance lasted about two years. In the beginning, V. hated B. He did his best to organize a shock brigade,* but she preferred dancing and diverted the energy of youth towards

* A group of workers pledged to work substantially faster and better than required by regulations.

that futility. When V. saw that he was unable to discourage that attraction he joined the movement, even started helping young people organize dances and athletic performances, and in return was helped by them in work. Then suddenly, when B. made her first jump, V. decided that life without her would be valueless, and proposed to her. She accepted. The secretaries of the regional and local Party organizations decided to sponsor the marriage. Stimulated by them, the collective farm took over all preparations and decorated the village beautifully for the great day. The people's commissar for agriculture was invited to come. He could not accept, but congratulated the young people by wire and offered them a magnificent gift, a phonograph and a set of records.

The story is continued in *Pravda*. Early in the morning guests started arriving. Among them were leaders of the Party, the Soviets, and the economic organizations, as well as the champion of the girl parachutists of the Union. About noon, a score of airplanes appeared in the sky. The betrothed were offered a ride, after which they were enthusiastically acclaimed by the crowd. About five o'clock, 800 guests were invited to dinner. Tables were overloaded with mutton, hams, ducks, chickens, pies, and other dishes. After a while the regional Party secretary rose and made a speech congratulating the V-s on their marriage, the most serious step in their lives. He expressed the hope that they would live in perfect unity and procreate an abundant Bolshevik progeny. The 800 present rose and drank to the health of the newlyweds. The people danced and rejoiced far into the night.[9]

Was not this an invitation to millions of young people to reconsider those ideas about marriage which, until quite recently, they were taught as belonging to the very essence of the Doctrine? To re-enforce the new ideas, very simple, but probably very effective symbolic means were used. The registration offices ceased to be filthy places. Now, young people found them clean, comfortable, well furnished; the officers became polite, friendly, underlining the seriousness of the act. Marriage certificates started being issued on decent paper, no longer on wrapping paper, as was the case previously. For a small additional sum the newlyweds could receive a marriage certificate designed by artists.[10] Then, in the fall of 1936, wedding rings started being sold in Soviet shops.[11] Since these rings are used in church weddings, this novelty could be interpreted as an invitation, on the part of the government, to have the civil marriage, or registration, re-enforced and made almost indissoluble by the Church.

2. The freedom of divorce was first curtailed and then almost abolished. The first phase appears in the law of June 27, 1936, which introduced a number of inhibitions. It calls for the summoning of both parties when a divorce is to be registered.

Moreover, according to the law of September 28, 1935, the fact of divorce must be marked in the passports and birth certificates of the consorts. Commenting on this regulation, *Izvestia* expressed the hope that before marrying a "fluttering scoundrel," a girl would ask him to produce his papers and then perhaps renounce the honor of becoming his thirtieth bride.[12]

Finally, the fee for divorce which previously had been rather nominal was substantially raised; instead of three rubles, one had to pay 50 rubles for the first divorce, 150 for the second, and 300 for the third and each subsequent divorce.

The effect of the antidivorce drive may be measured by the following figures: in the course of the second half of the year 1936, the number of divorces in the Ukraine was 10,992, against 35,458 in the second half of 1935;[13] in other words, it decreased more than three times.

The second phase appears in the decree of July 8, 1944.

Prospective applicants for a divorce will henceforth be obliged to state their reasons and satisfy the courts that these reasons are serious and valid. Both parties must appear personally before a lower court which hears all the evidence and then seeks to determine if it cannot effect a reconciliation. If this is believed impossible, the petition can be carried to a higher court. Witnesses must be heard in both courts. The divorce fees have been raised to 2,000 rubles.

It is probable that the courts, obeying the government's directions, will demand very good reasons and irrefutable evidence to grant a divorce. In consequence, obtaining a divorce in Russia will probably become more difficult than in many states of this country.

Moreover, the decree of July 8, 1944, abolished the institution of "unregistered marriage" introduced in 1926. Now, only "registered marriage" is legally recognized; as a corollary, the "bourgeois" distinction between legitimate and illegitimate children has reappeared in Soviet law. In addition to this, "the research of paternity" has been explicitly forbidden, so that illegitimate children and their mothers will receive no alimony. Very definitely, this will prove a mighty deterrent to extramarital relations, insofar as girls are concerned.

3. The freedom to dispose of unborn children through abortions no longer exists. Early in 1935, a campaign against abortion was started. Articles began to appear in Soviet papers written by high medical authorities, explaining the harm which abortion, especially repeated abortion, inflicts on women.[14] Praising maternity, these authorities declared that the longing for children had suddenly reappeared among the women of the Soviet Union—a manner of saying that now Stalin wanted them to bear as many children as possible. Trials resulting in severe sentences finished the careers of persons operating clandestine "abortaria": their very emergence disclosed that, without change in the law, Soviet hospitals no longer performed abortion at the simple request of the pregnant woman. Finally, a draft law prohibiting abortion was published and offered for public discussion. Numerous objections were raised, mainly based on intolerable dwelling conditions. Nevertheless, the law of June 27, 1936, abolished the freedom of abortion which had been considered one of the highest achievements of Communism by many pro-Communists.

Repealing the notorious law of November 20, 1920, the new law prohibited abortion in all cases except where there was danger to life or health of the pregnant woman or danger of hereditary transmission of serious sickness. As in the former

law, only medical men were permitted to perform the operation. Pressure exerted on a woman to induce her into abortion
was declared a crime punishable by two years in prison. To
make more childbearing possible, the law promised a large
extension of the network of maternity hospitals, day nurseries,
and kindergartens. Maternity grants were increased, and special allowances were promised to mothers of six or more children.*

4. The peculiar parent-child relationship which had obtained
under the Communist Experiment, and which granted superiority to the children, was reversed to one which is considered
normal in the world; once more, children have to recognize the
authority of their parents. Obviously, the change could not be
effected through legal enactment, and the method of persuasion through propaganda was used exactly in the same manner
as it was used to stabilize marriage. Statements like these could
be found almost daily on the pages of Soviet papers, beginning
with the spring of 1935:

Young people should respect their elders, especially their parents . . . The respect and care of parents is an essential part of the
Comsomol † morals . . . One must respect and love his parents, even
if they are old-fashioned and do not like the Comsomol.[15]

In 1939, the official journal of the Union Prosecutor declared:

Sound moral ideas must be inculcated into the minds of young
persons. They must know that lack of care for their parents is found
only among savages and that in every civilized society such conduct
is considered dishonest and base.[16]

To corroborate these ideas, the journal cited the laws of
Solon and Xenophon's works.

The method of positive demonstration was also used, and
Stalin himself found it necessary to set the example. In Octo-

---

* The second antidivorce law (1944) substantially increased the advantages granted to mothers of numerous children. Honorary titles were granted
to mothers of seven or more children.
† Young Communist League.

ber, 1935, he paid a visit to his old mother living in Tiflis,[17] and in the detailed accounts of this visit signs of love and respect to the old lady by the leader of the World Proletariat were emphasized. A high degree of intimacy in family relations was displayed through the reproduction of such questions as: how did Stalin's children like the jam made for them by their grandmother. Another day Stalin appeared in one of Moscow's gardens with his children, something he had never done previously. Up to that time, the majority of Soviet citizens did not even know that Stalin had any children.

Gradually, the unlimited freedom granted to young people under the Communist Experiment was curbed. One of the most conspicuous items in the process has been the decree of July 15, 1943, excluding children below the age of sixteen from evening performances in theaters and movies.

To strengthen parental authority, an indirect method has been used in the new inheritance law of March 20, 1945. While previous laws limited possible heirs to direct or adopted descendants, consorts, and needy dependents, the new law broadens this list to include parents, brothers, sisters, and public organizations. Although according to the new law the testator may not deprive his minor children or jobless heirs of their rightful portion, its impact on the family is clear: the greater the freedom to dispose of one's estate, the greater is the authority of the head of the family relating to presumptive heirs.

3

Destruction, then reconstruction; that was the pattern of the activity of the Communist rulers regarding the family. What happened to the second pillar of society, the school?

Very definitely, the school had to stop conveying the particular culture tradition of the nation to the younger generation and concentrate on becoming a mighty instrument of the Revolution. The Communist leaders expressed their ideas on the subject in this way:

The victory of the Revolution can be consolidated only by the school; the training of the future generation will anchor everything won by the Revolution . . . The fate of the Revolution depends upon the extent to which we can make fresh, human material of the new generation, competent of building a Socialist economy, a Communist society.[18]

Their task was facilitated by the fact that in Imperial Russia public education prevailed strongly over private education. On this basis, they readily made education a State monopoly. But there was also an important obstacle: when Russia was taken over by the new rulers, teachers of all grades, from the elementary school to the University, were in the majority "progressively minded persons," often members of the revolutionary movement. But almost none belonged to the Bolshevik wing of the Social Democrats, the predecessors of the Communist Party. They held democratic ideals and rejected Lenin's teachings. Therefore, when the Communist Revolution took place, they could be used as agents of the cultural revolution only with reservations. Another difficulty consisted in the fact that the Communists wanted to change not only the content of teaching, but also the pedagogical methods and forms of organization. In this regard they had no well-established ideas, and the trial and error method was used for years, resulting in reckless experimentation with the younger generation. Finally, the economic collapse of the period of War Communism was unfavorably reflected in the school situation.

The experimentation may be divided into two periods. The first lasted up to 1923. This was a rather negative phase, emphasis being laid on the destruction of culture tradition.

The destruction of the old school system was carried out in the guise of a bold and far-reaching educational reform. The Educational Act of October 16, 1918, replaced the complicated school system of old Russia by a "unified polytechnical school," with nine (later ten) grades: * No homework was permitted, and examinations were abolished, as well as any

* These nine grades corresponded to the twelve grades of the American school. In 1929, a tenth grade was added and the school was divided into three levels: the elementary (grades 1-4), the intermediary (grades 5-7), and the secondary (grades 8-10).

kind of punishment. Overnight, coeducation was introduced on all levels. The labor principle was stressed, and the schools were transformed into a preparatory stage for the productive work in which the pupils were to engage after graduation. The administration of the schools was entrusted to "school collectives" composed of all the teachers, pupils, and employees.

As a result, the schools became revolutionary clubs for young people, while their basic function, that of inculcating knowledge, was almost entirely neglected. As material conditions were desperate, school attendance substantially decreased. The teachers were ill paid and cases of abject poverty, mass sickness, and even prostitution were reported among them.[19] The labor principle degenerated into imposing purely mechanical tasks on the pupils, such, for instance, as the carrying of fuel from the yard to the stoves.

The reform of elementary and high schools was accompanied by a sweeping university reform. The decree of August 8, 1918, permitted every boy and girl over the age of sixteen to enroll in a University, irrespective of their academic background. Another decree of October 8, 1918, aimed at "blowing up" the Universities from within. This decree proclaimed (1) the abolition of academic degrees,[20] and (2) the introduction into the University councils of all faculty instructors, in the hope that these would be more inclined than the professors to carry out reforms in the Communist style. In 1920, a reform of the academic curriculum was carried out, based on the distorted information regarding American educational patterns, then in vogue among those in power. The liberal phase of education was neglected: emphasis was laid on strict specialization, mainly in the technical sciences. The result was the same as in the case of the "unified school"; teaching in the true sense of the word almost stopped, and in consequence, the training of specialists for all kinds of learned professions likewise ceased.

4

About 1923, the general improvement of conditions due to

the NEP permitted the Communist government to attack the problem of overcoming illiteracy and simultaneously shift from the negative to the positive phase of experimentation.

With respect to the aim of overcoming illiteracy, redundant declarations had already been made in the first, or destructive, period. But they remained on paper and, as has already been mentioned, the number of schools and pupils were gradually decreasing. The bottom was reached in 1923 when 6.8 million children were registered in elementary schools. Then the trend reversed and ten years later, in 1932–3, 18.2 million children were enrolled in the first four grades. In addition to this, there were 3.6 million pupils in the intermediary schools (grades 5-7) and secondary schools (grades 8-10) as compared with 0.6 million in 1922–3, and 458,000 students in institutions for higher learning, as compared with 159,800 in 1928. Education seems to have advanced on a level with the industrial expansion of the period.*

There were, however, low points even in the qualitative phase of the situation. Contrast the trebling of elementary education and still greater expansion on the intermediary and secondary levels with the very modest increase in the number of school buildings: there were 105,000 schools in 1923, and 166,000 in 1932. Consequently, in 90% of the elementary schools and 70% of the secondary schools pupils were taught in two or three shifts, each pupil attending school for three hours a day only. The increase in the number of well-trained teachers also lagged behind the expansion of the school system. In 1932, in elementary schools only 50% of the teachers had full training, 40% had only seven years of grade school, and the rest still less. In secondary schools, only 40% of the teachers had graduated from Universities; 20% had some pedagogical training, but on the background of secondary school only; 20% had nothing but secondary education and were obliged to give instruction to the limit of their own knowledge.[21]

Nevertheless, from a purely quantitative standpoint, these

* For details about the movement of the school population, see Table 6 in Appendix II.

achievements seemed marvelous. But, also, they coincided with the period of major experimentation in schools and this fact, as we shall see, completely annihilated the quantitative advance.

The aim of the experiment was clear: the school was to be a weapon in the hands of the workers preparing fighters for the realization of the ideals of the working class.[22] But what were the appropriate means to bring this about? On this question the Communists had no ideas of their own. They therefore decided to imitate the most radical pattern they could find in Europe and America, without regard to the fact that the new ideas were applied there only in a few "progressive" and very expensive schools. Since information about foreign progressive education was limited, Soviet policies changed so frequently and were so contradictory that the teachers had no opportunity to adjust themselves to each of the successive new sets of rules.

In the course of the experiment the old system, providing for regular periods of study, the division of pupils into classes, and guidance by teachers was abolished. The teaching of subject matter was replaced by "projects," even the three R's being taught on that basis. Thus, for instance, the general topics for a few years were as follows: first year, labor in the family; second year, labor in general; third year, economics of the province; fourth year, economics of Russia; eighth year, the history of labor; ninth year, the Taylor system and the Communist organization of labor.

The "projects" were naturally used to inculcate the Marxist doctrine into the minds of the pupils. As revealed in 1934, in Moscow children nine or ten years old had to discuss planned economy, including such questions as the reasons for developing heavy industry ahead of light industry. In Samara, the resolutions of Party congresses, written in the dull and clumsy language typical of all the official documents, were used to exemplify the rules on the participle. The province of Ivanovo distinguished itself by the introduction of "political contests" in the course of which insidious questions on current politics were asked. At the same time, to make instruction easier, special pamphlets were published containing all the necessary information. This permitted the teachers to simplify the procedure greatly; they no longer had to formulate the question, but could just ask: what is the reply, say, to question four of the second chapter? When, in 1934, these educational methods finally were discontinued, a group of teachers were moved to write:

We have lived to see the great day. Now we shall no longer be forced to torture ourselves and the children by demanding that they memorize sociological schemes which they cannot understand. What have we done? We have taught them everything except facts.

What happened in general in the course of the period of the Great Experiment has been marvelously told by a Soviet author in the imaginary diary of a Communist schoolboy: [23]

The Dalton plan is being introduced in our school. This is a system thanks to which the teachers will have nothing to do, and the pupils will have to find out everything by themselves. Our school desks will be replaced by long tables, and the classrooms will be called laboratories. [A little farther on he says]: The Dalton plan is worth nothing. We all—both the teachers and the pupils—understand nothing. All the fellows say that Dalton must have been a lord, one of the bourgeois . . . During one month we must read a whole heap of books, write ten reports, and draw the outlines of ten diagrams; and besides that we must be able to talk about all we have read and written.

Another illustration is contained in the following report about a conversation between a "traveling lecturer" and a village teacher.

At first the teacher answered timidly, as if he felt a little ashamed of speaking about his school. "Our school is a very ordinary one. I work very slowly." But as soon as it grew clear to him that all the schools were more or less in the same condition, he began to speak in quite another tone: "I have succeeded in collecting some kind of data during the last years. Please, notice the methods which we applied in organizing our school. At first we introduced the method ot self-help. Everything was done by the children themselves, so as to make them quite independent of help from the outside." And how was general instruction given? "Well, to tell the truth, no instruction was imparted at all. The children were too tired to learn. After that another method was introduced, the Discussion method. Then it was abandoned for the Active Labor and Laboratory method. Then it was the turn of the Concentration method. However, we did not stop for long at it and passed over to the Dalton plan, and had nearly put it into practice, but here the peasants intervened and demanded that the children should really be taught something. But I dare not teach them in the old manner, and nothing comes of the new methods." [24]

Simultaneously with the experimentation in the lower and middle grades of education, sweeping changes took place in Universities and other institutions for higher learning. In old Russia, since 1905, these institutions enjoyed an autonomy almost unknown in other civilized countries.* In the fall of 1922, this autonomy was completely abolished. A board of directors was placed at the head of each institution, all appointed by the Commissariat for Education. The University Councils, which in Imperial Russia actually headed the schools, lost all real significance and became ceremonial institutions. Real power was shifted to the Communist Party. In 1926, on the boards of directors, 152 Party members confronted 132 non-Party men, despite the fact that only 4.6% of the professors and 8.6% of the Faculty instructors belonged to the Party.[25]

The new organization was first of all used to exert actual pressure on the professorial staff. The professors were compelled to join the union of "the workers of public education and socialist culture" which, like all the unions, declared in its statutes that fostering the International Communist Revolution was its major preoccupation. As members of this union, professors had to sign declarations in which they congratulated the government *apropos* the execution of alleged counterrevolutionists in their midst, or protested against imaginary capi-

* The Universities were State institutions, and the State paid the salaries of the staff. But the professors formed an independent body, the University Council, which elected the rector (president), the deans of the faculties (schools) and new members of the staff when positions were vacant.

talist interference with Soviet affairs, or expressed their firm belief that, before the advent of Communism, true science did not exist.

But this was not enough. The government started a purge of the professorial body by submitting all professors to the procedure of re-election. This re-election was conducted by special committees consisting of representatives of trade unions, students, and academic teachers. Every professor appointed before 1918 had to submit a report to the committee about his scientific progress during the last decade, and his participation in public life. Then he had to appear personally and reply, in public session, to every question posed by the members of the committee, and sometimes questions asked from the floor. Finally the committee decided by open vote whether the candidate for re-election was or was not to be permitted to continue teaching. In an article published about that time in one of the leading papers, it was emphasized that scientific efficiency was secondary; the point at issue was the elimination of men who did not do their best to imbue the new generation with socialist ideas.[26]

Academic teaching was naturally co-ordinated with the general situation. In 1922, a National Council of Science was created, consisting mainly of high Party officials. Very soon it began to furnish its own detailed programs of lectures to be delivered by the professors. Students belonging to the Communist cells had the duty of checking the conformity of these lectures with the prescribed programs. Naturally, the study of the Marxist doctrine was imposed on all students. What actually happened may be seen from revelations made much later, when the Party leaders decided that "political education" in institutions of higher learning ought to be curbed. Here is a story told by a student:

An older man takes the chair and starts speaking. The students are ready to take notes. But they cannot: in a few moments the speaker mentions Aristotle, Plato, Epicure, the Cronstadt upheaval of 1921, the liquidation of the *kulaks* as a class. Aristotle is proved to be the precursor of the Mensheviks, Plato of the Fascists. Aristotle's ideas are illustrated by reference to subversive activities of the *kulaks* in the *kolhozes*.[27]

On the other hand, quite a few subjects of study in institutions for higher learning were dropped. Wherever liberal education was given before the Experiment, those Faculties or divisions of Universities disappeared. Simultaneously Universities and Polytechnical Institutes were divided into a large number of small functional schools. By the way, this was one of the chief means of quickly increasing the number of institutions for higher learning and thus proving to the ignorant outside Russia that the new regime cared much more for science than Imperial Russia had.

Moreover, the class principle was applied to the selection of students. The number of students to be registered in each institution was fixed, and preference was given to graduates of "Labor Faculties," special institutions where young workers and "poor peasants" were given preparatory training for academic studies. Some preparation was required to enter these schools, but the requirements were low and could not be insisted upon, since few qualified workers and peasants were available.[28] Finally, an attempt was made to give a definitely proletarian shape to university studies. In 1928, the principle of "uninterrupted practice" was introduced; every student had to spend, alternately, two weeks at a university and one week at a factory. This was an unfortunate idea, since the heads of the industrial units did not know what to do with this intermittent student labor. Instead of introducing them to the technological processes, they used them as unskilled labor and assigned them to the transportation of loads, sweeping floors, standing watch at night, etc.

The result of the Great Experiment in education was a cultural catastrophe. This fact has been established beyond doubt by numerous surveys carried out in the first half of the 'thirties. According to these surveys, candidates for enrollment in institutions of higher learning displayed a lack of command of the Russian language, poor reading knowledge, and the tendency to use stereotyped and unfounded generalizations. The evil proved to be a tenacious one. In 1938, the following statement was made:

In a number of schools there are a considerable amount of semiliterate children. Even in Moscow many children do not have a command of the Russian language.[29]

This situation was the more serious as the majority of the young teachers had graduated from Soviet schools where they had not learned much and therefore had not much to communicate to their pupils.[30] Here are a few examples.

In 1936, a "pact of socialist emulation" was signed between two teachers' schools. The school whose students would come nearest to the goal of faultless spelling would be the winner. The official journal of the Commissariat of Education reproduced, without corrections, the challenge and the acceptance. Each of the letters contained no more than a few hundred words, and although the rules of Russian spelling after the reform of 1917 * are rather simple, there were one hundred and thirty-two mistakes in the first letter, and one hundred and fifty-six mistakes in the second.[31]

Naturally, the young teachers knew nothing about history. Wrote the same journal:

This fall Soviet children were especially eager to return to school. They knew that a new subject was to be taught, and a fascinating one, Russian history. They were eager to learn who the mysterious Varangians were, what were the deeds of Rurik, Vladimir, and the other princes. Alas, they were disappointed, because the teachers could not satisfy their curiosity and, instead of giving them facts, talked in terms of vague sociological generalizations.

These poorly trained teachers had to face pupils in their classes who lacked any idea of order and discipline. Here is a letter from a girl who had just graduated from high school and was offered a teacher's position.

* This reform, carried out by the Provisional Government, but prepared under the Imperial government, brought the Russian language close to the ideal of phonetic spelling.

There is no poorer profession than that of a teacher. In classrooms there is such a smell that one always has a headache. It is so noisy that the teacher has to shout all the time. Hooligans among the pupils disorganize the class. No, thank you. [A newspaper wrote]: Because of poor discipline, many periods of study are entirely wasted. Larcenies in schools are frequent. In front of the school buildings the pupils fight and make a terrible noise. Not knowing what to do with rebellious pupils, the principals and teachers call the police and have them arrested and punished.[32]

Equally serious was the fact that because of the completely senseless curriculum the interest of the pupils was not aroused. In April, 1934, the Central Committee of the Communist Party recognized that "political education," which in the course of the Experiment had been paramount, was a complete failure. It was boring, and it destroyed the children's interest even in such social phenomena as they were able to understand.

The necessity to stop the school experiment was recognized by the Communist leaders when they saw that the program of industrialization could no longer be pushed forward because of the lack of adequately trained young specialists or even generally educated persons. Already in 1931 and 1932, partial reforms were tried. A resolution of the Central Committee of the Communist Party of September 5, 1931, warned the professors and teachers against the survival of pre-Revolutionary educational methods, and also against the indiscriminate application of the so-called "progressive" methods. The resolution acknowledged that the Soviet school did not give its graduates sufficient preparation for further study. To meet the demands of the Communist leaders, the Commissariat of Education introduced a new curriculum: history as a special subject reappeared; teaching of the "social sciences," i.e., the Marxist doctrine was curtailed, as was also the compulsory "social activity" of the pupils. The schools were separated from production and steered towards their natural function, that of teaching. As usual, a number of persons who had been active in the educational system prior to this reform were declared to be subversive deviators from the Party line and were treated accordingly. The center of the pedagogical thought of the previous period, the Institute of Marxist Pedagogy, was disbanded.

On August 25, 1932, the movement was continued by another resolution of the Central Committee. Some more items of "progressive education" were abolished. The class period was restored in its dignity as the basic unit of teaching. Principals were ordered to elaborate definite schedules and insist on their application. Teachers were ordered to teach their subjects systematically. These were very natural demands indeed. But does not the necessity of emphasizing them say more than volumes about the state of the schools before their formulation?

Important changes took place also in institutions of higher learning. The decree of September 19, 1932, restored the authority of the professors; they were to give the marks to the students, not the Communist cells. Furthermore, it was ordered that only those sufficiently prepared and who had passed the entrance examinations were to be registered as students; that lectures were to be given regularly and according to schedule; that such novelties as the "brigade method" in examinations be abolished;* that theses be written by candidates for degrees; that students be relieved from too much social activity; that when selecting young men to be trained for professorial positions, academic achievements, and no longer zeal in Communist propaganda be the decisive factor. These were sweeping changes indeed, but still in the framework of the Great Experiment. The methods of teaching were improved, but what the student was to be taught still continued to be determined by the Communist doctrine. That no departure from fundamentals was envisaged may be derived from the fact that the resolution of 1931 emphasized the importance of purely Communist education in schools and enjoined the local Party committees to supervise the school system closely, espe-

---

* In reality, this was a kind of collective examination: questions were offered to a group of students, and a collective reply was completed by them. Naturally, at least one good student was introduced into each group, and his knowledge covered the ignorance of the group.

cially the teaching of social sciences. The general spirit of the time was not yet favorable to drastic change.

In 1933, the People's Commissar for Education acknowledged that the "leftist deviation" in school had been ingrained more deeply in the system of education than first assumed. He enjoined the educators to eliminate the anti-Leninist idea that the school was withering away together with the State.[33] But under the general conditions of The Great Retreat, the gigantic disorder and the unspeakable inefficiency of the school system could no longer be tolerated. A program of drastic reforms was elaborated and then actualized, often with substantial additions, the necessity of which appeared in the course of the cure to which the school system was submitted.

5

First of all, the deficiency of room and teachers was to be eliminated. The sweeping decree of February 28, 1935, demanded that the two or three shift system be abolished in Moscow in the fall of 1936, in other large cities in the fall of 1937, and throughout the Union in the fall of 1938. In the fall of 1937, all teachers with less than seven years of grade school were dismissed as well as those who, despite more years of schooling, could be convicted of illiteracy, i.e., of the inability to spell Russian words correctly.

The feverish building of school edifices and the relentless training of teachers were the prerequisites of the realization of this order. Alas, the nation was too busy with other problems—political purge and the achievement of collectivization and industrialization—so that no forces were left free to accomplish the tasks in the realm of education. Consequently, in 1939, at the outbreak of the Second World War, the situation as to school room was no better than in 1932–3. The number of pupils in elementary schools rose from 17.9 million to 21.3 million, and those in intermediary and secondary schools from 5.5 to 12.2 million, so that the school buildings had to harbor about 50% more children than in 1932–3. But the number of school buildings was 172,000 in 1939, as compared with 166,000 in 1932. It is true that 20,000 school buildings were constructed between the two dates, but 15,000 "dwarf schools" were simultaneously closed. The new school buildings could give shelter to 5.9 million pupils; since their number had increased by 10 million and the closed schools had sheltered a substantial number of pupils, in 1939 the overcrowding of schools was at least as bad as in 1935, the date of the order.[34]

But the shortage of teachers was dealt with rather well. In 1938, 91,600 persons graduated from teachers' schools, while in 1933 the figure had been 43,700. These new teachers would not only cover the need created by the continuous expansion of the school system, but at least partly replace the unsatisfactory teachers who formed the majority of the teachers' body in 1932–3.

At the same time, efforts were displayed to enhance the prestige of the teachers and give them decent living conditions. Their salaries, especially in elementary schools, were increased. "Personal ranks," a counterpart to the academic degrees in Universities, were introduced. Through this measure a specific feature of the old order was revived; then the majority of the teachers of the secondary schools were on civil service and granted the same rank as the officers of the administration or the courts.

Relating to the institutions for higher learning, a simple return to the old order was "indicated." On January 13, 1934, the academic degrees abolished in the beginning of the Revolution were restored. The right to grant them was extended to all institutions for higher learning and scientific research. This liberalism proved to be detrimental, and in 1936 the government withdrew this right from the majority of institutions and made it the privilege of a few, first of all the Universities and Polytechnical Institutes. This was precisely the situation which had obtained under the old regime. There was, however, this difference: while under the old regime the granting of an academic degree by a Faculty was final, under the Soviets the final word belongs to a special committee attached to the commissariat of education.

Another feature of the reform of education was to bring back order and give a sensible shape to the school curriculum. What were, however, the specific order and curriculum to be adopted? In this regard the Communist leaders displayed the same lack of imagination and creative ability as in the beginning of their school experiment. Then, they used the model of "progressive education" as the most radical and, it seemed, the most revolutionary departure from historical tradition. This time, they chose for a model the school of Imperial Russia, probably for the simple reason that, having studied in it themselves, they knew that in that school there was order and that the curriculum (which was not very different from the French or the German) was rather sensible. Revolutionary diatribes against the old school now became out of place; they had served their purpose when the Revolution had been in its infancy; now that it had come of age, they became a nuisance.

To bring back order, measures initiated in 1931 and 1932 were reinforced and expanded. In the fall of 1934, "stabilized teaching plans and programs" were imposed on elementary and secondary schools, stating how many hours a week should be spent in each class for each subject and what particular topics should be taught. In January, 1935, new rules on pupils' self-government were issued. Self-government was entirely abolished in the four lower grades. Where it remained its purpose was defined as that of helping the teachers to raise the level of school work and discipline. In institutions for higher learning the Young Communist organizations, whose activity had made real study impossible, were prohibited from interfering with the orders of the administration and given the task of improving the conditions of study. In May, 1935, yearly examinations were revived, and the passing from one grade to another was made dependent on success at these examinations. Early in the twentieth century, first the reduction in the number of such examinations and then their complete abolition had been hailed in Russia as a significant victory of progressive ideas in education. Thus, in this respect, the new Soviet school order went back to the late nineteenth century.

The most conspicuous item, however, was the restoration of the uniform, for boys and girls alike, both in elementary and secondary schools. This was even more than returning to "the good old days," since in Imperial Russia uniforms were unknown on the elementary level.

How responsive the school authorities were to this aspect of the retreat may be seen from the following facts. In September, 1935, the journal of the Commissariat of Education gave a preview of the uniform to be introduced at some later date. Immediately people began discussing—not whether uniforms were desirable—but whether "electric blue," chosen for the girls in secondary schools, would be becoming; some people thought that this would do very well for girls with rosy cheeks but would not be suitable at all for the pale ones. A few days later it was learned that in many places the local authorities had introduced uniforms of their own invention, without waiting for the final order. The center rebuked the overzealous principals and explained that uniforms could be introduced only gradually. In 1944, in relation to girls, the reform was accentuated: pigtails became the officially recommended style of hair dressing.[35]

It was more difficult, however, to restore discipline. "In accordance with Stalin's personal desire," experienced Communist leaders were sent to the schools of the great cities where discipline was lowest. They were to instill into the minds of the pupils that they had to be polite and respect the authority of the teachers.[36] The teachers were ordered to supervise the conduct of the pupils and help them get rid of such habits as keeping their hats on in class, or jamming the principal into a corner. Budenny, then a great man, was asked to help. In a letter published in December, 1935, he advised the pupils to be quiet in class, pay attention to their teachers, and prepare their home work carefully: they were to spend their leisure time on "physical culture," advice becoming a military leader. Only a few years earlier, however, he would have added some advice about studying the Communist doctrine. It was symptomatic that he did not.

All these measures met with partial success only. This is beyond question since in October, 1943, the Commissar of Education said: "Much remains to be done as to discipline. The slightest sign of rudeness, or disrespect towards elders must be dealt with severely. There is still some reluctance to accept a strong attitude towards laziness and hooliganism." [37] To uproot disorder, a set of "Rules of Conduct" for the pupils of elementary and secondary schools was elaborated, containing such admonitions as to study well, obey the principals and the teachers, be respectful regarding them and their parents and all old persons in general, and to respect the honor of the class and the school. In some schools these rules were dictated to the pupils in class, and they were ordered to learn them by heart. About the same time, new rules for the University students were issued defining their duties and the order of study.[38]

In the course of the war, an additional step was taken towards the restoration of the pre-Revolutionary school order. This was the abandonment of coeducation, introduced at the beginning of the Revolution and highly praised at that time as one of the most significant steps leading away from bourgeois society, where the girls are allegedly trained to become housekeepers or mistresses of men "owning" them. The movement away from coeducation started in Moscow in 1942–3, and in the fall of 1943 became general. Articles published at about that time explained that experience with coeducation had shown that there were physiological and psychological reasons against it, namely, the different mental and physical development of boys and girls. Another object was based on the inevitable division of labor between men and women. A boy must be prepared for service in the Red Army, but a girl is essentially a future mother and must know how to look after her children and bring them up. In the course of the academic year 1944–5, different programs of study for boys and girls were introduced, the boys specializing in technical subjects, while the girls were to be trained in pedagogy, handicrafts, domestic science, personal hygiene, and the care of children.[39]

An equally important feature of the reform program consisted in the abandonment of "political education." This was probably one of the greatest sacrifices made by the Communist leaders in the course of the momentous years 1934–9, when the nation was being prepared for the inevitable war. Very courageously, the leaders recognized the necessity of the step and acted accordingly. The curtailment of political education in elementary and secondary schools was effected through the resolutions of the Central Committee of the Communist Party of April 22 and 24, 1934. Political education was altogether abolished in the seven lower grades of the school. One hour a week was left in the eighth and ninth grades, and two hours in the tenth grade.

Simultaneously, social work in schools was once more curbed. Why should elementary school pupils be compelled to be members of auxiliary groups of "voluntary societies," such as Aid to the International Revolution, or Chemical and Aerial Warfare, or study such topics as the master plan for the reconstruction of Moscow? Such questions were posed by *Pravda*. Children should study well and spend their leisure time skating and skiing,[40] was the advice given. Budenny's letter, quoted above, should be remembered in this context.

In institutions for higher learning, a similar trend gained the upper hand four years later. On November 15, 1938, the Central Committee of the Party decided to discontinue the separate teaching of dialectical materialism, Leninism, and the History of the Communist Party. Instead, the students were to have one course in Marxist-Leninist-Stalinist Theory on the basis of the official *History of the Communist Party* edited by Stalin. The reform was drastic but still insufficient, as seen from the following story:

The largest lecture room was full of students, since Marxist-Leninist Theory is a compulsory subject. The students did not listen; some read newspapers, others seemed to sleep, or study lecture notes on physics, or discuss some fascinating subject in whispers. After the lecture the Party investigator who made the preceding observations tried to establish why the students paid no attention to the lecture. The students said that they were more responsive to this particular course than to lectures delivered on the same subject by other professors, who sometimes had very unpleasant experiences. But why, insisted the Party man. The students explained that the subject did not interest them.[41] This is a very significant fact indeed: the official doctrine of the new State was considered a bore by the generation which would operate this State a few years hence!

The abandonment of political education made room for the study of those subjects which had been neglected under the Communist Experiment, especially the mother tongue, literature, history, geography, and foreign languages.

Relatively simple was the task of restoring the teaching of the mother tongue. If there are well-trained teachers and there is reasonable order, the pupils would undoubtedly succeed after a few years of study. The two prerequisites were gradually being fulfilled. But this was a long process. Could not short cuts be found by directly appealing to the pupils? Actually, in 1934-6, the Commissar of Education used this method and exhorted the pupils to get rid of their illiteracy. The most insistent appeal was published in 1936. "Our government and Stalin personally," wrote the Commissar, "demand that only wholly literate pupils graduate from schools so that they will be able to continue their study in institutions of higher learning. Therefore, the pupils should make the utmost effort to acquire the art of correct spelling. Those who have not mastered spelling will not be granted certificates of graduation." To help the pupils carry out this advice, the Commissar ordered that they be given "orthographic dictionaries," to be used in all kinds of compositions.[42]

Much more difficult was the reorganization of the teaching of history, geography, and literature, because in these subjects political problems were involved. The task seemed so important that on May 16, 1934, two decrees were signed by Stalin for the Party and by Molotov for the Soviet government. One ordered that history be taught according to chronological order, and that pupils be required to memorize the most important events with their dates as well as the names of the prominent actors on the historical scene. The other ordered that the teaching of geography be resumed. Children should memorize the geographical names and gain a solid knowledge of the map. In addition, it was decreed that new textbooks be written and submitted for the approval of a special committee. On August 14, 1934, this committee, consisting of the highest dignitaries of the State, among them Stalin, published a criticism of the outlines of Histories of Russia submitted by the prospective authors. When out of the competing drafts one was selected and made the standard text, *Pravda* wrote:

> To love one's great and free fatherland means first of all to know its past. For a Soviet pupil the textbooks on history must number among the most fascinating. The tendency to discuss history according to sociological stereotypes has nothing in common with Marxism. The main thing demanded from a textbook on history is the same as that demanded from Soviet literature: it must be so clear and simple that the mass of the people can understand it.[43]

There was also some trouble with the texts on geography and literature. The new text on literature by Florinsky and Trifonov was condemned, since it repeated the old error of abstract treatment of the subject. In three texts on geography, published to fill the new requirements, a committee of experts discovered three hundred and eighty-five mistakes.[44]

After many revisions, the goal for textbooks was proclaimed to have been reached. Texts now used in Soviet schools can be characterized as systematic and clear, but rather dull. All novelties in the style of progressive education have been banished. On the basis of such texts, in combination with refresher courses for teachers, the study of history and literature has been put on a rather solid foundation. There has been more trouble with languages. In 1938, it was established that orders regarding their teaching had not been carried out, especially in relation to French and English, while German was taught in quite a few schools. The reason was that they lacked teachers familiar with the Western languages. In consequence, only five per cent of the students in institutions of higher learning had a reading knowledge of foreign languages.[45]

In the Universities the pre-Revolutionary curriculum has also been partly restored. This was expressed in the fact that "Faculties" of History, Literature, Philosophy, and Law had been restored in those Universities where this was feasible, but in many instances this proved to be beyond the range of possibility. Here, as in many other aspects of Soviet cultural life, a hard lesson was taught the Communist reformers: a Faculty may be disbanded by affixing a signature to a sheet of paper, but no signature, exhortation, or order, is sufficient to resurrect a defunct cultural institution.

Somewhat outside the trends discussed so far, but definitely within the general framework of the "restoration" policy of the last decade, stands an additional measure of great importance. On October 2, 1940, a decree appeared, the preamble of which stated that "in conditions of increasing welfare, the interests of the socialist State and society demand that part of the expenses of public education be borne by the toilers themselves." In consequence, education ceased to be free in the three upper grades of the "unified school" and in all institutions of higher learning. The newly established fees are rather high: 200 rubles a year in high school in Moscow, Leningrad, and the capitals of the federated republics; 150 rubles elsewhere. In institutions of higher learning, the tuition fee was set at 300 to 400 rubles, even 500 rubles in the schools of art, music, and drama. A number of students may be granted state subsidies; to earn them they must receive the mark "excellent" in two-thirds of the subjects and "good" in the rest.

In no field was reconstruction after years of destruction more difficult than in education. Let us, however, not forget the fact that to a large extent the educational chaos was created by those very people who later on had to combat it. In no field, moreover, did the efforts to restore order and efficiency result

in a greater approximation to the old structure than in education. With the passing away of free education and coeducation,
the last vestiges of "revolutionary achievements" have gone.
Twenty-eight years after the Revolution, the internal order in
schools is comparable not so much to the relatively liberal
order of the early twentieth century, as to that of the reactionary period of the 'eighties and 'nineties of the nineteenth
century. Moreover, at the present time the curriculum differs
only slightly from that of Imperial Russia. Thus, for instance,
the list of classical works to be read in Soviet schools almost
completely coincides with that used in 1917, naturally with the
addition of a few works written after that date. The main
difference is that the study of Religion has been replaced by
the study of the Marxist doctrine. But even this difference appears to be rather a similarity, if one considers that in Communist society the Marxist doctrine has taken the place of the
dogma of the Orthodox Church.

The objection could still be raised that the scheme of the
"unified school" permits a bright boy or girl to reach the
summit of the educational system, whereas in old Russia, as in
prewar France or Germany, the school system was so organized
that graduates from elementary schools rarely continued their
education, while boys and girls from well-to-do families enrolled
directly in the lower classes of the secondary school, after a few
years of home training. But the fees introduced in 1940 restored
the pre-Revolutionary barrier in a new form, once more making secondary and higher education a privilege of the upper
social groups.

The restoration of the old order and old curriculum were
means of restoring the efficacy of the school system. These
means were applied to a system which had been expanded and
simultaneously permitted to deteriorate. When the results of
the systematic efforts of the past decade become fully effective,
Russia will possess a school system meeting the normal educational requirements both quantitatively and qualitatively,
though there will still be much room for improvement.

The goal of endowing Russia with an adequate school system

is therefore still ahead, and not one of "the achievements of the Revolution," as has so often been asserted by "friends of the Soviet Union" relying on quantitative data only and indulging in wishful thinking.

6

The curve relating to school policy has been strikingly similar to that regarding the family: after long years of destruction and experimentation, feverish efforts were made to restore the situation which existed at the outbreak of the Revolution or even earlier. What happened to the Church, the third pillar of society? Was it not possible to eliminate it entirely?

Very definitely the Communist leaders thought that this was possible and acted accordingly. Throughout the Communist Experiment and well into the period of The Great Retreat, they applied all the measures they could imagine to destroy the Church. The reasons were obvious:

1. Religion is incompatible with the Doctrine professed by them; the Doctrine explains "all" in terms of pure materialism, but Religion challenges this explanation and recognizes the primacy of the Spirit. Therefore, as long as Religion exists, the Doctrine has not gained final victory.

2. Religion is embodied in Churches, in Russia first of all in the Russian branch of the Greek Orthodox Church, and since this Church existed under the old regime and was intimately connected with the Imperial State, its persistence in Communist society signified a partial survival of the pre-Revolutionary order.

3. In terms of the Doctrine, the Church is one of the tools of oppression of the proletariat by the masters. Its members cannot but regret the high social status they enjoyed before the Revolution and display efforts to regain it. In consequence, the Church cannot but be counterrevolutionary.

Still more than with regard to the family, destructive intentions as to religion have been emphatically denied by the Communists and their fellow travelers. The official theory is that the Communist government had to prevent and repress rebellion wherever it was found, and that clergymen of various denominations were imprisoned, exiled, or executed not as clergymen, but as dangerous counterrevolutionaries. Some churches have been closed; but according to the official theory, this was spontaneously done by the masses forsaking religion, and without any official pressure.

The fallacy in such statements is obvious. That the government attacked religion against popular wishes was conceded many times by the government itself; and that not counter-revolution, but religion, was the reason is obvious from the fact that the Roman Catholics were persecuted as fiercely as the Greek Orthodox, although the former had no reason to desire a restoration of the *status quo ante*.[46]

There has been religious persecution. After an initial period when the Communists hoped that the churches would crumble after having been deprived of the legal and material support of the State and the bourgeoisie, a violent attack was launched in 1922–3, under the NEP, to compensate partly for the concessions in the realm of economics. From 1923 to 1928, there was a kind of intermission; but the shift to the Second Socialist Offensive was accompanied by a second attack, at least as violent as the first. Simultaneously with the partial retreat from wholesale collectivization (March, 1930) the attack was mitigated, and the mitigation was accentuated throughout the first years of The Great Retreat, to be superseded by a vigorous attack in 1937–8 as part of the Great Terror.

However, throughout all these fluctuations changes occurred only with regard to the intensity of the antireligious effort; never, up to quite recently, was there anything resembling religious tolerance. To exterminate the enemy, the Communist rulers partly used well-known devices, and partly displayed a spirit of inventiveness. The government (consisting of convinced and militant atheists) jailed and executed bishops, priests, and active laymen. It forcibly closed churches, desecrated objects of veneration, prohibited any kind of religious education and propaganda, as well as any kind of charitable, cultural, or social activity on the part of the churches. It organized, on a large scale, antireligious education and propaganda of a highly offensive style. It ridiculed religion and associated it with the forces of political and social reaction. In 1923, it fostered the rise of the so-called Living Church, a schismatic movement in the midst of the Russian Orthodox Church. After the death of Patriarch Tikhon (1925) the Russian Orthodox Church was not permitted to elect a new Patriarch.[47]

It is almost inconceivable that persecution systematically conducted for long years and using all possible approaches to the positions of the enemy was not crowned by complete success. And still this happened: religion and the churches survived. In 1937, it was established that at least half of the adult population had preserved their faith.[48] It was also established that the attack on religion did not liberate the young people from "religious prejudice" and transform them into "convinced and consistent atheists," recognizing nothing but the Marxist doctrine in its official interpretation. On the contrary, the Communists were surprised to learn that those young people who allegedly were converted to atheism were more contaminated by crude superstition and magic beliefs than the believers. Finally, they had to recognize that the persecution of religion bred hostility in large masses of the people towards the Soviet regime.[49] This unpleasant revelation struck them more than once. Up to the late 'thirties, every time they became aware of growing animosity, on the basis of religious persecution, they temporarily mitigated the pressure and prepared a new and, they thought, better plan for the destruction of the enemy. They could do so as long as the situation did not involve a direct threat to their power over Russia. But this time, i.e., in the late 'thirties, war threatened. Under such circumstances continuation of the antireligious policy would have exposed the government to a grave danger. Would it not be possible that, in the struggle to come, a large section of the population, namely those embittered by religious persecution, might remain neutral, perhaps even reach the conclusion that

German victory would be a lesser evil compared with continuing religious persecution, and would act accordingly?

This danger loomed the greater since, planning to invade Russia, Hitler tried to find weak points in the Russian structure and assumed that the hostility of religious-minded people to an atheist government could be of great help. Therefore, an exceedingly benevolent attitude was displayed by him towards the Russian Orthodox Church, in marked contrast to his intransigent attitude towards the Roman Catholics and the Protestants. Money was given for the erection of a Russian Orthodox Cathedral in Berlin, and appropriation was made for the repair of nineteen Orthodox churches in Germany. This was merely a symptom, but a symptom pointing to an extremely dangerous situation.

7

The Communists responded to this situation by a New Religious Policy which, up to Hitler's invasion, received this shape: contrary to the Communist dogma which considered that every religion was a nuisance, it was officially declared that Christianity was a peculiar religion, since it promoted the cult of the abstract man. Therefore, in specified periods, it could play the part of a progressive social force; actually, it contributed greatly to progress both in the Ancient World and, on many occasions, in Russian history. Directions were now given to recognize fully the contribution of the Russian Church and the Russian clergy to the historical advancement of Russia.[50] It was prohibited to exert any violence against religion, especially to close churches or destroy or desecrate objects of religious veneration; from now on even hurting the religious sentiment of the believers was to be avoided. The Godless Union, which for years had been the instrument of the government's antireligious policy, was now entrusted with the task of supervising the execution of the new directions. Naturally, all trials of clergymen and religiously active laymen for alleged political crimes were stopped. Antireligious propaganda was substantially toned down: attempts to destroy the religious sentiment by directly attacking or ridiculing objects of veneration and then "proving" that God did not exist, because He did not interfere, were abandoned. Orders were given to persuade the populace that religion was a survival of the past made unnecessary now by the advancement of science, which could explain "everything." When, under the pressure of circumstances, the government had to abandon the six-day week, with every sixth day as the official rest day, and restore the usual seven-day week (June, 1940), Sunday was chosen as the rest day, despite the opposition of the Godless Union which suggested Monday or Wednesday.[51]

The purpose of these measures was obvious. It was appeasement of an important section of the population where hostile sentiments prevailed. Since the enemy in his turn virtually hoped to gain the support of the same section, it appears that the foes had one idea in common: both recognized that the religious-minded Russian people were a strong and perhaps decisive force in the struggle to come. Therefore, they started a kind of competition for their favor.

Naturally, the competition situation was accentuated when war broke out. Hitler declared that his invasion of Russia was a crusade. In the Russian provinces occupied by him, the Orthdox Church received substantial support. In many towns and villages churches were reopened, bishops and priests reappeared and started to officiate. Several bishops, mostly quite recently ordained, often in dubious circumstances, accepted the "crusade" myth and began to pray for the "great German Leader" as the liberator of faith. Among the pro-German bishops, most conspicuous was Polycarp, who proclaimed himself archbishop of Lutsk, primate of the autocephalous church of the Ukraine.

What happened on the other side of the front? Since 1927, Metropolitan Sergius of Moscow, Acting Patriarch of Russia, directed the Church to refrain entirely from any action which would manifest even the slightest reactionary tendency; in his mind, Christianity was compatible with any social and political

order and need not interfere with the policy of the secular authorities, provided that they did not impose anything that went
against the moral teachings of the Church. Up to Hitler's aggression, he was unable to persuade the government that he
meant business. Now the opportunity was given him to prove
it by deeds.

On the very day of the outbreak of the war, Acting Patriarch
Sergius issued a pastoral letter in which he enjoined the believers to take full part in the patriotic effort. The Church, he
declared, always was one with the Nation in periods of crisis
and would be the same this time. Neutrality, he said, was insufficient; active participation was mandatory. Foreseeing
events in western Russia, he condemned in advance any co-
operation with the enemy. This letter was given great publicity.
In all the churches of the country special services were held
with prayers for victory to the Russian Army. These prayers
were repeated very frequently during the months of the war.
When news about Polycarp's secession reached Moscow, the
Acting Patriarch issued a new pastoral letter and put Polycarp
on trial by proxy.

The Soviet government recognized the significance of the
patriotic attitude of the Church. Through the agency of the
Godless Union it declared: "If the servants of the Church
honestly call upon the believers to fight against Fascism, we
must not belittle this fact." Three months after the outbreak of
the war the publication of antireligious journals was discontinued, officially, because of paper shortage. Antireligious museums were closed. Heavy taxes on the churches were substantially reduced. When, in December, 1941, the first Russian
offensive started liberating several provinces, the Soviet press
expressed indignation about the acts of antireligious vandalism
committed by the Germans, namely, the destruction or dese-
cration of churches and sacred objects. Both in 1942 and 1943,
the severe curfew prevailing in Moscow was lifted for Easter
night.[52] In November, 1942, Metropolitan Nicholas of Kiev
was appointed to the governmental commission for investigation of "crimes committed by the German Fascist invaders."[53]

Never, since 1922, had any clergyman been appointed to any official body.

About the same time a book appeared in Moscow entitled: *Truth About Religion in Russia*. In any country but Russia the publication of a similar book would not have astonished anybody. But in contemporary Russia this was a sensation. Had not the rulers of Russia prohibited reprinting the Bible and importing it from foreign countries? And now a beautfully printed and copiously illustrated book on religion appeared, comprising contributions of the highest dignitaries of the Russian Orthodox Church, as well as a number of priests and laymen belonging partly to the cultural *élite* and partly to the rank and file believers. There is reason to believe that the book was printed on the presses of the Militant Godless Union. Together with the already mentioned fact that the Union was ordered to protect religion against illegal interference on the part of local authorities, this was the most challenging and ironical feature of the religious phase of The Great Retreat.

On the occasion of the twenty-fifth anniversary of the October Revolution, Acting Patriarch Sergius "cordially congratulated Stalin, the God-given leader of the military and cultural forces of the nation." The next year, congratulations came on the part of Metropolitan Nicholas of Kiev. In the meantime, Stalin used different opportunities to express his gratitude to priests for their outstanding help to the Red Army.[54]

The improvement of the State-Church relationship reached its climax when on September 5, 1943, "Stalin received Acting Patriarch Sergius, Metropolitan Alexei of Leningrad, and Metropolitan Nicholas of Kiev. During the reception Metropolitan Sergius informed Stalin that leading circles of the Orthodox Church intended to hold a Council of bishops in the very near future and elect a Patriarch. The head of the government expressed his sympathy with the decision and said that the government would not hinder this in any way." [55]

A few days later, nineteen Russian Orthodox bishops convened in Moscow and unanimously elected Sergius Patriarch of Moscow and All Russia. On September 12, he was officially installed. Before separating, the Council addressed a message to the Soviet government expressing the Church's gratitude for the government's friendly attitude, and another message to all the Church members once more severely condemning all those who would support Hitler and his armies.[56]

Then the Archbishop of York of the Church of England arrived in Moscow to visit the hierarchy of the Russian Orthodox Church, and to invite a Russian Church delegation to come to England.[57] A few years earlier, an attempt of Russian Church dignitaries to have any relations with foreign churchmen would have been condemned almost as an act of treason!

About the same time—more precisely, on October 9, 1943, an order was issued creating a Council for Russian Orthodox Affairs to establish liaison between the Soviet government and the Patriarch of Moscow. On June 30, 1944, another Council was established to conduct the State's relations with the other religious groups represented among the Russian population.

The creation of these councils discloses the emergence of an entirely new situation, namely, that of friendly co-operation between the State and religious bodies, especially the Russian Orthodox Church. This statement may be substantiated by passing in review the types of activity by means of which the Church has helped the nation and the government in the struggle against the invader and then noting the rewards which it has received from the government.

First of all, by constant prayers for victory, the Church sustained and strengthened the morale of the people. Moreover, Sergius wrote several messages to the pastors and churchgoers, calling on them to increase their efforts to aid the Army in the fight against the invader.

Secondly, the Church induced the flock to collect money for direct help to the war effort. A few days before the election, Sergius announced that the Church had contributed more than eight million rubles for the building of the Dmitri Donskoy tank column, and that the priests and laity had also donated millions of rubles for aircraft squadrons and the relief of wounded and orphans.[58]

Thirdly, the Patriarch used the authority of the Church to prohibit collaboration with Hitler in German-occupied provinces. On many occasions he solemnly condemned those bishops and priests who had accepted Hitler's lie that his invasion was a crusade and expressed their admiration for his deeds.

Fourthly, the Patriarch helped stir up the resistance to the Germans in territories which were not Russian, but where the influence of Russia was strong. In an Easter message "to all Christians of Yugoslavia, Czechslovakia, Greece, and others of the Orthodox faith languishing in Fascist captivity," he said:

Our Orthodox Church is marching side by side with the people. In all churches of the Soviet Union prayers are offered for victory and collections are made for needs created by the war. Let the lamp of Orthodoxy burn still more brightly before you. The conscience of every sincere Slav and Greek dictates that he shall seek every way to evade working for Germany. May God strengthen our fraternal union.[59]

In this case Sergius could not but use the radio, controlled by the government. This shows that the government appreciated the support of the Church. A similar situation developed at the All-Slavic Congress which was held in Moscow in the summer of 1943. Metropolitan Nicholas was present, accompanied by six bishops. He gave an address extolling the duty of every Christian to fight the Fascists. Since he could not have appeared without the permission of the government, it is obvious that the latter was eager to use the authority of the Russian Church among the peoples of the Balkan and the Danubian basin.

Sergius displayed willingness to support the government in its sometimes difficult relations with the Allies. Shortly before his election he made the following statement:

I am not a military man, but it seems to me that the time for the complete annihilation of Hitler has arrived. I refuse to believe that the mothers of American and British soldiers want this to drag on. We Russians are the world's most patient people, but the end of our patience is overflowing.[60]

This was vigorous support on the demand for a second front which was then paramount in Russia, and somewhat embarrassed the Western Allies who were not yet prepared for the final onslaught on the common enemy. The visit of the Archbishop of York was arranged in a manner which could not fail to convince him of cordial relations between the State and the Church in Russia, and thus helped to dissipate the fears and objections among the Anglicans against close collaboration with Russia.

In 1944 and 1945, several statements, first by Patriarch Sergius, then by the National Church Council, have endorsed the strong anti-Vatican line of Soviet foreign policy.[61]

The services rendered by the Russian Church to the nation and government have been substantial indeed. What has the Church received as a counterpart?

The main reward has been official recognition of the Church and permission to elect a Patriarch. This, by the way, has resulted in an almost complete breakdown of the notorious Living Church, so strongly supported by the Soviet government twenty years ago. In a letter written by Patriarch Sergius in November, 1943, we read: "A number of bishops of the Living Church has congratulated us on the election. Many want to restore communion with us."

An additional feature of the new status may be seen in a further communication contained in the same letter:

We have moved to a new residence given us by the government; this is the former German embassy. It is a luxurious residence, and we understand that this is a sign of the benevolence of the government, a reward for the Church's conduct in the course of the war.[62]

The new status of the Church is well manifested in these events: On May 15, 1944, the death of Sergius, Russian Orthodox Patriarch of Moscow and All Russia, was reported. A few days later Metropolitan Alexei of Leningrad, fulfilling the last will of the late Patriarch, became Acting Patriarch, in expectation of the convocation of the Church Council which had to elect a new Patriarch. In accepting his appointment, the

Metropolitan addressed a warm, personal letter to Stalin whom he called "Dear Joseph Vissarionovich" and described him as "the wise leader placed by the Lord over our great nation." The new Acting Patriarch promised to follow the same principles as the deceased Patriarch, and defined them as compliance with canonical rules and loyalty to the Fatherland and to its government headed by Stalin.[63]

At the Patriarch's funeral, a high-ranking official represented the Soviet government.

To elect a successor to the deceased, a National Council of the Russian Orthodox Church was permitted to convene in Moscow, January 31, 1945. The forty-odd bishops of the Church were present as well as numerous delegates from the dioceses, both priests and laymen. The meeting was also attended by the Orthodox Patriarchs of Antioch and Alexandria and representatives of other Orthodox churches, according to an old tradition. The chairman of the Council on the Affairs of the Orthodox Church delivered one of the first speeches. After having elected a new Patriarch, the Council sent a message to the Soviet government expressing its gratitude to the government and to "the highly honored Joseph Stalin" for their aid to the Church.[64]

Of great importance has been the restoration of the training of priests, which up to quite recently could be conducted only in clandestine seminaries or by correspondence courses. In December, 1943, Patriarch Sergius announced that he had decided—and obviously the Soviet government had approved the decision—to open a theological academy in Moscow and begin special courses for the training of priests in the dioceses. Candidates would be accepted only after a thorough education in State schools. Training would be free of charge. The curriculum would differ little from pre-Revolutionary times, but in addition to theological subjects the Soviet Constitution and Law would be taught. Graduates would sign a special pledge to devote all their life to the Church.[65]

Furthermore, the printing of some religious material has become possible. According to the Chairman of the Council on Greek Orthodox Church Affairs, the Orthodox Church "may print whatever it wishes . . . In fact, we have given explicit permission for the Church to order any quantity of Testaments, prayer books, and liturgical books and are ready to facilitate this step in every way, even to the extent of making representation to the paper rationing authorities. As to the distribution of such material, there are no objections and no restrictions." [66]

Quite a few churches have been reopened in Moscow. In the summer of 1942, the number of functioning churches was twenty-six, and last Christmas it was said to be fifty.[67] In August, 1944, the Chairman of the Committee of Greek Orthodox Affairs revealed that "measures to facilitate the opening of new churches in Russia was among the principal concerns of the Council," and that the Committee "placed absolutely no barriers to church expansion." [68]

Closely connected is the fact that in August, 1943, the celebrated icon of the Iberian Virgin was made available for public worship. In 1930, its disappearance from a famous shrine in the center of Moscow was considered as the climax of the persecution. Now it is placed in the Sokolniki Cathedral in one of Moscow's suburbs.[69] In November, 1943, Patriarch Sergius expressed a hope of buying a plant for the production of tapers necessary for the Orthodox Divine Service.

The government has not only terminated the publication of antireligious literature and closed antireligious museums, but condemned the ridiculing of religion. In June, 1943, Kalinin said:

Since religion still grips considerable sections of the population and some people are deeply religious, we cannot combat it by ridicule. Of course, if some young people find it amusing it is not so terrible. But we must not allow it to develop into mockery.[70]

It seems that the last barrier before the Church, the prohibition of propaganda, including religious education, is about to crumble. In August, 1944, the Chairman of the Council on Greek Orthodox Affairs said: "Priests may go to their parishioners and engage in proselytizing work either in church or outside." One month later the same authority declared: "Parents may (religiously) educate children themselves in the privacy of their homes or send them to the homes of priests for such education. Children of different families may also gather or be gathered in groups to receive religious instruction." In October, 1944, the Chairman of the Council on Affairs of Religious Cults made an identical statement as to children of other denominations, among them the Catholics. He emphasized, however, that religious instruction could not be given inside a church, synagogue, or mosque. "This would be against our established laws," he said, "which maintain that the church is given to the congregation for purposes of prayer and no other reason." [71]

It is obvious that in 1944 the status of religion in the Communist State was entirely different from that of the years 1937–8. The Church is now an officially recognized social force. This status was granted it as the result of the concomitance of these factors:

1. Despite twenty years of reckless persecution, faith has persisted in Russia. This basic fact refuted the Doctrine insofar as religion was concerned; according to the Doctrine, religion could not but wither away once it was deprived of the political and economic support which it enjoyed previous to the Revolution.

2. The fact of the persistence of faith has been acknowledged, though reluctantly, by the Communist rulers and has become one of the determinants of their policy. The Archbishop of York, repeating what he had heard in Russia, has often emphasized this acknowledgment.

3. Another fact has also impressed itself on the minds of the rulers: religion is not necessarily a "counterrevolutionary force" directing people towards the restoration of pre-Revolutionary political and economic relations. In consequence, its destruction is not as essential as it seemed to the Communist leaders in the beginning of their Experiment.

4. In the course of The Great Retreat, the Communist rulers were struck by the following "discovery": in many respects the

aims of the Church were the same as the modified aims of the rulers. Now, the Communist rulers want discipline, a stable family, and restriction of sex. The Russian Orthodox Church always preached discipline, a strong family, and restriction of sex. To impose the corresponding standards on men, the Church possesses means that the Communist Party lacks: as every living religious body, the Church persuades its members that they ought to behave in accordance with the above-mentioned standards because it is God's will, and imposes on the violators supernatural sanctions which, for the believers, are of the greatest efficacy. The Communist Party could perhaps persuade its members to behave in accordance with the new ideas, but it is terribly handicapped by the fact of having preached the opposite standards just a few years back.[72] Supernatural sanctions are not at its disposal, and as to coercion, the Party knows very well that it is rather inefficacious regarding moral standards.

Chosen for purely opportunist reasons, the New Religious Policy accentuated in the course of the war proved to be a marked success. Not only did the head of the Russian Orthodox Church appeal to the flock for active resistance and struggle against Fascism, but this appeal brought a wholehearted response. The Church people chose the continuation of the Communist rule as the lesser evil, perhaps in view of the New Religious Policy, and not the rule of Hitler, combining hypocritical support of religion with loss of national independence.

On this basis, in the course of The Great Retreat, when realistic considerations almost entirely dismissed the doctrine, fairly cordial relations could easily obtain. In old Russia the close connection between the Church and the State was one of the pillars of the regime. In the phase of The Great Retreat now under discussion, the general evolution of Russia, after having led to the wholesale negation of the old regime, came back close to the starting point.

The similarity should not, however, be exaggerated. In contradistinction to the *ancien régime* when the Orthodox Church was related to the Orthodox State, the opposing points of view

between the State and the Church now remain entire: the
State still supports the materialistic philosophy of Marx, and
the Church has not, and could not have abandoned its spirit-
ualistic dogma. Latent conflicts of intense gravity are therefore involved in the situation. What will happen it children
receiving regular religious education from priests oppose
statements in class of their atheistically-minded teachers? And
what will happen if young churchgoers discover that the discrimination against them has not been lifted? And what will
happen if older believers learn that their beloved bishops and
priests died somewhere in the far north or in Siberia from cold,
deprivation, and hard labor in prison camps from which they
have not been released? And what will happen if the "paper
distributing authorities" reject the application for publishing a
book written by a theologian refuting the very premises of
Marxist philosophy?

We do not know what will happen in such cases, but the
very possibility of foreseeing them shows how long still is
Russia's road towards real religious liberty.

8

The complicated processes studied in this chapter may be
summarized as follows:

1. In the course of the Communist Experiment, great efforts
were displayed by the Communists to destroy those pillars of
society which are the family, the Church, and the school. The
three pillars were actually shaken. Quite a few people used, or
more exactly abused the liberty of divorce and abortion; quite
a few young persons enjoyed freedom from parental authority.
The churches lost approximately half of their flock and had to
live in poverty, on the margin of official society. The school
ceased to transmit to the younger generation the culture tradition accumulated in the course of centuries.

But, on the one hand, it appeared that the achievements
were only partial and could not be made complete. Too many
people proved immune against the propaganda of new family

relations and atheism. On the other hand, even the partial successes were more than balanced by detrimental effects unforeseen by the promoters of the Experiment.

2. The fluctuations of the policy aiming at the shaking of the three pillars of society have been almost similar regarding the family and education, but entirely different as to religion. Relating to the family and the school, there was for many years consistent accentuation of pressure, whereas with respect to religion, periods of high pressure have alternated with periods of relative relaxation.

3. Inevitably, the Communists came to the conclusion that the pillars of society shaken by them in the course of the Communist Experiment had to be re-enforced. They reversed their policy relating to school in 1931, the family in 1934, and the Church in 1939. The trend following these reversals forms one of the most conspicuous features of The Great Retreat.

4. When the necessity for reconstruction became clear to the Communists, they were unable to create new patterns, but directed society towards the revival of pre-Revolutionary institutions. To begin with, this restoration was only partial, but in the course of the war became wholesale. Most conspicuous have been the restoration of fees and the abolition of coeducation in schools, the factual abolition of divorce, and the restoration of the Patriarchate and religious education.

5. Viewed as a whole, the measures composing The Great Retreat in the realm studied in this chapter are comparable with the "return to normalcy" carried out in the Western world after the First World War: in both cases, it was taken for granted that the normal coincided with that which had existed before the disturbance—war in one case, revolution in the other. It may be assumed that the majority of the Soviet citizens applauded the return of the "good old times" as wholeheartedly as the Western "bourgeois" approved the corresponding acts of the governments. The main reason for the hostility of large groups towards the government thus disappeared, and a sacred union against the aggressor could materialize.

Chapter IX

THE CULTURAL TRANSFIGURATION:

Scientists and Artists in Uniform

1

THE SOCIAL AND ECONOMIC transfiguration to which Russia was submitted under the Communist Experiment had a counterpart in cultural transfiguration. While according to the Doctrine, ideas are mere reflections of social and economic relations, still they are able either to accelerate or retard change in these relations; since the Communist Revolution in Russia took place in the midst of a hostile world and was threatened by virtual "intervention" on the part of the capitalists, it seemed to be very important that new ideas accelerate the social and economic revolution, and not retard it. Consequently, the protagonists of the great Communist Experiment had to do their best to change rapidly the mentality of the men involved in this Experiment, i.e., of the Russian nation. The Russians had to become "new men," imbued with new ideas, having abandoned the culture tradition rooted in the past. "The outcome of the Revolution," exclaimed Bukharin, "depends on our ability to mold the younger generation into human material able to construct Socialist economics and Socialist society." [1]

In regard to the individual phases of this new culture, no specification existed, nor could it exist, since according to the Doctrine men living in capitalist relations could not imagine how men would think and act when living in the framework of socialist society. Just as in many other realms of social and cultural activity, the Communists had to proceed by trial and error, more often than not borrowing patterns invented by radical elements of bourgeois society.

However, in the particular field now under study the Communists made a significant invention. Under their rule, culture became managed, or official. To understand what official culture is, it is convenient to contrast it with the unofficial culture of liberal society.

In liberal society, as a rule, culture is free from legal regimentation. An indeterminate number of persons, not especially designated by any agency, produce, reproduce, rework, and propagate cultural values; their activity is judged by "the public," that is to say, by the unorganized mass, and on its acceptance or rejection of the cultural product depends the success or failure of the cultural agents in their competition. The law interferes in individual cases only, to prevent harm or imminent danger to personal or economic rights, perhaps to the essential conditions of the successful protection of the State.

The principle of noninterference of law and political agencies in culture production and distribution exists only in liberal society and is as exceptional in human history as is liberal society. Preliberal society permitted the elimination of whole trends of cultural activity characterized as subversive or destructive for the proper mentality of the population. In Communist society the departure from the pattern of liberal society is still greater. In this society positive interference is added to the negative one, i.e., to the elimination of trends. The State imposes definite trends on cultural activity and thus shapes the mentality of its subjects and, to achieve this end, designates the individuals who are permitted to participate in cultural activity and propaganda.

Official culture is partly directed by State machinery, and partly created by special cultural agents (scientists, authors, painters, and the like) under the guidance of that machinery. At the top is the Supreme Leader. He is assisted by the Department of Propaganda of the Central Committee of the Communist Party [2] and, on a lower level, by numerous specialized agencies, such as the Political Office of the Army, the Council of Political Enlightenment, and the National Council of Science. The Commissariat of Public Education and a number of Trade

Unions play the part of executive agencies which they share with such institutions as the State Publishing Office, the Central Committee of the Cinema, and the Central Board of the Radio. All these agencies are headed by Communists and are predominantly staffed by Communists, in execution of the constitutional principle that all the means of influencing public opinion should be transferred to the Communist Party representing the Labor class.

What does the State monopoly of the technical means of cultural activity and propaganda mean to the individual cultural agent? He intends to write a book or an article, but he knows that the publishing house or the newspaper office with which he will have to negotiate is a State agency. This agency strictly observes the rule that nothing incompatible with Communist principles of action be published and, additionally, displays efforts to get material, the publication of which would promote the official doctrine. High remuneration and honorific forms of social reward (among them titles and orders) await our author if he produces something according to the "general line," and the impossibility of publishing the work awaits him if he makes an attempt to oppose this line.

The Communist State does more than this. Under the pretext of fostering culture, it creates special bodies, membership in which is offered to the producers of cultural goods. Such are, for instance, the Association of Soviet composers, the Association of Soviet writers, the Co-operative of Soviet painters and sculptors. The members of these associations are given "contracts" according to which they have to produce a certain amount of words, square inches of pictures, and the like, and are paid a certain sum of money monthly, provided that their production is acceptable to experts commissioned by the government. Royalties are paid in addition to the monthly salary if the works appear to be good sellers. But without the help of an association, a young cultural agent has no chance to see his work published, reproduced, etc. And the association not only helps the authors in their negotiations with State publishers and the like, but also helps them to find acceptable themes which must, as much as possible, be related to the construction of the new society. On the other hand, regular production is demanded, and even royalties for earlier works are withdrawn, if the cultural agent ceases to produce and thus help that construction.[3]

Quite recently, the working of the system relating to music has been reported in these words:

> Musical compositions in Russia, from operas to Army songs, are written on stated themes and in stated periods, on the basis of government contracts . . . Naturally, when orders are given, the particular musical styles and inclinations of a given composer are taken into account. Many contracts are the results of applications by the composers themselves. Good fees are paid for compositions under government contract. For example, the usual price for a symphony is ten thousand rubles. In addition, the composer is paid a lump sum on publication of his score, and also receives royalties amounting to a certain percentage of the takings at every public performance of his works.[4]

In addition to this, in 1939 huge prizes (up to 200,000 rubles) started being awarded for outstanding achievements in arts, science, and technique.[5] These are "Stalin's prizes," the Communist counterpart of the Nobel prizes of the "bourgeois" world. Naturally, conformity with the official patterns is one of the requisites of victory in the competition for these prizes.

2

Under the Communist Experiment, the machine of culture management was used to direct all the creative forces of the scientists, men of letters, and artists towards the aim of engendering the universal proletarian culture foreseen by the blueprint.

Since in modern society science is functionally connected with University teaching, the measures reported above in regard to the Universities had the additional significance of regimenting the scientific activity. Moreover, the special institutions for scientific research were submitted to a treatment similar to that of the Universities. Most significant was the treatment of the Academy of Sciences, the very center of scientific research in Russia. In 1929, elections of new members took place. Under government pressure, quite a few persons were nominated for prominence not as scholars, but as Communists. Since the secret ballot was used, three such candidates fell through. To appease those in power, the board of directors offered to proceed to a second ballot, unforeseen by the statute. This time the three men, unknown in the universe of scholars, received the highest scientific honor available in Russia.

Three years later, one of those thus chosen made the following statement before the All-Russian Congress of Trade Unions:

> In our ranks, we have fifty thousand scientists. Now this army experiences a great *kolhoz* movement. Correct distribution of forces, interpretation of scientific activity in terms of production, socialistic emulation, shock brigades—such are the principles of our scientific activity.[6]

Throughout the years of the Communist Experiment, the government sponsored research in the technical sciences and in those theoretical sciences which form their indispensable foundation, such as mathematics, physics, and chemistry, provided that this research was conducted by men who uttered a few words from time to time praising the government.° Significant advance was made in these fields, continuing the advance of the prerevolutionary period. But in fields where official truth was involved, conditions were unfavorable. An obscure professor coined the term "Red Truth," in contradistinction to the White Truth of the bourgeois nations.† Observation shows that this Red Truth consists predominantly of quotations from Marx, Engels, Lenin, and later on also Stalin. In consequence, in philosophy, jurisprudence, sociology, eco-

° A few scientists with world fame, such as I. Pavlov, could permit themselves criticism of the government in lectures.

† To secure the propagation of Red Truth, an Institute of Red Professors was created.

nomics, and history the period of the Communist Experiment was rather sterile.

Let us substantiate these statements by a few examples. Up to 1930, Russian history was dominated by Pokrovsky, vice-commissar of Education up to his death (1932). Pokrovsky was an orthodox Marxist of the old style; all historical events, in his opinion, were determined by the development of the economic basis of society, which was considered impersonal and independent of human will. The role of great men in Russian history, as in every history, was only imaginary; the greatest among them, Peter I, was merely a drunkard and syphilitic. Naturally, up to the rise of the revolutionary movement, Russian history was nothing but exploitation, chaos, and darkness.

In the course of the First Socialist Offensive (War Communism) all the antagonists of Pokrovsky and his school were simply silenced. During the NEP a certain alleviation took place. Some of the "bourgeois" historians were permitted to publish the results of their research, naturally without explicitly opposing the Marxist interpretation of history. The interest of these scholars concentrated on the earliest periods of Russian history, and in this field very substantial advance was made.

However, already under the NEP the instrument of the forthcoming pressure was created; this was the Association of Marxist Historians (1925). With the Second Socialist Offensive, this Association started their attack, which culminated in the deportation, from Leningrad to provincial towns, of two prominent historians, Platonov and Tarle. The Association systematically attacked their writings, old and new. In 1931, a symposium summing up the "errors" of the two great men was published,[7] in which these statements could be found: "When Platonov stresses the role of the middle class in the liquidation of the Time of Trouble (seventeenth century) he vindicates Kolchak and Denikin. When he turns to the study of the history of the Russian North, he manifests the hope that the *kulaks* of that region will overthrow the Bolsheviks." Tarle was especially scolded for the abundant use of unpublished material from the archives (sic!). The very foundation of historical science was thus put in jeopardy by men who did not know how to find and use such material, and thought that writing history was tantamount to repetition and comment on Marx's and Lenin's statements about the past. Pokrovsky threw the weight of his authority into the struggle in 1931, speaking at the Institute of Red Professors. He advised the audience not to indulge in "academic history" because this is a species of "objective science," and there is no such thing as objective science: science is either red or white.

Similar principles were applied in the interpretation of the history of art and literature. Here is an example from a book devoted to the study of the most brilliant artistic group of the early twentieth century, *Mir Iskusstva* (The World of Art):

It was from the positions of a group of nobility which participated in the capitalistic development of Russia that the *M.I.* derived its particularities, which separated it from the consistent urbanism of the ideologists of the upper bourgeoisie. This was the position used by *M.I.* in its struggle both against the group of the *Itinerants* representing the danger of a peasants' revolution, and the Academy representing the danger of aristocratic reaction.

Not very clear, but consistent with the principles of orthodox Marxism: every artistic trend, by necessity, reflects the position of a particular social group in the class struggle.[8]

As to jurisprudence and political science, during the period of War Communism, 1917–21, a complete negation of legal form was actually dominant. Reisner, Goikhbarg, and Stuchka, the pillars of the juridical thought of that period, published their basic works during the NEP, but the ideas which they contain had been expressed by them earlier. These ideas, in their substance, amount to the negation of the possibility and necessity of the existence of law within the framework of Communist society. According to Goikhbarg, "law, even more (than religion) is a poisoning, stupefying opium for the people." Reisner says: "we still do not know whether we (the Communists) need law." According to Stuchka's conviction, the relations between individuals in socialist society will be regulated not by coercion (even if it be legal) but by conscious good will of the workers.

The period of the NEP which was characterized by a partial restoration of private-capitalistic relationships in production and exchange was at the same time a period of great development of Soviet law; codes were published and attempts were made to revive scientific legal literature. Under such conditions complete negation of law became impossible. According to Stuchka, a partial restoration of bourgeois law was taking place, while at the same time the socialist law regulating relations between the links of socialist economy was recognized. According to Reisner, Soviet law was becoming complicated: to the socialist law of the working class there was added the peasant class law and the bourgeois class law, and in many instances the Soviet regime retained the forms of the bourgeois individual law.[9]

Under the Second Socialist Offensive, it was first proclaimed that the primary aim was the building of a classless society. It was later asserted that this aim was almost attained—that classes no longer existed, although some individuals with hostile class-consciousness still remained. Once more the revolutionary-Utopian version of the Marxian doctrine of law and State was applied to Soviet actuality, and the assertion was made that the existence of law in the new society had lost all sense. This viewpoint found a talented and consistent supporter in the person of E. Pashukanis, who in 1930, at the congress of Marxian political scentists, was proclaimed the foremost representative of Marxian jurisprudence.

According to the teachings of Pashukanis, law and morals are not eternal abstract categories of human community life, but merely forms of existence in bourgeois society. No law existed in primary Communist society; in feudal society it was only in an embryonic state; in the early Socialist society it must at once begin to wither away as a body foreign to it; in the fully developed Communist society there will be no law. If law is merely a form of bourgeois relationships, it is incapable of being socialist in substance. Therefore, as soon as socialism begins to be realized, law begins to wither away. Law, in his opinion, began to wither away in the Soviet State, and the State itself with it, since 1917. After a delay caused by the NEP, this withering away proceeded rapidly. The term "socialist law" is fundamentally contradictory, and the Soviet jurists are called upon to bury law and replace it by other forms of regulation of human relations. Criminal law in particular, deprived of its judicial form, must turn into a system of expedient measures of defense.[10]

3

In the realm of science, a substantial difference may be noticed between the ideas officially recognized in 1940 (or later) and those which had been recognized around 1930. This difference is of complicated origin. It depends partly on the official emergence of the rule of the One which needed explanation and justification. But it also depends on the shift from internationalism to nationalism, forming the very backbone of The Great Retreat.

The study of this complicated process should begin by discussing a substantial change which, in the latter part of the Communist Experiment, occurred in that "science of sciences" which, according to the Doctrine, is the Marxist-Leninist Theory.

At this point, a preliminary question may be raised. How can the very possibility of fluctuations be explained? Communist society, which was being created in Russia, was an attempt to transmute the Marxian doctrine into reality. This doctrine had been developed into a system long before the beginning of the experiment, and it would seem that its application could give but one definite and invariable result.

Actually, however, the application of the Marxian doctrine to the social reconstruction of Russia assumed various forms—the dosage, the pace, the ways and practical methods changed; periods of advance alternated with periods of retreat. The present-day sociology of knowledge believes that each doctrine is at least partly determined by the social situation in which it was created. This principle can be reversed: each social situation is necessarily expressed in corresponding doctrines. Therefore, changes in the Doctrine had to correspond to changes in the social structure of Russia in the various phases of the Communist Experiment.

The decisive change in the Doctrine took place in the late 'twenties. Officially, a providential event conditioned it: in 1925, a manuscript written by Engels in 1878–82 was discovered by the leaders of the Marx Engels Institute in Moscow and published by them under the title, *The Dialectics of Nature.* In this work mechanical predetermination of natural processes was denied and a "creative ability of matter" was postulated. Now, for Marxists, consciousness is the highest product of matter organized in a specific manner (living organisms).[11] If in general matter is capable of spontaneous or creative change, then necessarily in men, i.e., matter on the highest level of organization, this ability must be highest. Thus, the revival of the hero theory in history was prepared, and the theory could be used to explain the personal role of the dictator, concealed in the earlier years of the Revolution.

However, in the beginning change in the Doctrine was limited to the theoretical level. The new interpretation of Marxism was given the name of "dialectical materialism," whereas the older variety, that making history a product of impersonal forces, was labeled "mechanical materialism." For quite a few years debate between the representatives of the two interpretations was permitted and actually took place, without attracting the attention of the public outside the ranks of the specialists in Marxist theory.

In 1930, a few months after the official proclamation of Stalin's leadership, one of the contesting interpretations was officially recognized to be the correct one and thus introduced into the Doctrine. This significant step was made by means of the resolution of the Central Committee of the Communist Party (January 7, 1930) "on the new tasks of Marx-Leninist philosophy." The resolution denounced both "the idealistic danger," rather nonexistent, and the "mechanistic revision of Marxism." The usual technique was applied: the old interpretation was declared "revision," i.e., deviation, and the new one presented as the orthodox and traditional version of the Doctrine, which it definitely was not.

When this resolution was published, even high ranking Communists were not sufficiently informed about Stalin's new position. They did not know that in these new conditions it was dangerous to oppose or even doubt his ideas. Therefore, in the journal *Under the Banner of Marxism* [12] quite a few Soviet philosophers argued that the new interpretation was anti-Marxist. The counterblow came in the form of a special resolution of the Central Committee of January 15, 1931, in which the protestants were severely rebuked. In the course of the next few months almost all the adherents of the condemned trend were declared counterrevolutionists, even terrorists; they lost their positions, and some of them were executed.

Since that time dialectical materialism was beyond discussion. Naturally, it started being applied to concrete political questions, not only present, but also past, since in the Soviet State the interpretation of past events in terms of the Doctrine is considered to be one of the most important tasks of philosophy. In 1937, the revised version of the Doctrine received its final form in an official *Outline of the History of the Communist Party*, edited by Stalin himself. There, among other things, the idea was expressed that the socialist doctrine was produced not by the Labor class, but by providential leaders. After the publication of the *Outline*, quite a few rank-and-file Communists expressed their doubts in letters to the editor of *Pravda*. Very patiently the editor explained that time and again ideas, especially political ideas, emerge independently of economic conditions, sometimes despite economic conditions. Thus, for instance, the collectivization of the Russian homesteads took place not because of economic necessity, but because ingenious ideas had been formulated by Lenin and Stalin; the same was true of "socialism in one country." In general, continued the editor, socialist ideology cannot be elaborated by the Labor class. What it could produce is merely "trade-unionism," the philosophy of Menshevism. Socialism entered the minds of the workers as a kind of revelation which originated in the minds of a few intellectuals. In Russia, socialist consciousness was given to the Labor class by Lenin and Stalin. As usual, threats were added to explanations: those Communists who did not share the new ideas and professed the impersonal theory of social progress were compared with bourgeois politicians for whom, it is well known, there is no room in the Soviet Union.[13]

Later statements contributed still more to the clarification of the meaning of the change.

Pseudo-Bolsheviks, such as Bogdanov or Lunacharski [one could read in 1939], asserted that for the establishment of socialism definite economic conditions were necessary which could not be replaced by slogans or ideas. Vulgarizing Marxism, they fell so low as to assert that consciousness was subordinate to existence, while true Bolsheviks held the opposite view and emphasized the explosive and transforming capacity of progressive ideas. In contrast to learned but dull men of the Second International, Lenin and Stalin correctly defined the actual role of ideas in the historical process, and on the basis of this correct definition socialism in one country could be realized and adequate relationship with the capitalist environment established.[14]

It is obvious that neither Marx nor Lenin would have subscribed to the propositions above. But both were dead, and in the framework of dictatorship and managed culture nobody would dare to prove by citations that the new Doctrine no longer had much in common with orthodox Marxism.

The amazing change in the Doctrine was of great consequence in the conception of history. In 1931, Pokrovsky found himself in a peculiar position. On the one hand, he continued fulminating against the "bourgeois historians." But on the other hand, he had to comply with the revised version of the Doctrine and publicly acknowledge that his *Russian History* was wrong because in writing it, he did not sufficiently recognize the "relative independence of the political factor from the economic." In his scheme there actually was no room for Lenin and Stalin as moving springs of History. He died early enough not to see all his works debunked and his pupils demoted or exiled.

In 1934, Tarle was permitted to return and resume his scientific activity. His brilliant works on Napoleon gave him the first rank among the living Russian historians. It was under his leadership that the rehabilitation of Russian history reported in Chapter VII took place.

Meanwhile, the school of Pokrovsky was being annihilated. In 1936, Bukharin and Radek, then members of the inner circle, published fulminating articles [15] against it, accusing it of scientific backwardness and, politically, of vindicating Trotskyism. The next year Pokrovsky's pupils were declared to be traitors and wreckers.[16] Shestakov, the winner of the prize contest on the best textbook in history, published an article in which he tore to shreds Pokrovsky's conception of Russian history. His article began with a sentence which showed that, though the Pokrovsky school was dead, the science of history had not yet recovered its liberty. "Stalin," he wrote, "continuously enriches and pushes forward the science of history, throwing bright light on facts of universal history and discovering the laws of historical evolution." [17]

About the same time, these directions were given to University professors. When teaching the Marxist-Leninist Theory or History; they should avoid any arbitrary interpretation, especially "the anti-Marxist deviation of the school of Pokrovsky." They were forbidden to minimize the role of the personality in history, the functions of the State, or the victory of socialism in Russia. They were warned against disparaging war in general and ordered to distinguish between just and unjust war.[18]

In 1942, a symposium entitled *25 Years of Historical Science in the USSR* was published. There Pokrovsky's ideas were once more debunked, but one could not find any mention of the symposium of 1931 directed against Tarle and Platonov: Tarle was one of the editors of the new symposium, in which the Soviet historians were directed to give a true image of the heroic past of the peoples of the USSR and continue revising all the wrong ideas about it.

Another field of science where the change in the Doctrine was of paramount importance was that of jurisprudence and political science. In 1936, Pashukanis, like many others, was requested to disavow his ideas. He did so, but in a form which could not please those holding power. "The enemies of the Party," he wrote, "are getting hold of the problem of the withering away of law." Here was his chance to renounce his former ideas. But, having posed the question: "If, in the USSR, the capitalistic elements have been destroyed and a classless society has been built, why does the State still exist?"—he simply forbore from giving any answer, thereby letting it be understood that (1) either classless society had not been built in the USSR, or that (2) the Marxian doctrine to the effect that the law and the State always express class domination was wrong.[19] No further attempts in the same direction were made, and all the ideas of Pashukanis and his followers are now considered as manifestations of counterrevolutionary Trotskyism.[20]

The recantation of former "fallacies" was demanded not only of theorists, but also of practical workers. The following decree of the People's Commissariat of Justice regarding the institute of legal psychiatry is characteristic in this respect.

The basic mistake of the leaders of the Institute is that, after the exposure of the hostile work of the school of Pashukanis and Krylenko, its leaders failed to make any deductions. The direct consequence was their interpretation of the problem of imputability, which actually coincided with Krylenko's fallacious principles.[21]

In another section of the same decree one finds:

Residues of legal nihilism, neglect of socialist legality, negation of the socialist nature of our law—are (expressed) in the ignoring of the principle of imputability.

The existence and the text of such a decree clearly show that the point here is not a change in private opinion, but a transition from one official doctrine to another. This is precisely the reason why the following proposition sounds so sternly throughout all the accusatory articles: "the theory of the impossibility of building a system of Soviet law is closely related to the Trotskyist theory of the impossibility of building socialism in one country."

From behind the scaffold of criticism there gradually begins to emerge a new official theory of the law and the State. It goes approximately like this:

The great proletarian revolution has for the first time in the history of humanity created a socialist State of workmen and peasants. This is the highest type of State—that of the dictatorship of the proletariat. Having emerged victorious, the working class destroyed the oppressionist bourgeois State machinery and built a new State apparatus of its own. This new form of State, discovered by Lenin, is the Soviet Republic. The task of the workers is the further strengthening of the dictatorship of the proletariat. Only thus can the rule of the working class prepare conditions for the future withering away of the State. But the State of the dictatorship of the proletariat will remain in existence during the entire first phase of Communism. Its withering away will begin only in the second, higher phase. Destroying the bourgeois State, the working class creates its own socialist law, which is the expression of the will of the working class.[22] .

It was after the appearance of these theses that Vyshinsky, now the supreme official authority on problems of law, gave the following explanation:

Law is the complex of rules of human behavior established by State power, that is to say, by the power of the dominant class in society, as well as of customs and rules of social life sanctioned by State power and put into effect in compulsory order, with the help of the State machinery, for the protection, strengthening, and developing of social relationships advantageous and desirable to the dominant class. Law in such a conception is possible also in socialist society: the dictatorship of the proletariat does not exclude law and legality as one of the forms of legal expression.[23]

Late in 1938, articles started appearing in Soviet journals

and newspapers, often in the form of replies to inquiries on the part of the readers, in which it was explicitly recognized that, as to the withering away of the State, not only Marx and Engels, but even Lenin had erred. Thus, Vyshinsky wrote: "Lenin had shared the idea of the withering away of the State. But Stalin introduced a correction and proved that, under Socialism, the State had to be re-enforced. In consequence, law also must persist and become socialist. Everywhere in the world those in power violate the law and individual rights. There is only one country where, like pure gold, justice is sparkling. That is the USSR." [24]

Political economy, along with political science and jurisprudence, was affected by The Great Retreat. Obviously, there could be no retreat from Marxist positions, since the transformation of Russia's economic structure on the Marxist model was maintained. But political economy, as taught in the course of the Communist Experiment, was tainted with that "vulgarized Marxism" which so easily substitutes itself for the rather austere Marxist theory. In this field the meaning of The Great Retreat was that of cleansing: exaggerations and vulgarizations which had prevailed around 1930, simultaneously with the dominance of the idea of the withering away of the State, were brushed away and instead rather conservative interpretations of economic phenomena in general, and of the Russian scene in particular, gained the upper hand.

To get correct insight into the scope and significance of the change, one may use a very simple procedure. Compare a standard textbook written around 1930, such as Professors I. Lapidus' and K. Ostrovityanov's *Outline of Political Economy* with a programmatic article by Professor A. L. Leontiev and associates, which appeared in August, 1943, in the journal, *Under the Banner of Marxism.*[25]

Ten years ago Soviet economists asserted that on the first day of the Socialist Revolution the laws and categories of capitalist economy ceased to function. The view that such laws continued to operate in the USSR as the law of the cost of production, of surplus value, and of rent, was denounced as a fundamental error. Now this position is attacked as un-Marxist and unscientific and economics is defined as "the science which explains the laws which govern the production and distribution of the necessary articles of consumption in human society in the different stages of its development." In this definition the idea is implicit that there are economic laws which operate both under capitalism and socialism.

The "vulgarizing Marxists" of the early 'thirties romantically idealized primitive Communism and were inclined to interpret the shift from it to class society as the Fall of Men. Today such ideas are declared to be in clear contradiction of historical facts. Leontiev's article emphasizes "the historical limitations of primitive Communism which corresponded to an extremely low level of the development of productive forces . . . At a certain stage, primitive Communism became an obstacle to social progress. It had to yield its place to a new method of production which gave more latitude to the development of productive forces."

In this way, a historical vindication of capitalism is offered. Very definitely, this is in accordance with Marx's teaching, but the point at issue is that ten years ago, nobody in the USSR would have dared to ascribe any value whatsoever to the capitalistic mode of production.

Denying the validity of economic laws in socialist economy, the "vulgarizing Marxists" whose ideas, then, represented the official Doctrine emphasized that in that economy there was no room for the law of value. According to present-day ideas, the notion that this law is inoperative under socialism is presumed to be incompatible with Marxist theory. This law is not liquidated under socialism, but is invested with a new set of conditions. This is a very important point. By resurrecting this law, the economists justify piece work wages, one of the chief targets of classical socialist agitation; they justify differences in wages based on the fact that the labor of citizens in socialist society is not quite uniform; they explain differences in income between workers and peasants, and market competition and market prices. They are probably aware that the particular treatment received by these institutions in the USSR would have been frowned upon by Marx and Engels. Very wisely, they make this remark: "It would be absurd to imagine that Marx and Engels could foresee and foretell the concrete way to employ the law of value in the interests of socialism."

The "vulgarizing Marxists" denied, furthermore, that surplus value could exist under socialism; in doing so they probably were aware of the tremendous propaganda effect of this idea under capitalism. "Labor is robbed of surplus value by the capitalist exploiters," was one of the most effective slogans of socialist agitation. Now Leontiev and his associates declare: surplus value must exist under any system of society. In particular, it is needed for socialist accumulation, to maintain the armed forces, schools, and other public services, and to meet the expenses of the system of social security.

These differences may be summarized as follows: According to the doctrine of the early 'thirties, there is an unsurmountable chasm between capitalism and socialism. According to the doctrine of the 'forties, the two economic systems are governed by similar, though not identical laws. Soviet socialism is no longer presented as the only progressive system, but as the most progressive, the most advanced one.

The significance of the revised doctrine is this: the striking similarities between the economic system of mitigated Communism and the capitalist system receive a full explanation and justification; secondly, the eventual collaboration between the Communist State and the great capitalist States is interpreted as co-operation between the best and the second best economic systems known to humanity. This interpretation is facilitated by the distinction which is being drawn between monopoly capitalism in Fascist countries and capitalism in the bourgeois democracies which have preserved the elementary liberties, among them the right of Trade Unions and Labor parties to exist and carry out their natural functions.

Ten years ago anyone who dared to say anything of this kind would immediately have been jailed, probably executed. Today this is the official Doctrine, and anyone would be jailed or executed who dared to deny any difference between the progressive capitalism of the democratic countries and the reactionary capitalism represented by Fascism. In many parts, the revised Doctrine is a return to pure Marxism, but quite a few statements would have been strongly opposed by Marx, Engels, and even Lenin. The revised Doctrine is Stalinism, no longer Marxism-Leninism.

In the natural sciences, a direct impact of the change in the Doctrine seems to be out of the question. But it only seems so. In actuality, the Doctrine permeates everything, and change in it must bring new light on every scientific problem. How is this possible? The following story gives the answer.

Late in 1936, British and American scientists, specialists in biology, were expected to attend the Seventh International Congress in Genetics, to be held in Moscow. They did not attend because the Congress was canceled, and it was canceled because it had been suddenly discovered that genetics was a counterrevolutionary science. The government's spokesman, Professor Lyssenko, a famous botanist, challenged the validity of classic genetics, including the Mendelian laws, and stigmatized them as formalistic and of no practical value. The actual reason for the attack was never disclosed, but it is not difficult to guess: the theory of heredity, as formulated by modern genetics, points to the immutability of the hereditary material of which the organisms are built. This was acceptable in Moscow as long as the theory of impersonal evolution prevailed, but with the shift to the theory of creative evolution this became embarrassing.[26]

About the same time as the attack on classic genetics, of which Professor Vavilov was the principal exponent, certain anthropological and biological theories started being rejected because they were similar to those held by Nazi scientists. Thus, Professor Shyvko was severely rebuked for having classed the Buryato-Mongolians as mentally equal to twelve-year-old Europeans. Actually his findings pointed to the cultural backwardness of the tribe. But the statement was interpreted as racialism, and as such declared not permissible on the part of a Soviet scientist. Simultaneously, Professor Levit of the Medical Institute in Moscow was attacked for having taught that heredity was the determining factor of criminality. The biological, or anthropological view on crime was, by the way, held in old Russia by many progressive criminologists. It is probably wrong; but characteristic of the Soviet regime is the manner of refutation: it is wrong not because it is contradicted by facts, but because other persons (in this case, the Nazis) hold the same view.

Vavilov and the other geneticists were not, however, silenced at once. For three years they were permitted to fight publicly for their scientific views, contesting that they did not conflict with Darwinism or Marxism. They even dared to assert that the rejection of Mendelian genetics would carry genetics back seventy years. In 1939, the case was decided: the acceptance of genetics would throw biology back to the Middle Ages. "The concept of the gene contradicts dialectical materialism," it was declared.[27] Since it does contradict, it must be rejected. In biology, as in history or jurisprudence, a Soviet scientist has to think in terms of dialectical materialism, or of creative evolution. This is probably better than thinking in terms of impersonal evolution or mechanistic materialism. But in both cases a pattern of thought is imposed on the scientists chosen by the Supreme Leader. In this regard, The Great Retreat changed nothing. For Russia, intellectual freedom is still ahead.

4

Let us now return to the years of the Communist Experiment and establish how literature, art, and music were molded by the managers of Communist culture.

In the realm of literature, during the period of War Communism, the monopoly of the printing press and paper were used in order to foster the development of two selected movements, while authors belonging to other trends were given no opportunity to publish their works.

One of the privileged groups were the Futurists. Their

declaration of creed was truly revolutionary. Mayakovsky, their head, proclaimed the identity of futurism and proletarian art in these words: "Futurism is the proletarian art; futurism is the ideology of the proletarian class." He declared unrestricted warfare against classical literature. "Guns have been placed everywhere," he said in the midst of the Civil War; "but why has Pushkin not yet been attacked?" Mayakovsky did his best to support the new regime for he actually loved upheaval, destruction, and outrage. However, the other members of the school proved to be of no value. They were revolutionists in literature in that they proclaimed and applied the principle of "the egotist word" deprived of any meaning. But their production was unintelligible. Lenin frankly said that he understood Pushkin, but not Mayakovsky, the clearest of all.

Proletcult * was the other privileged movement. The government hired outstanding writers and poets to teach young proletarians the art of literary production. The result was that a minority of truly gifted persons started imitating their "bourgeois" teachers, while the majority could not produce anything at all. Moreover, the members of the group displayed a pretense to control literature. This was too much for the government. Under the pretext of needing the services of young men in the Red Army, it disbanded the Proletcult (1919).

Two years later, the great change in the economic policy caused a correlated change in the literary policy. The State Publishing House became one of the "trusts," or economic units belonging to the State, but operating according to the principle of economic self-sufficiency. Its output had to cover at least the cost of production, and this was possible only if the public acquired the works published by it. From the very beginning of the NEP it appeared that the public was willing to buy books, but not of the kind published under War Communism. They wanted interesting and intelligible works and refused to buy futurist poems or propaganda.

In consequence, older men of letters, silenced for the years of War Communism, reappeared on the scene. But very soon

* Abbreviation for proletarian culture.

dominance was acquired by a new group to which Trotsky gave the name of "Fellow Travelers." These were younger authors who had begun publishing works before the Revolution. The Revolution became the central object of their creative activity. But in their eyes it was not the same thing as in those of the Communists: not the liberation of humanity, not a glorious beginning, but rather a phantasmagoria, an upheaval of chaos against order, something quite irrational. They tried to describe it in a realistic manner and to keep silent as to its value.

Works of this kind found buyers. Commercially, the movement was a success. But from the very beginning there were political difficulties. The Fellow Travelers were antagonized by the remnants of the Proletcult; by Mayakovsky who, in poems, now had to praise governmental campaigns against laziness, or the better paving of streets, and who understood his destitution well; and by a group of orthodox Communists. Among the latter, the theory of Professor Pereverzev was in vogue, who thought that by studying the form of a literary work, one could conclude to what social group the author belonged and what economic interests he represented.

However, the Fellow Travelers had supporters also. Chief among them was Voronsky, the editor of the magazine *Krasnaya Nov*. An influential Communist himself, he proclaimed this theory: the Fellow Travelers are certainly not persons enlightened by Marxism, but they are going the same way as the Revolution. They are members of the new society, a product of new Russia. They have to continue their way until the day when the proletarians have mastered the literary technique and are able to undertake the production of literature. Conflicts between the Fellow Travelers and their antagonists became so acute that the Central Committee of the Communist Party had to interfere. On July 1, 1924, a resolution was passed which endorsed Voronsky's theory. The Committee declared that neutral art could not exist in class society and that leadership had to belong to the proletarians. But, continued the Committee, for the transitory period of the NEP, authors of the type of the Fellow Travelers were admissible because they possessed the heritage of the bourgeois culture and were the natural teachers of the proletarians in literature.

An accidental event, the suicide of the poet Essenin (1926) gave the signal for a reversal in policy. Essenin's life story is significant. A young poet at the time of the Revolution, he had already published a few good poems, the tendency of which was to deplore the contamination of rural Russia by urbanism and capitalism. He applauded the Revolution, erroneously seeing in it the realization of his dreams. He was very much upset by the NEP. Having met and married Isidora Duncan, he left the country and spent a few years abroad, especially in the United States, leading a life which induced the immigration authorities to ask him to leave. Back in Russia, he found the NEP society at its apex. During an attack of despair he destroyed himself. The reaction of the literary world showed the Communists that the authors shared Essenin's ideas regarding the failure of the Revolution to create a better society.

A new period immediately began, which could be called the period of terrorism in literature. All works were critically analyzed from the standpoint of their compatibility with the official dogma. This was performed by volunteers among the authors themselves who hoped to gain by denouncing their fellows. For years the names of many outstanding authors, among them the Fellow Travelers, disappeared from the shelves of the bookstores and the pages of magazines. Among the victims were both Voronsky and Pereverzev, the foes of the preceding years. In 1928 it was "proved" that under the disguise of orthodox Marxism, Pereverzev was preaching art for art's sake, and that he repudiated the ideological and political function of literature.

The general trend to be followed by all authors was defined: this was Socialist Realism, a term coined by Stalin himself. Literature had to become "an auxiliary guild" in the building up of socialist society. The leader of the extreme left, Bezymensky, said that "the only task of literature was that of fulfilling the social directions of Stalin." Authors had to describe the socialist enthusiasm of the masses and provoke it where it was absent. Authors' "shock brigades" were formed and sent to places where new, gigantic plants were being constructed. The personality of the authors tended to disappear. Often works were signed by the brigade, without mentioning the individuals forming it. An escape was left for those who preferred going to remote parts of Russia to describe the folkways of primitive tribes; in this way, literature became dilletantic ethnology or "literary reportage"—almost verbal photography. In March, 1933, the new situation was consecrated by a resolution of the Central Committee: socialist realism became compulsory. On this note, the Communist experiment in literature reached its climax. It was naturally accompanied by a kind of demotion of the classics. Here is a typical statement:

Leo Tolstoy is almost useless because of his classless position. Such scenes as the conversation between Princess Oblonsky and peasant women are directly harmful, for there can be no understanding between women of different classes. The same must be said about the scene between Pierre Bezoukhov and Marshal Davoust, since any kind of talk on human brotherhood is detrimental.[28]

Somewhat different was the development of art and music. In the Communist view the proletariat, gaining political power, had also to conquer the realm of art and music as the proper instrument for the socialization of emotions. In consequence, under the Communist Experiment, art and music had to extol the impersonal greatness of the masses.

However, the first impulsion, given by Lenin himself, was rather simple; the bourgeois content of art must be replaced by proletarian content, without change in form, and since the proletariat is a giant, gigantic monuments should express its victory. Consequently, very soon the streets of the cities were adorned with monuments of revolutionary heroes, completed by third-class artists, and made of clay, plaster, or alabaster: other materials were unavailable. The result was embodied in ugliness. This was one of the causes of the change which took place very soon; another was the pressure of radical elements among the artists supported by influential Communists. For a few years radicalism in art was identified with Communist art. The law of revolutionary metabolism very soon started operating: each group was denounced by another as not sufficiently revolutionary and then dethroned.

The first group to gain victory was that of Cubo-Futurism. It revolted against the whole accustomed image of the outward world. In consequence, attempts were made to "deform space" by painting cubic color scrawls on the walls of houses, or painting purple lawns and flower beds. This style aroused considerable opposition among the workers. Attempts to introduce "geometric art" into the workers' clubs provoked a decline in attendance. Customers refused to buy objects in which "new art" was expressed.

The next group to rise was Suprematism. This group demanded the abolition of the usual art technique. Articles of daily use, such as pens, newspaper clippings, playing cards, and so on were to be combined in art products. Individual members of the group demanded "dynamic monuments" and "dynamic palaces." People were taught to see the supreme beauty in a typewriter or a locomotive.

Fortunately for Russia, all these discussions took place during a period of great material security. Almost nothing could be realized in architecture and not much in painting. With the NEP, a certain relaxation occurred. In 1922, the *Itinerants,* representatives of pre-Revolutionary art, were permitted to organize an exhibition. A certain interest in portrait painting was displayed. But in 1928 a new crisis occurred. New demands were imposed on the artists, and to show their "class face" became obligatory. In painting, the dominance of radical schools continued; they were fostered by the government, which acquired their production and displayed it in museums in place of products of "bourgeois" art, many of which were relegated to cellars or attics.

In regard to music, the Communists attacked the problem from three sides. First, they decided to liberate the orchestra of "the tyranny of the conductors." To this end the *Persimfans*

was created, an orchestra which, without being led by a con-
ductor, played—Beethoven's symphonies! Secondly, the idea
was advanced that proletarian music should imitate the noises
to which the proletarians were accustomed. Hence, the idea of
noise instruments and noise orchestras. The greatest experiment in this direction was carried out in Baku at the fifth anniversary of the October Revolution. It was a complete failure,
since the audience was unable to recognize the International.
The third means was the creation of the Association for Modern Music. In February, 1932, a new opera, *The First Cavalry
Army,* by Protopopov, a member of the Association, was performed in Moscow. On this occasion the composer declared:
"To create a truly revolutionary opera, one must overcome the
hopeless nonsense of the difference between major and minor
keys; such stereotypes cannot go along with socialist reconstruction." The opera was, however, a complete failure; obviously, the public still wanted to have that "bourgeois" distinction.

In regard to the theater, the new leaders preferred to refrain
from too radical experimenting. They were all fond of the theater, and this was only natural, since there is some affinity between the revolutionist type and the actor; and they recognized
that the theater of old Russia was outstanding. Naturally, the
government wanted to use the theater as an instrument of
popular education. But the first revolutionary plays appeared
only in 1923 and never reached the level of prewar creations.
For many years Meyerhold, a well-known producer of Imperial
times, was given an almost dictatorial position. He used it for
experiments in the field, rather continuing those he had started
before the Revolution.

With the approach of the Second Socialist Offensive, the attitude of the government stiffened. In 1927, it was decided that
the theater should contribute to the construction of socialism.
It had to concentrate on class struggle, collectivization, the socialist enthusiasm of the workers, etc.[29] However, great difficulties appeared. Good plays of the convenient style were
scarce; the political line was unstable, and this prevented the

playwrights from committing themselves on detailed aspects of the situations they treated. The response of the public was significant: despite the great fondness of the Russian people for the theater, actors often had to play before very small audiences when "revolutionary plays" were given.

5

In such realms of human activity as literature, graphic art, music, and the theater, The Great Retreat was probably not so imperative as in quite a few fields, studied in preceding chapters. The dull novels produced during the Second Socialist Offensive were read by nobody; but, for the majority of people living under the strain of the Offensive, being deprived of appealing literary production was but a minor hardship; they could either read nothing, or reread works of pre-Revolutionary origin. Many did the latter, and the Communist leaders knew it. Already in 1934 it was reported that in factory libraries Pushkin and Tolstoy were in greatest demand.[30] The pictures and sculptures produced under all three phases of the Communist Experiment did not interest anybody except a few connoisseurs, but at any time and at any place, only a few persons really care for the new products of these arts. In music nothing particularly interesting was created during the Experiment, but the audiences could continue listening to the performance of classics and modern, though prerevolutionary music, Russian or foreign.

And still there were great reasons for change. In Communist society writers, poets, painters, sculptors, composers, performers of music, and actors, were in the service of the State. For long years after the Revolution (in literature and painting with a significant interruption, in music with relative tolerance of neutral production) they were ordered to "create" products in the revolutionary style. Experience showed that for the advancement of the Revolution, this production did not contribute anything of importance. Moreover, in the course of the revolutionary years the interest of the masses in the higher aspects of culture had increased. These masses could not be persuaded to enjoy the pseudo art of the Communist Experiment. But they needed esthetic stimulation, and its lack caused a sense of frustration, and was a source of unrest. The simplest solution of the difficulty was to repudiate the cultural experiment and to direct culture production towards the gratification of popular desires, naturally without permitting anything which could undermine the power situation of the rulers. In particular, this signifies: (1) giving a place of honor to folk art, which always appeals to the masses, and (2) erasing the refinements brought into art in the lifetime of two or three generations, thus going back to the simpler art of the middle of the nineteenth century.

With the approach of the war, an additional trait was introduced; art was to be patriotic, to evoke the historical glory of Russia, and to stimulate love of "eternal Russia," past, present, and future. Since present-day Russia is socialistic, this did not preclude the glorification of the achievements of socialism. The slogan of the preceding epoch, socialist realism, could be maintained, but it was given a new interpretation. In 1939 Kalinin said:

> What is socialist realism? This is not clear. Perhaps it is the reproduction of Russian patriotism and of socialism as it is in life, not in books. This real socialism is sometimes awkward, but this should not deter the author and painters. The final formula is that to be a socialist realist one must love his fatherland and have full command of the Marxist-Leninist theory.[31]

The Great Retreat did not stop before the doors of the theater. The story was, however, somewhat different, because of all aspects of culture, it was the least deformed by revolutionary experimentation. On the occasion of the theater festival given in Moscow in September, 1935, the London *Times* reported that the visitors were disappointed because the Revolution did not penetrate the scene. *Sadko* was given in the conventional style of the late nineteenth century; the same style dominated Shostakovich's new opera. "The repertory of the

Moscow theaters is under the banner of classicism," wrote *Pravda* about the same time. Thus the theater continued displaying the trends of the early twentieth century and was consequently "fine art," too fine for popular understanding. Therefore, in this field, too, the clock was to be turned back.

It is very probable that the program of The Great Retreat in art was never consistently formulated by the rulers. They started with a few actions of minor importance. Observing their salutary effect, they increased pressure in the direction which proved to have been correctly chosen.

One of the earliest stops was the creation of the Union of Soviet Writers (summer, 1934) instead of the notorious RAPP (Russian association of proletarian writers) which, under the Second Socialist Offensive, had been the main instrument of literary terrorism. Officially, the new Union was organized for the purpose of fostering the creation of works saturated with the class struggle of the proletariat and praising the wisdom of the Communist Party.[32] But in the course of the first general assembly (Moscow, August 18-30, 1934) conciliatory notes could be heard. "It is time to terminate the division of writers into allies and enemies," said the government's spokesman.[33]

By means of a few admonitions the writers were given to understand where they had to look for models. Kalinin advised the young authors to study and imitate Pushkin and the other classics. Addressing a group of young officers of the Red Army, Voroshilov told them that a thorough knowledge of classical literature was essential for a Red commander, since the Red Army is a school of culture and in that school the classics must play the dominant part.[34] The works of the authors recommended by them have nothing in common with the ideas of the International Revolution; on the contrary, they are deeply rooted in the historical and national tradition. A few years earlier, anyone admiring these authors would have been frowned upon as a potential counterrevolutionist since, according to the Doctrine then in force, Russian literature started with Gorki and was continued by such authors as Mayakovsky and Demyan Bedny.

Simultaneously with directing literature towards the great masters of the past, the leaders permitted the writers and other "art producers" to guess that they were no longer restricted to the topics which had been obligatory under the Second Socialist Offensive. The lifting of the restrictions appeared in the following events: early in 1935, Bezymenski, then very influential, published an article in which he scolded Alexandrov and Dunayevsky, producer and musical contributor of the film *The Merry Boys,* for having borrowed quite a few features from bourgeois shows.[35] The Central Committee of the Film Workers Union appointed a commission to dispose of the case. It acquitted Alexandrov and Dunayevsky and thus sanctioned their "apolitical production." Bezymenski insisted on his accusation, but the defendants appealed to the Committee of Party Control, then one of the highest bodies in the Soviet State. The decision of the Committee never was published, but a few days later a letter to the editor of *Pravda* signed by Bezymenski appeared in which the voluntary prosecutor recognized that his indictment had been groundless.

About the same time, addressing the Central Committee of the Union of Soviet Writers, Kirshon insinuated that Soviet film producers and playwrights had displayed dangerous tendencies inimical to the nature of Soviet society. He explicitly mentioned *The Egyptian Nights,* by Meyerhold; a review, *Under the Dome of the Circus,* by Ilf, Petrov, and Katayev, and once more the film, *The Merry Boys.* These works were unpropitious because no elements of proletarian culture could be discerned in them. But, very significantly, Kirshon was rebuked. Ilf, Petrov, and Katayev protested against groundless accusations. The fact that the protest was published in *Pravda* and no rejoinder was permitted to appear proved that the Kremlin was not on Kirshon's side.

About the same time, Soviet poets were informally granted permission to write poems on subjects which they could choose freely; up to that time, socialist emulation and defense were approximately the only commended topics. In the course of the year 1935, the readers of journals were pleased to find poems describing the beauty of landscapes, or glorifying love, or expressing the despair of a mother who lost a child. In February, 1936, the Central Committee of the Union made the discovery that lyrics had to be poetical and gave corresponding instructions to its members.

Still another feature of The Great Retreat was the rediscovery of the people's interest in their art. "Young people are fond of songs. In factories, one sees notebooks in which all songs are written down that are ever heard by any worker. Lyrical songs predominate . . ." Records of popular songs started being made and produced in increasing numbers. In the Don region, known for the high quality of folk art, a contest among the best performers of folk songs and dances was arranged; the winners had to participate in the performance of the new opera, *Quiet Flows the Don,* in Moscow's Great Theater.[36]

The climax was reached when, on the eighteenth anniversary of the October Revolution (November 7, 1935) Stalin paid a visit to the Great Theater where popular songs, plays, and dances were performed. He applauded, and the next day an article appeared in *Pravda* explaining that popular art was the true source of inspiration for Soviet artists, and that all the previous trends were ridiculous imitations of the rotten art of the petty bourgeoisie. Stalin repeated his deed on the eve of the New Year, attending a performance of factory songs. In the course of the next month, he attended the first performance of the opera mentioned above. About the same time, an "Olympiad" of folk songs and music was organized in Moscow.[37]

Stalin permitted the publication of a story disclosing his personal role in the revival of folk art. Once upon a time Stalin expressed the desire to hear, at a forthcoming concert, a folk song which had been performed by a sailor's choir. The sailors in question were found, but it appeared that they had sung without notes, having learned the tune from an artist called Seversky. The latter was found, not without trouble, in a town near Moscow. A group of musicians were ordered to prepare the score for a choir accompanied by *balalaikas*—at the behest of Stalin. The musicians first said that they knew the song, but a few hours before the concert, it appeared that the harmonization was different. In the course of the last few minutes this difficulty was overcome, and Stalin applauded the performance and expressed his satisfaction with "the operational efficacy of the personnel involved." [38]

Companies of folk artists were invited to Moscow and other centers to display their art before large audiences, and numerous specialists were sent to all the corners of the Soviet Union to collect the remnants of folk art, which had been rapidly declining under the Imperial regime and almost entirely eliminated during the period of acute antinationalism. Sometimes discoveries made by such expeditions were triumphantly displayed in Moscow. Thus, for instance, the Moscow Theater for Folk Plays performed two plays discovered by leading members of the Leningrad Party Committee while attending Christmas plays in the region of Gdov. In these plays quite a few old men took part who were able to reproduce exactly a tradition going back to the period before the emancipation of the serfs. [39]

Not only Great Russian but also Ukrainian, Cossack, and Caucasian folk art was fostered. Early in 1935, a band of Ukrainian folk musicians and a choir of Don Cossacks performed in Moscow. A great "ensemble" of Cossacks and Caucasian dancers and singers was organized. An exhibition of Ukrainian folk art took place in Moscow. To help revive folk music, the production of accordions, one of Russia's national instruments, was resumed. The art had been almost forgotten, but a few old masters were discovered and entrusted with the task of training young people. [40]

There was a field where inspiration by folk art was impossible: that was architecture. There, change took place in the form of returning to the "Russian Empire style" of the early nineteenth century, perhaps the most successful of all Russian creations in the field. When in 1936 the Finnish embassy submitted designs for a new building in the modernistic style, they were politely asked to replace it by something in the classical style, since this was the style chosen for the reconstruction of Moscow. The Palace of the Soviets was planned in this style of architecture, to be built twice as high as the Empire State building, despite its unfitness for skyscrapers.

After having given more or less precise and positive directions to the art producers of Russia, the Communist leaders launched an attack on the culture production of the previous period. War was declared on something which was now denounced as "formalism," but which a few years earlier was considered to be the revolutionary style in art. In this case, as in many others, the rulers displayed their skill in the manipulation of symbols: in Russia, the elaboration of form at the expense of content was always frowned upon, except in narrow circles of specialists. Therefore, to call a trend "formalistic" was tantamount to exposing it to public wrath and drawing sympathy towards those who were curbing that undesirable trend—in this case, the government.

The war against formalism was waged in this way: late in January and early in February, 1936, a series of articles appeared in *Pravda* in which Soviet art in all its features was severely criticized. It was stated that this art was suffering with formalism and was an imitation of the decaying art of Western Europe. It could not be understood by the popular masses, even by rank-and-file intellectuals. Under the significant title, "Chaos in Music," Shostakovich's new opera, *Lady Macbeth of Mtsensk*, was debunked.[41] *Apropos* a suite for orchestra and choir composed by Aladov on the basis of Kupala's poem, *Pravda* wrote: "Kupala attended the first performance, but left before the end with a broken heart; for half an hour he heard nothing but siren whistles and monstrous machine noises." Speaking of the *kolhoz* ballet, *The Sparkling Spring*, the same paper emphasized that the composer had not paid any attention to the beautiful folksongs of the Kuban region where the action was supposed to take place, and that the music had been hastily readapted from an industrial ballet. "Formalism in music runs contrary to common sense," was the conclusion.[42]

In consequence, in March, 1936, conferences of writers, poets, painters, sculptors, and musicians were convoked, in the course of which the problem of art reform was discussed, naturally in the particular Soviet style. People who a few weeks earlier were considered to be the very bearers of Communist art were suddenly attacked and compelled to recant their artistic creed and the products of their art. Some of them displayed reluctance to follow suit. "The three days of the Moscow conference of film producers were characterized by a lack of concreteness . . . We hope that the leaders of the film industry will finally understand the depth and value of the demands of the Party and make them materialize their production," wrote the official paper. In another article *Izvestia* stated that the Moscow conference of writers had been unsatisfactory. One of the participants said that the problem of the struggle against formalism was already solved and that there was nothing to talk about. Another declared that neither his generation nor the following one could produce grand Soviet art. Naturally, resistance was finally broken. The painters' conference stated: "Be it resolved that Soviet art may develop only under the banner of the people's art." [43] The conference of composers was concluded by the acknowledgment that the articles of *Pravda* were of paramount importance for the development of music. "Remoteness from the collective art of the people, the true spring of every art, has been the sin of Soviet music, which must be overcome as quickly as possible."

There was, however, one exception: this was, for reasons already explained, the theater. In the acute phase of the struggle against formalism it was Meyerhold, the greatest among the formalists, who was permitted to make the basic report to the meeting of the Union of Theater Workers. Naturally, he criticized at length the mistakes of other producers. Another speaker made an attempt to criticize Meyerhold himself, but was silenced by the audience. Meyerhold finished the discussion by declaring that his theater could not produce revolutionary plays (this was one of the accusations against him) because really good revolutionary plays did not exist. [44]

However, it was necessary to give an example. Tairov's
Kamerny Theater was chosen to play the role of scapegoat.
This theater had the misfortune of having produced an antireligious play at a time when the government had already
started recognizing the progressive role of religion in the earlier stages of Russian history. The play, namely, the comic
opera *Bogatyri* was closed, and a few weeks later *Izvestia* denounced the general trend of the theater in these words:

Tairov and his theater failed to understand that the Socialist
Revolution had removed the problems of the bourgeois theater.
Everything born of the decadence of bourgeois art, everything that
poisoned art—the affectation, eccentricity, and estheticism hiding
the poverty of creative principles—all that was and still continues
being Tairov's fetish.[45]

In contrast with the relatively mild treatment of the theater, in the field of graphic art an additional attack on formalism appeared necessary. On the occasion of the creation of
the Union Art Committee, the newly appointed chairman
wrote:

The managers of the chief museums of the USSR acquired pictures without the necessary discrimination. The famous Tretiakov
gallery is full of pictures with the formalist tendency, provoking the
righteous wrath of the workers. There is Larionov's *Soldier:* the face
is roughly painted, the legs unnatural, and the only thing carefully
painted is a fence with obscene inscriptions on it. Udaltsov's *Auto-
portrait* is nothing but a combination of lines and squares. Rosanov's
Violin represents a very old one indeed, for it is broken in parts and
combined with sheets of paper, playing cards, and advertisements.
Kamensky, the poet, is shown as a cyclops; more detailed examination shows a complementary eye on the right cheek. The *Black
Square* represents just a black square on a white surface. On the
other hand, products of true realism, the pictures of Vereschagin,
Repin, Serov, Levitan, and Shishkin have been relegated to store-
rooms.[46]

The Committee decided to remove the products of formalist
art into a special chamber of monsters open only to specialists
who could study from these examples how they should not

paint. The pictures of prerevolutionary realists were ordered back into the public halls of museums. This interchange of positions is highly symbolic of the epoch of The Great Retreat.

The new trend was further manifested in the organization of exhibitions of such great masters of the past as Repin and Levitan, and of the drawings of the early nineteenth century, as well as in the acquisition, by the Tretiakov gallery, of a number of pictures by Repin, Surikov, Serov, Levitan, Shishkin, and Kramskoy, all great masters of the late nineteenth century.[47]

6

In art, the year 1936 was crucial in that then the principles of the New Esthetic Policy were clearly formulated. This did not emancipate the agents of culture production from management, though the margin of liberty was now substantially larger than it had been in the previous period. But still the writers, artists, and composers were not permitted to try new paths in their fields, as they and their predecessors had done before the Revolution. They had to be "moderate realists," to look for inspiration in folk art, and to create in simple forms understandable to large masses. One should therefore not imagine that, after 1936, art advanced smoothly, without uncertainties and disturbances. Since art is connected with politics, the Great Purge affected quite a few of its servants. In March, 1937, the Union of Soviet Writers expelled a number of their members convicted of having been "enemies of the people," in other words, friends of the fallen leaders. To prevent possible mistakes, the Union stopped entirely the admission of new members.[48]

One year later it was officially stated that the Party and the Soviet people were dissatisfied with Russia's writers. They lacked audacity, were unable to pose real problems, displayed the tendency to concentrate on details, and rather superficially reproduced reality.[49] Was this not natural within a society which was passing through the terrible ordeal of the great purge?

Still later, complaints were loud that this task of producing patriotic literature was badly managed. Even in the editorial offices of the leading journals nobody knew how to express patriotic views without falling into the cheapness of pseudo heroic novels.[50]

The leaders had no reason to be pleased with the achievements on the theater front. The theater and the films responded in a rather mechanical way to the new directions of the government. The government wanted patriotic plays. So, films were produced in which Soviet aviation was shown to destroy the imaginary enemy almost without losses. If this corresponded to reality, wrote *Pravda*, for what purpose should such films be shown, since victory was already certain? In the theater new productions lacked any individual traits. Situations were conventional, characters most primitive, and creative efforts nil. The dissatisfaction resulted in the resumption of the attack against formalism, this time especially in the theater. In 1938, Meyerhold's theater was closed, and in 1939, he had to pass through the humiliating procedure of recantation. At a meeting of actors he had to acknowledge that his chief mistake had been the emphasis on form at the expense of content. Therefore he had to consider the closing of his theater by the government as an act of wisdom. About the same time Vyshinsky explained to the actors that the Soviet theater had not sufficiently participated in the Party's struggle against formalism. Its leaders had not understood the class roots of formalism and, despite the government's advice, persisted in adhering to it. To emphasize the disapproval of Meyerhold's theater, the Maly Theater in Moscow revived Gogol's *Inspector General* in the unsophisticated style of the 'sixties of the nineteenth century.[51]

This time, even the world-famous Moscow Art Theater was put in jeopardy. Articles appeared according to which its latest production, *Anna Karenina*, had fallen to the level of melodrama. In this case, help came from the highest place: The Union Art Committee declared that the new play had been produced under the guidance of the highest Party authorities.

The question was settled: if Stalin wanted melodrama, then the most famous theater of Russia had to produce it.[52]

The general unrest in the field of art resulted in the convocation of a new series of conferences (1939). This time the central theme was a warning against the exaggeration and misinterpretation of the slogans introduced in 1936. At the authors' conference the well-known writer, Katayev, called the attention of the audience to the dissatisfaction of the public with the primitivism of Soviet literature. "Patriotism is now the most important subject," he said, "but very often this grand theme is mutilated by unskilled hands. The results are trivial and uninteresting stories about frontier skirmishes which nobody reads." At the actors' conference Moskvin said: "We dare not simplify art, or make it subservient to any scheme." At the musicians' conference the reporter expressed the idea that the musicians had to liberate themselves from the survivals of the previous period, and to restore the link with the older generation. Commenting on these statements, *Izvestia* found them laudable and declared that subservience and lack of courage were attributes of bourgeois, not Soviet art. In Soviet language this meant that the government wanted the authors to display a little more courage and personality in their production.[53]

Famous men were permitted to address their colleagues in order to explain the causes of their troubles and to help them overcome these obstacles. In a *Letter to Young Writers*, Alexis Tolstoy advised them to show real and no longer conventional heroes of our day. Asseyev made this statement:

We, the Soviet writers, are still trying to create a literature. We have tried first one way, then another, and have seen that our works were failures. Suddenly, we have become aware of the existence of such giants as Pushkin, Shakespeare, Dickens, Gogol, and Tolstoy. We realize that they have had centuries of culture behind them and have received education from men with cultivated minds. And now we, the Soviet authors, must try to produce something to equal them. Naturally, the idea provokes irritation and is somewhat depressing.[54]

There is, however, one phase of the New Esthetic Policy where no fluctuation has obtained, and this is emphasis on folk art. In the course of the war an exhibition of folk painters from the famous region of Palekha-Mstera [55] was organized; these painters displayed their illustrations of the glorious events of Russian history and of the classic works of Russian literature. Then, a special conference on folk art was convoked where performers of folk songs, tales, and dances met scholars in the field. A parade of folk art was organized in which 48,500 people participated. A new type of production was fostered, combining folk art with a sophisticated technique. A *New Tale on Ilya Muromets,* the legendary hero of early Russian history, was highly acclaimed by the leaders; in this tale the hero arises and liberates Russia from the German aggressors. An oratorium, *The Tale of the Battle for the Russian Land,* was composed in the style of folk tales, but using the sophisticated orchestration of our day.[56]

7

Kurt London, the author of an interesting book on Soviet art, deplored the fact that "in Moscow those men, so clever in other respects, did not know the meaning of modern music, literature, painting, and architecture; because they did not understand, they negativated it." [57]

If it were necessary to choose between definite trends and impose one of them, excluding the others, then perhaps "the wise men in Moscow" were right, and not London: art production was reinstated into the people's life. The revival of classic literature found an enthusiastic response in the population, especially among the younger generation. An acute observer reports:

A hard-headed Bolshevik said: "I never realized what innocent fools we were until I saw the present younger generation at a performance of *Anna Karenina.* They wept because they realized that some things in literature are eternal: that some sorrows, like some joys, are with us forever, regardless of the state of society in which we live. I cannot tell you how much I envied them. I wish I could revive my youth, I missed so much . . ." At a performance of *Eugene Onegin,* an audience composed overwhelmingly of young persons was tense and breathless with sympathy with the heroine whom previous generations had disowned as alien and excoriated as a parasite.[58]

At the front, in the course of the war, "men listened to songs with words by Lermontov and Fet, discuss Turgenev and Leo Tolstoy, read Chekhov, Gorki, Balzac, and Hugo." [59] No contemporary Soviet name appears on this list.

The government was also gratified with the results of its policy regarding the revival of popular art and expressed its satisfaction in this dithyramb: "The Russian people has created a magnificent folk literature. In it, the people's dignity and intelligence have been expressed. It has fortified the people morally; it could be compared with the festival clothes of the soul. It has given a deep significance to the people's life, being in accordance with custom, with every day's activities, and the veneration of her fathers and forefathers." Is this not in the Romantic style of the early nineteenth century, perhaps in its German variety? But no, this was written and published in the Soviet Union, A.D. 1942!

Equally successful was the revival of prerevolutionary music. When Glinka's *Life for the Tsar* was performed the audience was enthusiastic and, according to Soviet papers, openly expressed its preference of this great old master to contemporary composers.[60] The authorities took due notice of this. It has been reported recently that Glinka's life and works formed the central theme of study in the Union Research Institute for Music.[61]

Reliable evidence also exists about the response of the public to the recent change in theaters. It is to be found in their repertoires, since the majority of theaters are only partly subsidized and have to make money by selling tickets, just as in "bourgeois" society. Here is a revealing statement. Every year each theater elaborates a "progressive plan of production" in which Soviet plays dominate. In actuality, classical plays are given much more frequently than Soviet plays, and moreover, the poorest day in the week (such as Monday) is chosen to give such plays as *Battleship Potemkin*.[62] Shortly before the outbreak of the war, the repertoire in Moscow's theaters was comprised of 75% of classical plays, with Ostrovsky, Chekhov, and Shakespeare in leading positions, and only 25% of postrevolutionary plays performed.

It is very interesting indeed that war has brought no change in this situation. A few really good plays have been produced, such as *Front*, by Korneichuk, and *The Russian People*, by K. Simonov. But Ostrovsky continues to dominate the theater. His plays are in greatest demand at the front, and today this is decisive. Classical operas have already been given in the restored theaters of Leningrad. In 1944–5, the repertoire in Moscow's Maly Theater consisted of four plays by Ostrovsky, Gogol's *Inspector General*, two Shakespearean dramas, a new historical play by Alexis Tolstoy dramatizing Ivan the Terrible's reign, and two plays on Soviet life in war conditions.[63]

Art offered to the people under the New Esthetic Policy pleased them in general. In this way one of the most important goals of The Great Retreat, to give the people satisfaction whenever possible, was fulfilled. Without a doubt this policy has successfully met the immediate requirements of the war period. Had war broken out in the midst of the period of "socialist realism," 1932 style, writers, painters, and composers would have met it entirely unprepared. After having been permitted, perhaps ordered, to renew the broken link with the past, they could very easily concentrate their efforts on the Second Patriotic War, glorifying its heroes, and elevating the sentiments which naturally emerge in a nation at war. Such essays as Alexis Tolstoy's *On the Motherland* will certainly remain in the treasury of Russian literature. Patriotic poems by K. Simonov and others will surely be recognized as significant contributions to victory.[64]

As to the adequacy of the New Esthetic Policy as a springboard for further cultural advance, an absolutely objective statement is not yet possible. Quite a few good novels, especially in the historical genre, have been written, such as *Peter the Great*, by Alexis Tolstoy, *Sevastopol Days*, by Sergeyev-Tsensky, and *Port Arthur*, by Stepanov, all stressing the heroism and steadfastness of the Russian people. But no great painting or sculpture is known to have adorned Russia's museums.

In 1943, an article appeared in the leading journal in the field which confirms the impression that, in the leader's opinion, Soviet literary production is still below expectation. "The people look at the Soviet writers with hope and expectation. What they want is not simple description, but insight; not lots of details, but the revelation of the New Man." [65] These things are just expected; consequently, they definitely are not yet here.

Regarding figurative arts, observers are struck by the dominance of "undigested classicism." Especially poor is the situation in architecture.

Soviet architects have done all they could to spoil their lines with classical gimcracks plastered over most of their façades. The new Tchaikovsky concert hall, the proportions of which are grand and lofty, is covered with ranks of inappropriate columns and extruding pieces of masonry and glass.[66]

In music, the recent production of Soviet composers has rather disappointed foreign listeners. Thus, for instance, Shostakovich's *Seventh Symphony* is generally found to be below expectations. The listeners and perhaps the critics as well are unaware that Shostakovich has to comply with the requirement of simplicity now paramount in Russia. Furthermore, are Prokofieff and others really Soviet composers? Have they not received their musical training and general culture in the stimulating atmosphere of the interplay of schools and trends characteristic of pre-Revolutionary Russia? And do their recent works show the way for future advance, as those of Tchaikovsky, Scriabin, or Stravinsky did in their time?

In the theater, additions to the old repertoires have been small indeed, and in these additions no actual foundation for further development may be found. "We are returning to the glorious tradition of Russian realism," [67] exclaimed Moskvin, one of Russia's greatest actors, in 1943. This is a glorious tradition indeed, but still a tradition.

The brilliant advance which, before the Revolution, had given world leadership to the Russian theater has been arrested. Up to the present day, no heir apparent has appeared in Russia.

The tentative conclusion is that despite the New Esthetic Policy, Russian art in all its branches is in danger of petrification, the death of every art.

8

What might be the final judgment about the development of Russian culture under the pressure of official management?

1. In all creative phases of culture but the technical one, the Communist Experiment was a signal failure. In the beginning the Communists made the mistake of identifying "revolutionary trends" in the different fields of art with their revolution. The gulf between the two became obvious when theories were put into practice. Moreover, the response of the public was entirely negative and, contrary to the intention of the Communists, art production became production for art's sake, without real significance for the planned "socialization of emotions." Later on, in a few specified fields such as literature, trends directly related to Communism were invented and imposed on the producers. But what was produced under such conditions was no longer art and, once more, the reaction of the public was hostile. Thus, the cultural phase of the Communist Experiment resulted in deadlock. Ways out of it were found only when the Experiment was abandoned.

2. The Great Retreat did not bring any change in the mechanism of culture management. This mechanism formed an essential part of the dictatorial structure, and therefore it could not be abandoned. The leaders knew very well that, in pre-Revolutionary Russia, science, literature, and art played a sig-

nificant part in the preparation of the Revolution, and they were not inclined to permit a similar development to undermine their authority.

3. But the mechanism of culture management could be used to give new impulsions to creative activity in accordance with changing requirements. Naturally, the directions had to receive different forms in the various phases of culture. In the realm of science, the new impulsions have been adjusted to the political necessity of vindicating the rule of the One and the return to nationalism. In some specified fields, such as jurisprudence and political economy, a movement back to the doctrines of the 'forties or 'fifties of the nineteenth century has taken place, depending on the maintenance of Marxism as the official philosophy.

4. In literature, art, music, and the theater, The Great Retreat produced a sweeping change resulting in the glorification of popular art and the revival of trends which dominated the middle of the nineteenth century; these trends appealed most to the esthetic level of the masses. In architecture, the style of the 'twenties of the nineteenth century was revived.

5. In this way, the end of appeasement and preparation for war has been well subserved. But the possibility of a further advance of Russian culture has become problematical.

CHAPTER X

POPULATION, SOCIAL CLASSES, MORES, AND MORALS:

The Revolution Reflected in the Mirror of Figures

1

THE PROCESSES STUDIED thus far in the course of our analysis of the Communist Experiment and The Great Retreat were the particular policies of the rulers and the direct reactions of the people. There are, however, social processes which arise from the various activities of the individuals and groups as their unpurposed, sometimes unexpected resultants.[1] Such processes should now be studied as the impact of these policies and reactions on the movement of the population, the class structure of society, the spread of culture in its most elementary form of literacy, the manner of living, and the respect of the people for the moral rules by which they were bound when the revolutionary disintegration started. Data relating to these important phases in the life of a nation may help us clarify some of the statements of the earlier chapters and prepare the establishment of a final balance sheet of the Revolution. For the latter purpose, data concerning the revolutionary period must be confronted with data expressing the conditions in Imperial Russia. Whenever possible, the data in question will be given quantitative expression, to make it a really solid background for the final judgments.

2

To begin with, what was the population movement before the Revolution and in the course of the revolutionary period of Russian history? *

* For the following, see Table 1 in Appendix II, and Chart V.

The only complete census in Imperial Russia took place on February 8, 1897. It showed a population of 106 million within the territory occupied by the Soviet Union on September 1, 1939; 12.2 million (11.5%) lived in towns and 93.8 million (88.5%) in rural districts.[2]

Seventeen years later, on January 1, 1914, i.e., just before the World War, the estimated population was 138.1 million (18.4% urban and 81.6% rural). This meant a yearly (geometric) increase rate of 16 per thousand; for the last three years before the war this rate was 20.0, 18.9 and 18.3 per thousand, respectively.

War resulted in a substantial decline in the rate of increase. On January 1, 1917, the estimated population of Russia was only 1.5% greater than in 1914, or equal to 140.2 million. Had the trend of the previous years continued, a population of 145 million could have been expected. The difference of about five

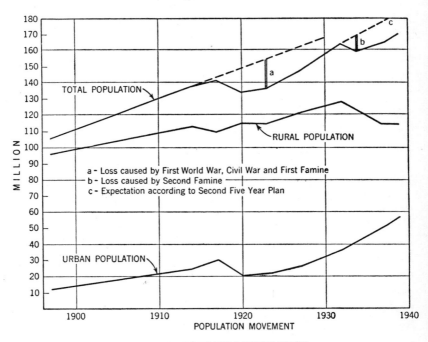

a - Loss caused by First World War, Civil War and First Famine
b - Loss caused by Second Famine
c - Expectation according to Second Five Year Plan

V. POPULATION MOVEMENT

million can be only partly explained by the direct loss of lives at the front. Another important demographic phenomenon was apparent; the percentage of the urban population suddenly rose to 21.7%, a figure which represented a peak for many years to come; the sudden accumulation of people in cities certainly played an important part in the outbreak and success of the revolution of 1917.

During the following years Russia was in the throes of a civil war and went through all the hardships of a speedy and reckless social transformation. A partial census, taken on August 28, 1920, in combination with estimates for those parts of the country where no census was taken, showed a population of 134.2-134.5 million, about six million less than in 1917. This was the demographic cost of the first three years of the revolution, leaving out of consideration the expectation of an increase proved both by earlier and later facts. The census disclosed a reversed migration movement of the population: only 14.7% were found to be living in towns, a percentage substantially smaller than in 1914. It is obvious that during the acute revolutionary period many people hoped to find refuge in rural districts, where the Communist methods of administration were applied in a less drastic manner than in the cities.

The figures for 1920 did not coincide with the bottom of the crisis engendered by the Communist experiment. As a result of the decrease of sowing areas, crops, and cattle, a famine broke out in 1921 during which, according to official figures, about five million persons died from starvation and epidemics.[3] The famine, however, did not strike the whole area of Russia or even its greater part. In some sections of the country the situation greatly improved from March 15, 1921, when the first Communist experiment was abandoned in favor of the New Economic Policy, which created much more favorable conditions of life. The ascending trend was resumed in many parts of the country, and this compensated for the losses mentioned above; the population of Russia on January 1, 1923, may be soundly estimated as equal to 135.9 million. However, the population would have been around 150 million if the pre-

war rate of increase had been resumed about the end of the
First World War. The difference of about 14 million can be
considered the approximate cost of the revolution.

The next few years were characterized by a very high rate
of increase of the population; it was 19.4 per thousand in 1924,
20.4 in 1925, and 22.7 in 1926. The census of December 17,
1926, showed a population of 147,027,915 of whom 26,314,114
(17.4%) lived in towns and 120,713,801 (82.6%) in rural districts. This total substantially surpassed that of prerevolutionary years, but the process of urbanization lagged behind
prerevolutionary progress; the percentage of the urban population did not reach that of 1914, not to mention that of the
abnormal 1917 figure.

The extraordinary speed of increase can be explained as follows: First, the consecutive disturbances of the World War,
the Civil War, and the famine created a large vacuum which
permitted a rapid increase of the population, without providing for *new* means of existence. Second, during the years of the
New Economic Policy, the social structure of rural Russia was
molded according to the pattern of the *mir* which, other things
being equal, encourages a fast increase of the rural population.

The census of 1926 was taken a short time before the trend
reversed. In 1927, the increase of the population was 21.7 per
thousand, and in 1928, 24.0; it dropped to 21.1 per thousand
in 1929, 19.0 in 1930, and 17.1 in 1931.[4] The point of saturation seemed to have been reached. Moreover, at that time the
New Economic Policy was abandoned and the Second Socialist
Offensive was begun, one of the principal elements of which—
the collectivization of farming—resulted in the decline of crops
and cattle similar to that of the years of War Communism.

The population of the Union of Soviet Socialist Republics
was about 163.2 million on January 1, 1932. For the following
years reliable data concerning the movement of the population
are almost completely lacking. However, there is sufficient evidence to show that during the following two years a demographic catastrophe took place which was for a long time
denied by official sources. In 1933 a number of foreign corre-

spondents published reports on the famine which they could observe. The series was opened by the Manchester *Guardian* in March, 1933. In April, Gareth Jones described the famine in the *Daily Express*. In June, Muggeridge made his observations in the *Morning Post* regarding the famine in the Ukraine and the Northern Caucasus; he wrote that he had seen almost deserted villages, whose inhabitants had died from hunger. On September 15, Duranty informed the readers of the New York *Times* that the mortality in the Ukraine had at least trebled because of the food shortage.[5] In October, 1933, Lang, correspondent of *Forward,* testified that large sections of Russia visited by him had suffered from a terrible famine.

Moreover, in the course of the events in question, the present writer was able to read and make excerpts from quite a few genuine letters coming from Russia. The reproduction of some of these excerpts will give a sufficient idea of the extent of the catastrophe and of the mechanism by which it was caused.

Ukraine, September, 1933: The harvest has been brought in, but we have not yet seen any bread.

Crimea, October, 1933: About the time of the harvest, nobody had a piece of bread. Miserable conditions persist; our children are sick and underfed. For their recovery, flour and fats are necessary, but we haven't them. A moment ago my son came home from school; he is hungry, but I have nothing to offer him but pumpkin.

Ukraine, November, 1933: The harvest was very poor. Men have suffered badly. They have forgotten what it means to eat bread. If nobody helps us, we are doomed to die. We are very weak.

Crimea, November, 1933: We have no roofs over our heads. There is no bread, no clothes. Only my sister and I are alive, all other family members having died. My child is four years old. He asks for some bread, but I have none to give him.

Ukraine, November, 1933: Our homestead was liquidated three years ago. Nothing has been left us. We have nothing to eat but weeds. Our misery is beyond description. So many die from hunger.

Crimea, November, 1933: We are poor in the extreme and have no place to live. Bread is a luxury. We never stop being hungry.

Ural, November, 1933: Many people have died from hunger. In our family two cousins, grandmother, and mother died first; sister

Ann was the last to die. In our village, many families have completely died out.

Ukraine, February, 1934: Everybody is miserably poor. No potatoes, no beets, no cabbage, almost no flour. Perhaps one month more and then there will be hunger death. No dogs or cats are left. Most people have died. Their huts have been torn to pieces for fuel. We do not understand how we managed to survive so long. But now the time to die seems to have come.

The famine was at first denied by the Communist government, but on December 5, 1935, a significant article appeared in *Pravda*. It concerned the Don and Kuban districts, which are numbered among the granaries of Russia, and contained the following sentence: "The wickedness of the class enemy reached such a point that many *kulaks* concealed thousands. of puds * of grain and let themselves and their children die of starvation." The story itself is quite incredible but permits the inference that in 1933 there actually were famine and starvation in the richest parts of Russia.

The actual number of hunger deaths in 1933 cannot be computed. However, the population of the Union of Soviet Socialist Republics on January 1, 1934, can be estimated at about 159 million, this figure being derived from that of the census of 1937. The difference between the actual population in the beginning of 1934 and a figure of 167.8 million, which would have been reached if only the prewar rate of increase had governed the population movement, shows that the demographic price of the Second Socialist Offensive was about eight million human lives. Still larger was the discrepancy between the actual increase of the population and the expectations of the Second Five-Year-Plan which, up to 1937, were officially considered as having been attained.

When Communist methods began to be mitigated, the situation gradually improved, and the upward movement of the population was resumed. The rate of natural increase was 12.3 in 1935, 14.1 in 1936, 21.0 in 1937, and 20.5 in 1938.[6] The relatively low figures for 1935–6 show that the process of recov-

* One pud is equal to 36.16 pounds avoirdupois.

ery after the famine of 1932–3 was much slower than that after the famine of 1921–2. The startling increase in 1937 obviously reflects the anti-abortion law of June 28, 1936.

Meanwhile, on January 6, 1937, a new census was taken in the Soviet Union. The findings of this census never were and never will be published; for in September, 1937, it was officially announced that the census had been disrupted by the activity of counterrevolutionary and Trotskyite wreckers.[7] A few important figures, however, were disclosed by Molotov at the Eighteenth Congress of the Communist Party in March, 1939. He gave one to understand that, in 1937, the population of the Soviet Union was 164.2 million, of whom 49.7 million lived in towns.

To make up for the alleged shortcomings of the census of 1937, still another census was taken on January 17, 1939. This time, in contradistinction to 1937, not only the actual population but also those persons who usually resided at a certain place but were absent the day of the census were to be counted by the census takers. This points to an important element in the situation, namely, that it was assumed that by eliminating persons of the above-mentioned category the wreckers of 1937 succeeded in obtaining an incredibly low population figure.[8] As early as June some preliminary figures were published which showed that 170,467,186 persons were found living in the Union, 55.9 million (32.8%) forming the urban and 114.6 (67.2%) the rural population.[9]

The change in the methods of registration of facts did not result in a substantial change in findings; the difference between the figures of 1937 and 1939 can be explained by the actual increase of the population during the two years separating the censuses. It is noteworthy that the difference between the "permanent" and the "actual" population (these are the officially used terms) did not exceed 0.75%.[10] The ruling group could do nothing but recognize that the population was much smaller than had been estimated. Unfortunately the data available does not permit the exact reconstruction of the dynamics of the rural and urban population. The following statements, however, may be made.[11]

One hundred and twenty and seven-tenths million persons lived in rural areas in 1926; the peak of the rural population was reached in the beginning of 1931, when 128.5 million lived outside of towns, and this despite the fact that during the years 1927–1930 5.1 million had already migrated to towns.

During the years 1931–1936 the rural population decreased from 128.5 million to 114.5 million. The migration figures are available only for the first five years of the above-mentioned period; their sum total is 12.6 million. There is some reason to believe that the speed of the process was the same in 1936; this gives a sum total of 15.1 million during six years. The comparison of the figures concerning migration and the decrease of the rural population shows that there was almost no natural increase of the rural population in the years 1931–1936. In 1937 and 1938 the rural population remained stable, for the entire natural increase was absorbed by the migration to towns. How large the natural increase was can only be estimated.

Still another process may be observed in rural areas, especially in 1932–1937, and that is a rapid decline of the peasant population. This decline can be deduced from the continuous decrease in the number of homesteads or families, the average membership of which could hardly have increased. There were in 1932, 24,483,000 homesteads with 117.5 million people in them. In 1937, the number of homesteads was only 19,930,000 with 95.7 million individuals in them. This decrease may be explained partly by the catastrophe of the years 1932–3, partly by the increase of the nonpeasant rural population which, from about 10.2 million in 1932, must have increased up to 18 million in 1937, as the result of a partial industrialization of rural areas and of the increase in the number of Soviet officers, of persons active in public services (education, medicine, and the like) and of workers of machine and tractor stations. Since the rural areas of Russia were overpopulated, the decrease of the peasant population could be considered as a process of positive social value, all reservations being made in regard to the methods applied to reach this improvement.

The urban population has more than doubled from 1926 to 1939. The increase was the result of the co-operation of three factors: (1) migration from rural areas, 18.5 million; (2) administrative transformation, 5.8 million; and (3) natural increase, 5.3 million.

The general conclusions of this study may be formulated as follows:

1. During the period of its existence the Soviet State was twice subjected to demographic catastrophe.

2. Each time the catastrophe was followed by a rapid restoration of the demographic equilibrium, though the speed of the process was not as great the second time as the first.

3. In both cases the catastrophes were accompanied by migration of the population away from areas where Communism was applied with greater intensity, to areas where the application was less intense.

4. The later years of the period studied were characterized by a partial improvement in the abnormal demographic situation in rural Russia.

3

As the result of the population movements studied above, the age composition of the Russian people has changed significantly.* In 1897, the population of Russia was characterized by an extraordinarily high percentage of children and youths. 22.8% of the total population was below the age of 8, and an additional 25.8% between the ages of 8 and 20, with only 13.4% above the age of 50. The census of 1926 showed a slight decrease in the relative number of children below the age of 8; they formed 21.7% of the population. Most drastic, however, was the decline of the group of children between 8 and 12: they formed 7.7% instead of 9.1% in 1897. The explanation is

* See Chart VI.

simple, since the group consisted of children born in the course of the First World War. In contradistinction to this decline, the group of persons between the ages of 12 and 20 formed 19.4% of the population as compared with 16.7% in 1897; this was a consequence of the very high birth rate in the years directly preceding the war. The percentage of old people (above the age of 50) did not substantially change, the figure being 13%.

The census of 1939 displayed a significant decrease in the younger groups. Those below the age of 8 formed only 18.6% of the population; this relatively small figure reflects the numerous deaths of children in the course of the second famine (1932–3) and the relatively low birth rate in subsequent years. The group between 8 and 12 now formed 9.7% of the population, but those between 15 and 20 were strongly underrepresented: they were only 8.9% instead of 11.6% in 1926. The low figure reflects the low birth rate and high infant mortality in the years of civil war and famine (1921–3). The percentage

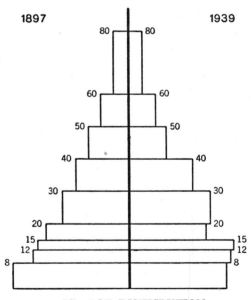

1897   1939

VI. AGE DISTRIBUTION

of the old people displayed a remarkable stability; once more the figure was 13%. The group of those between 20 and 50 was, in consequence, higher than ever. It formed 41.9% of the population, as compared with 36.2% in 1926 and 38.7% in 1897, a situation which, by the way, was very favorable for waging a totalitarian war, with its unlimited demands on manpower.

4

The change in the class composition of the population cannot be measured exactly, as change in rural-urban or age distribution can be.* It must first of all be described, and in this description these ideas will be used:

1. A social class is a horizontal stratum of an all-inclusive society, the members of which meet one another on equal terms and look on outsiders as being persons of "higher" or "lower" status.[12]

2. The criteria on which the distribution of the individuals among the social classes (stratification) depends vary in time and space. In each society definite criteria or social prestige are acknowledged and are ascribed different coefficients, so that the final judgment of a person's social status may be conceived as the solution of a specific "social equation."

3. In each society the individual classes are assigned different functions relating to political, economic, and cultural activities; the difference may be qualitative or quantitative.

4. Though as a rule members of the same social class easily associate (enter the specific relationship of "being acquainted") and intermarry, certain barriers within a social class sometimes exist. In such cases equality within the same class is still recognized, so that an eventual shift from one section to another is not considered promotion or demotion; but no social intercourse on friendly terms is permitted, or at least it is met with strong disapproval.

Officially, prerevolutionary Russia was an "estate society" —in other words, a modification of caste society in which the

* See Chart VII.

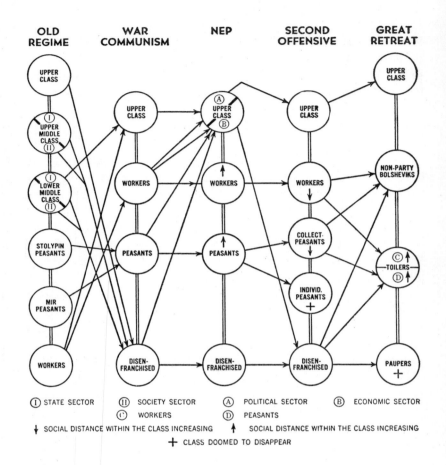

VII. SOCIAL CLASSES

social equation depended on birth. There were such estates as clergy, nobility, merchants-burghers, and peasants; but the basic estates were split into a number of subdivisions, the lines of demarcation lacked any precision, numerous groups were present which could not be located in the official scheme and, finally, it was almost impossible to formulate the specific rights and duties of the members of the individual groups. In actuality, pre-Revolutionary Russia was already a "class society" in the same meaning as Western societies are, with some survivals of the earlier caste system, but perhaps not so strong and conspicuous as in Germany or Austria-Hungary. Five main social classes formed that society.

The first, the upper class, centered around the Imperial court and consisted of the higher bureaucracy, high-ranking military men (especially of the Imperial Guard), the higher clergy, and that part of the nobility which had preserved wealth, especially in the form of landed estates. With some qualification, highly successful professional men, businessmen, and artists could be considered as also belonging to this class. In contrast with a consistently "capitalist" society, wealth and income were not the only criteria of upper-class position; being born into the class was at least as important and usually was conducive to fair advance within the bureaucracy or the military machine. Fine education was a necessary requisite (among other things, command of at least one foreign language, usually French). The caste-for-class compensation phenomenon was well known: members of impoverished noble families married "bourgeois" heiresses and thus preserved their social status. But members of impoverished noble families who failed in bureaucracy or the Army eventually lost their status.

The second, the upper middle class, comprised the middle grades of bureaucracy, the remainder of the military and professional men, part of the clergy, and businessmen, and the owners of smaller estates. Once more, education was a necessary criterion, but it did not have to be so refined as that of the upper class. High school education was sufficient and, although knowledge of a foreign language was widespread, it was not a prerequisite. Together with the upper class, this class could be opposed to the rest of the population as "educated people" to "plain people." The two classes consisted of men permeated with the Petrinian civilization, a merger of old Russia with Western Europe, whereas the "plain people" continued living within the pre-Petrinian civilization, being only superficially influenced by the West.

Within the upper middle class a barrier of the type discussed above was present: the bureaucracy and the military men were frequently opposed as "the State" to "society," represented primarily by the professional men, whereas the landed gentry and the businessmen were divided between the two compartments according to their personal preference. In the pre-Revolutionary assessment of social forces, the former section of this class belonged to the same camp as the upper class, and the latter considered itself as supplying a natural leadership to the "plain people."

The third, the lower middle class, was predominantly urban and was separated from the preceding group on a basis of lower income or lower education or, more exactly, by a lack of contamination by the Petrinian civilization. Artisans, small shopkeepers, the rural clergymen, persons occupying the lowest ranks in the bureaucracy, and the so-called "semi-intellectuals" * formed this class. A barrier similar to that just mentioned existed here also.

The fourth class comprised the great mass of the peasants. At about the time of the revolution a substantial differentiation within the group existed: three levels—rich, medium, and poor —were commonly recognized, the first hiring labor to help till their allotments, the third being compelled to spend a large part of their time as hired workers on the landlords' or the rich peasants' fields, and the second being in the state of economic equilibrium, hiring no workers and looking for no jobs. With Stolypin's agrarian reform, the dissolution of the agrarian

---

* Semi-intellectuals are persons who have received some training, usually technical, and who carry out auxiliary functions in the administration, business, or the professions.

communities began, and the rich and medium-level peasants enriched themselves, whereas the poorer ones were driven towards the status of proletarians.

The fifth, the proletariat, predominantly urban, was, in Russian society, a relatively new phenomenon.[13] Though young, this class was well differentiated: the social distance between the skilled labor of older industrial centers, such as St. Petersburg, and the unskilled labor of the new centers was large. The higher strata of the class were receptive to the propaganda of the revolutionary leadership evolving from the society sector of the middle class, and were at least as "class-conscious" as the proletariat in advanced industrial societies.

Unfortunately, it is impossible to give an exact quantitative distribution of the population among the classes. Since the peasant class almost coincided with the rural population, on the eve of the Revolution about 82 per cent of the population must have belonged to it. The proletariat made up no more than six per cent of the population. As everywhere, the upper class was very small comprising, together with the upper and lower middle classes, about 12 per cent of the population. The smallness of the middle class, as compared with such a "bourgeois" country as France, was striking. But the structure just described was highly dynamic; mighty social processes were influencing the nation, dislocating the peasant class, undermining the upper class, and giving increased importance to the middle classes and the proletariat.

The February Revolution gave rise to a social order which was not given time to crystallize, since it was once more overthrown by the October Revolution of the same year. Tentatively, it may be said that the February Revolution lifted to the highest level the "society sector" of the former middle classes, and ascribed highest prestige to former participation in the revolutionary movement instead of to birth, wealth, or participation in the Imperial government. But the prestige of education remained intact, and no immediate change in the respective positions of "educated people" and "plain people" followed.

The October Revolution was tantamount to a complete re-evaluation of the criteria of social prestige. The nationalization of land, trade, and industry and the socialization of the professions (by transforming professional men into State functionaries) resulted in the abolition of wealth and income as criteria of prestige; moreover, the fact of having previously belonged to one of the economically privileged groups, beginning with the lower middle class, became a symptom for negative rating. Within the symptom of participation in the revolutionary movement, a discrimination was introduced: only participation in the ranks of the victors, the Communist Party, was deemed of positive value; participation in the antagonistic groups became another negative value.* Education was now a symptom of dubious and rather negative value; more often than not it was considered as circumstantial evidence for "bourgeois" mentality.

The impact of this rescaling of values on the individual groups was tremendous. The former upper class, the State sector of the upper and lower middle classes, and the bulk of the society sectors of these classes fell to the very bottom of the social pyramid. The proletariat exchanged positions with the peasant class; it was proclaimed to be the privileged class of the new society and was reinforced by quite a few former artisans and intellectuals, but it lost a substantial contingent through migration to the countryside. A new upper class arose, centered around some subgroups within the society sector of the former upper and lower middle classes. Thus, the first socialist society, the child of War Communism, was born. It consisted of the following four classes:

1. The upper class, comprising the upper level of the Communist Party machine, a few "fellow-travelers" originating from the society sector of the former middle class, especially from the semi-intellectuals, and a few recruits selected from the peasantry and the proletariat. This class received the highest social prestige, the totality of political power, and the

---

* The earlier participation in political life on the "wrong" side could be made up by timely joining of the bandwagon (late in 1917 or early in 1918).

highest income possible in a society where the Communist creed officially became paramount. Obviously, it was not granted ownership of the means of production, but actual management of the industrial equipment of the country and indirect management of its agricultural equipment became its social function, as well as did leadership in cultural activity.

2. The proletariat, consisting of "workers and employees," naturally of the State only, since no private bureaucracy could survive the wholesale nationalization of the means of production. A large part of the former proletarians, in addition to some former intellectuals and semi-intellectuals, formed it. High social prestige was officially ascribed to it, but it did not participate in political power, and the income of its members was on the survival level. Within the class the tendency was towards equalization: the same Labor Code regulated the status of workers and employees, and the differential between highest and lowest wages tended to disappear. When, because of the desperate food situation, the system of rationing had to be introduced, higher rations were awarded to manual than to intellectual workers.

3. The peasant class, formed out of the former peasantry plus refugees from the cities, proletarians, and even intellectuals. The division within the class created by the Stolypin reform was abolished, and all the peasants returned to the traditional agrarian community structure. Within the class the trend was towards equalization. To the thus unified class, the actual monopoly of the means of agricultural production was ascribed, but the individual members were denied the right to dispose of their shares, and the agrarian communities were limited in their rights through the overlordship of the new upper class. When the urban-rural migration of the early revolutionary years was terminated, membership in the class returned to the hereditary type: in the future only those individuals who were born into a peasant family could become members.

4. The class of the disenfranchised, thus called because its members were deprived of the right to participate in elections. To this class belonged the members of the former upper and

upper and lower middle classes who did not secure positions within the new upper class, the proletariat, or the peasantry. The status of the members was approximately the lowest in the caste society. Only the lowest social functions, primarily manual work, were considered becoming for them. When distributing goods according to the ration-card system, the government either ignored them or gave them an infinitesimal share. Whether the status was hereditary was not quite clear and, since the order existed for a few years only, the problem was never finally solved.

Once more only approximate quantification is possible. The peasant class somewhat increased in size and formed about 85% of the whole. The new upper class was as small as that of Imperial Russia. Perhaps 3% of the population were disenfranchised,[14] and 12% belonged to the proletariat, comprising not only the manual workers but also the new bureaucracy, minus its top level.

The social structure just described was short-lived. Under the NEP the following trends could be observed relating to vertical social mobility (the movement of individuals on the social ladder).

The new upper class of the War Communism period did not disappear but, in addition to it, another group emerged at the top of the social pyramid. These were the "nepmen," or the individuals who had to manage "the private sector of economics." The creation of this "private sector" was full of implications: once more, income started playing a significant part in social classification, and since part of the enterprises were returned to their former owners, birth, not in the meaning of titles of nobility, but in the "bourgeois" meaning of having been born into a well-to-do family, also resumed playing its part. Furthermore, education resumed its role in social classification.

The nepmen were not, however, simply introduced into the upper class. Under the NEP an almost insurmountable barrier existed between the two sectors of the upper class, one forming the summit of the political machinery, the other the economic top of the structure. Members of the latter enjoyed higher incomes, but members of the former drew higher prestige from their location in the immediate vicinity of the power center. The two criteria of social prestige were ascribed approximately the same value, but it was understood that the two groups could not merge: one had to be either a member of the ruling *élite* or a member of the "Soviet bourgeoisie." To make the situation clear, the nepmen were disenfranchised, so that they could not participate in the determination of policy.

Owing to the revival of industry, a slight backward movement from the peasant class into that of the workers took place, which meant, in the new social setup, an ascending social movement. Within each of the two classes the trend reversed from equalization to differentiation. To the workers and employees, wages once more were paid according to services rendered, and intellectual work was now considered to be of higher service than manual. Among the peasant class, differentiation advanced rapidly owing to permission to rent-lease land and hire agricultural workers. A group of rich peasants, now called *kulaks*,[15] emerged; but, at the same time and at the opposite end of the social ladder, a group of poor peasants reappeared—marginal men earning their living as farm hands. The process was so quick that one cannot but suspect that, during the preceding period, equalization had not been so complete as it officially seemed to be. From among the rich peasants of the Imperial period, probably quite a few succeeded in preserving at least part of their wealth in the form of cattle and machinery. Other individuals had performed the miracle of "primary capitalist accumulation" in conditions where accumulation of wealth was considered an antisocial act. Now that differentials in wealth were legalized, the hidden differentiation of the previous period became open.

The higher level within the peasant class displayed the tendency to restore landlordship destroyed by the first agrarian revolution. There were peasants who tilled hundreds of acres and possessed thousands of domestic animals. These rich peasants, the rural counterpart of the nepmen, had some trouble with the local authorities. However, some of them invented an ingenious technique to overcome the difficulty. Taking only a small allotment in the *mir,* a rich peasant pretended to be a pauper and, officially, was engaged by a real pauper as his hired hand; the contract was registered in the local Soviet and gave the desired status of a pauper to the rich man; this made him an acceptable candidate for official positions. Using his actual influence in the village, often bribing the members of the local Party cell, he managed to be elected chairman of the local Soviet; as such, he was able to report himself as a man absolutely deprived of means and therefore not subject to taxation, which in the higher brackets was heavy. On the other hand, the real pauper whose "hand" the rich man officially was, was instructed to hire workers and rent land; he appeared to be a little capitalist and was disenfranchised, which did not worry him, since the rich man provided for his livelihood. All these manipulations were possible only on the basis of the strong community ties which continued to prevail in rural districts, and of strong and corporate opposition to the Communist ideas.

The class of disenfranchised did not disappear but decreased numerically, having lost quite a few members of the new upper class. Moreover, the treatment of the members of this class was more lenient than during the former period, and the hereditary character of the group was not emphasized.

On the basis of the census of December 17, 1926, the following percentage distribution of the social groups was computed by the Communist leaders: workers and employees, 17%; peasants, without the *kulaks,* 76%; nepmen and *kulaks,* 4.5%; others (mainly the disenfranchised), 2.5%. The group distribution of the census does not completely coincide with that in the text; especially, it does not help in establishing the size of the upper class. The numerical predominance of the peasant class continued to be striking.

The years 1928–9 witnessed another reversal of the trend in vertical social mobility—a reversal as drastic as that of 1921. The nepmen class was destroyed through confiscatory taxation, open confiscation, or deportation, and sometimes execution of its members for actual or alleged offenses. Those who were not physically exterminated were deprived of their high social status and returned to the bottom.

Within the workers' and employees' class, equalization was once more the rule, with some advantage in favor of manual labor. As in the first phase of the revolution, education was rather a negative than a positive symptom in social classification.

Within the peasant class one of the most reckless "social executions" known to history took place; overnight, the *kulaks* were deprived of their belongings, movable and immovable, and reduced to the state of paupers. Within the rest of the class a line was drawn separating the relatively privileged "collectivized" peasants from the underprivileged "individual" ones.

Towards the end of the period the leaders proclaimed that social classes had been abolished and that classless society had emerged. Actually, Russia was as far from the social ideal of Marxism as she ever had been. The social structure was this: the top level was occupied by the political sector of the former period, the economic having been destroyed. Once more, the political leadership was indeed very similar to a class, since it disposed directly of all means of production in industry and, indirectly, in agriculture; its standard of life was substantially higher than that of any other social stratum, though no ostentation was possible, since it would have contradicted the official achievement of classless society; though the group was not hereditary, membership depended, as a rule, on the historical fact of having been among the followers of the Supreme Leader for a sufficiently long time.

Immediately below came the Labor class, including those intellectuals who did not rise to the upper class. They had to work hard with poor remuneration, but they still were better off than the peasants, since the tremendous momentum given to industry had abolished unemployment. However, those who did not comply with the regulations or who expressed doubts about the soundness of the official policy were dropped from this class and fell to the bottom of the social scale.

Below the workers were the peasants. Among them the collectivized unit formed a relatively privileged group, in that corn levies were a little lighter in collective than in individual farms, and improved machinery, fertilizers, selected seed, and the like were distributed exclusively among the collective farms, in order to create an additional stimulus for joining them.[16] The lower group was that of the individual peasants. The society of the period of the Second Socialist Offensive resembled that of Imperial Russia in that two groups of peasants existed, one more and the other less favored by the government. However, the individual peasants of the years around 1930 were, actually, members of old-fashioned *mirs*, whereas around 1910, individual peasants were those who had separated their allotments from the *mirs*. In both cases the underprivileged group was doomed to disappear.

Membership in the two classes of peasantry remained hereditary but it could be forsaken by migration to the city and enrollment into the labor class. This step was, in practice, irreversible, since collective farms were not supposed to accept applicants for membership from the outside.

Finally, the social bottom was occupied by the disenfranchised, or the outcasts. Numerically, the group was much larger than under War Communism. It was composed not only of the survivors of the upper classes of the old regime, but also of survivors from among the nepmen, ruined by the second wave of nationalization, and of the *kulaks*, ruined by wholesale collectivization. Additionally, the class was augmented by those members of the Labor class or of the peasantry who made attempts to resist the official policy, or who expressed opinions incompatible with the official one. The status of the class was that of complete deprivation of rights: disenfranchisement, prohibition from working in governmental shops, no ration cards, and no higher education for the children. This time the group was definitely treated as a hereditary caste; very often inquiries were undertaken regarding the ancestry of the pupils of high schools and Universities, and the establishment of the fact that, say, an aunt of the person in question had been a shopkeeper or the like was a sufficient reason for expulsion.

According to Molotov, in 1934 the distribution of the population among the classes was: workers and employees, 28.1%; collectivized peasants, 45.9%; individual peasants, 22.5%; *kulaks,* 0.1%; others (mainly the disenfranchised), 3.4%.[17] As always, the upper class was included in that of the workers and employees. Very probably, the group of the disenfranchised was much larger than stated. The proportion of peasants had subtantially decreased, owing to the industrialization and rural-urban migration throughout the period.

Like the First Socialist Society, the Second was not given the opportunity to receive a definitive shape since, beginning with 1934, the social structure of Russia was submitted to another reconstruction through The Great Retreat.

First, the upper class which had emerged as the result of the October Revolution was submitted to the ordeal of a wholesale purge.[18] Firing squads terminated the lives of quite a few persons who, in the course of the previous phases of the Revolution, had been near the top. Others were demoted and allotted positions at the very bottom. Vacant positions, naturally, were filled by individuals emerging from other social strata.

Moreover, a new social class arose which later on was officially designated as "the Nonparty Bolsheviks." * Since it was assigned a position immediately below the upper class and above any other social group, it can be compared with the middle class of capitalist society. The members of the new group were recruited mainly from "intellectual workers" of the previous period, but quite a few manual workers, peasants, and especially disenfranchised persons were permitted to join.†

---

* This is a term introduced by Stalin in May, 1935, and heavily loaded with meaning. "Bolshevik" is the older designation of the ruling party; therefore, taken at face value, the term is a typical *contradictio in adjecto.* The term designates a man who, though not a member of the party (of the only party permitted to exist) shares its ideals, serves them well, and consequently must be ranked approximately as high as a party member.

† The so-called "Stakhanov movement" was used as a device for selection.

The main characteristic of the class is a relatively high income in the form of salary for services, either in administration, industry, or in activities which in liberal society are performed by professional men, such as doctors, actors, musicians, authors, artists, lawyers, etc. Thus, income as well as education have become undisputed criteria of social prestige. But the class has not been granted participation in political decisions, which has remained the monopoly of the upper class. It received, however, the function of managing the industrial, commercial, and cultural institutions of the country, according to the directions of the policy-making agencies consisting of upper-class men.

The line of demarcation between this class and the upper class is not sharp. No official or unofficial obstacle could prevent the members of the two groups from carrying on social intercourse. On the other hand, the two groups display the tendency to isolate themselves from the rest of society and to transmit their high social status to their children. Two devices are used: personal savings and the equipping of children for succession in the group functions. Saving and investing in state bonds is not only permitted but is socially commended; the bonds may be transmitted to the children of the actual group members, thus guaranteeing them a higher income and thereby an enhanced social status. Another form of saving is that of acquiring buildings, both in cities and in the countryside. The law restricts each person to one house, but cases are reported in which this law has been evaded, with the approval of the government.

On the other hand, the decree of October 2, 1940, which abolished free education in the upper grades of high school and in institutions of higher learning, is highly symptomatic. Since the managerial functions of the new *élite* presuppose high-grade training, it is obvious that the new *élite* is creating a high barrier to protect their children from two close competition with children born into other classes.

The rise of the Nonparty Bolshevik class was one of the main social processes characterizing the period of The Great Retreat. Another was the equalization of the classes of the workers and peasants which was officially performed by the Stalin Constitution of 1936. Within the class of workers an unprecedented differentiation of income levels has taken place. Within the peasant class the difference between the collectivized and individual peasants has lost its significance, since in practice almost all the homesteads have been collectivized. Membership in the class is hereditary; one is a member of a collective farm when born into a peasant family. However, the social status of a peasant may be exchanged for another one; he may be offered a position which makes him a member of the Nonparty Bolshevik group or be transferred into the proletarian class; such a transfer may either be made on his initiative or on the basis of the law of October 2, 1940, on the State Labor Reserve. No shift from the worker class to the peasant class is possible, but members of the class may be rewarded, for special services, by transfer into the Nonparty Bolshevik group.

In addition to this, a group has reappeared which is more typical of "bourgeois" than of socialist society—that of the artisans. Membership in it is, in the majority of cases, derived from participation in the lower middle class of pre-Revolutionary society, which thus reappears on the surface after twenty years of oblivion. The group is socially equal to those of the workers and peasants.

With the Stalin Constitution the group of the disenfranchised has officially ceased to exist. Unofficially, it continues to exist, since those members of this group who have not been permitted to join the Nonparty Bolshevik group are assigned no social function whatsoever, and in a society where income is once more the main criterion of social classification, they naturally continue to rest at the bottom of the social pyramid. However, the hereditary character of the class has been abolished: it has been explicitly stated that sons and daughters of the former *kulaks*, nepmen, and the like may receive higher education and be appointed to any position. Consequently, the group will disappear when the last individuals now belonging to it die.

To sum up the changes in the social structure that have

taken shape under The Great Retreat, the following propositions may be formulated:

1. On the eve of World War II, Russian society was once more a stratified society consisting of definite social classes.

2. The following criteria of social status were recognized: (a) the fact of durable and loyal participation in the ruling *élite,* especially since Stalin's final victory; (b) higher education providing efficiency in those activities which are ascribed the highest value by the ruling *élite;* and (c) income, without distinction of its sources.

3. The social strata are: (a) the ruling *élite* plus a few fellow-travelers; (b) the Nonparty Bolsheviks; (c) the "toilers," consisting of the workers and employees, the peasants and the artisans; and (d) the paupers, or the formerly disenfranchised.

4. These groups are real social classes: membership in the peasant group is hereditary, and membership in the two upper groups displays the tendency to become hereditary, with the possibility of partial rejuvenation through outsiders selected by these groups. Definite social functions are assigned to these groups.[19]

5. Vertical social mobility is much less intense than it was ten years ago. Ascent depends on recognition of services by the leading group.

Approximate quantification is possible on the basis of statements made by Molotov in 1939, and on the findings of the census of January 17, 1939.[20] In 1937, there were in Russia 1,751,000 "enterprise managers," 250,000 engineers, 80,000 agronomists, 80,000 scientists, 159,000 actors and artists, 297,-000 journalists, 132,000 physicians, and 46,000 judges and prosecutors—a total of 2,800,000 persons in positions eligible for membership in the two upper classes. An additional 2,500,-000 were found in the bureaucracy. Assuming that their families consisted on the average of four persons, the size of the two classes may have been 20,000,000, or 13% of the population. This is, however, only a maximum: quite a few persons in the categories mentioned do not belong to the ruling or the Non-party Bolshevik groups, their income being insufficient. The upper class has been estimated to number 800,000 to 1,000,000 persons,[21] with the middle class consisting, perhaps, of 8,000,-000, or 5% of the population.

In 1939, the number of peasants (both collectivized and individual) was found to be 78,600,000, or 46.4% of the population. This signified a very substantial decrease both in absolute and in relative figures as compared with previous periods.

The number of "nontoilers" and persons of indeterminate occupation has appeared to be 1,200,000, or 7% of the population. This is probably the approximate size of the group of the formerly disenfranchised.[22]

Such is the society which has evolved out of a quarter of a century of revolution. In this society, as in every post-revolutionary one, some elements of the *ancien régime* have been merged with elements directly derived from the revolution, whereas still others may be considered as a social invention of the post-revolutionary period. Directly derived from the *ancien régime* is, in the majority of cases, one's location in the peasant class and perhaps also in the artisan group. Directly derived from the revolution is one's position in the ruling group. Directly depending on post-revolutionary invention is one's position in the new middle class.

This post-revolutionary society is still in flux. Further changes are probable. But the velocity of change has substantially decreased, and for the individual the chance of gaining higher social status is no greater than in bourgeois society. Since this velocity is one of the best criteria of revolution, later historians will probably say that the Russian Revolution as such lasted from 1917 to 1940.

5

In the fluctuations of the class composition of the Russian population, the most dramatic features of the Revolution have come to the surface. Almost as dramatic have been the efforts of the Russians under the Soviet regime to overcome the appalling illiteracy of the masses.*

As has been shown in Chapter II, in 1914 the index of literacy of the Russian people stood somewhere near 40%. Its fluctuations in the course of the Revolution can be studied on the basis of the censuses of 1920, 1926, and 1939.

The census of 1920 was only partial and its results are only partly comparable to earlier and later data. From a report submitted to the Tenth All-Russian Congress of the Soviets (December 22-27, 1922) the following data may be obtained: in European Russia proper (without the Ukraine and White Russia) plus Northern Caucasus and Western Siberia, the index of literacy for men was 31.8% in 1897 and 40.9% in 1920; for women, 13.1% in 1897 and 24.4% in 1920.

We may infer that the years 1914–1920 were characterized by a decline of literacy, a natural phenomenon in a period of war, civil war, and revolution.

Six years later the situation was substantially different, and data relating to it are as complete and reliable as those for the year 1897. The census of December 17, 1926, established that from a total population of 114 million above the age of ten, 58.2 million, or 51.1% were literate. The differentials observed in 1897 remained, but were attenuated: 66.5% of the men *vs.* 37.1% of the women, 76.3% of the urban *vs.* 54.2% of the rural population were literate. The differential between metropolitan Russia and semicolonial territories remained very high; the index of literacy was only 10.6% in the Uzbek and 12.5% in the Turkmen Republic.

The age distribution of literate persons was substantially different from that of 1897. The maximum of literacy was attained by the age group from 20-30, and a more detailed study shows that those between the ages of 25-30 were more literate than those between the ages of 20-25. Persons who were 25-30 in 1926 had been born in 1901–1906 and, as a rule, had entered school between 1909 and 1914. Once more, facts confirm the proposition that in 1914 a climax was reached, to be followed

* See Tables 6 and 7 in Appendix II and Chart VIII.

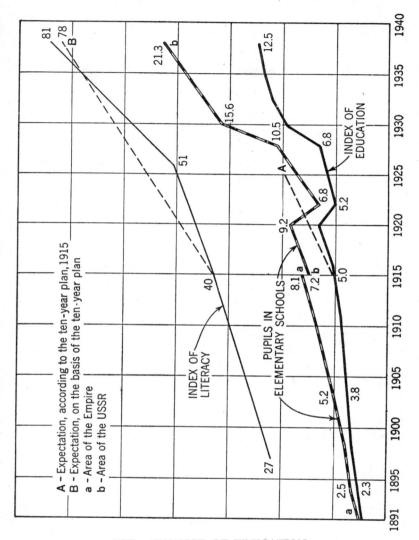

VIII. ADVANCE OF EDUCATION

The number of pupils in elementary schools is shown in millions. The term "index of education" is defined in the text (page 34).

by a period of decline and to be surpassed only in the late 'twenties.

The census of 1939 has yielded the following figures: [23] 81.1% of the population above the age of ten were found to be literate. The differentials once more substantially decreased: 90.8% of the men vs. 72.6% of the women, 89.5% of the urban vs. 76.8% of the rural population had achieved literacy. Still, approximately one-third of the women in the countryside remained illiterate, chiefly in the semicolonial territories. However, in these same territories a remarkable general progress was achieved: the index of literacy was 67.8% in the Uzbek and 67.2% in the Turkmen Republic.

As regards the age distribution, 54.4% of the illiterate men and 50.8% of the illiterate women were above the age of 50 (born before 1889 and having reached school age before 1897). From this statement and the general age distribution of the population in 1939, it appears that among the population between the ages of 10 and 50, 95% of the men and 83% of the women, or 89% of the two sexes were literate. This means that in the Army raised by the Soviet government to resist Germany there were no longer any illiterate persons.

6

A revolution necessarily affects the people's mores and morals. This is especially true in the case of a programmatic revolution such as the Russian has been because, in the course of such revolutions, the leaders try to impose new manners of living and moral rules on the people. They usually meet enthusiastic support on the part of certain groups, but in the minority only, while the majority either continue living as they did or reluctantly and only partly follow suit. To establish the amount and distribution of the departures from habitual conduct caused by the Communist Revolution belongs to the most arduous tasks of the inquirer. What follows cannot but be a preliminary sketch.

The realization of the Communist blueprint was conducted

in specific conditions—those of destruction, violence, and class war. Disorder, even chaos, resulted. But in the eyes of the leaders and their followers, this was a kind of Sacred Chaos, to be memorized by later generations in heroic sagas. The victors, at least officially, were proletarians living in conditions of over-crowding and filth, lacking sufficient education and good manners. According to the Doctrine, they gained victory not only for themselves, but for the nation, virtually for humanity. Before the achievement of victory throughout the world they could not think of any improvement in their living conditions. A kind of Communist asceticism consequently arose; wearing rags, being disheveled and dirty became a virtue; seeking entertainment, social intercourse, or romance became a sin. Naturally, Sacred Chaos and Communist Asceticism became closely associated with Communism as such, though actually there is no necessary connection between them. In any case, anyone who wanted to "belong" had to be dirty and disdain order or any kind of superfluous embellishment of life, just as the opposite traits must be displayed by anyone who wants to "belong" in typical bourgeois society.

In general, the tendency has persisted throughout the Communist Experiment, though under the NEP a certain relaxation took place, and timid efforts to restore some features of the pre-Revolutionary manner of living were made. One can best learn about the general style of life under the Second Socialist Offensive from a few incidents which occurred when the tide was turning and that style started being denounced by the leaders—after they had changed their minds and directions. Then, it was revealed that in Kuschevka (Northern Caucasus) the Communists never visited film shows, they stayed away from gatherings in the Commons, and did not take part in athletic performances, since they believed that this would cause trouble. In Odessa, being unshaven and poorly clad was considered a symptom of seriousness and a businesslike attitude. A group of Young Communists inquired whether they were allowed to pay social visits, enjoy various kinds of entertainment, play accordions, and the like; they asked these questions because their mentors told them that young men should stay home and listen to broadcasts on instructive topics.[24]

The aspect of austerity did not stop even with children's toys. *Izvestia* described a game called "I am an atheist, and you?" sold in the leading stores of Moscow. The instruction (addressed to boys ten to twelve years of age) began: "The economic oppression of the labor class results in oppression in all realms of life; in the intellectual realm, the instrument of oppression is religion." [25]

Another feature of the revolutionary folkways was totalitarian leveling. Since everyone had to live in conditions of proletarian austerity, there was no reason for any difference in the external appearance of one individual as compared with others. To merge into collectivity—that was the best way of complying with the style of the epoch.[26] One of the external manifestations was the abolition of all kinds of ranks and titles in which Imperial Russia was rather rich.

In the particular field of sexual mores contradictory tendencies appeared. The leaders never preached sexual laxity, but neither had they reason to insist on bourgeois views on the subject. Among the younger generation the following views started being identified with Communism: sexual life was merely the expression of one of the basic urges and should be treated as such, discarding the nonsense of romance and artificial repression; girls who refused to indulge in sexual promiscuity were frowned upon as having preserved bourgeois morals and were threatened with expulsion from the Young Communist League.[27] There were Communists who expressed astonishment when women whom they approached rebuked them on the "pretext" of loving their husbands and desiring to remain faithful; was this not continuing the bourgeois tradition? On the foundation of such views on sex, quite a few young men became what later on was called "fluttering scoundrels," swinging from one love affair to another without considering the consequences for the girls and the probability of children. Around 1930, making sex gratification a kind of complementary award for civic virtue was preached. In quite a few novels of the period of the Second Socialist Offensive the girl declined a proposal because the boy "had not fulfilled the norm of production," or told him that she would consider falling in love with him if he could prove his valor by rounding up and denouncing a couple of counterrevolutionary wreckers.

It must be emphasized that these features of life were not inherent parts of the Communist blueprint. But since they emerged simultaneously with the Communist Experiment, in the minds of the people they were identified with it. Only a few appreciated these innovations; the majority saw in them one of the most unpleasant, almost intolerable aspects of the Communist Experiment.

One of the features of The Great Retreat was the rejection of these accessories of the Experiment and the return to normalcy in this particular aspect. This certainly was one of the most popular aspects of the Retreat. It was, however, not so much retreat from Communism as the destruction of a social configuration which had grown simultaneously with attempts to realize the blueprint. Obviously, this was one of the concessions which the government could grant wholeheartedly, since actually it conceded nothing and gained very much.

In the beginning of The Great Retreat, Stalin himself gave directions to the idea that under socialism life should be beautiful and joyous. In consequence, Soviet papers subscribed to these views: "We endorse beauty, smart clothes, chic coiffures, manicures . . . Girls should be attractive. Perfume and make-up belong to the 'must' of a good Comsomol girls . . . Clean shaving is mandatory for a Comsomol boy." [28] To help the people to realize these new directions, conferences started being held debating such questions as clean shaving, smart dressing and well-washed hands. Time and again there were curious incidents. Thus, for instance, at one of such conferences this question was asked from the floor: "Why is the reporter unshaven and his clothes filthy?" In Uman (Ukraine) a man refused to get rid of his beautiful black beard. A "social boycott" was or-

ganized against him, and the central authorities had to interfere and explain that no crime was involved in the man's conduct.[29]

Moreover, these directions were given: "Young people must
gather and dance." [30] The young people carried out this edict
enthusiastically, and soon after its publication it was reported
that winter vacations were spent by boys and girls in dancing
to exhaustion. Soon quite a few dancing schools were opened
in Moscow and they were well attended: early in 1936, the
number of students was reported to be 6,000. Unfortunately,
many of the teachers were dilettantes—bookkeepers, psychol-
ogists, and so on.[31] In the summer of 1935, carnivals started
being arranged in Moscow's parks. At one of them there were
people disguised as boyars,* pages, or wearing dominoes; some
appeared as Pushkin's heroes; one impersonated the great national poet himself. Similar doings were reported in 1936.[32]

When smart dressing became an official slogan, the public
suddenly realized how ugly and monotonous their wearing
apparel was. They also discovered that their furniture was ugly
and poor. Realizing this, they started demanding improvements, and to meet these demands and improve the esthetical
value of Soviet production, a journal started appearing under
the title, *Fashion*.[33] Cases were, however, reported where
"backward" provincial authorities opposed the change in the
style of living. Thus, in Krivoy Rog, when young people started
dancing one of the Caucasian dances, the authorities thought
that this was too much and had the dancers arrested.[34]

But in general the change was drastic. Already in the fall of
1935, a French visitor was struck by the orderly conduct and
cleanliness of the Moscow crowds, the obvious care of women
in their dress, the courtesy of the public in the theater, and so
on. Other foreigners reported the appearance of a kind of "new
aristocracy" at horse races, where they occupied the best seats
and tried to imitate the conduct of the upper classes in bourgeois society in dress and manners.[35] Fashion houses were

---

* Boyars formed the higher nobility of Russia up to the end of the seventeenth century.

opened in Moscow. Resurrected restaurants invited the public to come and enjoy delicious food. In these places cooks, waiters, and managers of the good old times suddenly found employment, and were very well remunerated indeed, since they had to teach their art to young men and women without the slightest idea about the refinements possible in this phase of life.[36]

Another feature of The Great Retreat was the abolition of the totalitarian leveling characteristic of the Communist Experiment. This phase of the Retreat was best manifested in the revival of such "reactionary" institutions as titles, ranks, and orders of merit. In 1934, such titles as "meritorious artist or scientist" started being distributed in scores; in the same year academic degrees were restored. A new dignity, that of the "Hero of the Soviet Union" was created and first awarded to the crew of the famous *Chelustkin* and their rescuers. On September 22, 1935, military and naval ranks of the old regime were restored; proceeding by trial and error, the government refrained from reviving the ranks of generals and admirals in the beginning. But in 1940 even this step was made. Moreover, a number of orders of merit were created, first those of Lenin and the Red Banner, emphasizing revolutionary symbols, but later (1942) also those of Suvorov, Kutuzov, and Alexander Nevsky, underlining the link with the glorious past. The bearers of titles, high ranks, and orders were granted privileges with respect to rooms in State rest houses, railway reservations, income tax, etc. They were the ones who could really enjoy the gaiety belonging to the official style of the late 'thirties, whereas the income level of the majority of the people did not permit them to participate directly. But it is very probable that the possibility of gaining access to the attractions of the new way of life became a mighty force pushing many individuals to a display of efficiency and loyalty, the two necessary conditions of succes in Soviet society under The Great Retreat.

A very important change took place regarding sexual morality, accompanied by the glorification of marriage and the restriction of divorce (Chapter VIII). Beginning in 1935, Soviet papers were full of flaming declamations against the "flutter-

ing scoundrels" engendered by the Communist Experiment.
An experienced educator was invited to deliver a series of lectures called *To the Parents* which later on were published and
distributed by the million. "Many people," he said, "have mis-
interpreted the new freedoms and imagined that sexual life
could receive the shape of promiscuity. But social morals demand that sexual life be restricted to marriage, an overt union
of man and woman for the purpose of happiness and the
breeding of children." [37]

In 1935, the official paper of the Young Communist League
acknowledged receiving a few letters extolling free love. The
paper rebuked the writers severely: "They drive us into mean-
ness, filth, and barbarism," was their judgment.[38]

As usual, the drastic change was accompanied by grotesque
exaggerations; for example, in Minsk the militia (police) arrested many young women in modern attire and brought them
before the courts on a charge of "immoral appearance." In the
Ural province quite a few people were brought before the
courts in pairs and asked the question: "Do you plead guilty of
fornication?" From many places it was reported that *kolhoz*
chairmen ordered all the girls to submit to medical examinations to check their virginity.

But the fight against moral laxity had to be continued
throughout the later years of The Great Retreat. On November 21, 1938, the paper of the Young Communist League published a significant article condemning both loose young women
and vulgar young men for promiscuity. The article used the
word "honor" in referring to a girl's chastity, once more in the
good old Victorian sense. The paper had solicited an expression of the views of the members of the League, and then published a number of their letters. The girls wrote resentfully of
young Don Juans who went about practicing their art on im-
pressionable girls, and some urged that offenders of the two
sexes be placed on a platform for ridicule at Young Communist meetings. A mother wrote to the paper that her sons
derided her for being behind the times when she objected to
their loose behavior with girls. "You are not behind the times,"

answered the paper. "Your sons are backward, for their reasoning and behavior have nothing in common with Communist
morals." Summing up the discussion the paper said: "Some
still regard lightness in morals as the mark of a happy person,
but in reality it results in spiritual emptiness and the dimming
of high aspirations." [39]

7

It is commonly recognized that to judge the morality of a
population, we possess no better yardstick than that offered by
criminal statistics.[40] In our particular case, it would be fascinating to use the Communist Experiment to test the validity of the
idea that replacing the capitalist order by the socialist one
would result in a drastic decrease of criminality and delinquency. Unfortunately, a correct comparison of criminality in
pre-Revolutionary Russia and in the Soviet Union is almost impossible. After the Communist Revolution the content of criminal law was submitted to drastic change, so that figures for
the years before and after the Revolution are not comparable.
Furthermore, the system of collecting and publishing criminal
statistics has been completely modified. After a period of total
interruption, criminal statistics were restored only gradually
and then were submitted to a number of successive reforms,
so that even figures for the years after the Revolution are almost incomparable with each other. It is symptomatic that the
author of a textbook on Soviet criminal statistics published in
1935 was able to give figures only for the years 1923-8, and accompanied them with a notice concerning their unreliability.[41]
On the basis of the very unsatisfactory data available, only
approximate statements can be made. Crime and delinquency
increased until 1922, then declined until 1929, and then again
increased until 1935.[42] In Moscow, from 1931 to 1934, juvenile
delinquency increased 100%.[43] It is noteworthy that changes
in juvenile delinquency, as compared with the *ancien régime,*
have not been as large as one could have expected. Offenses
against property continued playing the major part. A special

investigation of juvenile delinquency carried out in 1935 in Moscow and Leningrad proved that theft and related offenses formed 66.7% of the offenses committed by first offenders and 77.1% of those committed by recidivists. In the Kiev area, offenses against property formed 78% of the total contribution of juveniles to crime. Recidivism continued being high: 33.34% and 30.2% of children detained in institutions of two types were recidivists; respectively 10.5% and 8.5% had been sentenced five times and more. As to the causal background, 26.5% of the first offenders and 46.9% of the recidivists were homeless children.

Among other causes of delinquency Soviet authors mention, in the first place, the curtailment of parental authority so typical of the years before 1935, and then the free sale of alcohol and tobacco to juveniles, as well as the influence of the movies.[44] The whole forms a picture not greatly unlike that shown by the results of modern studies on the causation of juvenile delinquency in "bourgeois" society and proves (1) that the transfiguration of the social and economic order did not substantially affect criminality; and (2) that the Soviet authorities did not discover any miraculous means of combating juvenile delinquency, as is often asserted by pro-Communist writers.

During the past few years, when the Soviet government proceeded to The Great Retreat, crime and delinquency have again declined. On this decline, relating to the first years only, we possess these data: in the first half of 1935, the number of crimes committed in the Soviet Union was smaller by 13.2% than in the first half of 1934, and by 39.3% smaller than in the first half of 1933. This decline was due almost entirely to a sharp curb of offenses against property, while crimes against persons and hooliganism, the typical offense of Soviet juveniles, did not substantially decrease.[45]

In general, it may be stated that crime and delinquency followed the economic curve in inverse ratio which, as we know, followed in inverse ratio the curve of Communist methods applied in economics. Consequently, crime and delinquency have increased or declined in direct ratio to the attempts to transform the economic life of the country according to the Communist blueprint. It is noteworthy that this correlation obtains especially relating to offenses against property.

However, another factor was probably involved, and that is the experimentation of the Communist rulers in the field of practical criminology. This experimentation has followed a very complicated pattern indeed because the actual needs of a dictatorial government interfered strongly with the demands of the Doctrine.

In the course of the First Socialist Offensive (War Communism) the punitive activity of the State was chaotic. Old laws were abrogated, but no new criminal law was promulgated, and the courts were given the direction to judge on the basis of "revolutionary consciousness." The study of their practice shows that in the majority of cases this consciousness was nothing but a vague reminiscence of pre-Revolutionary law: the courts continued punishing for murder, rape, and even theft, approximately as the courts of Imperial Russia had done. This proves that the moral principles of pre-Revolutionary society were deeply ingrained in the people's consciousness, revolution or no revolution. A few (but just a few) model penal institutions, such as the reformatory colony at Bolshevo,* were created and readily shown to foreign visitors. These institutions probably were successful in many cases, but the large majority of criminals were confined to institutions about which the best idea can be given by rereading the works of Dickens or Howard.†

Under the NEP, the restoration of order was a necessity and in consequence a Penal Code was put into force on June 1, 1922. It was a rather old-fashioned code; crimes were described and particular punishments prescribed. Naturally, quite a few offenses known to pre-Revolutionary law were dropped, but a substantial number of offenses against the State

---

* This one has been described by American enthusiasts of Communism more than a score of times.

† John Howard, famous English prison reformer (1726–1790).

or the collectivity were added.[46] The main innovation was the permission granted to the courts to punish offenders for anti-social acts not directly foreseen by the law.

Already under the NEP an interesting development began. This was the restoration of penal transportation,* which had played a major part in Russia's punitive system up to 1900, but then was used in exceptional cases only and was entirely abol-ished by the Provisional Government as incompatible with mod-ern ideas in criminology and strongly opposed by public opinion. On August 10, 1922, transportation without judicial trial was re-stored for political offenses.[47] On January 15, 1927, it was in-troduced for "socially dangerous crimes." A decree of January 10, 1930, made transportation the ordinary punishment for major crimes. The Correctional Labor Code of August 1, 1933, differentiated four types of penal transportation. On the other hand, this code abolished imprisonment, so that in addition to penal transportation, only reformatory colonies of different types were left.[48]

But this happened already under the Second Socialist Offen-sive as part of the general experimentation of the period. This was, however, the only real phase of experimentation in prac-tical criminology. A draft penal code prepared around 1930 foresaw a complete transfiguration of criminal law; it consisted only of a catalogue of offenses and of another catalogue of punishments, the court being given complete liberty of choice of the punishment to be meted out. But this draft was never enacted.

Under The Great Retreat a few measures in this field were taken which certainly cannot help being frowned upon by modernists in criminology. First of all, the decree of August 8, 1936, restored imprisonment. The decree is conspicuous by its laconic brevity: higher courts are allowed to sentence defend-ants to prison "for the most dangerous crimes" (not the most

---

* Transportation of offenders to penal institutions situated in colonies or re-mote parts of the State. In old Russia, Siberia was the goal. The Communists favor the far north of European Russia.

dangerous criminals, which would have been in accordance with progressive ideas in criminology). It is also permissible to send to prison (without trial) individuals sentenced to labor camps, or other reformatory measures, if they do not comply with regulations. The decree of October 3, 1937, allowed the courts to sentence convicts to twenty-five years' imprisonment, whereas until then the ten-year limit of Soviet criminal law was considered one of the most progressive achievements of Communism. On July 15, 1943, the notorious *katorga*, hard labor of the old regime, was restored.

Another field where change has been drastic is that of juvenile delinquency. As has already been mentioned, in the early 'thirties, delinquency increased greatly and became a kind of social plague. Seeing that the government did not interfere, here and there the population took the problem into their own hands. What happened is shown by this story: in the Ural province the president of a *kolhoz* ordered a girl to be submerged in icy water who was suspected of being a member of a criminal gang, and then confined her to a cold shed where three days later she died of pneumonia.

On April 7, 1935, one of the most drastic decrees in the history of Soviet criminal law appeared: the courts were permitted to sentence to death children having reached the age of twelve who were found guilty of murder, robbery, or burglary. A few days later a court in Moscow sentenced to death a youth convicted of robbery in a railway train.[49] Incidentally, in Imperial Russia capital execution could never be applied to persons below the age of twenty-one. The decree of May 31, 1938, abolished the "children's commissions" which played the part of juvenile courts and practically destroyed the application of any systematic reformatory measures to the majority of children.

Meanwhile, a new draft penal code was completed. This draft uproots all elements of progressive criminology from Soviet criminal law and frankly returns to the retributive system of punishment used about the middle of the nineteenth century.[50] Juvenile courts and the like are no longer in keeping with the new trends, whereas capital execution, labor camps, and prison are. The necessity of maintaining order in a dictatorially ruled State has thus finally prevailed over the Utopian dream of changing the moral nature of men.

Chapter XI

THE UPS AND DOWNS OF A REVOLUTION:

The Convulsions of a National Body

1

We have gone through various phases of social and cultural life in Russia after the Communist Revolution and have established the complicated movements which took place in them. What do these findings mean from the standpoint of the shock hypothesis announced in the first chapter of this book? Do these findings corroborate the idea that the Communist Revolution introduced heterogeneous elements into Russia's life and that subsequent events may best be understood as a long process of elimination or partial adaptation of these elements to the historical framework of Russia? Or could they be understood equally well as minor fluctuations within its organic development?

Two main corollaries have been drawn from the hypothesis.

1. If a historical shock obtains aiming at the realization of a preconceived plan of social reform, then dictatorial rule is unavoidable.

2. If such a shock obtains, later developments display the pattern of convulsive movements, with frequent changes of direction and movements in opposite directions simultaneously going on in various phases of life.

The analysis carried out in the preceding chapters has first of all shown that a strong dictatorship emerged at the very beginning of the Communist Experiment, and that this dictatorship has not been lifted or even mitigated up to the present time. For many years those in power have explained the preservation of dictatorship by "the encirclement of the first socialist country by capitalist nations," and the probability of "a capitalist coalition against the Socialist State." Events have not confirmed their views: war came to Russia, but it was not brought about by an all-capitalist coalition; on the contrary, in World War II the Soviet's allies were those nations in which capitalism was nearest to its classic structure, whereas the enemy had deviated from it to a great extent. Capitalism *versus* Communism has not become the point at issue. In actuality, those in power in Russia reason as all the dictators do: they assert that they know what the people need to be happy. They know that all peasants can be happy only in collective farms, that only the State management of all economic activities is conducive to the common good, and that all is lost if people do not believe in Marxism-Leninism-Stalinism. But they are afraid that those whom they want to make happy are unable to recognize the only way to happiness, and consequently they compel them to be happy according to the dictators' ideas.

The existence of dictatorship throughout the years following the Communist Revolution permits one to conclude that not only did a shock situation obtain from the start, but that it has persisted up to the present day.

The analysis has also established that the pattern of convulsive movements best characterizes the social and cultural processes which have taken place in Russia after the Communist Revolution. The movements have been so complicated and the reversals so numerous and so capriciously distributed in time that a considerable effort is necessary to keep them in mind.* This is a preliminary statement only, to be elaborated below. But it hardly could be disputed by anyone who knows the facts presented above.

Thus, the two expectations derived from our basic hypothesis are verified by facts. In consequence, we are entitled to retain the hypothesis as the scientifically valid explanation of the facts studied. Let us not forget that in earlier chapters (II-IV) we have found another confirmation of the hypothesis by comparing the historical trends of Russia with the content of the

* See Chart IX.

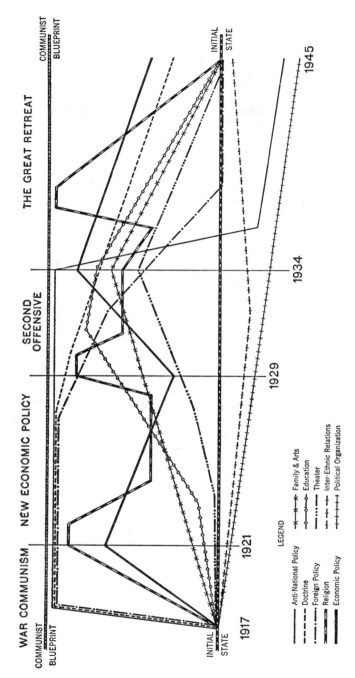

IX. FLUCTUATION OF POLICIES

blueprint, the realization of which was the end of the Communist Experiment. The hypothesis may now be called "theory." As in every scientific theory, it may be challenged by different means, such as bringing in additional evidence allegedly ignored or omitted in this investigation, or deriving additional corollaries from the hypothesis and proving that the corresponding expectations are not verified by facts. However, this situation obtains in regard to every statement belonging to empiric science where nothing is final.

Elaborating our theory, we must first of all try to introduce some order into the uncorrelated findings concerning the various realms of social and cultural life. Since we have to deal with a revolution, the problem may well be posed in this way: which of the possible patterns of a revolutionary process has been chosen by the Russian Revolution? [1]

Every revolution is a series of dislocations and reconstructions, but the process of dislocation and reconstruction may assume different rhythms. History knows many revolutions rather of the *coup d'état* type, where dislocation and reconstruction took place simultaneously; such revolutions may be classified as one-phase processes. More common and conspicuous have been revolutions in which the primary process of dislocation and reconstruction was superseded by another one, in the opposite direction, partly restoring the old system of values and even personal statuses within it; these are two-phase revolutions. But there may be more complex revolutions in the course of which the trend reverses more than once, so that they form a three, or a four-phase process.

The only way to find out what has been the actual course of the Communist Revolution in Russia is to classify the individual processes studied, establishing how many phases may be detected in each of them, and how these phases are correlated. But what is a phase? For the purposes of this study, a phase will be identified with a period of time during which a particular social or cultural process was running in the same direction, either towards the realization of the Communist blueprint or away from it, or during which the movement (change) was effected without increasing or decreasing the distance from the Communist goal. In all cases, the velocity of change may vary, and differences as to velocity can be used for the refinement of the classification.

On this basis, the individual processes may be classified as follows:

1. *One-phase process.* Here, two varieties appear:

(a) The movement may correspond to the straight line pattern, in other words, be constantly directed towards the ultimate goal, or away from it. Strangely enough, only one process corresponds strictly to this pattern, and this single process has constantly run away from the goal. This was the process of organizing and strengthening the political dictatorship. Contrary to the writings of numerous pro-Communists, who describe the events of the years after 1917, at least up to 1934, as a continuous advance towards the splendor of Communism, no process has followed this pattern. This is true even of such conspicuous successes of the Communist regime as social security and socialized medicine. The real advantages offered by social security have fluctuated depending on (1) the economic curve and (2) the government's eagerness to gain and maintain the favor of the labor class; in the course of The Great Retreat, it has degenerated more and more into a system granting special privileges to the new upper class. As to socialized medicine, under the NEP it was once more combined with private medicine, as it had been in old Russia.

(b) The movement may begin with a "spontaneous creation" in almost no time and then receive the form of maintaining the early achievement.* This has been the case in the management of culture, insofar as the form and not the content is considered. Culture began being managed from the first days of the new regime and remained in that state up to our day. Variations in the margin of liberty do not affect this stability and must be considered as separate processes affecting the individ-

---

* To maintain a social achievement necessitates corporate effort; therefore, in such conditions a social process does not stop running; what ceases is a change of distance from the goal.

ual realms of cultural activity. It is noteworthy that the process involved is functionally connected with political dictatorship.

2. *Two-phase process.* Here, three varieties appear:

(a) In some aspects of social and cultural life, the best possible approximation to the goal was reached from the start, and for a certain time the configuration remained on the level attained; then, a change occurred and a declining phase was substituted for the level one. This pattern has obtained in (aa) international policy, which up to 1927 was characterized by aggressive internationalism in complete agreement with the Doctrine, but after 1927 went through a declining phase in which the subphases of ambivalent, auxiliary, and esoteric internationalism could be established; (bb) the basic policy as to national and historical values, which up to 1934, was antinational, and in 1934 suddenly became ultranationalistic; (cc) the content of the basic Doctrine, which up to 1927 coincided entirely with the orthodox Marxist formulation, but later on evolved towards a "hero-theory" not far distant from Carlyle's teachings. This particular development was to a certain extent auxiliary to the development of the dictatorial system.

(b) In quite a few phases of social and cultural life the development started by an ascending phase (directed towards the Communist goal) but later on passed through a descending phase (partial undoing of the achievements of the first phase). This pattern could be observed regarding (aa) the family, where the reversal took place in 1934; (bb) the school system, with an ascending phase which may be divided into two subphases separated by the year 1923, and differing as to the velocity of the process, and a descending phase which began in 1931 and one more consisted of two subphases, the first allowing partial reforms only and the second (after 1934) giving room to an almost wholesale restoration of the pre-Revolutionary situation; (cc) figurative arts and music where the ascending phase (up to 1934) was expressed in attempts to socialize emotions according to allegedly Communist patterns, and the descending phase signifying the return to the purpose of gratifying the esthetical urges of the people; (dd) history as a science and political economy, which were first entirely sub-jugated to extreme Marxist views (ascending phase) and later on returned to relative independence (history) or moderate Marxism (political economy); (ee) the general style of life characterized by lack of joy, boredom, filth, and leveling up to 1934 (ascending phase) and the elimination of these "accessories of Communism" after that year (descending phase).

(c) In one particular field the opposite pattern has obtained: this is the realm of inter-ethnic relations where, up to 1932–3, a program opposite to the blueprint was applied, and later on a substantial approximation to the latter obtained. Had the Constitutional Reform of 1944 brought real change into the situation, a three-phase process would have obtained; but no doubt the reform has remained on paper.

3. *Three-phase process.* This pattern was realized in the realm of the theater only, where up to 1923 almost no interference was exerted; then came an ascending phase accentuated around 1927, and still more around 1930, and a descending phase after 1934.

4. *Four-phase process.* This complicated type of social process has appeared in one variety only: a first ascending phase followed by a first descending phase, a second ascending phase and a second descending phase. This has been the pattern of the most conspicuous and best-known of the social processes having taken place in Russia under Communist rule, the process of the economic transfiguration consisting of the phases of War Communism, the NEP, the Second Socialist Offensive, and the Mitigation of Communism. The same pattern has obtained in:

(a) The social structure insofar as approximation to, or departure from the Communist ideal of material equality is considered;

(b) The theory of law and the organization of the punitive system;

(c) Literature, insofar as content imposed on it by the machine of culture management is considered. These qualifications are, however, necessary:

First, within the basic (economic) process minor fluctuations have obtained; temporary concessions (a minor descending phase) were made in 1930 and 1932, in the course of the Second Socialist Offensive, but the restoration of Communist purity was attempted in 1939 relating to collective farms.

Secondly, in the organization of the punitive system, a particular aspect (the restoration of penal transportation) has persistently led away from the blueprint beginning with 1922; once more, this development was determined by the basic process concerning the political organization of the country.

5. *Six-phase process.* The most complicated form of the six-phase process obtained in the realm of the religious (or, more exactly, antireligious) policy of the government. There, the development started by an ascending phase which was strongly accentuated in 1922–3; then came a descending phase followed by a second ascending phase in 1929–30, a second descending phase, a third ascending phase in 1937–8, and a third descending phase which started in 1939 and was consistently accentuated up to the present day.

Not only have the individual processes followed different patterns, but the reversals of the trends have not taken place simultaneously and, in consequence, it is easy to offer many instances of simultaneous movements in opposite directions. A glance at Chart IX suffices to confirm this statement.

Still more important is the fact that, in many instances, similar reversals took place in dissimilar, sometimes opposite situations. Thus, for instance, the first attack on religion was launched in the midst of a substantial retreat from Communist principles in economic life, the second simultaneously with strong efforts to make Russia a Communist society, and the third in the course of another mitigation of Communist principles in economics and simultaneously with the first steps of fake democracy under the name of Stalin's Constitution. The Communist pressure on the school system was accentuated in the course of the descending phase represented by the NEP, and was decreased in the midst of the Second Socialist Offensive. The successive mitigations of internationalism in foreign policy took place both in the course of descending and ascending phases regarding the social and economic structure of the country.

The diversity of the patterns followed by the individual processes was not foreseen by the protagonists of the Great Experiment. According to the Doctrine, the revolutionary period of Russian history ought to have been a one-phase process, consisting of successive steps bringing Russia nearer and ever nearer to the goal. Such a development could have obtained if the Communist program were also the people's program. Lenin knew that it was not, but expected that by means of demonstrating uninterrupted successes, the people could be induced to endorse the program they had originally rejected. This hope did not materialize. Hence, the complexity of the social processes described. Their functional interrelation may be described in this way:

1. An offensive was launched in 1917 in almost all the realms of social and cultural life; but as a necessary response to the challenge of the people's resistance, the blueprint had to be replaced by its opposite in the political field. There, instead of the withering away of the State, coercion was intensified and organized into dictatorship.

2. The political development gradually attracted towards itself quite a few social processes which in the beginning pointed to the achievement of the Communist goal. Managed culture appeared to be the necessary corollary of dictatorship. The punitive system departed from Utopia and was directed towards fulfilling the requirements of dictatorship. The official Doctrine was submitted to incredible distortion to help justify the dictatorial system.

3. In one particular field, that of foreign policy, the resistance of an insuperable force, namely, the corporate will of capitalist society to survive, made an early appearance as a major obstacle which could by no means be overcome. Hence, the early reversal of the trend and, later on, continuous movement away from the goal.

4. In the majority of the realms of social and cultural activity the active, passive, or impersonal resistance of the Russian na-

tion greeted the efforts of the rulers aiming at the realization of their goal and time and again endangered their power position. Therefore, backward movements had to be substituted for advance. Depending on the strength of the resistance and the intensity of the danger involved in it, these movements were started at different times and, whenever possible, they were abandoned for a renewed offensive, in some cases two or three times. In this way the two, four, or six-phase processes have obtained.

5. The particular descending movements were merged into The Great Retreat when the danger of losing political power through military defeat and indifference or even hostility of the people appeared on the political horizon.

6. In a few realms of possible interference, particular considerations imposed the choice of rather exceptional patterns. Pure opportunism induced the Communists to depart from the blueprint concerning inter-ethnic relations where, later on, the configuration received by the total situation permitted them to shift to a program more compatible with their basic ideas.[*] Special attachment to the theater—the pre-Revolutionary theater of Russia—induced the Communists to refrain from interference for quite a few years and never to insist too much on Communist purity even during the years of the greatest pressure.

Still more conspicuous was the convulsive character of Russia's post-revolutionary development in those rather impersonal processes which arise as the resultant of governmental policies and the people's reactions. A short survey suffices:

1. The movement of the population has been characterized by two major demographic catastrophes.

2. In industrial production, an almost unprecedented catastrophe took place under War Communism. Eight years were necessary to make up for it, and the aftermath was the unsound speed of the industrial expansion under the Five-Year-Plans.

---

[*] Another major case of determination by purely opportunistic consideration was the adoption of the agrarian program of the Populists.

3. In agriculture, in addition to the catastrophic decrease of crops under War Communism, the fluctuation of figures relating to cattle has been most conspicuous; twice in the lifetime of a generation these figures were cut by 50 per cent as the result of Communist Experimentation.

4. In education, the steady advance of the pre-Revolutionary period was interrupted by the Revolution and resumed only in 1923. The goal of universal education was reached in 1931, but at the cost of a terrific deterioration of quality. To make up for it, heroic efforts had to be carried out after 1931.

5. For the individuals composing the Russian nation, the revolutionary convulsions of the national body have been most conspicuously reflected in the rapid change of their position within the social framework, now for the better, then for the worse. It is true that the intensity and velocity of vertical social mobility is characteristic of every revolution. Those who once were omnipotent ministers of a monarch suddenly find themselves in jail, and former convicts ascend to the summits of political power. Individuals and families who enjoyed high incomes become paupers or penniless exiles; persons and families with a vague economic status start enjoying the luxuries available. Once highly estimated interpreters of "official truth" are now ridiculed, and their positions are taken by others who, before the revolution, were considered absurd dreamers or prophets of a Utopia never to be realized.

Vertical social mobility may also be intense and rapid outside revolutionary periods, but then individuals only, not groups, are involved. In the case of a revolution groups, as such, move up and down the social ladder, owing to the revolutionary rescaling of values. Outside revolutionary situations, vertical social mobility may be compared with the up-and-down movement of individuals within a building: some use the staircase and move slowly, while others take local elevators, and still others use express elevators; they interchange their positions, but the positions continue to form a stable system. But a revolution dislocates the very building, whole stories crumble down, and other stories are miraculously lifted up.

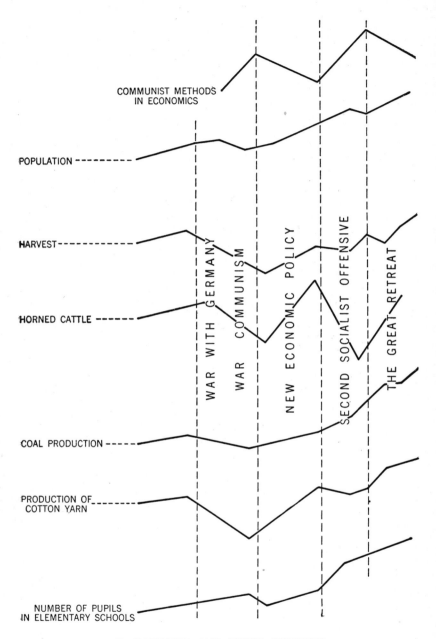

COMMUNIST METHODS IN ECONOMICS

POPULATION ------

HARVEST------

HORNED CATTLE ------

COAL PRODUCTION -----

PRODUCTION OF COTTON YARN -------

NUMBER OF PUPILS IN ELEMENTARY SCHOOLS

WAR WITH GERMANY

WAR COMMUNISM

NEW ECONOMIC POLICY

SECOND SOCIALIST OFFENSIVE

THE GREAT RETREAT

X. POLICIES AND THEIR EFFECTS

As shown in Chapter X, in the course of the Russian Revolution sudden changes both for the better and worse have affected almost everybody and many people more than once. The best way to grasp the situation is to pass in review the typical life stories of individuals who now belong to the new middle class. For some, attainment of this status signifies social ascent after lifelong (perhaps hereditary) membership in one of the lower groups. For others, the same fact means the termination of a turbulent career-line through rapid descent under War Communism, ascent under the NEP, another downfall under the Second Socialist Offensive, and a second restoration of status under The Great Retreat. For still others, the situation may be intermediary between the two polar types. But membership in the labor class is also of diversified origin, persons of former bourgeois and labor or peasant extraction being now mixed in that stratum.

Catastrophes, individual or even collective, may take place in societies whose development has been organic. But the accumulation of catastrophes and convulsions in Russian life after 1917 is quite exceptional. They cannot be explained by assuming that the corporate will of the people was behind the Communist Experiment. These catastrophes can be understood only on the basis of the shock theory.

2

The convulsion pattern characteristic of Russian life under Communism does not preclude the possibility of viewing the process as a whole and of determining its main phases. Naturally, there are many obstacles: (1) there is no reason to consider all the component forces of the whole process equal; (2) neither is it possible to ascribe to them coefficients which would express their differential strength; (3) moreover, it is impossible to determine exactly the distance from the Communist goal reached at different epochs by the individual aspects of social and cultural life. Nevertheless, arbitrarily ascribing equal importance to the individual processes and relying on rough estimates of the distance from the Communist goal, the position of Communist society as a whole between the initial stage and the goal of Communism may be determined for each year. The comparison of such positions may yield a kind of "curve" expressing the general trend of Russian life under the great Communist Experiment and after. The curve thus constructed may be interpreted in this way:

1. The Communist Revolution in Russia has been a four-phase process, consisting of two ascending and two descending phases.

2. The curve expressing the general movement has the same shape as that expressing the social and economic movement in particular. This is only natural in the case of a society remolded according to a plan in which the economic and social structure was considered fundamental.

The four major phases may now be described. In the course of the first phase the main social and cultural processes all ran in the same direction, towards the realization of the Communist blueprint, with one major exception; this was the organization of dictatorship. In the course of this period, dictatorship was rather covert, and officially full power was ascribed to the pyramid of the Soviets. Since the Doctrine emphasized the social and economic structure as the foundation of every society, the principal efforts were directed towards the transformation of that structure; however, opportunistic considerations compelled the new rulers to postpone a too drastic transformation in rural economy. Internationalism and anti-nationalism were other features of the blueprint which were given full and immediate force. Heavy blows were inflicted on the pillars of the old order—the family, the school and the Church. Regarding the arts and science, the principle of official management was invented and put into force as a natural appendix to political dictatorship. It was used to impose definite patterns on the creative aspects of culture which were considered congenial with the revolutionary transformation of the social and economic order.

In the course of the second phase, large parts of the social and economic achievements of the previous period were undone; the trend, from the standpoint of the Communists, was therefore downward. Literature, in general, followed suit, but this partial retreat was compensated by additional pressure on the family and the Church; however, relating to the latter, the pressure very soon decreased to the level of the first period. In the course of this period, the school became one of the most conspicuous fields of Communist experimentation; in the fields of music and figurative art, the experimentation was not discontinued and, towards the end, it expanded into the realm of the theater. In the political field, the dictatorial structure made further progress, after heavy struggle for supremacy within the ruling group. First symptoms of breakdown in the Doctrine and its application to the great problem of internationalism appeared; but they did not yet materialize into substantial changes in policy.

In the course of the third period, the social and economic offensive was conducted with greater vigor than in the first one. This time, no exception for agriculture was allowed, and at about the end of the period the approximation to the blueprint seemed almost complete. In politics, the supremacy of the One was officially acknowledged and justified. Further departures from the purity of the Doctrine and its earlier application to the problem of internationalism took place, these movements running contrary to the main trend. In the field of religion, the pattern of the second phase was repeated: first there was increased persecution, then relaxation. The attempts to destroy the family, the experimentation in school, and the imposition of revolutionary patterns on arts and science were continued. However, from the middle of the period symptoms of an incipient backward movement in the field of education became perceptible, and a few short-lived economic concessions were made. It may be concluded that in this period the policies and sociocultural trends were less consistent than in the first period.

The fourth phase, that of The Great Retreat (1934–   ) did not destroy the dictatorial structure of power, but gave the population the slight satisfaction of the verbal acknowledgment of democratic principles. In actuality, the concentration of power in the hands of the One is now beyond question; the famous trials of the years 1936–38, the great Party purge, and the purge of the Red Army chiefs were the most conspicuous manifestations of the process. In economic life, quite a few significant concessions to the desires of the population were made which substantially lifted the efficacy of national labor. Internationalism was thrown overboard and values forming the particular Russian heritage were permitted to become paramount. Very significant changes materialized in the social structure, preparing for the rebirth of class society. Experiments relating to the school and the family were discontinued and old style patterns were put into force; the same happened in the realm of art. Relating to religion, a last assault was tried simultaneously with the great political purge, to give way to a complete retreat. When this particular retreat began (1939) the trend was downward throughout the sociocultural texture, varying only as to velocity. This phase was consequently as consistent as the first one. Only then all the trends were upwards, now all are downwards.

We have called the first and the third phases ascending, and the second and fourth descending. This they definitely are, if one looks down on the development from a summit symbolizing Ideal Communist Society. Are they also, respectively, ascending and descending if one looks down on them from another summit symbolizing the fulfillment of basic needs, individual and social? They definitely are not. In the course of the first phase, which was directed towards the realization of the Communist blueprint, crops were halved and cattle decimated; industrial production fell to 20% of the pre-Revolutionary level; the population decreased, literacy went down, and crime increased. In the course of the second phase which was directed away from the blueprint, crops, cattle, and industrial output increased and returned to the pre-Revolutionary level, the population also increased, the secular process of overcoming illiteracy was resumed, and crime decreased. The third phase, once more ascending towards the summits of Communism, was characterized by fluctuating crops, despite increased sowing areas, further slaughter of cattle, and another demographic catastrophe. The output of heavy industry increased by leaps and bounds, but that of light industry remained stagnant or even decreased. Literacy continued advancing, but the quality of education was deteriorating; crime once more went up. The fourth phase, The Great Retreat from Communism, gave the Russian nation increasing crops, expanding herds, increasing population, progress in the output both of heavy and light industry, advance in education, and recession of crime.

On the basis of these facts, this general conclusion may be offered; extreme Communist methods resulted in the conspicuous malfunctioning of society; their mitigation brought relief and fostered progress.[*]

3

The major phases are separated from one another by the main breaking points of the years 1921, 1928–9, 1934. Obviously, each of these points corresponds to major—in the official slang—"historical," decisions of Russia's rulers, and these decisions obviously were caused by challenging events or situations which obtained about that time. It is worthwhile making a summary review of these decisions and situations in which the various developments separately described in the course of the analytical study intersect and interplay.

The causal background of Lenin's "historical decision" of 1921 is relatively simple. The attempt to endow Russia overnight with an economic system of the Marxism style created a vicious circle; industrial production decreased, curbing the stimuli for agricultural production; the curb of agricultural production was then reflected in a further decrease of industrial production, and so on, up to an almost complete paralysis of the economic body. The withdrawal of food from the countryside to prevent starvation in cities caused a terrible hunger

[*] See Chart X.

catastrophe in the eastern part of European Russia. Unfavorable meteorological conditions were partly responsible for the crop failure of the year 1921. Such conditions used to recur in Russia; but after 1891, they no longer resulted in death from starvation or from contagious diseases conditioned by starvation. The general deterioration of the economic process turned the clock back and made the country unable to support the population which had rapidly expanded under better conditions. Speaking in cold scientific terms, this catastrophe was a necessary adjustment of the population to the means of existence available, in the absence of such methods of adjustment as emigration or the purchase of food abroad.* But the conditions which made this adjustment necessary were created by deliberate human acts, the policies of the Communist leaders carrying out the Great Experiment.

The subjective response of those involved naturally corresponded to these objective conditions. The response was revolt: in 1920–1, strong peasant upheavals took place in twenty-one out of the fifty governments (provinces) of European Russia. In the government of Tambov it was so successful that for a year and a half no administration obedient to Moscow existed there. In March, 1921, a revolt of sailors in Constradt made it clear that the New Order created on the basis of the Communist Doctrine was doomed.

The Communist government did not realize the situation up to the spring of 1921. In the winter of 1920–1, they still planned to enforce the execution of the basic program by compelling the peasants to sow what the State needed despite their lack of interest in doing so. A Central Sowing Committee and a cluster of local committees were set up to see that the cultivation of all land included in the general scheme was carried out as a national duty. However, the plan could not be enforced. In March, 1921, in a speech delivered to the Tenth Party Congress, Lenin recognized that tremendous blunders had been committed, that the social and economic transfiguration had

---

* The purchase of food from abroad was partly substituted by the generous help of the United States through the ARA.

advanced too fast, and that a serious retreat for many years ahead was necessary. Lenin's authority being supreme, the First Retreat, that of the NEP, was inaugurated.

The NEP was inaugurated because this was the only escape from total collapse, not only economic, but also political. Much less conspicuous are the causes of the shift from the NEP to the Second Socialist Offensive. For the NEP society, though awkward and responding to no ideal whatsoever, was a relatively efficient society, providing people with food and industrial commodities in steadily increasing amounts. The destruction of such social structures is rather exceptional. Moreover, not only the cause, but even the date of the change cannot be stated with precision, since the shift was gradual and, in the course of quite a few months, there was a significant discrepancy between official statements as to the continuation of the NEP and acts incompatible with its principles. About the end of the year 1929, acts of the latter trend had accumulated to such an extent that the abandonment of the NEP could no longer be denied.

The NEP structure was doomed to destruction because of the duality of value systems embodied in it. Marxism remained the official doctrine; but, in practice, adepts of Marxism had to act as if they were confounded "capitalists." The Communist leaders never were converted to capitalist views; during the NEP their value system was repressed, and with the beginning of the Second Socialist Offensive, this repression was terminated. Since repressions always tend to be terminated, the problem of the cause of the change performed in 1928–9 is reducible to the problem: why did it happen that in 1928–9 the Communist rulers were no longer motivated by considerations which, in 1921, compelled them to abandon War Communism and to begin the NEP?

The answer is this: in 1928–9, the Communist leaders once more acted under pressure of the expectation of a revolution conducive to the overthrow of their power. Significant social processes induced them to come to this conclusion. First of all, within the ruling group of the upper class, those Communists who were entrusted with the management of the collective sector (the "red directors") separated themselves from the rest of the group. They were contaminated by the "bourgeois spirit" embodied in the nepmen. They conspicuously directed their efforts towards increasing personal gains and, if possible, transmitting them to their progeny.

This was bad enough. Still worse was the trend observable among the peasants. There, very definitely, a new upper class was developing. Moreover, the intellectual workers, now relatively well remunerated, remembered the much easier and more pleasant manner of life in the old days and regretted the lost brilliancy of the Empire. The process was especially manifest in the changing mentality of the students who, under the NEP, were recruited mainly among the sons and daughters of the new upper class and the *kulaks*. To the consternation of the rulers, the students preferred idealistic philosophers and writers to Marx and liked symbols of "petty bourgeois" society, such as flowers on balconies, neat dress, useless bric-a-brac in their rooms, and the like.[2]

A dangerous coalition was in the air, or at least was suspected to be in the air by the Communist rulers: this was the coalition between the bourgeois-minded Red managers, then non-Party specialists working in Soviet institutions, the upper group of peasants, and the idealistically-minded students. This coalition could not have been "counterrevolutionary" in the strict meaning of the word: its members did not want "restoration," i.e., the return of the former rulers, bureaucrats, landlords, and capitalists, but perhaps they wanted the restoration of the "bourgeois" order, with themselves occupying the top positions within it. In other words, perhaps they wanted to put an end to the NEP by eliminating from it all the survivals of Communism.

According to the Marxist doctrine, the political structure is merely a superstructure on the economic substructure of society. The processes just mentioned were interpreted as unavoidable manifestations of the "social order of production" existing under the NEP and as precursors of a forthcoming revolution which was to transfer political power from the ruling group (the Communists) to the emerging upper class.[3] In 1928–9, in the speeches, articles, and pamphlets of the leaders, this question was often asked: who will go ahead faster—we, the Communists, or our foes, the protagonists of the restoration of the bourgeois order? To prevent the victory of the antagonists, the abolition of the NEP, despite its economic success, was indicated.

Additional items entered into the range of motives from which the "historical decision" of 1928–9 emerged. One was the difficulty, already mentioned, of finding an adequate adjustment between the collective and private sectors in economics. Another was the discovery of the idea of planned economy and its sublimation to the level of a miraculous means of reaching the paradise of Communism.

Foreseeing an impending political revolution, being unable to master the difficulties appearing on the junction of the two sectors of the NEP society, possessing a new tool for provoking enthusiasm, the Communists decided to start a new offensive. The immediate goal was to create artificially a new balance of social forces which would guarantee the continuity of the political regime. This could be reached only by increasing the relative weight of the proletariat, especially of the industrial proletariat, the very basis of the regime. To such an end, the industrialization of the country was the natural means. The idea as such was not new; as has been shown, during the last twenty-five years preceding the First World War and the Revolution, Russia lived under the banner of rapid industrialization.[4] The following items, however, were new: the velocity of the advance; the planned character of the progress which, they thought, would prevent waste; and the State ownership and management of industry.

The Second Socialist Offensive had to be abandoned—for reasons to be studied in the next chapter. But even after having discontinued the offensive, the leaders did not stop justifying their deeds of the years 1929–34. The official justification was that sacrifices had been necessary to prepare a better future for the Russian nation. Before the outbreak of the Second World War, this better future was usually interpreted in economic terms: endowing Russia with heavy industry was a necessary premise for the later satisfaction of the needs of the Russian people through the development of light industry. After the outbreak of war in the West, they began to emphasize the military situation and to point to the importance of Russia's industrial advance for national defense.

In actuality, the Second Socialist Offensive was started as the result of purely political considerations, as a means of self-preservation on the part of those in power. It was not a voluntary sacrifice of the nation. No sacrifice could have been brought about by the nation since it never participated in the decision to launch the offensive. That sacrifice would be necessary was not expected even by the leaders. Military considerations could not have been decisive since, in 1928-9, no war was in prospect even in the distant future and the partial return to normalcy under The Great Retreat was carried out on the basis of military considerations: continuing the Second Socialist Offensive would have made Russia defenseless.

The study of the causal background of The Great Retreat is now ahead. But, prior to this study, a brief recapitulation of our findings as to the scope of the Retreat should be introduced.

CHAPTER XII

THE SCOPE AND THE MEANING OF
THE GREAT RETREAT:

A Study in Statesmanship

1

IN THE COURSE of this war, the Russians have displayed a corporate attitude which cannot be better designated than as a Sacred Union around national values. Union around national values in an emergency situation does not astonish us. It seems to be natural, and if a sizable group, the so-called Fifth Column, displays the opposite attitude, we are not only shocked, but also puzzled. But as regards contemporary Russia, Sacred Union around national values is astonishing and at the same time comforting, as is every unexpected advantage. Was not Russia, for many years, the stronghold of a culture which denied particularistic national values and, in addition to them, many values which were held supernational? Had not Russia become a Red Paradise, a preview of the Universal Communist Society to come? Was her unity—if any—not the unity of fighters for the Communist transfiguration of Humanity, not that of fighters for a national culture? Such were the fears of some, the hopes of others, when Hitler brought war to Russia and, later on, made her an ally of the United States.

Yes, Russia had been all that, and her leaders had been proud of having achieved the complete transfiguration of a nation consisting of 170 million individuals. But there is a tremendous difference between them then and now. To understand it, let us look at it through the eyes of an imaginary historian of ages to come who would have at his disposal detailed and accurate descriptions of the social and cultural order in Russia, in 1930 and 1940, while the memory of events which took place between the two years and the names of the leaders would be lost. We may easily assume that, on the basis of such evidence, our historian would conjecture that between 1930 and 1940, a major revolution occurred in Russia, accompanied by a complete change in leadership.

Yet we know that between 1930 and 1940, there was no revolution in Russia, and no change in leadership. What actually happened was that for many years Russia was the scene of a Great Retreat.

Let us now modify the setup of our mental experiment and guess what the report of a keen observer could have been who, after having visited Russia in 1930, and having heard nothing of the country for quite a few years, would have returned there in 1940.

In 1930, on the streets of Moscow and of provincial cities and towns, only badly-clad men and women could be seen; the lack of any care for external appearance was emphasized and interpreted as a particular virtue. All these people seemed to have only two aims: to be at their workshops on time and to get some food in the co-operative stores, after having spent many hours in lines and then presented their ration cards. They never seemed to think of entertainment or of such a thing as a party.

Ten years later, on the same streets, people just as poorly clad could be seen, but also to be seen were women trying to copy Paris fashions, and men cleanly shaven and wearing starched collars. Those who were not so distinguished in their appearance obviously envied those who could afford it. Among children, the majority were in uniform; people explained that now uniforms were compulsory for all pupils of elementary and secondary schools. Among men, there were many in brilliant uniforms; some of them were addressed as captains or colonels and displayed on their chests insignia of different orders. When asked what these orders were called, they proudly replied that they were the orders of Alexander Nevsky, Suvorov, and Kutuzov. This seemed quite unexpected to our visitor, since in 1930 he had been told that all ranks and orders had been irrevocably abolished by the victorious proletarian revolution and that the memory of princes and generals had fallen into oblivion.

Following some of the individuals met on the street, our visitor saw them entering shops. Nobody showed any ration card: some spent their rubles with the same easiness as a well-to-do person in a bourgeois country, others counted every kopek, just as destitute people do among "capitalists." This was in great contrast to the observations collected in the course of the first visit: then, ration points counted more than money, and the amount of money in the purses of different buyers was approximately the same.

But now people not only went shopping. Many looked for entertainment, and their wishes were easily gratified. They could attend a performance of folk dances and songs, or humorous films, or shows in the perfect style of pre-Revolutionary days. But to do so they had to buy tickets, and not all could afford it: the distribution of free tickets had been discontinued, as well as the practice of offering propaganda instead of entertainment. In other places, people danced or studied dancing; ten years ago, an attempt to do these futile things would have been immediately stopped.

In 1940, quite a few people would stop to buy a book or a paper. They were quite different from those which were available in 1930. Even now there was much propaganda in them; but their content was not limited to propaganda. In the newspapers, an intelligent reader could enjoy good articles on sports, art, science, and technique. Books were no longer romanticized, but nevertheless bore descriptions of the great adventure of building socialism in one country. Quite a few people acquired classics, Russian and foreign, in good editions recently published. In general, cultural life was no longer dominated by the demand of being Marxist, as it had been then, though the negative demand of not being anti-Marxist was still obvious; still, cultural life was incomparably more diversified than it had been in the course of the first visit.

In newspapers such words as fatherland, patriotism, and

Russia were often recurring; in 1930, mentioning them was considered a definite symptom of a counterrevolutionary attitude. The visitor wanted to get some information at the headquarters of the Comintern; but he had some trouble finding it: the Comintern looked old and forgotten, already lying on its death bed. (We know that it died in 1943.)

Time and again articles condemning abortion and divorce could be found in the papers, and others glorifying respect to parents and older people. In 1930, the same papers conveyed just the opposite views.

Now, children going to school complained that they had to work hard. Among the main subjects of instruction were the Russian language and literature, and history and geography, about which their predecessors had never even heard; but now they no longer had to study sociology, or the Marxist doctrine, and they were very happy that this was the case for they heard from their older brothers and sisters that the subject was a bore. Some of the older children expressed regret that they had to obey their teachers, and take different tests on which their advance depended; they could no longer spend their time in debates about the international revolution, or religion as the invention of priests. In 1930, one heard that many children were refused at the doors of a school because they belonged to the "master class" of pre-Revolutionary society; now, this no longer mattered, but quite a few parents complained that their children could not continue beyond the seventh grade since the fee for advanced education was prohibitive.

Now, time and again one could see people within or before a church building; if they were numerous, militiamen secured order; one could no longer observe intentional disturbance in the form of antireligious processions or carnivals. To understand the change, our informer wanted to buy one of the antireligious papers with which he was familiar; but it was difficult to find one; nobody seemed interested in them any more. (Had he come two years later, the difficulty would have turned into an impossibility.)

Visiting a factory, our informer noticed a significant change in the situation. Then, the principle of equal remuneration dominated, and nobody cared to work. Now, everybody cared since remuneration depended entirely on the quantity and quality of the work performed. In whispers, several workers complained that the wage differential was very high. And actually, it was substantially higher than in advanced industrial societies of the West. And the labor class was no longer on the top of the social pyramid. Engineers, high bureaucrats, successful writers, actors, and so on formed an exclusive group, the members of which could enjoy life in conditions which seemed to them royal in comparison with what they had to endure ten years ago.

In the countryside, improvement was undeniable. The peasants looked much happier than they had been then. When asked why it was so, one received the same answer: everybody is now free to till an allotment individually in the midst of a collective farm and breed one's own cattle; in general, the *kolhozes* are much better managed and no longer depend entirely on Moscow.

Our observer is supposed to be a keen one. Therefore, he could not fail to notice that not everything had changed between his two visits. Stalin was as omnipotent as he ever had been; when our visitor inquired about the liberties granted by the Constitution bearing his name, his informers only smiled. They also told him that the Commissariat of the Interior was just as bad as the GPU and the still earlier Cheka had been. All the factories and shops continued to belong to the State. The materialistic philosophy of Marxism, though in modified form, remained the official acknowledged Doctrine. The system of culture management continued to be in force.

On the basis of such observations, the scope of The Great Retreat may be easily established. As in 1921, the key positions have remained in the possession of those who gained victory in 1917. The difference was this: in 1921 the principle of key positions was applied in the economic realm only. In the course of The Great Retreat, all the realms of sociocultural life were passed in review and political dictatorship, State monopoly of production and distribution, and management of culture were selected for durable occupation as key positions.

On the other hand, quite a few positions outside the central fortress have been abandoned. Among them, there is one which could be called Communist asceticism, the repression of joy and beauty, the imposition of boredom and ugliness. But Communist libertinage was simultaneously outlawed and replaced with the strong family pattern of olden times.

Another position entirely abandoned under The Great Retreat was the belief that men could be induced to work for the same remuneration regardless of their achievements. This was probably one of the most painful concessions made by the rulers.

A third Communist stronghold entirely abandoned in the course of The Great Retreat was that of Internationalism. "Russia first" is now the actual principle of Russian policy. This was probably almost as painful a concession as that previously mentioned.

The complete abandonment of positions held under the Communist Experiment, however, has been rather exceptional. The main pattern of The Great Retreat has been the amalgamation of traits of the historical and national culture of Russia with traits belonging to the Communist cycle of ideas and behavior patterns. The slogan reported above, "Russia is a great nation because it gave the world Pushkin and Lenin," means this: Pushkin is the personification of Russian culture; there is no necessity to impose attachment to Pushkin on anybody, because it is there. Lenin as the personification of Communism is, however, dubious. If the association of ideas between "Pushkin" and "Lenin" can be made very strong, then the support given by the nation to Pushkin will be extended to Lenin. Obviously, the two sets of traits cannot be amalgamated in their totality and without change. Naturally, the Communists wanted to retain as many of Lenin's principles as possible, and correspondingly, to revive Pushkin's principles only to the extent of sheer necessity. They were, for instance, particularly reluctant to revive the religious aspect of Russian culture but finally had to give way. Throughout the years of The Great Retreat, they proceeded by the trial and error method, advancing here, retreating there, and selecting from the historical tradition such configurations as could be amalgamated more easily with their principles. As has been shown above, in many cases this resulted in the revival of relatively old patterns, superseded by others already in existence before the Revolution.

The pattern of amalgamation may be demonstrated in a large number of fields of sociocultural activity. The Russian Orthodox Church is once more a recognized, even partly privileged body; this is in accordance with historical tradition. But the State teaches antireligion in schools; this is in accordance with Communist principles. The *kolhoz* is a Communist institution, but individual allotments and cattle breeding revive parts of the old order. Painting repeats the style of the 'eighties of the nineteenth century, but it is used to produce portraits of the heroes of our day. In literature, Alexis Tolstoy's masterpiece, *Peter the Great*, is written in the grand style of pre-Revolutionary days, but is conceived in such a way as to show that Stalin is a dignified successor of the greatest of Russian monarchs.

2

The meaning of The Great Retreat can be discussed from the standpoint of the rulers, of the people, and of the objective historical process.

From the standpoint of those in power, the individual changes in policy forming The Great Retreat have been concessions, since in each particular case they had to abandon part of their plan or even some position already gained, and remold the social configuration according to ideas which were not theirs. This does not, however, mean that they had to yield to demands becoming too loud to be ignored. Under dictatorship, nobody is enabled to formulate demands, and the government has to infer their existence from the reaction of the people to their actions.

Only rarely were statements made from which the recognition of failure could be derived. These have concerned: (1) the failure of the antireligious policy; (2) the failure of aggressive internationalism; (3) the failure of political education; (4) the failure of education in general, and (5) the failure of the original *kolhoz* system to satisfy the elementary needs of the rural population.

In some of the cases already mentioned and in other instances, the change in policy was accompanied by a surreptitious change in the Doctrine, ascribing the former policy to the interference of deviators, wreckers, enemies of the people, and the like, and introducing the new policy as the correct application of orthodox Marxism. This device has been used regarding the revival of the cult of national heroes, the abandonment of the family and school experiments, the repudiation of revolutionary art patterns, the toning down of antireligious propaganda, the change of the official position relating to many scientific problems, the decentralization of economic planning, etc. Also often used was the pattern of acting without explanation: slowing down the tempo of industrialization, changing the modes of remuneration of industrial workers and collectivized peasants, curbing the excesses of local nationalism in "national republics," restoring the old-fashioned measures of punishing offenders—are all conspicuous examples. In a few cases, the rulers have used the device of making verbal concessions without permitting them to materialize in practice; such as has been the case of the Constitutional reforms of 1936 and 1944 and of the introduction of *kolhoz* and Party democracy.

Up to this point, the reforms composing The Great Retreat have been classified from the standpoint of their presentation by the government to the people. How do they fit into the general pattern of the period, into the general plan of the Retreat? This pattern has never been officially formulated, but it may be inferred from individual actions. First of all, the dictatorial structure and the personal position of the Supreme Leader and the inner circle was to be consolidated and whenever possible re-enforced.

Secondly, the antagonistic forces acknowledged to exist had to be appeased, the enemies being transformed into neutrals by eliminating the main causes of their hostility, and neutrals being transformed into friends and allies by meeting their desires. The latter feature of the pattern is easily recognizable in proclaiming a slogan for a joyous and comfortable life, in giving the people the art and literature that they can enjoy, in abolishing rations, in decentralizing economic planning, in muzzling laxity in sexual relations, etc., whereas the former feature is especially apparent in the mitigation of the very meaning of collectivization carried out to break the passive and impersonal resistance of the countryside which threatened to inflict irremediable harm on the food balance. It is also apparent in the abrupt shift from religious persecution to tolerance which was necessary lest the corporate strength of the embittered believers should join the enemy in the course of the anticipated war.

Thirdly, the efficiency of national labor had to be raised; this was achieved through a whole series of economic reforms, but also through the school reform and the restoration of the strong family pattern.

Finally, quite a few items of the original blueprint had to be revised, because experience had shown that they either could not be realized, or in the process of materializing produced unexpected effects of a highly detrimental character. The impossibility of achieving the Plan has brought the Communist leaders face to face with "the nature of things" and its reflection in the hearts of men, and with those basic moral precepts which do not vary much in time and space.[1] They had to acknowledge that it was impossible to build up a society based on irreverence to parents and elders, sexual promiscuity, the denial of the value of the fatherland, but also on the denial of economic self-interest and the assumption that man's nature could be transformed by order and propaganda. It also appeared that it was impossible to uproot the idea of God from a Christian nation, or to impose on other nations a blueprint which by historical accident had gained dominance in Russia. As to detrimental collateral effects, they have been most conspicuous in relation to the efforts to shake the three pillars of society.

On many occasions, when pondering the devices which could subserve the complicated purposes of The Great Retreat, the rulers must have been struck by the fact that so many items of the old order could, with slight modification, be used by them. The old school order, the old-fashioned type of family, the gamut of titles, ranks, and orders of merit, even Church discipline all proved to be very helpful in consolidating the dictatorial system, appeasing substantial groups of the population, or securing the efficiency of national labor. Step by step they were introduced into the pattern of neo-Communist society in the style of 1940 or later.

The new pattern of society did not first appear in the minds of the rulers and then become a reality. In the beginning, only a few general lines of the course to be followed could have been clear in their minds; only gradually, by trial and error, could it have received a more or less definite shape. In some cases the individual purposes underlying the new pattern coincided in their practical application and re-enforced each other; then, the decision was easy. In other cases, conflict situations arose, especially if the conflicting interests and desires of different groups had to be taken into consideration. Thus, for instance, the reform of morals met the desire of many people, but was opposed by quite a few youngsters enjoying sexual freedom granted under the Communist Experiment.

The necessity of changing policies which had been conducted on the solid foundation of the Doctrine could have opened the eyes of the rulers regarding the alleged infallibility of their prophets. We do not know whether this actually occurred, though change in the official Doctrine with regard to the role of the personality in history and the recognition of a few mistakes in Marx's and Lenin's predictions make the hypothesis plausible.

Perhaps many Communists are finally disgusted by the failure of other nations to make their "proletarian revolutions" and no longer believe in International Revolution to come. Perhaps in their hearts many of them never shared the application of the Doctrine to art: like all Russians, they loved popular songs and dances and in consequence enjoyed their revival. Lenin personally never believed in the destruction of the family, which course he had to carry out according to the Doctrine. In these instances there was not so much conversion as liberation from the yoke of verbal formulas imposed on the Communists themselves as part of the general framework of the Doctrine. Such instances should not, however, obfuscate the fact that The Great Retreat has been a sequence of concessions, great and small.

3

Concessions! This means victory, though partial victory only, of the nation against a reckless dictatorship. The plight of a nation is sad whose line of development is distorted by external conquerors; her plight is especially sad if the conquerors are barbarians. The plight of Russia under the Communist Experiment was very sorry indeed, despite the fact that her conquerors were not external but internal barbarians.[2] Consequently, such essential parts of The Great Retreat as the abandonment of the antinational and antireligious policy, and of experimentation in the family, the school, and the arts, were tantamount to liberation from a foreign yoke. And this liberation was accompanied by the disappearance of the most hateful features of economic experimentation. On that foundation, living conditions both in the city and village have substantially improved. They still are far removed from that joyous and comfortable life which the people have been promised, and are incomparably worse than in advanced capitalist societies; in the course of The Great Retreat, the latter has been courageously recognized by the leaders. But, in the course of The Great Retreat, the economic trend was consistently upward, and further improvement could be reasonably expected. This is what counts in the molding of the emotional "climate" on which the attitude of the people with regard to the government and the specter of defeat depends. Hostility against the government was rapidly decreasing, and the will to fight an eventual invader was rapidly increasing. The policy of The Great Retreat had borne abundant fruit.

From the standpoint of the objective historical process, the meaning of the Retreat was this: the Communist Experiment was not a logical continuation of Russian history. It was not a sequence of reforms carried out by a nation that had removed the artificial barriers which had checked its advance. It was a major deviation from the straight line of Russian history. It was a distortion of the natural development which could be expected on the basis of Russia's past. This distortion was one of the possibilities ingrained in the very character of the revolutionary process, especially of that phase which we have studied in an earlier chapter, namely, the opportunist accommodation of the competitors for power to "the natural program" of "the revolutionary mass." It is obvious that the original program of a competitor is only temporarily repressed in favor of the opportunist accommodation. If as the result of accommodation the competitor wins, the repression gradually ceases to operate when the new order is somewhat consolidated, especially in its political phase. In such conditions, the new leaders are able to realize not only those elements of the program which gave them power, but also a part, at least, of the residue, that is, those points which were not at issue during the period of competition.

This mechanism has been conspicuous in the Communist Revolution in Russia. The people never endorsed the antireligious attitude of the Communist leaders which, previous to the revolution, was not included in the Communist "offer" to the masses. But after power had been acquired and consolidated, attacks on religion could be launched. The temporary repression of the agrarian program of the Communists could be dropped only twelve years after the acquisition of power.

This phase of the process cannot be overemphasized. It introduces into the problem of the final outcome of a revolution a "personal coefficient" which operates approximately as follows: accommodation of the virtual leadership to "the natural program" of "the revolutionary mass"; acceptance, by this mass, of the offer thus formulated; delegation, to the successful competitor, of the authority to proceed to reconstruction, on the basis of this program; gradual withdrawal of the repression and return to the original program; exertion of power according to this program, and not to "the natural program" of "the revolutionary mass." And since the revolutionary situation is no longer present, in other words, since society has returned to "normalcy," the propositions concerning revolutionary situations no longer obtain. Whether it likes it or not, society has to endure the power structure chosen in the course of a revolutionary competition for power. Whether the nation continues to accept this leadership will be decided during the next crisis when society once more has become plastic. Obviously, the test of a nation's attitude towards its government receives quite another form, if the revolution results in establishing a true democracy. Unfortunately, this is a rather exceptional case.

It is also obvious that the departure from the official program of a revolution on the basis of opportunist accommodation is conspicuous by its absence in cases when there is actual conformity between the original program of the victorious competitor and "the natural program" of "the revolutionary mass." It is also obvious that the possibility of concealing the discrepancy between the two programs varies in inverse proportion with the level of general and especially the political education of the nation.

In the particular case of Russia, the situation was most favorable for the display of the peculiar process just described. There was no conformity between the original program of the victorious competitor for power and the "natural program" of "the revolutionary mass." And the level of education of this mass was very low indeed since, in the Russian case, it was the nation minus the *élite*. This made concealing and obfuscating the discrepancy a mighty easy task.

In the course of The Great Retreat, the disruptions in the national structure effected by the shock of the Communist Revolution have been, in the main, healed. The history of Russia continues, naturally, modified by the shock. But once more it is Russia's history, not that of an anonymous body of international workers.

4

Why was there a retreat? Leaders, military or political, do not retreat without being compelled to do so. What were the particular pressures under which the Communist leaders had to undo a large part of what they had previously done?

A discussion of these causes may be conducted on two levels, the abstract and the concrete. Abstractly, we may say that all revolutions must in part undo what they have done if the society in which the revolution has taken place is to survive. This is the golden rule drawn by historians from the French revolutionary and post-revolutionary epochs: post-revolutionary France is a child both of the Revolution and of the *ancien régime.*

The outcome of the Russian Revolution must be the same. Any vital society, after suffering an eruption, returns to the climate best suited to its nature and its historical evolution.[3] Therefore, one may say that the very logic of history forced the Communists either to retreat or to cede leadership to another group, after another revolution. Communists have always been able opportunists; in 1921, under similar circumstances, they preferred "a serious retreat for a long time ahead" to the distant threat of political breakdown. In the 'thirties, they once more preferred retreat to loss of power.

This is an abstract explanation which does not help us to understand why the retreat took place in 1934 and not earlier or later. A consideration of concrete events may elucidate this timing.

It has been one of the peculiarities of the Russian Revolution that the decisive reversal of the trend, the beginning of the period of the undoing of revolutionary mischiefs, was never acknowledged and announced. Officially, the Communist Experiment continued going on, but its very meaning was surreptitiously changed: as has already been mentioned, in the official Doctrine in the edition of 1934 and later, many items of the former Communist Experiment were declared to have been "petty bourgeois deviations" from pure Communism and, vice-versa, many elements of Tradition previously ridiculed and combated were introduced into the official Doctrine. Thus, when retreating, the Communists tried to maintain the fiction of a triumphant ascent towards the felicity of Communism. Difficulties decreased and living conditions improved owing to the fact that pure Communism was no longer alive. But, officially, improvement was ascribed to the accumulated victories of Communism.

It is amazing how well the Utopians succeeded in their masquerade, at least concerning the outer world: only a minority of authors writing outside of Russia, and therefore free to express their opinions, qualified the later developments either as the Revolution Betrayed—if they continued cherishing the Doctrine—or as the Nationalization of an International Revolution, if they liked that particular phase of the change. But the majority did not realize the reversal of the trend and continued describing Russian events as a straight line advance.

Since The Great Retreat never was acknowledged and announced, it is impossible to establish exactly what reasons compelled the Utopians to change their minds and when and how this change took place. Therefore, a tentative reconstruction on the basis of circumstantial evidence is the only possibility left. In many cases, the very nature of the measures taken enable one to hazard a guess as to the problems which the rulers had to solve.

Evidence available allows us to formulate this hypothesis: The Communists had to terminate the Second Socialist Offensive and to begin The Great Retreat because, in 1934, two chains of events converged. One was the conspicuous failure of major phases of the Experiment. The other was the rise of the real danger of being attacked by a mighty coalition.

But has the Communist Experiment been a failure? Was not Russia at least introduced into the family of industrialized nations? Today, in the light of later events, one is inclined to feel nothing but admiration for the wisdom of the policy which endowed Russia with a strong industrial basis. Without the hastily created industrial equipment, one could say, the magnificent resistance of the Russians to German aggression would have been impossible. The tragedy of the nations conquered by Hitler has proven that valor alone is not sufficient.

There can be no doubt that the industrialization of Russia in the course of the Five-Year-Plans has been beneficial. Let us, however, not forget that rapid industrialization had been the way of pre-Revolutionary Russia, and that it was the Communist Revolution which retarded that process by many years. Proceeding to rapid industrialization, the Communist leaders made up for one of the greatest mischiefs of the Revolution. So far their policy deserves unqualified approval.

But a policy cannot be judged on the basis of its end only. Besides the end, there are the means, and the tempo, and the cost, and the collateral effects. If such yardsticks are used, then the basic approval must be qualified and, what is important in this context, very probably it has been qualified by the framers and executors of the policy also.

Gigantic industrial plants have emerged in Russia and her productive capacity has grown much higher. But the tempo chosen in the beginning proved to be detrimental, since the industrial advance was balanced by the wholesale destruction of agriculture and the undermining of the nation as a biological aggregate. Men were working day and night, increasing quantities of raw material were used, but millions had to die from starvation: a truly diabolical picture to appear in the midst of a society which had been promised paradise on earth. In the course of The Great Retreat this was tacitly recognized and the tempo slowed down. Directing Russia towards industrialization, the Communist rulers acted in accordance with one of the major trends of recent Russian history; but skyrocketing the tempo, they acted as the Utopians which they are. In slowing down, they made up once more for the harm they had inflicted. If from the start the tempo had not been chosen on

Utopian grounds, achievement would have been higher and more harmonious than it actually was.

When men have to die from starvation, this means that something is wrong with the economic machinery, be it capitalist or socialist. The Communist rulers could and did deny the catastrophe caused by their policy, but they certainly perceived it. Simultaneously, they had to face another catastrophe: this was the disintegration of the educational system, despite redundant reports about its achievements. Of course, rapidly increasing millions of children of school age were given access to education, and the number of students in institutions of higher learning showed an almost vertical ascent. But the methods of teaching and training in the style of the Communist Experiment once more made the efforts of both teachers and students nothing but a waste of time. There were hundreds of thousands of students in institutions of higher learning, but they hardly knew the three R's. Despite strenuous efforts, they could not gain that command of the elementary forces of nature which is the key to advanced technique, because their minds were not prepared to receive the training. There were millions of children in elementary and secondary schools, but actually they acquired mastery in one art only—that of discussing, in stereotyped terms, political and social problems. Here was a conspicuous danger: the program of industrialization was likely to collapse if there were no longer human agents able to operate it.

Moreover, the persistent efforts aiming at the destruction of the family resulted in creating an army of quite a few million neglected and homeless children whose rising delinquency gradually appeared to be an unbearable social plague.

Chaos instead of frictionless motion in industry; millions of men dying from collectivization; culture catastrophe; disruption of community ties and rising criminality—were these not signals understandable even to the blindest of Utopians? And still they could have continued their Experiment, at least for a while; this time, in contradistinction to 1921–2 and 1928–9, no revolution seemed to threaten. What threatened, and what in due time they recognized as threatening, was foreign conquest and, for them, loss of power.

How, precisely, did the threat of war and defeat and loss of power appear on the horizon? In 1931, Japan invaded Southern Manchuria, and the next year, Northern Manchuria, close to the Soviet border. For the first time since 1920, a real threat of war appeared on the political horizon. However, this virtual war was merely colonial and did not menace the regime. In 1933, Hitler came into power in Germany and began his vociferous attack on Communism. At first, the permanence of Hitler's government was questioned; between Russia and Germany there was Poland, whose army in 1933 was obviously stronger than Germany's. But in January, 1934, the German-Polish pact was signed. Then, the imminence of war was appreciated in Moscow, and the pact was understood as an alliance hostile to the Soviet State.

It was the coincidence of two negative phases, one external and the other internal, which made The Great Retreat inevitable. Were the Communist Experiment a success, as the rulers claimed, the emergence of a danger from the outside would not have compelled them to change policy. Had the nation adopted the Communist ideal, then the adequate response would have been—more and purer Communism. But the nation did not accept it; of this the rulers were fully aware. They understood that they had to imbue the nation with the fighting spirit without which war is lost before it begins. Therefore they had to bring back the very force which they had tried to uproot—the national sentiment. In addition to this they had to bring back the incentive of economic self-interest vilified by the Doctrine.

On the other hand, were there no danger from the outside, the rulers would probably have continued their experimentation. On previous occasions they changed their policy drastically, but in one set of conditions only, namely, when anticipating the destruction of their power position by an insuperable revolutionary movement. The emergence of an external threat once more created a situation wherein the Communists had to choose between remaining Russia's rulers and showing the world the example of a consistently socialist society. Once more, they preferred to adjourn the Experiment *sine die*.

Usually a threat from the outside is independent of internal developments; it just coincides with them. In the Russian case, however, the situation was different; the danger from the outside developed mainly as the result of the activity of those who ruled over Russia and operated the Communist Experiment.

The existence of the danger was openly recognized and publicized. What was not and could not be conceded was that the very existence of Fascism was largely due to the foolish international policy of the Soviet in its first fifteen years. The threat of war, in the East and West, was a retaliation for the threat of revolution. In the East, it was the foolish policy of trying to sovietize China which gave Japan at least a plausible pretext for her interference with Chinese politics. In the West, it was the foolish policy of undermining every organization of the Labor class opposed to Communism which shifted the balance in favor of Fascism. Both policies were integral parts of the Great Experiment, directly derived from the Doctrine.

5

We have seen what the objective facts were which made The Great Retreat necessary, or at least made it the only means of avoiding military defeat, enslavement of the nation by foreigners and, as a corollary, the collapse of the existing power structure. But these facts had to be realized by those in power and they had to be induced to make the necessary adjustments. As has already been explained, nothing about their deliberations and decisions has ever been published, and we have to rely on circumstantial evidence only.

Almost never had the political leaders of a great nation been more mistaken about reality than those of Russia around 1930: on the eve of the most decisive change on the European, possibly the world scene, they continued to act as they had done for fifteen years, fostering internal trouble in every "bourgeois" country, combating first of all the "social traitors," and thus helping the enemies of the latter wherever they could find them. Did not the German Communists, directed from Moscow, associate themselves with National Socialists in a big strike, and did not the leaders of the Communist International credit to themselves every defeat of the Socialists, even if these defeats were inflicted by Fascists? Did not the rulers continue their nefarious policy within the country, provoking despair and defeatism among the people under their rule?

There are reasons to believe that on the eve of 1932 the leaders did not yet grasp the real situation with regard to internal affairs. In December, 1931, at the session of the Central Executive Committee, a peasant woman delegate shyly introduced a motion to slow down the expansion of heavy industry and concentrate attention on the production of goods of direct use to the peasants. Molotov severely rebuked her and said that this could not be done since the achievements of heavy industry were not yet sufficient. In February, 1932, a Party conference * took place at Moscow. According to schedule, it had to last from the first to the ninth of the month, but was already closed on the fifth, since the members had nothing to talk about any longer. Since the discussion of the Second Five-Year-Plan was on the schedule, it appears that at that time nobody doubted that the plan had to continue the vertiginous ascent of industrial production.

Doubts first seem to have arisen in the course of 1932. In any case, it is significant that from May to December, the Second Five-Year-Plan was never mentioned, except on the occasion of a few reprimands at the address of extremists.[4] This took place despite the fact that the Plan was to start as of January 1, 1933. In actuality, it was confirmed only in 1934, so that for more than one year the country lived under the banner of the Plan, but without a concrete plan in force.

Very symptomatic events took place at the seventeenth Congress of the Party which confirmed the plan (February, 1934).

* A Party conference is a gathering of high-ranking Party functionaries, primarily of provincial and district secretaries.

The draft was much more modest than that discussed two years earlier by the Party conference.[5] At the Congress, the discussion was started by optimistic reports delivered by Molotov, and a number of provincial delegates introduced motions to increase the speed of industrialization. Then suddenly Ordzhonikidze, the commissar of heavy industry, brought in a motion to decrease the figures concerning coal and iron. A committee was formed, with Molotov as chairman, and at the end of the Congress its report was submitted. It decreased figures relating not only to iron and coal, but also to agriculture and the means of transportation, the number of workers, and the payrolls, and made rather modest promises as to food and other consumers' goods. This report was unanimously confirmed. Quite obviously a secret session had taken place at which delegates from the provinces informed the leaders that the country was upset by the announcement of the Second Five-Year-Plan which was to be as painful for the nation as the First had been.

The events at the Congress almost coincided with the signature of the German-Polish pact, to which Soviet papers ascribed the most sinister meaning. Since the first measure in the sequence of The Great Retreat took place in April, 1934—this was the resolution of the Central Committee concerning political education—it may be assumed that if and when the proceedings of the Political Bureau are published, a secret decision of the greatest importance will appear to have been made in February or March, 1934.

There is an additional piece of evidence which fully corroborates the assertion that the Great Decision was reached in 1934, and that it was mainly motivated by the anticipation of war with a Fascist coalition, and that is the sudden and drastic increase in armaments and military appropriations which started in 1934. For ten years, 1924–34, the strength of the Red Army was 562,000; in 1935, it was 1,500,000 and was still increasing in the course of the next few years.[6] A feverish activity aiming at the technical improvement of the Army started. Among the measures there was the restoration of discipline, which was inaugurated in 1935 with the revival of military ranks, and was

continued through the succeeding years, going so far as order-
ing the Red Army men to salute their officers when not on
duty, and restoring epaulettes and swords as part of the uniform of generals and commissioned officers.* The military appropriation jumped from 1.4 billion rubles in 1933 to 9.0 in
1935, 15.9 in 1937, 40.8 in 1939, 54.0 in 1940, and 71.0 in 1941.

For our purposes it is significant that the process began in
1934. About that time, the leaders may have looked around
them and discovered that they were completely isolated. The
nonaggression pacts with their neighbors were of no value.
The flirtation with France had not yet progressed far enough,
and France was ruled by utterly anti-Communist groups. And,
within the country, there was nothing but the hostility of collectivized peasants, the bitterness of the former enthusiasts of
the Socialist Reconstruction whose expectations had been so
terribly frustrated, and defeatism of a nation which had been
deprived of her past and taught to despise her culture. Very
realistically, those in power must have recognized that under
such conditions war would mean defeat, complete collapse,
and termination of their rule. Time was to be gained and fortunately could be gained, since their prospective enemies were
not yet ready and had to rearm. Meanwhile, a completely new
policy was to be inaugurated: the integration of the Soviet
Union into the combination of forces antagonistic to Fascism;
a complete change in the direction of the campaigns conducted
by the Communist International in individual countries, Fascists
and no longer "social traitors" being the targets; a complete
change in internal policy, restoring the Russians' national pride
and curbing the disintegrating processes fostered through the
exaggeration of the inter-ethnic policy; retreat in the *kolhoz*
structure, revival of the incentive of economic self-interest,
granting successful men the opportunity of enjoying life in
conditions of reasonable comfort, and virtually transmitting
their social status to their children.

Whether or not they were converted to some new political

---

* In 1917, tearing away epaulettes from officers' shoulders was considered
one of the major symbols of the victory of the proletariat.

philosophy, the Communist leaders made those adjustments which were required by the situation. The Great Retreat saved both Russia's independence and the rule of those who were in power. That was the natural reward for an ability to see things as they really were, and not as they should be according to one Doctrine or another. But it was an almost miraculous performance on the part of rulers who had been obstinate doctrinaires for many years.

Chapter XIII

THE OUTCOME OF THE REVOLUTION:

A Balance Sheet

1

THE SECOND PATRIOTIC WAR is more intimately connected with Russia's internal development than the Russian-German war of 1914 with which the First World War began. Through a complicated concatenation of events the war, which for Russia is the Second Patriotic one, was engendered by the success of the Russian Communists in 1917 and the consistent application of their program until 1934 or 1935.

Nevertheless, for the sake of analysis we may consider the Second Patriotic War as another and independent shock inflicted on the Russian nation similar to the combined shock of the First World War and the Communist Revolution. It is obvious that the German aggression has brought new and gigantic disturbances on the Russian scene, and that the main feature of Russia's postwar development will be adjustment to the new situation.

In consequence, the process of Russia's adjustment to the shock of the Communist Revolution which forms the main object of this study will never be resumed, at least in a pure form. Before having terminated the process of recovery after the revolutionary shock, Russia will have to display new energy to make up for the wounds inflicted on her by the war.

Under such circumstances, it appears that it is possible to draw a final balance sheet of the Revolution right now. In such an enterprise, both the state of Russia on the eve of the German aggression and changes which occurred in the course of the war must form the basis of discussion.

With what is the post-revolutionary state of Russia to be compared? More often than not the effects of a revolution are measured by comparing the state of a nation immediately before with its condition afterwards.[1] This procedure, however, is correct only if the nation was stagnant before the revolution. We know that pre-Revolutionary Russia was a rapidly advancing society for which the procedure is obviously incorrect. To measure the effects of a revolution in such a society, post-revolutionary society must be compared with that hypothetical society which would have existed if the pre-Revolutionary trends had not been interrupted. Such a society is obviously only conjectural, and its comparison with post-revolutionary actuality will yield results of only limited significance. But such "mental experiment"[2] is unavoidable in any evaluation of historical events, and the conjectural statements reached in this way are still more significant than statements imputing to the revolution all the achievements and evils by comparing the situation after a revolution with the conditions that existed before the event.

If the revolution is "programmatic," that is, conducted "according to plan" with the purpose of actualizing a blueprint drawn up by its promoters, then another comparison, that between the actual achievements of the revolution and the blueprint is also of interest. The purpose of this chapter is to make these two comparisons in respect to the Communist Revolution in Russia.

2

To prepare the correct balance sheet we must first of all, therefore, formulate certain conjectures about the state Russia would have reached if her development had not been interrupted by war and revolution.

We may assume that without the revolution the political forces of Russia would have achieved the transformation of the "dual" or "constitutional" monarchy, which ruled Russia since 1906, into a parliamentary monarchy in which the Crown would have yielded actual power to representatives of public opinion. The franchise of the Duma would have been gradually democratized. The establishment of *Zemstvos*, that is, provincial and district self-government which, between 1864 and 1914, had contributed so much to Russia's advance in the fields of public education and public hygiene, would have been extended throughout the Empire, with perhaps the exception of some semicolonial territories; these agencies would have received a significant re-enforcement through the modernization of obsolete institutions of peasant self-government. The excellent judicial system which Russia had already enjoyed since 1864, curbed during the reactionary period before the Russo-Japanese war, but partly restored under the Duma, would have been expanded and improved.

The agrarian reform inaugurated by Stolypin in 1906, if peacefully continued, would have proved to be one of the greatest agrarian revolutions in history. By 1935, no agrarian communities would have existed, and the Russian countryside would have consisted of twenty million farms run on the basis of civil law of the *code Napoléon* type. Only a few landed estates would have survived: were the pre-Revolutionary trend maintained, by 1935 the peasants would have acquired almost all the remnants of the former quasi-feudal estates. The atomization of land ownership would have been balanced by a strong development of rural co-operation which had already attained notable successes in Siberia and Northern Russia. It is difficult to judge what the impact of these changes on agricultural production would have been. But since, in 1916, only 10 per cent of the arable surface was tilled by the landlords, the impact of parceling could not have been very important. A moderate but steady advance of agricultural production could have been expected. It would have been accelerated by the spread of general education and special training in the period actually covered by the Revolution. The natural agronomy.

In industry, the rapid advance of Imperial Russia in the last twenty-five years would probably have continued throughout resources of Russia offered the opportunity, and the expanding population of Russia, in combination with improvements in agriculture, would have created a big internal market. Russia would have remained a welcome field for investment for Western European capital: American capital, very probably, would have been added.

A quantitative statement on the probable increase in production is possible. During the twenty-five years from 1888 to 1913, Russia's production of coal increased from 5.3 to 29 million tons, or five and a half times, that of pig iron from 0.7 to 4 million tons, also five and a half times, that of oil from 3.2 to 9 million tons, or 2.8 times. Assuming the maintenance of the geometric ratio of expansion, in 1938 Russia could have produced 160 million tons of coal, 22 million tons of pig iron, and 25 million tons of oil. The possibility of a slowing down of this expansion in heavy industry cannot be denied, but a tremendous increase of the productive capacity of light industry might have been expected with certainty. Such figures as 5 million tons of sugar, 8 billion meters of cotton fabrics, 0.5 million ton of paper in 1938 are rather conservative estimates.

A tremendous expansion of railways was also to be expected. In 1915 a governmental committee drew up a ten-year plan of expansion which would have added 30 thousand miles to the 49 thousand miles which were then in operation. That plan would not have imposed on Russia anything beyond her capacity, because an increase of the railway net by 2,500 miles a year actually took place for many years previous to the decision. Assuming some slowing down after 1925, a network of 100 thousand miles by 1938 could have been achieved without difficulty.[3]

Expanding industry and railways would have produced a rapid numerical increase in the labor classes, and with this quantitative advance, qualitative progress could have been expected: skilled labor was gathering in old industrial centers and tremendous efforts had been made to disseminate technical education in various fields. Russian labor was "class-conscious" and, with the liberalization of political institutions, would easily have evolved mighty and well-organized labor unions. The social security laws of 1912 were considered by the government, business, and labor as just a modest beginning. On the basis of the consciousness of "social service" which prevailed in Russia at that time, a magnificent development along this line could have been foreseen. A significant improvement in wages and labor conditions could be expected in conditions of expanding industry and organized labor, which would continue the advance of the pre-Revolutionary decades.

Had agriculture and industry expanded rapidly, Russia even today would have been far from becoming a "saturated area" in which the increase of population was impossible. Consequently, the continuation of the population trends of pre-Revolutionary years could have been expected and on this basis, an *ex-post-facto* "prediction" of 180 million in 1938 is rather conservative. Gradual urbanization, as a result of industrialization, would probably have resulted in 30 per cent of the population living in urban areas by 1938.

In the field of culture, the main achievement would have been that of overcoming illiteracy. The magnificent efforts of the *Zemstvos* would have been continued and significantly accelerated on the basis of a law passed in 1910 which could be termed a "ten-year plan for national education." By 1920, all children in Russia except in semicolonial areas would have had access to schools; by 1930, this ideal would have been achieved everywhere. Since no special device was foreseen for the older age groups among which illiteracy was high, a complete elimination of illiteracy could not have been expected before their deaths. Still, by 1938, an index of literacy of 78 per cent could have been foreseen.[4]

By a parallel assumption, a great expansion of high schools, universities, and other institutions for higher learning might have been assumed. It is impossible to conjecture the probable achievements in science, literature, and art, since in these fields unpredictable "personal coefficients" are decisive. But one thing is certain: in each field, different schools of thought and work would have persisted, criticizing each other, even fighting each other, but enriching themselves and the nation through competition.

In the field of religion, the liberalization of political institutions would probably have resulted in the decline of the privileges of the Established Church. The resulting liberty would have compensated for the loss of part of her flock to competing denominations, and perhaps to religious indifferentism. But the back-to-church movement which had started among the Russian intellectuals would have definitely re-enforced the position of religion in Russia.

This picture may seem overoptimistic, and perhaps overemphatic about Russian similarity to this country. But a striking similarity of conditions did actually exist.[5] Like this country, Russia is a continent. Her natural resources are second to none. She is far from the state of demographic saturation. The pioneer spirit had been displayed by the Russians when colonizing the southern steppes (now the larger part of the Ukraine), the trans-Volga region, the Northern Caucasus, and Siberia. The democratic spirit was well developed in institutions of peasant self-government, later on in the *Zemstvos,* and in co-operative societies. Among the intellectuals, the spirit of social service was at least as well developed as among the best social workers of this country. Taking into account the similarity of underlying conditions, the similarity in part of our hypothetical picture with the actual state of things in this country is an additional argument in favor of these conjectures. They were formulated on the assumption that the development would not have been disturbed by external and internal causes. But the second part of this assumption is contrary to fact: the geographical location of Russia did not permit her to isolate herself from the rest of the world as this country did during the period of rapid expansion, and in her history many tensions were accumulated which, in combination with the disorganizing effects of war, caused an internal explosion. In these matters conditions were not equal in the two countries

and there resulted significant differences in the actual course
of events in them.

3

The Revolution of February, 1917, overthrew the Imperial·
government and for eight months introduced into the Russian
tragedy a quasi-democratic intermission. Had the order of
things then created lasted, many of the trends discussed above
would have been given accelerated actualization, but quite a
few significant departures would probably have taken place,
especially concerning the social order: a drastic agrarian reform would have immediately destroyed the remnants of quasi-
feudal landownership and restored the agrarian communities,
reversing Stolypin's policy. Very probably, after having secured possession of all arable land, the peasants would have
insisted on "full ownership"; thus, after a significant deviation,
the goal of 20 million "little masters" in the Russian countryside would have been achieved. It is hard to judge to what extent socialist ideas would have been carried out in industry,
but very definitely the laboring class would have made an extraordinarily rapid advance, both social and economic.

But the February Revolution was only a prelude which was
not permitted to develop into a real play. For twenty-five years,
Russia's fate was determined by the tremendous shock of the
Communist Revolution of October, 1917. This Revolution
was highly "programmatic"; in other words, its leaders had a
complete plan of social reconstruction which, they believed,
was the best means of making men happy. In their program,
two aspects must be distinguished, the exoteric and the esoteric.
The exoteric program was simplicity itself: the four slogans of
land, peace, bread, and "all power to the Soviets," which meant
the abolition of bureaucracy, gave them the decisive support
of the masses for a short while. The acquisition of power was
the necessary premise for the realization of the esoteric program. What was to happen to Russia if this realization were
permitted to proceed according to plan?

First of all, Russia had to disappear, becoming a part of the International Proletarian Society of Marx's and Lenin's dreams. In this society no room was reserved for political institutions: the State, a "bourgeois" institution, had to wither away. No bureaucracy was to be maintained, all citizens would direct in turn the corporate activities foreseen by the plan: according to Lenin, every cook was able to govern the State. The standing army was to be abolished and replaced by civil militia. In that society of which Russia was to be a part, no individual ownership of the means of production would exist any longer; these means of production were to be collectivized and transferred to the society of the future which had to be purely economic and devoid of political functions: State capitalism was considered as bad as private capitalism. In the new economic order, the "capitalist anarchy of production" was to be overcome: no efforts would be wasted and artificial scarcity would be replaced by plenty and, after a short period of transition, permit the realization of the ideal of remunerating everybody for his work according to his needs; since human needs are essentially equal, this implied social and economic equality. Naturally, this new social and economic order could not be realized within a society holding to the cultural traditions of the bourgeois age. But since, in the opinion of the leaders, "existence determines consciousness" and culture is a function of the socioeconomic order, after the shift to collective production and exchange human ideas would change rapidly, old superstitions would die out, and new systems of motivation would arise to replace those acquired by men in the bourgeois state of their existence. This natural development could be accelerated by planned actions of the leaders. As a result, religion had to disappear quickly, and the stable family of patriarchal Russia was to be replaced by free unions integrated in the proletarian style of life. Living in conditions of plenty, working only as much as would be required by collective needs, liberated from any kind of exploitation and political coercion, free from "religious superstition" and from artificial inhibitions of the sexual instinct, men would be happy for the first time in history.

4

We are now prepared to compare the actual state of things twenty-five years after the outbreak of the Revolution * with both the conjectural state of things described and with the blueprint of Russia's new masters.

In contrast to the Communist plan, but in accordance with the basic expectations of the pre-Revolutionary period, Russia did not disappear. In the turmoil of 1917–21, Russia proved to possess much more internal cohesion than was assumed by her foes. She was not merely an agglomeration of provinces ruled by an autocrat, but the political organization adequate to the natural unity of a "continent." The centrifugal trends were easily overcome and, by 1922, with the exception of the western borderlands, Russia was again one. In the turmoil of 1939–40, the larger part of the western provinces, lost in 1917–21, were regained; the final outcome is not yet certain, but there is a large probability that, except for Finland and Poland proper, Russia will have the same frontiers as in 1914 after this war.

Even more striking is the fact that these frontiers will coincide almost exactly with those which Russia would have demanded and obtained if the Provisional government were not overthrown by the Communist uprising. That government had already proclaimed the independence of Poland proper, and nobody in Russia doubted then that she was entitled to acquire from Austria the provinces of Eastern Galicia (with Lwow) and Northern Bukovina (with Cernauti).

But the major fact is that the frontiers are there and quite certainly will be there; Russia has not been dissolved in the International Society which failed to be born. It is true that, for a certain period of time, the name of Russia was carefully avoided and replaced by that of the Soviet Union. But gradually the old name reappeared on the surface and, in 1943, in the new national anthem, the two have been officially merged. The people living in that State have rejected the Communist

* In other words, at the beginning of the Second Patriotic War.

injunction to become "citizens of the world" and, in the course
of this war, have displayed their flaming patriotism or nationalism. Their revived nationalism, however, is not ethnic or
racial nationalism limited to the most numerous of the ethnic
groups living within the borders of the Soviet state; it is a kind
of corporate nationalism, involving all the groups forming the
family of "the peoples of Russia." This neonationalism is more
akin to the older "imperial" policy which prevailed in Russia
up to 1880 than to the narrower "nationalistic" policy of the
last few decades before the revolution. In Imperial Russia, with
the exception of the Poles, Lithuanians, and a few other groups,
the non-Russian masses were characterized by double allegiance—to their particular group and to the Empire. Twenty-
five years of the policy of racial and ethnic equality have consolidated this situation, and it is very probable that a great
number of non-Russians consider Russia's past as their own.

This neonationalism seems to be stronger than nationalism
ever was before the revolution. The explanation is that the attempts to uproot the national sentiment merely repressed it
and, so to speak, condensed it; when, anticipating the coming
war, the rulers of Russia reversed their policy and began to
foster this sentiment, it not only awakened but became overwhelming. Very fortunately, it was not only intensified but also
modified: lacking the narrow shape of racialism, this sentiment
remains compatible with the recognition of human values and
therefore will not necessarily prove to be a new source of disturbance in the postwar world.[6]

The Russian nation, which has become so self-conscious,
continues to be politically organized—in other words, to be a
State. The withering away of the State, foreseen in the blueprint, did not materialize; bureaucracy, police, courts, jails, a
standing army, all these essential attributes of the State are
there, and nobody can doubt that the degree of "coercion," that
is, of the enforcement of the officially recognized order, has
increased as compared with pre-Revolutionary times.

That the State would continue to exist was part of the basic
expectation of the pre-Revolutionary period. This expectation,

and not the opposite expectation of the revolutionists has been fulfilled. But the State was to evolve towards democracy. Has anything of this kind taken place? The answer to this question cannot but be emphatically negative, and this despite the Stalin Constitution which, taken at face value, grants to the population both freedom and participation in the exercise of power, the essentials of democracy. Only a superficial observer, however, takes a constitution at face value. What actually matters is constitutional practice and, in contemporary Russia, the practice is as antidemocratic as it ever was since the overthrow of the Provisional government. In consequence, it can be said that the Communist Revolution has not only reversed the trend towards democracy, but has disposed of a number of institutions which in pre-Revolutionary Russia could be considered as precursors of democracy. In very modest limits indeed, the essential liberties existed in Russia after 1905–6; since 1864, the courts were independent and, in general, good. Today they are neither independent nor good, because their personnel does not master the "stuff of law." After 1864, Russia possessed an excellent system of self-government, but contemporary Soviets are merely agencies of decentralized administration, not of self-government. To find a political order in Russia's past similar to that of our day, one must go back to the reign of Paul (1796–1801).

The dictatorial structure was employed to realize the socio-economic phase of the blueprint. In this phase success, that is, the materialization of an order conforming to the plan, has been more complete than in any other. Except for a small number of "individual," that is, noncollectivized peasants, and of "nonco-operated" artisans, nobody can claim as his own any means of production, no private trade whatsoever is legally permitted to exist. Arable land, almost in totality, is distributed among 242,000 *kolhozes.* Trade and industry, as well as transportation, are managed by the State. Still, there is a significant departure from the blueprint resulting from the great deviation in the field of politics: industrial enterprises as well as agencies of distribution are State agencies, and not agencies of the stateless society of producers which had to obtain according to the blueprint. Collective farms seem to fulfill the expectations of the fathers of Marxism better, but this judgment must be reversed if one examines things not at their face value, but as they actually are: these farms are managed by a special branch of bureaucracy, obeying the orders of the political leaders and paying only slight attention to the desires of the members. Therefore, in the opinion of the majority of the Socialists, not socialism but State capitalism has emerged in Russia.

Let us not argue about terms. The facts are clear: the means of production and exchange have been taken away from the former owners, according to plan, but placed at the disposal of a mighty bureaucracy, and not of that society of producers which, according to Lenin, could be run by every cook. In this phase of human activity, the development has been in direct opposition both to pre-Revolutionary expectations and to the blueprint of the new rulers.

A new social order has arisen. In the minds of its creators, this was not the ultimate end: the order had to be created to make men happy, primarily by satisfying their material needs. Thus, an extremely difficult question is posed: what has been the impact of the Communist Revolution on the material well-being of the population of Russia? The best way to answer this question is to establish what the new system yields as national dividends. But since the new rulers claim that they had to sacrifice present needs for the preparation of a better future, the question of change in national equipment must also be discussed.

Food supply is the basic function of any national system of economy. The crop of 1913 has yielded 0.52 ton of grain per capita, that of 1937—0.57.* The number of cattle per capita shows a certain increase as compared with pre-Revolutionary times, which is further significant if one takes into account that the export of food has almost stopped. It is, however, not

* Statements in text may be confirmed by figures to be found in Appendix II.

quite certain whether the improvement is real relating to crops.

After 1933, Soviet statistics are concerned with the "biological" and not the "real" harvest, i.e., with the quantity of grain which was ready to be reaped on the fields (the figures being necessarily estimates) and not with the quantity actually collected. A difference of 10% between the two figures is assumed to exist by authorities in the field such as Professor S. N. Prokopovicz. If 10% is deducted from the figure for 1937, no improvement is left. On the other hand, let us not forget that improvement was to be expected on the basis of pre-Revolutionary trends. It is noteworthy that the improvement appearing from figures for 1937 was, then, quite recent: a few years earlier, the situation was quite definitely worse than that before the revolution.

Light industry has been sacrificed to heavy industry throughout the three Five-Year-Plans. Therefore, up to 1934, absolute figures were not higher than in 1928, when the pre-Revolutionary level had once more been reached, after the catastrophe of War Communism. Between 1934 and 1938, figures were rapidly increasing. But if we compare these figures with the hypothetical figures which obtain when we project pre-Revolutionary trends into the future, the result is that the production of sugar and cotton fabrics has lagged behind expectation. It is only in the production of paper work that the advance has been very rapid—a natural feature in a country ruled by the greatest bureaucracy in history.

The industrial equipment of the country has improved tremendously. This improvement can be measured by comparing figures of production for the years 1913 and 1938, since in all these years plants were operated at full capacity. The comparison yields these impressive figures: in 1938, the production of coal was 4.6 times larger than in 1913, that of cast iron 3.4 times, and that of oil 3.6 times.

One might be inclined to say that never in history has there been an equally magnificent advance. To refute such a statement, one has only to recall the ratio of advance of industry between 1888 and 1913, given above. Without revolution, the curve would have been different: instead of a slump in 1917–21, followed by a seven-year period of recovery and ten or twelve years of feverish activity to make up for the delay caused by revolutionary events, a relatively smooth advance would probably have taken place.[7] But it is significant indeed that around 1938 two curves, the hypothetical curve based on pre-Revolutionary trends and the curve of actual production reach approximately the same level, and that after this point had been reached further advance slowed down.* Does it not signify that the almost incredible efforts displayed in 1928–38 were analogous to the display of energy by an organism recovering from a sickness, up to the point when the normal state of things had been regained?

Other items of national equipment have evolved according to different patterns. In respect to railways, none of the Five-Year-Plans has been even approximately fulfilled, and the present-day network (60,000 miles) is incomparably smaller than that which could have been expected to exist by 1925 if the ten-year plan of the Imperial government had materialized. In consequence, the system has to carry three-quarters as much as the freight traffic of the railroads of the United States on about one-sixth of the track mileage.

As a counterpart, post-Revolutionary Russia possesses a large system of airways and produces around 400,000 automobiles a year, whereas pre-Revolutionary Russia did not possess any airline and had only 8,000 cars. But airlines belong to postwar achievements throughout the civilized world, as does the diffusion of the "automobile civilization" throughout Europe. No definite comparative judgment is possible, but to put automobiles and airlines on the credit side of the Revolution is obviously wrong. The same applies to tractors of which there were nearly one million at the outbreak of the war, compared to a few thousands before the Revolution. By the way, the mechanization of agriculture has hardly compensated the country for the loss of half her horses (31.7 million in 1913, 17.5 mil-

* This is shown on Chart XI.

lion in 1938). In the course of this war, mechanization has proved to be of dubious value, by making agriculture in the richest provinces of Russia dependent on oil supply (so badly needed for the war effort) and on transportation. Had Hitler succeeded at Stalingrad, not to speak of the occupation of Baku, half of Russia's agricultural production would have been forced to stop.

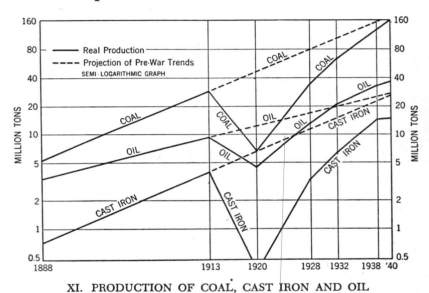

XI. PRODUCTION OF COAL, CAST IRON AND OIL

On the semilogarithmic graph, equal intervals of the vertical axis correspond to equal geometric rates of change, while on the horizontal axis equal intervals represent equal durations of time. In consequence, a straight line represents constant geometric change of a variable.

An additional item in the national equipment which has fared rather badly is housing. There is unanimity among the recent observers of Russia that the Russian cities are incredibly overcrowded and that the Russian workers often have to live in subhuman conditions.[8] Despite feverish building activity Russian workers, not to speak of intellectuals, have less living room per capita at their disposal than they had before the revolution. This shortcoming is all the worse since, once more according to the unanimous opinion of recent reporters, the new buildings are very poor and display signs of decay a few years after their erection. In 1935, one of the members of the Political Bureau said: "If you pay a visit to a workingman's flat, your first impression is that it is not bad at all. But when you get a little more inquisitive, you notice that the doors do not close, the window frames are poorly adjusted, and the glass in them is poor." [9] The standard of the building industry has not improved since then. "Nearly all the new buildings," says a recent observer, "are already showing defects. Doors do not work, walls are beginning to crack, elements of masonry have fallen down from the main structure." [10] Another reports of "big buildings, on which plaster was cracked or from which it had fallen, in a state of apparent neglect and disrepair," [11] despite signs boasting that the buildings were erected in 1937 or 1938. Therefore, not only must additional buildings be built, but those of which the five-year-planners are so proud must be replaced in the near future.

Meanwhile the dwelling space in towns, in ratio of the population, has steadily declined. It was 5.8 square meters per person in 1923, 5.7 in 1928, 4.7 in 1932 and 4.0 in 1937. In the course of the year 1940, only 250,000 square meters of dwelling space were built in the RSFSR, though about one million men migrated to the cities.[12] "Most single people and small families have to share apartments with other families, bathrooms, kitchens, and dining rooms being used in common." [13] The terrible overcrowding in cities and the unhygienic conditions of life there are only partly compensated by the fact that only about four per cent of the worker's income is spent for rent: European and especially American workers would spend even a smaller percentage of their incomes for similar accommodations.

To sum up the economic achievements of the Communist Revolution, it may be said that: (1) heavy industry has advanced according to expectations, but with an unequal and unsound distribution in time; (2) the advance in light industry, railways, and housing has lagged behind these expectations;

(3) the food supply is nearly up to the same expectations; (4) the mechanization of agriculture is a dubious advantage; (5) no paradise on earth, foreseen by the blueprint, has emerged from the Communist Revolution.

In addition to this, the "anarchy of capitalist production" has not been overcome, but simply replaced by recurrent blunders of the planners and executors of the plan. Never have people wasted more energy and raw materials by starting anew to work on a plan three or more times before possessing a final blueprint, or by producing mountains of wrecked commodities, than they did in Russia in the early 'thirties.

In the later 'thirties this chaos was somewhat mitigated, but has not yet been overcome. Thus, in 1938, 15 per cent of the coal output as well as one million tons of ferrous metals were lost en route from the mines to the furnaces. In 1939, the following story was told. The Krym preserve trust sold to the Minsk preserve trust several hundred tons of canned tomatoes. The Minsk trust sold the commodity to the Gomel retail trust; the latter sold it to the Krym trade office. Thus, a full trainload of tomatoes traveled from Simferopol to Minsk and back to Simferopol.[14]

In 1941, the following story appeared in the leading Soviet paper: in the outskirts of Odessa there are special railroad yards for the reconditioning of tank cars which are supposed to arrive empty. But they do not, because the consumers (Soviet agencies of the region between Rostov and Odessa) often fail to call for the merchandise addressed to them. Since the tanks ought to be empty, the yard management ordered that oil found in the cars be dumped below the hill. Whole lakes of crude oil, gasoline, and so on were formed beside the yard. Citizens came daily from the nearby streets and took home as much of the mixture as they could carry in pails.[15] At the same time serious oil shortages developed in many parts of Russia, owing to the delivery of oil to Germany in fulfillment of the agreement of 1939.

The final judgment about planned economy as practised in the USSR is this: never has there been a less harmonious economic system than that created according to the famous plans. To be convinced of this, one does not have to apply any foreign yardstick to the system in question, but merely compare the achievements with the plans, especially the first one; what they expected and recommended was harmonious and rational advance, securing the complete integration of parts into the whole; enormous departures, sometimes meaning acceleration, sometimes retardation, sometimes substitution and modification, made the results bear almost no resemblance to the blueprint. The art of rationalizing the economic machinery has not yet been invented, whereas the existence of such an art was one of the fundamental premises of the whole enterprise.

In this enterprise, the collectivization of the means of production was conceived not only as a means of producing plenty, but also as a means of creating social justice through the abolition of classes and the materialization of socioeconomic equality. To what extent did the new rulers succeed in this direction?

We have already found the answer to this question (Chapter X). The rise of a new social class, consisting of high-ranking Communists and persons whom Stalin has designated as "non-Party Bolsheviks" is imminent. This signifies the complete disruption of one of the fundamental aspects of the original blueprint and the return of Russia to a situation which would have obtained if no revolution had occurred. As usually happens in revolution, the distribution of individuals among social classes has been strongly affected, but despite the revolution, social classes have persisted.

Neither is there equality within the labor class: the wage differential between the upper and lower strata of this class is now as large as in capitalist society. Whether real wages have increased is a highly controversial question. It is rather probable that they have not. According to excellent authorities, in 1936 the average industrial wage was about eight times higher than the wage of 1931, but retail prices were fifteen to twenty times higher than prewar prices. In consequence, the number of "provision baskets" which could be bought by the wages of the average worker was 3.7 in 1913, 5.6 in 1928, 2.1 in 1935, and 2.6 in 1937.[16] But even if the wages had increased, let us not forget that in pre-Revolutionary Russia wages were increasing, and without revolution they probably would have continued to increase, as they did between the two world wars in industrial societies. But in any case, Labor has lost the rudiments of organization which it possessed in pre-Revolutionary society and lost also the prospect of acquiring the role of one of the main social forces which belongs to it in industrially advanced societies. On the other hand, Labor has gained security; unemployment no longer exists and is hardly likely to return for a long time to come. Social insurance covers all the other risks involved in industrial activity, such as sickness, invalidism, maternity, old age, and so on. This is one of the real achievements of the revolution, and very probably that degree of security would not have been obtained on the background of "capitalist" development. It is noteworthy that only industrial labor, not the peasants transformed into workers in agricultural enterprises of the State, have gained in this regard. Members of collective farms continue to depend on the fluctuations of harvests, and in case of bad harvests, the Communist government applies no other measures than those which, under similar conditions, were applied in Imperial Russia after the hunger catastrophe of 1891; loans in kind (seed, food, and fodder) formed their central part. It is also noteworthy that, under the new social order, two unprecedented demographic catastrophes occurred in Russia, one in 1921–22, another in 1932–33; the cost of each is measured in millions of human lives.

The two catastrophes did not, however, check the general trend in the population movement. After the catastrophes, the increase was resumed and so accelerated that, in 1939, the population reached the figure of 170 million, a little below the figure which would have been reached if the pre-Revolutionary ratio of increase had never been interrupted. The level of urbanization (33%) has surpassed expectation.

Public health has improved significantly: the death rate, especially the infant mortality rate has substantially declined, which permitted the population to grow despite the decline of the birth rate. This is largely due to the magnificent expansion of the network of "socialized medicine." But was not old Russia, as represented by her *Zemstvos,* the inventor of the system? [17]

The people of a country are the bearers of culture and also the object of cultural efforts of the *élite.* In backward countries, to which Russia quite definitely belonged and continues to belong, the main cultural effort aims at endowing all members of the national community with elementary education. In this regard, the Communist government is very proud of having overcome the secular illiteracy of Russia. The census of 1939 has shown that 81% of persons above the age of 10 could read and write, and that half of the illiterate persons belonged to the older age groups (above 50). This is, however, just one of the phases of sociocultural life where the imputation of an achievement to the Revolution is obviously wrong: without the Revolution, the index of literacy would have been 78% in 1939, a figure only slightly below the actual one; moreover, universal school education would have been reached quite a few years earlier. Thus, in our day, two curves have reached the same point: the curve of the actual indices and the curve of the hypothetical indices calculated on the assumption that the development continued with the same velocity which the process had reached early in the twentieth century.

By now, Russia has accomplished a historical task, the importance of which was recognized back in the 'sixties of the nineteenth century. No revolution was necessary to accomplish it: the enemy, i.e., illiteracy, was retreating long before its outbreak and would have been beaten without revolution, approximately at the same time when it actually was defeated— through the Revolution or perhaps despite the Revolution.

As concerns secondary and higher education, comparison is very difficult. It is noteworthy that, after the failure of the pedagogical experiments of 1923–32, the Communists drastically reversed their policy and, in general, restored the school system which had prevailed in the 'eighties of the nineteenth century. This is especially the case relating to school discipline and, in general, internal order, whereas the curriculum now strikingly resembles that of the last few years before the Revolution.

Among cultural activities of the higher level, natural and technical sciences have prospered; a large number of important contributions have been made by Russian scholars. Up to the present time, however, scholars who were famous before the Revolution or at least graduated from institutions of higher learning before then are still on the top, and it remains to be seen what the contribution will be of that generation which was the object of pedagogical experiments up to 1931.

On the other hand, the humanities in the broadest meaning of the term have suffered severely by the imposition on them of the official doctrine of Marxism. No great work in philosophy, history, economics, law, or government has appeared in the course of the twenty-five years; how could they, since a great work is necessarily a piece of independent thinking which could not be tolerated in the framework of a totalitarian dictatorship? In some specialized fields, namely, in that of law, a very curious phenomenon can be observed. What Soviet lawyers have to say about the law is now, after 1936, very much like what German Hegelians said sixty or eighty years ago. Thus, for instance, in criminal law punishment is once more conceived as retribution or retaliation for crime, and the sociological approach to crime which dominated in Russia since the early twentieth century up to 1936 is now declared to be one of the contemptible "petty bourgeois deviations" from Marxist orthodoxy.

The cause is clear: the "central theme" * of contemporary Soviet culture is the Marxist theory created one hundred years ago. Consistent efforts to focus the scientific thought on that theory have naturally resulted in the amazing "reaction" just mentioned. It is hard to say whether this "reaction" corresponds to the Communist blueprint; but one may assert that

* Which, according to Sorokin, determines the main phases of culture within the cultural "super-system."

nothing of that kind would have happened if the humanities had developed according to the pre-Revolutionary trends.

Similar statements must be made concerning art and literature. No great monument, sculpture, or picture has been engendered by the revolution; today, in painting, the style of the 1880's prevails, and in architecture the "Empire" style of the 1820's. In literature, quite a few good works have appeared during the periods of relaxation (1922–27, and after 1936); but as a whole literature very obviously suffers from the necessity of being "produced" in an imposed style, today that of socialist realism. The great richness of schools and nuances which characterized pre-Revolutionary Russia is gone as the result of Communist interference with culture.

Finally, what has happened to the family and religion, the two great guardians of culture? After many tribulations, the new rulers were compelled to restore the ideal of the stable family, in direct contrast to their blueprint. After the failure of persistent efforts to uproot religion, the Communists had to look for a compromise with it on the basis of a partial reformulation of their creed. The Revolution has severed the ties between the State and the Established Church, which probably would have occurred without revolution through the gradual liberalization of political institutions. The sufferings inflicted by the Revolution have purified the Orthodox Church; this is an advantage; but very probably, without the Revolution, acute atheism or religious indifferentism among the younger generation of our day would not have obtained the "successes" which are undeniable. Whereas the Communist blueprint has proven a complete failure in regard to the family, and the historical tradition has prevailed, in regard to religion the blueprint has materialized, say, about 50 per cent.

5

On the basis of the preceding survey, the following generalizations are permissible:

1. In regard to many important phases of sociocultural life,

twenty-five years after the Communist Revolution Russia was approximately where she would have been if no revolution had occurred. Russia continues to exist as a State; the population of this State is almost exactly the same as could have been expected without revolution; this population possesses that industrial equipment which could have been foreseen twenty-five years ago; the struggle against illiteracy is near termination, but it also accords with pre-Revolutionary expectations.

2. But as concerns political organization, Russia has been thrown back at least a century; her philosophy is that of the middle of the nineteenth century; her school system repeats that of "the dark age" of the 'eighties of the nineteenth century. Light industry and railways lag behind pre-Revolutionary expectation. Her creative capacity in the highest aspects of culture has been very definitely crippled through the imposition of a "managed culture." In painting, let us repeat, she is back to the 'eighties of the nineteenth century; in architecture, back to the 'twenties of the same century.*

3. Out of the Communist blueprint, the collectivization of production and exchange has been completely realized; religion has been shaken, but by no means uprooted. The country is endowed with heavy industry and has overcome her illiteracy; but in these respects the blueprint did not differ from the historical trend. In other aspects the blueprint has proven a failure. Russia is more nationalistic than ever; social classes and social inequality continue to exist; an economy of plenty has not been created; no grand art or literature has arisen; the family has returned to the stable type; the school is rather "reactionary."

4. The Revolution has produced a new society which is neither that which could have been mentally constructed by projecting the main trends of pre-Revolutionary times into the future, nor that which would have corresponded to the plans of the revolutionary leaders. To a certain extent, this new society may be viewed as a blending of the two models, but ele-

---

* The results of the breakdown of the Communist Experiment are shown on Chart XII.

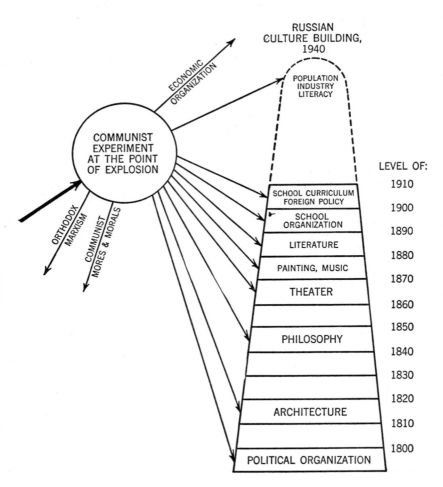

XII. THE OUTCOME OF THE COMMUNIST EXPERIMENT

ments are also present which do not fit into either; these are, first of all, elements of "reaction" and, secondly, elements invented in the course of the revolution, mainly as instrumentalities for the achievement of revolutionary ends.

The cause of the departures is clear. As revolutionary leaders usually are Utopians, they do not recognize the natural limitations of human actions and strive for goals which cannot be attained. They succeed best in those phases where they continue historical trends which were temporarily inhibited before the outbreak of a revolution. But to achieve these successes, 'the nation has to pay a heavy price. Everybody knows that revolution means destruction of human lives, material, and spiritual values. It is less well known that revolution, as shown by the Russian example, may mean retrogression. In any case, revolution is the most expensive mode of social change. Very probably, the cost of the Russian Revolution has been without precedent.

This cost is to be estimated even higher, as the Russian Revolution took place in a society fully conscious of its backwardness and displaying sincere efforts to overcome it. Only to a slight extent was the Communist Revolution launched to eliminate the partial inhibitions which opposed advance; to a much greater extent it was launched to fulfill a "social plan," to create an entirely new society. To take care of this aspect of the Revolution, its balance sheet must include a special account of the original patterns used by the revolutionary leaders and of those which they borrowed from various sources.

The leaders of the Russian Revolution were Marxists and, in their opinion, very orthodox Marxists; no wonder that in their blueprint and the activities based on it, Marxist patterns have prevailed. The idea of abolishing private ownership of the means of production and exchange and of founding a classless society is purely Marxist; of purely Marxist origin also has been the emphasis on internationalism, the implacable fight against religion, the animosity towards the stable, that is, "bourgeois" family.

But before the Revolution Marxist thought was known to be

highly abstract and to avoid any concrete planning of socialist society. Therefore, when the revolutionary leaders had to realize their blueprint, it became immediately apparent that the means to the end had to be either borrowed or invented. Since inventions are not necessarily made any time they are needed, borrowing is often the only possibility. Borrowing was very frequent during the initial phase of the Communist Revolution; under War Communism the German War Economics pattern, highly appreciated by Lenin, was imitated. The pattern of "planned economy" which underlies the Five-Year-Plans was borrowed by Lenin from two "bourgeois" writers. In art and literature, the problem of new patterns was solved by declaring that Futurism was congenial to Communism, a proposition which very soon was refuted by facts. In regard to the schools, "progressive education," especially the Dalton plan, was hastily borrowed and imposed on the absolutely unprepared Russian system, to start the Communist experiment in that field.

There have also been social inventions. More often than not, they must be seen in acts rather than words, for the Communists were never very proud of their inventions. The most important one has been the One-Party system, in which Lenin embodied the vague ideas of the international revolutionary movement of the early twentieth century. This invention has given rise to a social structure which probably will persist as long as the political system created in November, 1917, lasts. And this is an invention which has received widespread appreciation outside of Russia; structurally, the Fascist Party in Italy and the National Socialist Party in Germany were exact counterparts of the Russian Communist Party, as well as the "ruling parties" in minor dictatorships and the Communist and Fascist movements which have struggled for power in democracies.

Another original invention has been that of the Soviet State, developing the rudimentary representation of the Labor class tried out by Russian revolutionists in the course of the abortive Revolution of 1905–6. The Soviet State, based on the ideas of (1) representing the toilers only, (2) organizing elections on the basis of labor units, (3) emphasizing the sovereignty of local bodies, and (4) creating the central political bodies out of representatives of the local ones, was embodied in the Soviet Constitution from 1918 to 1936. In that year, it received a deadly blow from the Stalin Constitution which preserved only the name, but not the principles of the Soviet State.

A third invention can be seen in the "Two Sectors Economy" of the NEP period, leaving the "key positions" in the hands of the rulers and returning the rest of economic activity to "private masters" from whom they had been expropriated under War Communism. In Russia, this structure was destroyed by the shift to the Five-Year-Plans-policy. Outside of Russia, it has impressed the Socialists very much; the de-Man *Plan du travail* [*] is a very strict imitation of the Russian pattern of 1921–8.

Finally, the principle of managed culture is also one of the social inventions of the leaders of Russian Communism, an invention amply used by the National Socialists in Germany. Just as that of the "One-Party," the principle of managed culture has persisted and obviously will persist as long as the political regime does; as has already been mentioned, it has found entrance into Fascist and National Socialist Society.

A few minor inventions could be added to the list, such as (1) uninterrupted work, (2) socialist emulation, (3) the commercialization of the revolution and, (4) the cultural strangulation of religion, i.e., the prohibition of any social, cultural, or charitable activity on the part of religious bodies. Nos. 1 and 2 proved to be failures and were abandoned with the Second Socialist Offensive. No. 4 was one of the most notorious phases of religious persecution and was discontinued (perhaps not entirely) under the New Religious Policy. No. 3 has survived and has become one of the pillars of neo-Communist society. But the Communists are not proud of this invention and conceal it under the inconspicuous term of "the turnover tax."

There is no need to evaluate the basic four inventions. Two

---

[*] A comprehensive plan of social reconstruction elaborated by the Belgian Socialist, Henri de-Man, in 1933. The plan has been endorsed by the French Socialists and by the British Labor Party.

of them, the Soviet system and the Two Sectors Economy, have proven to be unworkable or, more exactly, incompatible with dictatorship, and have been abandoned in Russia. Two others, the One-Party system and managed culture, have become essential parts of any totalitarian structure. Their location in the value system is thus clearly established.

Such is the meager and rather negative contribution of the Russian revolution to the human treasury of social patterns. This special balance sheet does not, therefore, offer any reason for changing anything in the judgments previously made when comparing the achievements of the Communist Revolution with pre-Revolutionary expectations.

6

If the achievements and contributions of the Communist Revolution in Russia have been so meager, for what did the Russians fight? Why did the Russians display that indomitable will to resist and survive which seems to have been absent in a number of more advanced nations of Europe? Does not the fact of this resistance, of this will to gain victory, invalidate the previous deductions?

These facts do not contradict the judgments above at all if both the facts and the judgments are correctly interpreted.

1. In the conceptual scheme used in this discussion, the statement that the Russian Revolution has been rather poor in valuable accomplishments is not identical with the statement that the Russia of 1941–3 has not changed as compared with the Russia of 1914. The Russia of our day is much better educated and much better equipped economically than the Russia which fought in World War I; but in these improvements Russia's *élan vital* has been manifested; in other words, under the revolution deeds have been accomplished which might have been effected without revolution.

2. The social environment for the maintenance of which the Russians fought is only partly determined by the Communist plan of social reconstruction. Russia entered this war after

seven years of retreat from integral Communism, after a far-reaching restoration of national tradition had taken place. The Russians of 1941–4, in contrast to the Russians of 1918–33, were not only permitted but encouraged to be proud of their culture and history. They fought for their own home, the value of which has been once more officially recognized, and not for an imaginary World Home of the Proletariat which they were unsuccessfully invited to love up to 1933. The very character of official propaganda throughout the years of war testifies to this fact: Russia came first, and the International Communist Revolution was never mentioned; very probably, the dissolution of the Comintern (May 22, 1943) has been hailed in Russia as enthusiastically as among Russia's allies.

The significance of the return to national values as the background of resistance is enhanced by the particular configuration of the conflict in which Russia was involved. Whereas in previous wars the point at issue was a claim on some province or sphere of influence, in this war Russia's foe denied the value of Russian culture and even the right of the Russian people to continue living in areas occupied by them for one thousand years. Acts of the enemy, especially the systematic killing of the inhabitants and the systematic demolition of monuments of Russian culture in the occupied provinces, have proven that he meant business. The Communist leaders, being acknowledged masters of propaganda, have skillfully used these facts to bring Russian morale to the highest possible level, the same level which was reached, say, in 1812: officially, this war was called "The Second Patriotic War."

It is very probable that in this war many Russians fought not only for their country as such, but also for the New Order in its totality, holding that it was the best in the world, or at least the most convenient for them; others may have fought for the maintenance of substantial parts of this order, though desiring changes in other parts; still others may have fought despite the rejection of the basic premises of the New Order—such as, for instance, official atheism. This divergence of views did not prevent the Russians from forming a sacred union, for they all knew what the victory of the enemy would mean. Even those who did not accept the New Order felt that it was possible to improve it, if Russia were to continue to exist as an independent nation; and they knew that there was no hope whatsoever if Russia's future were to be dictated by the Nazis.

The Russians fought for their home, which is largely the expansion of their old home with slight modifications introduced by Communist architects. It is not quite certain that they would have displayed the same stubbornness and will to victory if the Communist architects had been permitted to reconstruct the old building fully.

3. It must be emphasized finally that people are accustomed to act much more on the basis of short than long perspectives. In other words, their attitudes are much more determined by the comparison of today with yesterday than with the day before yesterday. In contemporary Russia, people no longer think of pre-Revolutionary times and possibilities; but they know very well that, economically and culturally, they are much better off today than they were in 1933. To take an example: the religious situation is still far from religious freedom; but in 1939, a new religious policy was started which was substantially accentuated after the outbreak of the war. Religious-minded people could not fail to be influenced by obvious improvement and were willing to obey the directions of the Church leadership to support the government in the struggle for the preservation of Russia's independence.

Thus it appears that the magnificent war performance of the Russian nation does not contradict our judgments about the Russian Revolution. It is very possible that a large number of Russians would like substantial change in many phases of the existing order. But they understand that first things must come first: to secure national independence is the first thing, and getting rid of obsolete survivals of Communism can follow after victory.

In this war, Russia has proven by deeds her right to be one of the Big Three among the United Nations. But she had to prove it against the dominant expectation that her strength had been badly undermined through the Revolution. Russia's part in the war has shown that, in her history, the Communist Revolution had been a dangerous sickness, but that Russia possessed enough vital energy to overcome it. At the outbreak of this war she was obviously recovering from it. Whether a new challenge, this time in the form of a titanic war, will accelerate the recovery or be conducive to a relapse, we do not yet know.

Chapter XIV

LOOKING FORWARD:

Russia in the Postwar World

1

THE RUSSIANS HAVE fought magnificently for their home; as has been shown in the preceding chapter, this was their old home with modifications introduced by Communist architects. Does this not mean that now, when war is over, they will be satisfied with repairing their home and will consequently neither demand nor permit any change? For many reasons, this is highly improbable.

First of all, war with Germany started in the course of a major social process which was going on in Russia—the fusion into an organic whole of those elements of the past which were strong enough to survive the revolutionary disturbance, with those elements brought into existence by the Revolution which were strong enough to resist the mighty pressure of reviving Tradition. The termination of a revolutionary cycle is always a compromise between old and new. The level of the compromise is, however, not determined in advance. There is, therefore, no reason to assume that the compromise situation which existed in 1941 would become the final solution. On the contrary, many events which took place after the outbreak of the war make this rather improbable. The Communist International was dissolved, the International replaced by a new national anthem, divorce almost abolished, coeducation in schools dropped and, last but not least, a Patriarch was once more heading the Russian Orthodox Church. Thus, for defense and victory further departures from Communist Utopia towards National Tradition were necessary. These departures were the price paid by the government for the people's contribution to the corporate enterprise which is totalitarian war. That this price had to be paid proves that the compromise situation which existed in 1941 was not at all final.

Furthermore, a generalization may be derived from Russian history. For the past 150 years every major war, whether successful or unsuccessful, has pushed Russia further towards the liberalization of her institutions. The victorious wars of the late eighteenth century, with Suvorov's immortal campaigns as their climax, were followed by the liberal reforms which took place in the beginning of the reign of Emperor Alexander I. The First Patriotic War (1812) and Russia's contribution to the victory of Europe over Napoleon (1813–4) resulted in granting a liberal Constitution to "Tsardom Poland," under the scepter of Alexander, and in the Draft Constitution of 1820 for the Empire. The delay in the realization of this magnificent plan provoked the revolutionary outbreak of the Decembrists (1825) whose mentality was formed during the victorious campaigns of the years 1812–4. Russia's defeat in the Crimean war (1853–6) was the signal for the "great reforms" of Emperor Alexander II. After 1866 the tempo slowed down, but it was accelerated after the victorious war against Turkey (1877–8). Russia's defeat in the Japanese war resulted in the Constitutional reform of 1905–6, the Stolypin agrarian reform, the restoration of the excellent judicial system created in 1864 (1912) and in the start of the decennial plan of universal education. The First World War overthrew the Imperial regime, which chose the way of reaction under conditions in which bold advance was indicated. The Provisional Government was preparing the fulfillment of the secular dreams of the Russian intellectuals, all in the direction of democracy and social justice, when the shock of the Communist Revolution interrupted the trend.

The recurrence of such events cannot be accidental. In all cases, in the course of successful or unsuccessful wars, events bared tremendous shortcomings and provoked movements demanding their elimination. Very probably this war will not be an exception since many shortcomings in Communist politics and economics have been conspicuous. Thus, for instance, Hitler's attack was a surprise to the Russian high command. But a fortnight earlier, the British government warned Stalin of the coming invasion. Stalin did not deign to pay attention and thus put Russia in jeopardy. Does this not point to an enormous defect in Russia's political structure, making the fate of the nation depend on the foresight and will of the One?

This political blunder was augmented by military blunders of the same magnitude. The Russian armies were deployed along the newly acquired frontiers instead of expecting the enemy on the Dvina-Berezina-Dnieper line as advocated by military authorities, and were commanded by pseudo generals of the type of Voroshilov and Budenny, who owed their positions to their exploits in the Civil War and still more to their loyalty towards Stalin. They were demoted, but after having lost immense armies and retreated hundreds of miles. The valor of the Russian nation has overcome even these blunders. But now that almost everybody is a military man and is able to judge about problems of warfare, is it probable that these crimes against common sense will be completely forgotten?

Thirdly, it is probable that through contact with men living in other conditions, comparisons in favor of other orders have probably been made by many Russians. There were numerous reports about the eagerness of wartime Russians to learn more about foreign countries and to understand them better. The magnificent performance of the Invasion and the glory of the aftermath must have shown the Russians that military valor and victory are not limited to Communist society. The excellent American equipment and first-grade food received by Russia through lend-lease must have shown the Russians the achievements of an economic system which they were taught to despise for years. The very appearance of American soldiers and foreign correspondents and especially their attire must have acted as a revelation. Such things as their solid and comfortable shoes, as told many times by correspondents, inspired admiration which increased when the Russians learned that the men whom they contacted were not the sons of lords or Wall Street magnates, as they first suspected, but had come from entirely different and sometimes very humble strata of British or American society.

Moreover, the Red Army has crossed the Russian frontier and occupied large areas which never ceased to produce and consume under conditions of capitalism. With the exception of Germany and Czechoslovakia, the economic and cultural level of these areas is not very high; nevertheless, "a lot of tawdry brilliance blinds the eyes of Red Army Men," as stated by *Pravda* and other papers, such as "women with faces carefully made up to be pale despite the burning sunshine, the pompous uniforms of the policemen, high cushions in taxicabs," etc.[1] The purpose of the discussion of this brilliance by Soviet papers was to "unveil the dirty background"; but the very necessity of a warning speaks for itself.

2

We have seen that there are good reasons to expect that the Russian people will demand further changes in their homes. What could these demands be? Depending on the dictatorial structure of Russia, only conjectures are possible about the attitude of the nation at large. Obviously, under a dictatorship, the people (using this term to designate the nation minus the ruling class) cannot have definite programs; the dictatorship is there to prevent the crystallization of programs and social groups supporting them. Still, certain tendencies may be tentatively established which could be organized into a program of action if the opportunity were given to the people to gather and discuss the situation under intelligent and tolerant leadership. These tendencies may be derived from observation of the major trends of change effected in the course of The Great Retreat to meet the desires of the people, from analysis of objective elements involved in the situation, and from official revelations about the plans of clandestine opposition groups which again and again have appeared only to be crushed by the government. With these qualifications, the following statements may be tentatively offered:

First, the Russian people would like to be granted participation in political decisions. This is evident from the very fact of the Constitutional Reform of 1936 which took place during a period of internal appeasement through concessions to the people. Actual participation in political decisions was not granted, but everything was done to make the people believe that at last they had a share in political power.

Why were these nominal concessions made? The official theory seems to be that the dictator, Stalin, has found it convenient to "grant" his subjects a new Constitution. This is, of course, no explanation at all.

In actuality, the concessions testify to the existence of real aspirations on the part of the people, and especially on the part of the younger generation on whom falls the obligation of military defense. Russia has not become a democracy; but Soviet constitutional reform bears witness to the fact that the Russian people are eager for a taste of democracy, for all the things that generations of Russians fought to obtain previous to the catastrophe of October, 1917.

There is also reason to believe that the Russian people, especially the peasants, would like to get back their traditional form of self-government, which is of the type of direct and not representative democracy. This expectation may be derived from the fact that, up to the time of wholesale collectivization, the rural Soviets were opposed and often dominated by "village meetings," consisting of all the adult inhabitants of a village or even a township, deciding questions of local importance as to highways, school buildings, the police, and the like, imposing taxes, and electing semiofficial functionaries.[2] One may object that more than a decade has elapsed since these democratic institutions were crushed by the dictatorial regime and that they must have fallen into oblivion. But the short-lived Soviets of 1905 reappeared in 1917! Is it not probable that an institution with many centuries of history behind it could be preserved in the minds of the people and revived in favorable conditions?

Second, among the individual phases of democracy the Russian people would especially like to have religious freedom in the American meaning of the word. This may be deduced from the magnificent resistance of the believers in the course of religious persecutions and from the far-reaching concessions which were really made by the Communist government in this field. These concessions are, however, precarious and incomplete. The elimination of antireligious education from schools and the termination of any kind of discrimination against the believers, as well as the consolidation of the concessions already made so that they would no longer depend on the mood of the rulers is the order of the day. An arduous task indeed!

History teaches, however, that religious freedom rarely remains unaccompanied. All the other freedoms have been derived from religious freedom and, in consequence, a development toward genuine liberty of the press, assembly, and so on may be expected, though in the more distant future.

Third, the Russian people would like to be given more economic freedom, though not to the extent of restoring the freedom of economic enterprises relating to big-scale trade and industry. It is hard to expect that the people would like to invite capitalists, Russian or foreign, to come and take over enterprises which have cost the people almost superhuman sacrifices. Moreover, the contemporary trend within capitalism, involving the departure of big-scale industry and trade from management by the owner towards impersonal management through private bureaucracy, makes the difference between the Russian and Western systems less striking.[3] Finally, the majority of Russian intellectuals have always detested the specifically "bourgeois" feature of Western civilization. Having found another solution which finally proved workable (though not superior to the Western one)[4] they hardly will be persuaded to take the bus they once missed.

There are, however, very good reasons to assume that the restoration of the system of free enterprise relating to small industrial and commercial units would be welcomed by the people. The demand of "free trade," meaning just that, was paramount in the riots and insurrections of the earlier period, and "speculation," once more "free trade," reappeared on the scene whenever possible. It has often been reported that in the market places where the peasants are supposed to sell their products to the housewives they meet "speculators" and sell their "surpluses" to them to save much time and trouble. Police (militia) are conspicuous by their absence, and in many cases local authorities implicitly legalize the situation by imposing differential taxes on individual farmers, collective farmers, and "others" who cannot but be speculators. As to small-scale industry, these stories are typical:

An industrious man, after having paid 500 rubles to a "co-operative," hired thirty photographers and fifteen traveling salesmen and started mass production of illustrated postcards, naturally sold as a co-operative production. Another, after having bribed the secretary of a Trade Union, received a blacksmith's certificate; then he hired quite a few real blacksmiths and started producing commodities of which there were a great shortage. In April, 1935, 1,700 persons were jailed in Moscow for illegal commercial or industrial activity.[5] These events took place in the course of the earlier part of The Great Retreat. But later on such concessions as the revival of the artisan form of production and the decentralization of local industry showed that the government was aware of the popular desire for a measure of private trade and industry.

Sweeping changes will probably be demanded regarding the organization of agriculture. This does not mean that the people will necessarily demand the partition of all collective farms among the members,[6] since in many parts of Russia, namely, in the most fertile ones, the amalgamation of little lots into larger economic units is technically and economically reasonable. The reasonable demands of the peasants could be formulated as follows: (1) permission for every village to choose between collective farming, old-style agrarian communities, and individual farming of the Stolypin type, and (2) transformation of the bureaucratic *kolhoz* into a genuine producer's co-operative involving the democratization of management and the granting of the liberty to dispose of one's share, which is conspicuous by its absence in the present-day structure. Within it the peasant is a shareholder, but his share can neither be sold nor taken in kind. Upon leaving the *kolhoz* or being excluded from it, a member receives no compensation for the land which he once had incorporated within the common area. Therefore, the membership in a *kolhoz* is *de facto* a compulsory one. This results in an inferior situation of the individual member in dealing with the *kolhoz*-management which, until now, had been appointed by local Party committees. For instance, every member has to accept the work proposed by the management, even if this work is poorly remunerated; in this sense labor in *kolhozes* is half-compulsory. On the other hand, the legal nature of the individual allotments is rather indefinite.

Within a genuine producer's co-operative each shareholder would be entitled to declare his intention to withdraw, which would result in paying him (if necessary, in installments) the value of his share. With this money the former participant could either apply for membership in another co-operative (where additional capital would be required) or he could invest it in a small-scale industrial or commercial enterprise. It must be emphasized that the co-operative form of husbandry was highly appeciated by Russian peasants and intellectuals, so that the program outlined above could be justified as one more approximation of Russia's historical tradition.

Furthermore, the collectivized peasants will probably demand more freedom as to the disposal of their collective property. It is noteworthy that, according to numerous reports, the *kolhoz*-managers display a tendency to act as owners regarding *kolhoz* land; they often sell part of the land (to other *kolhozes*) or lease it to groups of collectivized or individual peasants.[7] All these acts are indeed illegal, but they permit one to pierce through the crust of official statements and get an insight into the real ideas of the peasants relating to land.

As to the form of land tenure, in some parts of Russia, espe-

cially in the west (Belorussia and Ukraine, where the individualistic tradition is strongest) and in the north (where nature
is unfavorable to large-scale farming) the peasants will obviously demand the right to get rid of the collective farm and
return to individual husbandry.*

It is more difficult to predict whether, in some parts of Russia, the inclination to restore the *mir* structure could gain
momentum.

It is also difficult to foresee what the demands in the cultural field could be. There, the aspirations of the sociocultural
élite are of decisive importance. Will the new *élite,* for a long
time ahead, be satisfied with the simplified and stereotyped art
production which has been imposed on Russia through the
mechanism of culture management? Or will they get tired of
the official style and demand that authors and artists be granted
genuine freedom of creation? And if they make the demand,
will they be supported by the people? There is no evidence
available for the solution of these problems.

One thing is, however, certain: the younger generation of
the *élite* has already displayed its strong dislike of the official
philosophy of the regime, of the boring and stupefying Marxist
doctrine, even in its revised version. With all real departures
from it in virtually all fields of application, it has degenerated
into a shell without content. Getting rid of this obsolete survival of Communism will very probably be the life task of the
rising generation.†

What could be the attitude of the government confronted
by the tentative program just outlined? Official Russia will
oppose a democratic evolution by all the means at its disposal.
Whether these means will be sufficient to check a natural development cannot be stated on the basis of the evidence now
available.

As to the other demands, the response of the leaders will

* The preservation of Stolypin farms in these regions up to 1939 is very
symptomatic.

† This is compatible with the persistence of collectivism in industrial production; in Russia, the problem of the organization of industry is considered
more and more to be one of technical expediency.

probably be of the same circumspect nature as it was before the outbreak of the war. They will continue pondering what concessions are unavoidable and at the same time not destructive to their position, and proceed by trial and error.

The great unknown on which the development will mainly depend is whether the rulers will try once more to materialize their blueprint as they did when the shift from the NEP to the Second Socialist Offensive was decided.

In order to predict the probable attitude of the government, these considerations may perhaps be helpful. Very probably, even within the inner circle, faith in the Doctrine has substantially declined. Perhaps there is no longer any faith, but merely stereotyped repetition of formulas which have been associated with the days of struggle and victory. In the beginning, the regime was of the type of an "ideocracy";* today it is much more the exertion of power on the basis of a newly acquired legitimacy.[8]

The withering away of the faith in the Doctrine does not mean that the power position of the rulers has been imperiled. A new government of revolutionary origin can hardly establish itself firmly in the saddle without professing belief in an appealing idea. But, once established, and having organized an effective apparatus of coercion, a power structure may persist because of social inertia and can be broken only through the rise of a new power center endowed with flaming faith in another idea. The Communists have maintained power not because they continued believing in the Doctrine, but because in 1917 they found in their faith the strength to conquer power and because, through its exoteric simplification, they gained the temporary support of the people; and also because up to the present day no force has appeared on the political horizon strong enough to destroy the power structure then established.

At the present time the withering away of faith is an asset rather than a liability. It makes the necessary concessions

* This is a state where dominance belongs to an impersonal idea (though necessarily embodied in a social group).

easier and facilitates unavoidable compromise. A fact of great importance established in Chapter XII is that not all the concessions of The Great Retreat were of the appeasement type. If they were, then, with the passing away of the danger—in other words, after victory—these concessions could easily be withdrawn. We know, however, that in the compromise structure of The Great Retreat such elements were present as recognition of the indomitable though impersonal resistance of human society, acknowledgment of the unexpected but highly detrimental effects of basic reforms, and even the liberation of the rulers themselves from the yoke of quite a few verbal formulas. The presence of such elements, and the fact that they are interwoven with elements of appeasement, make the withdrawal of the bulk of concessions rather improbable. It is, therefore, rather probable that the Russian Revolution will remain a four-phase process—in other words, that no Third Socialist Offensive will follow The Great Retreat.

3

Taking for granted that a development towards more democracy and still more National Tradition will take place, what could be its impact on Russia's foreign policy?

It has already been explained that the Soviet leaders have recognized the vitality of the Anglo-Saxon democracies and have abandoned the hope of submitting them to Communist transfiguration.

But, besides the Soviet Union and the great Anglo-Saxon democracies, there are vast areas devastated by the invaders which, after liberation, are subject to strong convulsions on the basis of their despair and the desire for revenge. In this field, the Soviets and the democracies are in a competitive situation, and one of the peculiar features of this situation is the existence of the Communist parties, former members of the Comintern. These parties are stronger than they ever had been; first of all, their members have played a prominent part in the underground; secondly, today objective conditions for the rise and spread of Communist ideas exist, stronger in some places, weaker in others.

Relating to these parties, Moscow is in an embarrassing position. These parties see in Moscow a great authority, a group of men victorious both on the Russian scene and in the titantic war of the past few years; and these parties continue to believe in the Marxist Doctrine in a much purer form than the Communists in Moscow do. These parties are naturally inclined to foment trouble in their respective countries. But, from the standpoint of the Moscow leaders, this may be premature. Today, when Russia is almost exhausted by her war effort and the deliberate devastation carried out by the invaders, an overt conflict with "progressive capitalism" could hardly appeal to her rulers. On the other hand, entirely abandoning the moral protectorate over the foreign Communist parties would mean abandoning a substantial asset. In consequence, Moscow's policy in the incipient stage of the period of esoteric internationalism appears to be full of inconsistencies, now supporting such "reactionary forces" as monarchy in Rumania and Italy, then rebuking the governments of France and Belgium for their attempts to disarm the Forces of Resistance, among them the Communists, now supporting the UNO, then brutally imposing its will on the nations of Eastern Europe.

Despite these inconsistencies, the following principles will probably mold the foreign policy of the Soviet Union so long as the esoteric phase of internationalism lasts:

1. National security, on the basis of frontiers considered necessary by military experts, and of the organization of the area west of this frontier on the pattern of a cluster of small States endowed with "pink" governments depending on the Soviet Union and inclined to far-reaching social reform;

2. Gratification of the national sentiment which demands (a) unification, within the Soviet State, of all territories inhabited by Great Russians, Ukrainians, and Belorussians, and (b) elimination of all vestiges of defeat and humiliation brought to Russia after, or more exactly through the Communist Revolution;[9]

3. Participation in a system of general security provided that the Big Three accept Russia's territorial demands.

Since the national sentiment has approached its climax, there can be no doubt that the people support the government in a policy which, to a Russian nationalist, appears to be justified by Russia's past and present. The provinces annexed from Poland and Rumania are claimed on the basis of the historical right of the Belorussian and Ukrainian peoples to live in national States, forming part of the Soviet Union. The Baltic States and the slice of Finland annexed in 1940 are claimed on the ground that Russia, like the United States, is a continent and that these provinces belong to it. Since this neonationalism is historically founded, there is reason to assume that the people, though emphatically supporting the government in its insistence on the frontiers of 1940, would not be enthusiastic about further expansion into areas beyond these frontiers; Russian nationalism has not displayed any tendency to become sheer imperialism, and claims on Poland proper or Czechoslovakia would probably be interpreted as the revival of internationalism and consequently be strongly condemned.

In the course of The Great Retreat, the Russian nation has broken the backbone of the Communist monster and, having broken it, experienced the joy of recovery and victory. The Russians of our day are more immune against propaganda of wholesale Communism than any other nation which has not passed through the hell of War Communism and of the Second Socialist Offensive. No longer having any desire to see their home rebuilt according to the Marxist blueprint, they will hardly help the government impose such a transfiguration on their neighbors.

The government is very well aware of the unfavorable attitude of the people towards such a policy and, in the course of The Great Retreat and the war, has learned the lesson well that even in a dictatorship the government cannot neglect these attitudes in the case of a policy which might eventually lead to a major war.

On the other hand, the Russian people will probably give

the government strong support if it adheres to the policy of collective security and guarantees durable peace. In addition to the fact that peace is a necessary prerequisite of Russia's reconstruction after the war, one should not forget that in the past two great systems of collective security, namely, the Holy Alliance (1815) and the Hague conferences of peace (1899) were of Russian origin and that, in the course of The Great Retreat, the Russians have been more and more inclined to restore those links with the past which had been flagrantly destroyed under the Communist Experiment.

4

Let us finish this study by discussing what the challenge of Communism means *now* to the Western World.

The challenge of forcible transformation through the International Communist Revolution inspired, financed, and helped by Russia has almost vanished. The Communist International no longer exists and the Russian nation will not stand behind the government in a war on behalf of Red Imperialism. Of course, Communist parties continue to exist in many parts of Europe and elsewhere and very often they have proven to be the best organized elements of the underground movement; this is only natural since the Communist parties were always trained for underground activity. They might decide to gain "October victories" in respective countries, but this would be frowned upon in Moscow. In consequence, eventual Communist regimes may arise by spontaneous imitation, not by orders from Moscow.

As to the challenge of invitation to imitation, the situation is this. For advanced countries, insofar as correct knowledge of the situation exists, there is no reason whatsoever to imitate Russia. No material paradise has arisen, the problem of the smooth functioning of the economic system has not been solved, there has been real achievement only insofar as the Revolution continued historical tasks interrupted by the First World War, Civil War, and their concomitant devastation. On the other hand, the petrification of culture on the level which prevailed two or three generations ago, as well as the lack of the basic freedoms, is repellent to men living in a free society.

But not all the countries are advanced, and in advanced countries, only a few comprehend the real situation. Therefore, if the advanced countries fail to solve the major problems of the postwar world—that of collective security and of full employment—a "time of trouble" [10] may emerge and in its course the challenge of Communism, not as it really exists, but as distorted by ignorance or false pretenses, may become a major threat. And if the advanced countries do not help the nations in distress and the backward peoples, especially in southeast Europe and Asia, then the challenge of the Communist example may become the signal for a general conflagration.

International revolution is not dead, but rather in a state of suspended animation. Whether "the bacilli of Communism" of which Lenin spoke twenty-seven years ago will revive and multiply depends not so much on the plans and actions of the Moscow leaders, as on the wisdom and energy of the great democracies.

To find an adequate response to a major challenge, one must first of all know the facts and interpret them correctly. Let us hope that Russia's example will be conclusive and teach the salutary lesson that a nation cannot gain more through a Communist Revolution than through reforms in the framework of democracy, under the guidance of men of good will and correct and inspiring vision.

REFERENCES

Abbreviations

To AVOID a tedious repetition of transliterated Russian words, the titles of Russian newspapers (to which more than incidental references have been made) have been replaced by the following symbols:

I.   *Izvestia* (News, official paper of the Soviet government).

K.G.   *Krasnaya Gazeta* (The Red Paper, evening paper appearing in Leningrad).

K.P.   *Komsomolskaya Pravda* (The Truth of the Comsomol, official paper of the Young Communist League).

K.Z.   *Krasnaya Zvezda* (The Red Star, official paper of the Red Army).

N.R.S.   *Novoye Russkoye Slovo* (Russian daily published in New York; it often reprints material from Soviet papers).

P.   *Pravda* (The Truth, official paper of the Central Committee of the Communist Party).

S.Z.   *Sotsialisticheskoye Zemledelye* (Socialist Agriculture, daily paper of the Commissariat of Agriculture).

U.G.   *Uchitelskaya Gazeta* (The Teacher's Paper, daily paper of the Commissariat for Education).

V.M.   *Vechernyaya Moskva* (Evening Moscow, an evening paper appearing in Moscow).

Z.K.P.   *Za Kommunisticheskoye Prosvescheniye* (For Communist Education, official paper of the Commissariat for Education).

When Russian titles have been translated, the symbol (R.) appears.

REFERENCES

CHAPTER I

1. An occasional footnote in Marx's works pointing to the alleged affinity between the *mir* structure and socialism was often cited by the Russian Marxists.
2. The idea often appears in the works of the great Russian philosopher, N. Berdyayev, especially in *The Origin of Russian Communism* (1936).

CHAPTER II

1. This is approximately the official Communist doctrine inculcated into foreign visitors lacking knowledge of the historical background of the situation they observe. Similar "information" on Russia, except the statement on the role of the Communists, was given to foreigners by Russian revolutionists prior to the Revolution. Since then many of the latter have completely changed heart.
2. Paul N. Miliukoff, *Outlines of Russian Culture* (1942), vol. 3, p. 73.
3. F. Engels, *On the State of the Labor Class in England* (in German, 1848).
4. In 1911, 67% of the population of Portugal was illiterate.
5. For more specific reasons of the early blossoming of Kievan Russia cf. Henri Pirenne, *Medieval Cities* (1925).
6. Says Harry Best: "The liberty of those who tilled the soil did not proceed far." (*The Soviet Experiment*, 1941, p. 15.)
7. This error often recurred in Lloyd George's speeches about the time when diplomatic relations between Great Britain and Russia were resumed.
8. Cf. A. N. Antsiferoff and others, "Russian Agriculture During the War," in *Economic and Social History of the War*, 1930.
9. Land which peasants bought from landlords after the Emancipation Act was not subject to the *mir* legislation and became their private property. On the *mir*, see *Systematic Source Book in Rural Sociology*, edited by Pitirim A. Sorokin, Carle Zimmerman, and C. J. Galpin (1930).

10. *Op. cit., supra,* note 8. On Stolypin's agrarian reform see N. Karpov, *The Agrarian Policy of Stolypin* (R. 1925); Gregory A. Pavlovski, *Agrarian Russia on the Eve of the Revolution,* 1930; Geroid T. Robinson, *Rural Russia under the Old Regime,* 1932.

11. Antsiferoff and others, *op. cit., supra,* note 8. Also S. N. Prokopowicz, *An Essay on the National Income of Russia* (R. 1918).

12. Figures for 1895 have been borrowed from *The Productive Forces of Russia,* a symposium published by the Ministry of Finances (R. 1896). Figures for 1916 are based on the findings of the agricultural census of that year.

13. Figures for 1863 and 1888 are derived from D. Mendeleyev, *The Tariff Explained* (R. 1891–2). Figures for 1913 are taken from the official reports of the Ministry of Trade and Industry.

14. Manya Gordon, *Russian Workers Before and After Lenin* (1941), p. 347.

15. *Ibid.,* pp. 58-61.

16. After the Revolution of 1905-6, the formerly usual eleven-and-a-half hour labor day rapidly disappeared. About the time of the outbreak of the war, Russian workers labored on the average of 9.6 hours for 270 days a year. From 1900 to 1913, the nominal wages increased by 54%; after correction for the increase in living costs, an increase of real wages by 15% is left (Gordon, *op. cit.,* pp. 66-69).

17. Prokopowicz, *op. cit., supra,* note 10. In this work, the national income of European Russia proper is estimated, omitting from consideration Poland, the Caucasus, Siberia and the Central Asiatic possessions.

18. In 1914, the population of Russia was officially estimated to be 178 million. Later on, outstanding statisticians showed that this estimate was grossly exaggerated. Cf. S. N. Prokopowicz, *Bulletin of the Russian Economic Institute in Prague,* No. 80 (R. 1930), and Vladimir P. Timoshenko, *Agricultural Russia and the Wheat Problem* (1932), pp. 18-19.

19. Expanded by the laws of June 10, 1909, and June 14, 1910. On these laws cf. D. M. Odinets, "Russian Primary and Secondary Schools During the War," in *Economic and Social History of the War* (1930), and Count Paul N. Ignatieff in *Russia, USSR* (1933), p. 654 (ed. by Petr Malevski-Malevich).

20. A. Ch. "The Enactment of the Laws on Universal Education," in *Zhurnal Ministerstva Yustitsii,* September, 1910. From 8.8 million rubles in 1906, the expenditure for public education rose to 72.3 million in 1916.

21. The procedure used by the present writer to reach the estimate

in the text is described in his article, "Overcoming Illiteracy," *Russian Review*, Autumn, 1942. After the publication of that paper, a book published in Moscow in 1940 reached the author; there, the index is given as having been 38-39%, but no reasons behind the estimate are communicated (A. G. Rashin, *The Growth of the Russian Proletariat*, R. 1940, p. 420).

22. Rashin, *op. cit.*, pp. 420 and 430.

23. Ingatieff, *op. cit.*, *supra*, note 19, p. 662.

24. On this change see B. Noldé, *L'ancien régime et la révolution russe*, 1928, p. 92.

25. The diagnosis in text coincides in general with that of George Vernadski, *Lenin* (1931), p. 1; Michael T. Florinski, *The End of the Russian Empire* (1931), pp. 23-24; Waldemar Gurian, *Bolshevism* (1931), pp. 23-24; and Manya Gordon, *op. cit.*, *supra*, note 14, pp. 64, 345, and 360.

CHAPTER III

1. The "legal blindness" of the Russian *intelligentsia* has been masterfully analyzed by B. Kistiakovski, *The Social Sciences and Law* (R. 1915).

2. On these doctrines see Julius F. Hecker, *Russian Sociology* (1915).

3. Several private guesses went farther in the description of the society of the future, but they were never endorsed by the Socialist parties of the different states. Among such descriptions, August Bebel's *Women and Socialism* was very much read in Russia.

4. Especially A. Chekhov's novels and short stories.

5. To use terms coined by Vilfredo Pareto in his *General Treatise on Sociology* (1915); English translation entitled *Mind and Society* (1936).

6. In one of his latest works, Lenin gave a very clear account of the reasons of his dispute with the Mensheviks. The work is significantly entitled, *On the History of the Problem of Dictatorship* (*Collected Works*, R. vol. 23, pp. 422 ff.).

7. *On the Social Ideal* (R. 1911). This is the best critical discussion of Marxism and Anarchism available in any language. It should be translated into English.

8. Cf. Gaudens Megaro, *Mussolini in the Making* (1938).

9. Lenin and Zinovyev, "Socialism and War" (Lenin's *Collected Works*, R. vol. 18).

10. *The State and the Revolution*, pp. 74, 82. Quoted by permission of International Publishers.

11. Karl Marx, *Amsterdam Speech,* 1872.
12. Lenin, *op. cit., supra,* note 10, p. 26.
13. *Ibid.,* pp. 20, 74.
14. The most complete presentation of this phase of Lenin's political doctrine is to be found in his paper, "The October Revolution," (*Coll. Works,* R. vol. 24, pp. 639 ff.).
15. On the activity of Lenin and the Bolsheviks between the two revolutions see Manya Gordon, *Russian Workers Before and After Lenin,* 1931, pp. 50 and 61.
16. However, the Socialist Revolutionists were still more debunked, since it was divulged that one of the members of their Central Committee, Aseff, was simultaneously a member of the Imperial Secret Police. For a fascinating account of his story see Boris I. Nikolayevsky, *Aseff, The Spy* (1939).

CHAPTER IV

1. The theory of the revolutionary process applied in this chapter is based on the study of about one thousand major and minor revolutionary movements carried out by the author when preparing material for Chapters XII-XIV, vol. 3, of P. A. Sorokin's *Social and Cultural Dynamics* (1937). In a more complete form the theory appears in the author's paper, "Revolution and Competition for Power," *Thought,* vol. 18, pp. 435 ff.
2. P. Sorokin, *op. cit.,* vol. 3, pp. 498-99.
3. This is a procedure called "mental experiment"; it is commended by Max Weber and Robert MacIver (*Social Causation,* 1942, pp. 179-180).
4. For instance, David J. Dallin, *Russia and Postwar Europe* (1943), pp. 168-170. It is impossible to prove a negative statement. However, the publication of the Russian archives by the Communists did not substantiate the allegation that a War Party existed in Russia in 1914.
5. The retrogressive process in Russia's political structure in the course of the war is well described by B. Noldé, *L'ancien régime et la révolution russe* (1928), pp. 105-109.
6. The sequence of events is well described by Michael T. Florinski, *The End of the Russian Empire* (1931), pp. 69 ff.
7. Florinski, *op. cit.,* pp. 207 ff., 221 ff. *Contra* D. Fedotoff-White, *The Growth of the Red Army* (1944), pp. 3 ff.
8. Cf. E. Ludendorff, *Meine Kriegserinnerungen* (1919), vol. 2, p. 240.
9. That the revolution was not inevitable is the main idea of Sir Bernard Pares in *The Fall of the Russian Monarchy* (1939).

10. Lenin, "Imperialism the Latest Phase of Capitalism" (*Collected Works*, R. vol. 19), and N. Bukharin, *The ABC of Communism* (R. 1922).
11. In 1912, 5.4 million *kustari* supplemented the work of approximately three million industrial workers (Manya Gordon, *Russian Workers Before and After Lenin*, 1941, p. 356).
12. Leo Trotsky, *Revolution Betrayed* (1937), p. 6. Quoted by permission of Pioneer Publishers.
13. Reproduced from N. S. Timasheff, *Religion in Soviet Russia* (1942). Quoted by permission of Sheed and Ward, publishers.
14. Same source as in note 13.
15. More than one hundred years before the Revolution of 1917, Pushkin predicted that in Russia a revolution could not be anything but a "senseless and pitiless revolt." An amazingly correct prophecy on the character of the revolutionary leadership was made by Dostoevski in *The Possessed*.

CHAPTER V

1. At the XI Congress of the Party, Zinovyev declared that the freedom of the press (in the "capitalist" interpretation) would signify the end of the "workers'" party and the beginning of counterrevolution (*Proceedings*, R. p. 352). In an article which appeared in *War and the Working Class*, January, 1945, the official view that "genuine liberty of the press" was granted to Soviet citizens, but denied to the citizens of democratic countries, was once more expressed.
2. In 1926, all the 120,000 Communists living in the countryside were elected to the rural Soviets (*The Party in Figures*, R. 1925–6).
3. I. 1927, No. 50.
4. In 1926, the average number of days when a rural Soviet was in session was 5.8 per year (Murugov and Kolesnikov, *The Apparatus of the Local Soviets*, R. 1926, p. 44).
5. Lenin, *The State and the Revolution*, p. 96.
6. Compiled from statements by Kamenev, Bukharin, and Trotsky at the IX and X Party Congress (1920 and 1921).
7. Lenin, *Collected Works* (R. vol. 26, p. 348, and vol. 27, p. 280); Zinovyev in P., May 12, 1923.
8. Here are a few figures about the size of the Party: 312,000 in 1919; 733,000 in 1921; 386,000 in 1923; 772,000 in 1925; 1,130,000 in 1927; 1,872,000 in 1934. All these figures appeared in the Proceedings of the Party Congresses of the corresponding years.

9. The supervising function of the Party has been carefully elaborated in the revised statute of 1939.

10. At the X Congress, it was said that the cells had only duties, but no rights; that they carried out all that was ordered, but never displayed initiative (*Proceedings*, R. p. 172). Here are a few quotations from other Party Congresses: "Problems of highest importance have been decided, and the Party was unaware of it" (*Proceedings of the VIII Congress*, R. p. 950). "The party center displays the tendency to kill every initiative" (*Proceedings of the IX Congress*, R. p. 52). "If somebody criticizes the policy of the center, he is dismissed" (*Proceedings of the XII Congress*, R. p. 113).

11. Zinovyev said about the first Party leader: "If there was some dissent in the Party, this did not make any trouble, for everybody knew that there was one man entitled to speak in the name of the Party, his words representing the Party's opinion; this man was Lenin" (*Proceedings of the XII Congress of the Communist Party of Russia*, R. p. 46).

12. *Under the Banner of Marxism*, 1939, No. 2.

13. "Soviet Russia's New Deal," *The Nation*, November 21, 1936, p. 356. With slight changes, the article has reappeared in Sidney and Beatrice Webb's, *The Truth About Russia* (1942).

14. I. Feb. 7, 1935.

15. I. Nov. 24, 1933.

16. *Vlast Sovietov*, 1936, No. 15, p. 19.

17. P. June 5, 1936.

18. Dec. 3, 1936.

19. Nov. 26, 1936.

20. Cf. Lenin's *Collected Works* (R.), vol. 27, p. 26.

21. This latter view has been especially emphasized by S. and B. Webb, *Soviet Communism* (1935), vol. I, pp. 449-451.

22. Cf., for instance, *Vlast Sovietov*, 1936. No. 13, pp. 9-10; No. 14, p. 3; *Sovietskoie Stroitelstvo*, 1936, No. 8, p. 7. Cf. Stalin's speech, Nov. 26, 1936.

23. Kalinin, *Vlast Sovietov*, 1936, No. 15.

24. This seems to have been the idea of Stalin when the Constitution was drafted. In an interview with Mr. Roy W. Howard he said that he expected an acute electoral struggle around candidates nominated by different organizations, and expressed the hope that this would increase the efficiency of the boards depending on the Soviets (I. March 5, 1936). This idea has been abandoned. The shift was called "a surprising fact" by the well-

informed Moscow correspondent of the New York *Times* (Nov. 25, 1936).

25. "Soviet Russia's New Deal," *The Nation*, Nov. 21, 1936, p. 598.
26. *Bulletin of the Laws of the USSR*, 1939, No. 43, art. 182.
27. I. Oct. 18, 1937.
28. New York *Times*, Dec. 5, 1937.
29. I. Dec. 17, 1937.
30. I. Dec. 15, 1937.
31. I. Aug. 28, 1938.
32. Due to the annexations of the year 1940, to the redistribution of the Soviet territory among provinces, and to the increase in the number of the People's Commissariats.
33. New York *Times*, April 4, 1940.
34. I. Sept. 1, 1939.
35. I. May 28, 1939; the sessions again coincided in April, 1940, and in January, 1944.
36. The Constitution contains clauses concerning the territorial division of the individual republics and the number and functions of the people's commissars; such statements were introduced in order to guarantee some stability in regard to these matters (cf. Stalin's speech, I. November 26, 1936). However, the realization of this aim proved to be beyond the capacities of the rulers; they continually changed the territorial divisions and the number and functions of the commissars.
37. P. March 6, 1937.
38. The statute was published in P. March 27, 1939.
39. To prepare the elections to the 18th Party Congress (February, 1939) the local cells used this procedure: they expelled from the Party all the members they suspected of independence, accusing them of being "enemies of the people." After the selections the indictments were dropped, as based on false denunciations, and the members reinstated in the Party. But meanwhile the elections had been carried out (August 31, 1939).
40. The main puzzle concerning the trials are the famous confessions of the defendants. The best guess is that of William H. Chamberlin in *Soviet Enigma*, 1944, pp. 206 ff. In somewhat modified form, it is this: the defendants were actually guilty of a capital offense, that of having privately expressed their dislike of Stalin's rule and their desire to get rid of him. A man guilty of capital offense may easily be induced to make any statement desired by the prosecution, if leniency is put in view (in Soviet conditions, the promise not to involve the defendant's family is an additional motive). The purpose of the

trials was not only to destroy Stalin's virtual competitors, but to vilify their names. Therefore they were ordered to confess to conspiracy with the enemy, the most hateful crime in a country with flaming national sentiment—which Russia already was at about the time of the trials. A few reprieves were granted each time, in order to induce subsequent defendants to indulge in similar confessions.

41. It is noteworthy that the liquidation of the Old Guard was carried out by the same man who, some ten years earlier, had opposed the use of any kind of repression against the opposition. This proves that in the late 'thirties, Stalin was more autocratically-minded than in 1925.

42. P. May 26, 1935; I. June 27, 1935.

43. On this subject, David J. Dallin (*The Real Soviet Russia*, 1944, pp. 186-8) offers a series of telling quotations from books published by recent American observers.

CHAPTER VI

1. The Socialist Revolutionists recognized in the decree the text of an article published in one of their papers. It was replaced by the more elaborate decrees of February 14 and March 11, 1919.

2. Cf. "The Communist Policy towards the Peasant and Food Crisis in the USSR," Birmingham Bureau of Research on Russian Economic Conditions, *Memorandum No. 8*, Birmingham, England, January, 1933; see also B. Brutzkus, "Agrarian Revolution in an Agrarian District," *Economichesky Vestnik* (1925), vol. 3.

3. The main decrees were these: on the nationalization of the banks, December 14, 1917; of the means of water transportation, January 26, 1918; of foreign trade, April 23, 1918; of large scale trade and industry, June 28, 1918; of apartment houses in towns and cities, August 20, 1918; of small scale trade and industry, November 29, 1918.

4. Very illuminating is A. Gurovich, "The Supreme Council of National Economy," *Archives of the Russian Revolution* (R. 1922), vol. 6.

5. Corn levies were inaugurated under the Provisional government, but became oppressive after the Communist Revolution. They increased from year to year; 0.8 million metric tons in 1918, 1.8 in 1919, 3.4 in 1920, and 6.1 in 1921. Cf. A. S. Wainstein, *Rural Taxation before the War and during the Revolution* (R. 1924), p. 63.

6. The most important decrees on denationalization were these: of houses, August 8, 1921; of small scale trade and industry, December 10, 1921.

7. Particularly the German Civil Code of 1900, the Swiss Code of 1907, and the Draft Civil Code for the Russian Empire which was being elaborated when the Revolution broke out.

8. The far-reaching similarity of the agrarian structure, introduced by the Agrarian Code of 1922, to the old structure is proved in detail by C. Zaitsew in his article "Agrarian Law," in *Law of Soviet Russia*, published by N. N. Alexeiev, A. V. Makletsov, and N. S. Timasheff (1925), vol. I, pp. 215-235. (R.; German translation Tübingen, 1925.)

9. Birmingham Bureau of Research, *Memorandum No. 8* (cited above, note 2), p. 10.

10. Cf. Stalin's article in P. June 2, 1928.

11. V. I. Grinevetsky, *Postwar Perspectives of Russian Industry* (R. 1919).

12. The industrial output had to increase from 18.3 billion rubles in 1927–8 to 43.2 in 1932–3; that of agriculture from 16.7 in 1927–8 to 25.8 in 1932–3. The plan years began as of October 1, hence their cumbersome designation.

13. Directions of the Central Committee of the Communist Party, December 5, 1929.

14. In the course of World War II the practice of socialist emulation was revived, but in combination with other devices aiming at lifting the productivity of labor.

15. For the following cf. the article of B. Brutzkus, "Hunger and Collectivization," *Sovremennya Zapiski*, vol. 52 (R. 1933), pp. 418-9.

16. For a more detailed account of the early stages of collectivization, see P. A. Sorokin's paper in Sorokin, Zimmerman, and Galpin, *op. cit.*, vol. 1, pp. 621-34.

17. Thus, for 1939, the plan foresaw an increase of 13.3% in industrial production, a lower ration than for any year after 1929.

18. Gregory Bienstock, Solomon Schwarz, and Aron Yugov, *Management in Russian Industry and Agriculture* (1944), *passim*. Very good remarks can be found in Wendell Willkie's *One World* (1943), p. 65.

19. I. Dec. 12, 1943.

20. P. May 9, 1939; I. March 9, 1943.

21. P. July 2, 1939; Jan. 24 and 29, 1940.

22. In 1943, 70,000 new local enterprises were created producing

about six billion rubles of consumers' goods per year (V.M. Dec. 20, 1943).

23. I. 1935, No. 62.

24. I. 1935, No. 44.

25. I. Solonevich, in *Sovremennya Zapiski*, vol. 59 (1935), p. 386.

26. In 1938, the *kolhoz* members owned 55.7% of all cows, and the *kolhozes* as collective enterprises only 16.9%; the rest belonged to individual (noncollectivized) farmers and to State farms. In 1937, the homestead plots produced 21.5% of the total agricultural output (*Sotsialisticheskoye Zemledelye*, 1939, p. 87).

27. The surplus was 778,000 ha. (S.Z. Sept. 24, 1939). In addition to this, farms of the Stolypin type continued to exist in large numbers, covering 380,000 ha. in the Ukraine, Belorussia, and the western provinces of the RSFSR (I. June 15, 1939).

28. In some regions the minimum was fixed at 60 or 100 days. Those who did not conform had to be expelled from the *kolhoz*. In 1942, the minimum obligation was lifted to 100-120 days (I. April 17, 1942).

29. 452,000 ha. were reintroduced into the collectivized fields. Cf. *Quarterly Bulletin of Soviet-Russian Economics*, ed. by S. N. Prokopowicz, No. 6, p. 78.

30. P. June 15, 1939; S.Z. Sept. 17, 1935; I. July 8, 1939.

31. Changes in the remuneration of the *kolhoz* members started on March 1, 1933, when the workday unit first appeared, but it was only in 1935 that the adjustment of remuneration to the services rendered became real. A special decree on the differential compensation of *kolhoz* members was enacted on December 31, 1940.

32. P. March 7, 1936.

33. *Partiinoye Stroitelstvo*, 1941, No. 10; I. March 1, 1943.

34. John Scott, *Duel for Europe* (1942), p. 128. Quoted by permission of Houghton-Mifflin Co., publishers.

35. This right had been conceded in 1932, but was once more denied in 1933.

36. *Poslednya Novosti*, January 19 and 20 and March 11, 1941.

37. The bread price was .09 ruble a kilo in 1928 (State bakeries were then on a nonprofit basis), .125 ruble in 1932, .25 ruble in 1933, .50 ruble in 1934. The price mentioned in the text was introduced simultaneously with the abolition of bread rations.

38. The turnover tax was introduced in 1930, but up to Stalin's inspiration played only a minor part in the Soviet budget. On the present-day rates see Bienstock and others, *op. cit., supra*, note 18, p. 84.

CHAPTER VII

1. Lenin, *Collected Works* (R.), vol. 22, p. 37.
2. *Proceedings of the XIV Congress of the Russian Communist Party* (R. 1926), p. 354.
3. *Proceedings of the XV Congress of the Russian Communist Party* (R. 1927), p. 46.
4. Adapted from Lenin's authentic report, *Collected Works* (R.), vol. 24, pp. 128 and 247.
5. Speech to the Moscow Party officials, May 9, 1925.
6. Nonaggression pacts signed with Germany and Turkey, still under the sign of aggressive internationalism, had the meaning of covert alliances. The pact with Lithuania (1926) was due to the peculiar position of that little country, which saw in the Soviet Union a virtual protector against Poland. The real series began with the pact with Finland (Jan. 21, 1932).
7. *Proceedings of the Executive Committee of the Comintern,* July 29, 1929 (R.).
8. *Proceedings of the Executive Committee of the (Red) International of Trade Unions* (R. 1929), p. 583.
9. Letter to Comrade Ivanov, published on February 14, 1938.
10. K.P. Oct. 18, 1934.
11. Z.I. Jan. 25, 1936: P. Apr. 7, 1936; V.M. March 11, 1936.
12. P. Jan. 24, 1937; I. Feb. 28, 1937; K.P. Apr. 18, 1937.
13. P. March 19, 1938.
14. P. Nov. 7, 1938.
15. K.Z. Sept. 8, 1940.
16. *Antireligioznik,* 1939, No. 6.
17. New York *Times,* Nov. 10, 1936.
18. K.Z. March 21, 1938.
19. P. Apr. 28, 1938; I. March 3, 1937; K.G. Oct. 11, 1937.
20. K.Z. Nov. 22, 1938.
21. *Ibid.*
22. U.G. March 25, 1938.
23. K.Z. March 28, 1939; I. Dec. 12, 1942.
24. New York *Herald Tribune,* July 13, 1942. Recently Alexis Tolstoy's dramatized novel entitled *Ivan the Terrible* appeared; a film on the same Tsar has been produced by Eisenstein (I. Aug. 3 and Oct. 6, 1943).
25. I. Aug. 22, 1943.
26. K.Z. 1939, No. 212.
27. K.Z. June 9, 1939; P. July 2, 1939.
28. I. Nov. 12, 1934; V.M. Feb. 25, 1936; P. March 21, 1938; K.Z. Apr. 24, 1938.

29. *Trud* 1938, No. 183; P. Aug. 31, 1938; V.M. June 16, 1939.
30. I. July 3, 1934; Apr. 4 and 17, 1939; P. July 11, 1939.
31. I. March 6, 1937.
32. P. June 18, 1939.
33. New York *Herald Tribune,* July 13, 1942.
34. S.Z. Feb. 18, 1936; *Molot,* Feb. 11, 1936; I. March 5, 1936.
35. P. Dec. 17, 1935; I. June 6, 1936.
36. P. Dec. 19, 1935; S.Z. Feb. 2, 1936. As reported in 1945, from 1917 to 1944, Pushkin's works were sold in 31,618,000 copies.
37. *Krasnaya Nov,* 1936, No. 1; I. Nov. 11, 1935, and P. Jan. 29, 1936.
38. *Krasnaya Nov,* 1939, No. 1.
39. I. Jan. 25, May 25, 1942; May 26 and July 28, 1943.
40. I. Apr. 14, 1943 and May 1, 1944.
41. I. Apr. 14, 1943.
42. I. Apr. 4, Oct. 11, 1942; July 11, Nov. 4, 1943; June 6 and 13, 1944.
43. I. Apr. 17, 1939, June 6 and Nov. 9, 1941. See also numerous essays by Alexis Tolstoy and Ilya Ehrenburg.
44. The number of federal republics was 4 in 1923, 7 in 1924, 11 in 1936, and 16 in 1940. In 1940, the greatest of the federal republics, the RSFSR, included 17 autonomous republics (today there are 15), 9 national districts, 93 national regions, and 830 national Soviets (I. Feb. 18, 1936).
45. In 1936, education was given in 112 different languages, out of which half possessed special alphabets, but only thirty elaborated grammars (P. Oct. 10, 1936).
46. The main speeches were delivered at a session of the Central Executive Committee of the Ukrainian Republic, Apr. 26, 1925, and at a session of the Union Congress of the Soviets, May 25, 1925.
47. The timing of the reform points rather to outward than inward preoccupations of the authors. It has been reported that at the Moscow conference (October, 1943) Molotov displayed great interest in the structure of the British Commonwealth of Nations, especially in the rights of the dominions concerning foreign policy. The change in the Constitution took place after the USSR had been denied particular representation for each of the constituent republics in the Committee for the study of German atrocities.
48. K.P. Feb. 14, 1938.
49. I. Feb. 2, 1936; March 14, 1938; Apr. 11, 1939; P. March 18,

1934; K.P. Oct. 4, 1937; Z.K.P. May 30, 1934; Oct. 24, 1935; Aug. 27, 1938; K.Z. Apr. 21, 1939.

50. These statements are typical of the new attitude: "The Russian people is the first among the equal members of the Soviet family of peoples" (Scherbakov, I. Jan. 22, 1942). "The Russian people is atop the fraternity of the Soviet peoples" (Alexis Tolstoy, I. Dec. 10, 1942). *Apropos* the twenty-fifth anniversary of the Bashkir autonomous republic, it was emphasized that the Bashkir people was able to advance "under the protection of the great Russian people" (I. March 23, 1944).

51. *Krasnaya Nov,* 1939, No. 1; I. Jan. 14, 1944.

CHAPTER VIII

1. See, for instance, Nathan Berman, "Juvenile Delinquency in the Soviet Union," *Am. Journ. Sociology,* March, 1937.

2. A. Kollontay, "The Family and the Communist State" (R. 1919), p. 8; N. Bukharin, *Proceedings of the XIII Congress of the Communist Party* (R. 1924), p. 545.

3. Cf. John Hazard in "Law and the Soviet Family," *Wisconsin Law Review* (1939, p. 245).

4. First by the decree of December 17 and 18, 1917, later on consolidated and expanded by the Family Code of October 22, 1918.

5. Decision of the Supreme Court of the RSFSR, reported in *Sudebnaya Praktika,* 1929, No. 20.

6. I. July 7, 1935.

7. P. June 4 and 26, 1935; *Molodaya Gvardiya,* 1935, No. 1.

8. *Sotsialisticheskaya Zakonnost,* 1939, No. 2.

9. I. Sept. 9, 1935; P. Sept. 11, 1935.

10. I. July 7, 1937; K.G. Nov. 4, 1934.

11. New York *Times,* Nov. 18, 1936.

12. I. Feb. 12, 1937.

13. New York *Times,* July 11, 1944.

14. For instance, by Arkhangelski, member of the Academy of Sciences, I. June 5, 1935.

15. K.P. June 7 and Sept. 29, 1935; P. Aug. 4, 1935.

16. *Sovetskaya Yustitsia,* 1939, No. 4.

17. I. Oct. 23, 1935.

18. *Na putyach k novoi shkole,* 1923, No. 1.

19. Quoted by Paul N. Ignatieff, in P. Malevski-Malevich, *Russia, USSR* (1933), p. 666.

20. This permitted the appointment to faculties of persons with little training in science, but of high loyalty to the regime.

21. S. Hessen, in *Sovremennya Zapiski,* vol. 59 (1935), pp. 445-458.
22. *Na putyach k novoi shkole,* 1923, No. 2.
23. By N. Ognev (R. 1926). English translation available.
24. This report is quoted (though in another translation) in N. A. Hans and S. Hessen, *The Educational Policy in Soviet Russia,* (1930), pp. 23-24.
25. *Narodnoye Prosveschenye v 1925–6 godu,* p. 110.
26. *Ibid.*
27. Z.K.P. Oct. 18, 1935.
28. *Narodnoye Prosveschenye,* 1927, Nos. 11-12.
29. U.G. May 25, 1938.
30. This was fully acknowledged in 1944 when the ignorance of many teachers was explained by the fact that they had been trained under methods later on condemned by the highest authorities (I. Apr. 5, 1944).
31. Z.K.P. May 23, 1934; July 2, 1935; Jan. 1, 1935.
32. K.G. Sept. 9, 1935.
33. From a speech delivered by the Commissar of Public Education, Bubnov, April 21, 1933.
34. I. Sept. 11 and 13, 1935.
35. I. Jan. 8, 1944.
36. P. Oct. 30, 1935.
37. New York *Times,* Oct. 17, 1943.
38. I. Apr. 7, Aug. 10, Dec. 1, 1943.
39. I. Aug. 8 and 10, 1943; Jan. 8, 1944. On June 21, 1944, all the reforms relating to the school order were consolidated in a decree "On measures aiming at the improvement of education in schools." However, in 1945 the government had to emphasize that pupils not having acquired the art of faultless spelling could not graduate from schools (K.P. Apr. 29, 1945). Teachers who displayed leniency in checking mistakes were severely scolded (U.G. May 26 and June 2, 1945).
40. P. Feb. 7, 1936.
41. P. 1939, No. 115.
42. Z.K.P. Feb. 8, 1936.
43. P. March 7, 1936.
44. *Krasnaya Nov,* 1936, No. 3; Z.K.P. Dec. 12, 1936.
45. I. Sept. 9, 1938.
46. Reproduced from N. S. Timasheff, *Religion in Soviet Russia* (1942), p. 23. By permission of Sheed and Ward, publishers.
47. For a complete study of these measures see the book quoted above, pp. 21 ff.
48. *Ibid.,* p. 65.

49. *Ibid.,* p. 97.
50. The new formulation of the Doctrine was completed in December, 1938, and put into force in January, 1939.
51. For a complete survey of the New Religious Policy up to 1942, see the book quoted in note 46, pp. 112 ff.
52. *Ibid.,* pp. 136 ff. See also New York *Times,* April 25 and 26, 1943, and April 17, 1944.
53. New York *Times,* Nov. 5, 1942.
54. I. Nov. 10 and Dec. 29, 1942; Nov. 12, 1943.
55. I. Sept. 5, 1943.
56. I. Sept. 12, 1943.
57. The Archbishop's visit to Moscow and his statements relating to it have been reported in the New York *Times,* Sept. 15, 19, 23 and 24, Oct. 11, 1943, and April 8, 1944.
58. New York *Times,* Sept. 12, 1943.
59. *Soviet War News* (published in London), Apr. 27, 1943.
60. New York *Times,* Sept. 5, 1943.
61. Patriarch Sergius published a special article against the Vatican in the April, 1945, issue of *The Messenger of the Patriarchate* (R.). The pastoral letter of the council was published in P. Feb. 5, 1945.
62. Letter to Metropolitan Benjamin, the Patriarch's representative in North America, published in N.R.S. Feb. 22, 1944.
63. I. May 21, 1944.
64. P. Feb. 1, 2, 5 and 7, 1945.
65. *Information Bulletin, Embassy of the USSR,* Apr. 20, 1944.
66. Released by the *Religious News Service* in August, 1944; quoted by permission.
67. New York *Times,* Jan. 8, 1944.
68. Released by the *Religious News Service* in August, 1944; quoted by permission.
69. New York *Times,* August 4, 1943.
70. *Ibid.,* June 17, 1943.
71. Released by *Religious News Service* in September and October, 1944; quoted by permission.
72. *Bezbozhnik,* 1940, No. 4.

CHAPTER IX

1. *Proceedings of the XIII Congress of the Communist Party* (R. 1925), pp. 538-9.
2. The German Ministry of Propaganda was an imitation of that department.
3. Kurt London, *The Seven Soviet Arts* (1937).

4. New York *Times,* Aug. 15, 1944.
5. I. Jan. 13 and May 11, 1942; March 20 and 23, 1943.
6. *Vozrozhdenye* (Russian daily published in Paris), April 4, 1932.
7. Zaideman and Zwieback, *The Class Enemy of the Historical Front* (R. 1931).
8. N. Sokolova, *Mir Iskusstva* (1934), pp. 9, 10 and 32.
9. M. Reissner, *Law, Our Law, Law of Others* (R. 1925), p. 244.
10. E. Pashukanis, *General Theory of Law* (R. 1929); *The Proletarian State and the Building of Classless Society* (R. 1932).
11. Lenin, *Collected Works* (R.), vol. 10, p. 39.
12. *Under the Banner of Marxism* (R.) 1930, No. 5.
13. P. Oct. 19 and Nov. 22, 1938.
14. K.P. Apr. 24, 1939.
15. I. Jan. 27, 1936.
16. P. March 27, 1937.
17. *Krasnaya Gvardiya,* 1937, No. 10-11.
18. P. Nov. 15, 1938.
19. *Sovetskoye Gosudarstvo,* 1936, No. 4.
20. *Sovetskaya Zakonnost,* 1938, No. 1.
21. *Sovetskaya Yustitsia,* 1938, Nos. 13 and 16.
22. *Sovetskaya Zakonnost,* 1937, No. 8.
23. *Sovetskoye Gosudarstvo,* 1938, Nos. 3 and 4.
24. *Bolshevik,* 1938, No. 22, and 1939, No. 1; *Propaganda i agitatsia,* 1929, No. 2; K.P. June 14, 1939; U.G. Apr. 17, 1939.
25. In the course of the year 1944, interesting polemics were waged between American observers of Russia (Walt Lissner in the New York *Times,* and Maurice Hindus in the New York *Herald Tribune*). The text is an attempt to show the real change in correct historical perspective. Cf. P. A. Baran, "New Trends in Russian Economic Doctrine," *The American Economic Review,* December, 1944.
26. New York *Times,* December 14 and 27, 1936.
27. S.Z. June 14, 1939.
28. *Novyi Mir,* 1934, Nov. 5.
29. From 1923 on, there were plays on Zagnug's revolt in Babylonia, Spartacus in Rome, the French Revolution, and Russia's revolutionary past. A State repertory Committee was created to select appropriate plays.
30. Z.K.P. Aug. 11, 1938.
31. P. June 10, 1939.
32. I. Sept. 3, 1934.
33. I. Sept. 5, 1939.
34. P. Dec. 17, 1935.

35. *Literaturnaya Gazeta,* Feb. 28, 1935.
36. K.P. June 14, 1935; I. Aug. 28, 1935; P. Oct. 13, 1935.
37. I. Jan. 1, 1936; P. Jan. 20, 1936; S.Z. Jan. 15, 1936.
38. P. Jan. 16, 1939.
39. V.M. Apr. 4, 1939.
40. P. Dec. 4, 1935; Z.K.P. Jan. 8, 1936; P. Feb. 8, 1936; S.Z. Feb. 3, 1936.
41. P. Jan. 28, 1936.
42. P. Feb. 6, 1936; Z.K.P. Feb. 18, 1936.
43. P. March 25, 1936.
44. V.M. March 16, 1936.
45. I. Nov. 18, 1936.
46. P. June 7, 1936.
47. V.M. May 11, 1936, and Feb. 15, 1938; P. Feb. 13, 1938; I. May 22, July 28 and Nov. 2, 1943.
48. I. Apr. 3, 1937.
49. I. Nov. 24, 1938.
50. V.M. May 8, 1939.
51. K.P. Feb. 17, 1938; P. Apr. 16, 1939; V.M. June 15, 1939 and May 23, 1940.
52. V.M. Apr. 9, 1939.
53. I. Apr. 17, 1939.
54. P. March 25, 1940.
55. Famous for ikon-painting.
56. I. March 5, Apr. 25, Dec. 30, 1943; March 12 and Apr. 21, 1944.
57. *Op. cit., supra,* note 3, pp. 64-5.
58. New York *Herald Tribune,* July 13 and 17, 1942.
59. Ilya Ehrenburg, "The Word is a Weapon," reproduced in N.R.S. Aug. 6, 1944.
60. V.M. May 29, 1939.
61. N.R.S. July 2, 1944.
62. P. March 16, 1938.
63. N.R.S. May 6 and June 5, 1944. No change has occurred in the course of the season of 1945–6.
64. The most famous among these poems is "The Letter of a Red Army Soldier to His Friends," by K. Simonov, published in K.P. Feb. 3, 1942. It is full of references to old Russian customs and expressions of flaming patriotism; Russia is called "the dearest of all countries"; there is no reference to the Soviets or their symbols.
65. *Literatura i iskusstvo,* Oct. 23, 1943.
66. Ralph M. Ingersoll, *Action on All Fronts* (1942), p. 125.
67. I. Oct. 26, 1943.

CHAPTER X

1. Adapted from Robert MacIver, *Social Causation* (1942), pp. 303-305.
2. For the years from 1914 to 1926, see *Bulletin No. 80 of the Economic Cabinet of S. N. Prokopovicz* (R. 1931). Important additions and corrections can be found in V. P. Timoshenko, *Agricultural Russia and the Wheat Problem*, Stanford University, 1932, pp. 18 ff. Cf. also E. Z. Volkov, *The Dynamics of the Population of the USSR* (R. 1930).
3. *Bulletin of the Central Statistical Board*, No. 72, p. 91.
4. *USSR for 15 Years* (R.), pp. 211-212.
5. New York *Times*, Sept. 16, 1933.
6. *Quarterly Bulletin of Soviet Russian Economics*, ed. by S. N. Prokopowicz, No. 4, p. 109.
7. I. Sept. 26, 1937.
8. *Vlast Sovietov*, Aug. 1938, p. 10.
9. I. June 2, 1939.
10. Sautin in *Partiinoye Stroitelstvo*, 1939, No. 12. In 1897, when a census was taken in Imperial Russia, the discrepancy was about 4%; this testifies to a decreased horizontal mobility of the population in modern Russia as compared to the prerevolutionary situation.
11. Cf. S. N. Prokopovicz, *Bulletin of the Russian Economic Institute in Prague*, No. 139 (R. 1937).
12. This is an adaptation of M. Ginsberg's and R. Sutherland's and Woodward's best-known definitions.
13. On the rise of the Russian proletariat, see A. G. Rashin, *The Origin of the Industrial Proletariat* (R. 1940).
14. Up to 1922 no electoral statistics were published. In 1922 the proportions of the disenfranchised in the countryside fluctuated between one and seven per cent (see *Vlast Sovietov*, June-July, 1922). In towns and cities it was obviously much higher.
15. In prerevolutionary Russia, the term was used to designate a *subgroup* among the rich peasants, namely, those who recklessly abused their economic superiority, often in the form of usury. After the Revolution the term was officially used to designate *all* the rich peasants; the purpose of the change was to exploit the hostile attitudes evoked by the term and to orientate them towards the rich peasants in their totality. Great skill in the manipulation of symbols is one of the characteristics of the Communist regime.
16. The role of the differential treatment as a stimulus to accelerate

collectivization was often recognized by the Soviet press. (See, e.g., *Economicheskaya Zhizn,* April 5, 1930.)

17. *Sotsialisticheskoye Stroytelstvo* (1939), p. 16.

18. The purge was a case of the metabolism of revolutionary leaders. (Cf. G. Bienstock and others, *Management in Russian Industry and Agriculture,* 1944, pp. 28-9.)

19. In the opinion of A. Yugov (*Russia's Economic Front for War and Peace,* 1942, pp. 228-29) the new upper group is not a definite class, since its members have no class aspirations, no class psychology, and no definite status in production. As shown in the text, these statements do not correspond to facts; moreover, Yugov obviously uses the narrow Marxian concept of class.

20. These statements were probably made on the basis of the abortive census of 1937, the findings of which never were published. See *Proceedings of the Eighteenth Congress of the Communist Party of the USSR* (R. 1939), pp. 309-10.

21. A. Yugov, *op. cit., supra,* note 19, p. 228.

22. David Dallin, *The Real Soviet Russia* (1942, p. 96), asserts that the lowest class in contemporary Soviet society, that of "forced labor," forms from eight to eleven per cent of the total population.

23. P. June 2, 1939; *Planovoe Khozyaistvo,* 1940, No. 5

24. P. Aug. 4, Sept. 8 and Oct. 14, 1935.

25. I. May 22, 1934.

26. An investigation carried out by the present writer in 1935 has shown that, when using the opportunity to change the first and last names, Russian men (but not women) chose the most familiar and inconspicuous ones.

27. This tragedy is well shown in Panteleimon Romanov's story, *Without Cherry Blossom* (R. 1926) (English translation available).

28. P. Nov. 13, 1934; July 9, 1935; K.P. Oct. 10, 1934.

29. P. Nov. 13, 1934; K.P. July 28, 1935; I. Sept. 27, 1935.

30. P. Nov. 28, 1934.

31. K.P. Jan. 20 and Aug. 27, 1935; I. Feb. 6, 1936.

32. P. July 7, 1935, and May 1, 1936.

33. I. July 2 and Oct. 2, 1934; K.P. Aug. 28, 1935.

34. P. Sept. 3, 1935.

35. E. Mercier, *USSR, Reflections* (1936), pp. 97-99.

36. V.M. June 7, 1939.

37. Anton S. Makarenko, *Letters to the Parents* (R. 1940).

38. K.P. July 27, 1935.

39. New York *Times,* Nov. 22, 1938.

40. Pitirim A. Sorokin, *Social and Cultural Dynamics*, vol. 3 (1937), pp. 525-26.
41. A. Gertenson, *Soviet Criminal Statistics* (R. 1935), p. 65.
42. M. S. Callcott, *Russian Justice*, 1935, pp. 203 ff.
43. *Sovetskaya Yustitsia*, 1935, No. 10.
44. *Ibid.*, 1935, No. 20; 1936, No. 4; 1937, No. 12.
45. From a speech by A. Vyshinski (general prosecutor of the Soviet Union) delivered in January, 1936.
46. For a detailed account of the change, see Pitirim A. Sorokin, *op. cit., supra*, note 40, pp. 563-4.
47. This is perhaps the reason why foreign observers were unable to discover special institutions for political offenders. (Cf. J. Gillin, "Russia's Penal Court and Penal System," *Journal of Criminal Law*, 1933–4, p. 305, note 5.)
48. This code seems to be unknown to the majority of the investigators of the Soviet system of punishment; an exception is represented by M. S. Callcott.
49. V. M. Apr. 19, 1935.
50. *Sovetskaya Zakonnost*, 1937, No. 3.

CHAPTER XI

1. The significance of the phase concept in the study of social phenomena is stressed by P. A. Sorokin, *Social and Cultural Dynamics* (1941), vol. 4, pp. 389 ff. The failure to understand that revolution is not necessarily a two-phase process is the major shortcoming of Crane Brinton's *Anatomy of Revolution* (1938) where the whole perspective of the Russian Revolution is vitiated by its subsumption under the two-phase scheme. The scheme appears also in P. A. Sorokin's *Russia and the United States* (1944) wherein a destructive and post-destructive phase are distinguished. In another variety, the scheme is used by Sir Bernard Pares in *Russia and the Peace* (1944). The author holds that, after 1921, Russia was ruled by Communists who no longer practiced Communism. Somehow, the whole Second Socialist Offensive has disappeared from his mental horizon.
2. Cf. N. Bukharin's speech at the XIIIth Congress of the Communist Party (*Proceedings*, R., p. 555).
3. The danger of "counterrevolution" was recognized in Kamenev's speech at the XIVth Congress of the Communist Party of Russia (I. 1925, No. 296).
4. In 1944, on the occasion of a Mendeleyev celebration, it was acknowledged that the great scientist had anticipated the program of industrialization (I. March 30, 1944).

CHAPTER XII

1. On these precepts see Pitirim A. Sorokin, *Social and Cultural Dynamics* (1937), vol. 2, pp. 576 ff.
2. The terms "internal and external barbarians" are used in the same sense as "internal and external proletariat" in Arthur Toynbee's *Study of History* (1936–9).
3. This is the application of one of the basic theorems of modern sociology formulated as "the principle of the restoration of equilibrium" in Vilfredo Pareto's *Mind and Society*. P. A. Sorokin (*op. cit., supra,* note 1, pp. 677 ff.) objects to the term, but recognizes the existence of the phenomenon.
4. A few blueprints elaborated by extremists were published in Moscow to ridicule them. A province offered to develop its coal industry so as to cover fifteen to eighteen times the needs of the Union, and this in five years.
5. The gradual disillusionment of the planners appears from these figures. The first draft of the Second Five-Year-Plan (1931) foresaw for 1937 (the last year of the plan period) the production of 450 million tons of coal and 150 million tons of cast iron. The second draft discussed by the Party Conference in 1932 reduced these figures to 250 and 100 million tons respectively, and the third draft discussed by the Party Congress in 1934 dropped the figures to 152 and 38 million. In actuality, 127 million tons of coal and 14.5 million tons of cast iron were produced in 1937.
6. Cf. D. Fedotoff-White, *The Growth of the Red Army* (1944), pp. 368-9.

CHAPTER XIII

1. This, for instance, is the procedure used by A. Rhys Williams in *The Russians* (1943).
2. This is one of the main methods recommended by Max Weber.
3. Nowadays, Stalin acknowledges that after the war Russia will have to double her railway network.
4. The procedure behind the computation is shown in the present author's paper, "Overcoming Illiteracy," *Russian Review,* Autumn, 1942, p. 88.
5. The similarity between the conditions and the lines of development of the two countries is the main topic of Pitirim A. Sorokin's *Russia and the United States* (1944).
6. Here is a recent statement: "Russian patriotism does not preclude respect for the cultures of other nations" (I. Nov. 4,

1943). In an editorial from *Izvestia*, one can find these statements: "We are fighting for freedom, culture, justice, honesty, friendship" (March 31, 1942).

7. The expectation formulated in the text is identical with that of Manya Gordon, *Russian Workers Before and After Lenin* (1914), p. 341, and H. R. Knickerbocker, *Is Tomorrow Hitler's?* (1941), p. 123. It is opposed by D. Fedotoff-White, *The Growth of the Red Army*, p. 350.

8. See, for instance, Sir Walter Citrine, *I Search for the Truth in the USSR* (1936), *passim*.

9. P. Dec. 30, 1935.

10. Walter Graebner, *Round Trip to Russia* (1943), p. 168.

11. Ralph M. Ingersoll, *Action on All Fronts* (1942), p. 79.

12. *Quarterly Bulletin of Soviet Russian Economics*, edited by S. N. Prokopowicz, Nos. 1-2, p. 56.

13. W. Graebner, *op. cit., supra*, note 10, p. 168.

14. P. May 20, 1939.

15. P. May 9, 1941.

16. The provision basket is an ingenious device introduced in 1928 by the International Labor Office to compare real wages at different times and places. The authorities referred to in the text are the *Quarterly Bulletin* (*supra*, note 12) No. 1, p. 55, and Leonard E. Hubbard, *Soviet Labor and Industry* (1942), p. 165. Cf. also Manya Gordon, *Russian Workers Before and After Lenin* (1941), *passim*.

17. Henry E. Sigerist, *Socialized Medicine in the Soviet Union* (1937), pp. 70-77.

CHAPTER XIV

1. New York *Times*, Sept. 27, 1944.

2. Numerous investigations carried out in the 'twenties and early 'thirties showed that the village and township meetings met more often than the rural Soviets. Cf. Murugov and Kolesnikov, *The Apparatus of the Rural Soviets* (R. 1926), pp. 44 and 112; see also Fenomenov, *The Contemporary Village* (R. 1925), p. 34, and Yakovlev, *Our Village* (R. 1925), pp. 129-140. In some places, these meetings were held every week (I. 1926, No. 233). In these meetings, the disenfranchised were permitted to participate (I. 1926, No. 177). This testifies to the democratic spirit of the Russian countryside. Early in 1940, newly elected local Soviets revived the practice of convoking informal meetings of citizens to discuss such acute problems as the fuel shortage and the breakdown of transportation (*Poslednya Novosti*, Rus-

sian daily published in Paris, Feb. 19, 1940). In later years, the theme of the revival of local Soviets on the basis of active participation of the local *intelligentsia* occupied a prominent position in Soviet papers. Cf. I. Apr. 2 and 8, Aug. 4, Sept. 10, 1943; May 14 and 24, 1944.

3. This is one of the major points in P. A. Sorokin's *Russia and the United States* (1944).

4. Very appropriate remarks were made to one hundred Soviet trade leaders by Eric Johnston, President of the United States Chamber of Commerce, at a meeting held in Moscow in June, 1944.

5. I. Sept. 12, 1935; P. May 28 and Oct. 1, 1936.

6. G. R. Treviranus, *The Russian Revolution* (1944), does expect a forthcoming peasant revolution in favor of the wholesale return to individualistic agriculture.

7. S.Z. Sept. 9 and 12, 1935, and May 21, 1936; P. March 30, 1936; I. May 10, 1944.

8. Cf. Guglielmo Ferrero, *The Reconstruction of Europe* (1941).

9. On the territorial demands of the Soviet Union see article by the author, "The Russo-Polish Dispute," *Review of Politics,* April, 1944.

10. This is a term used by Russian historians to designate a specified period in Russian history (early seventeenth century). Arthur Toynbee in *A Study of History* (1936–9), has applied it to designate a determined stage through which, in his opinion, all societies pass after the "breakdown" of their civilizations.

APPENDIX I

N.B.   Only events mentioned in the text appear in this table.

PRIOR TO THE COMMUNIST REVOLUTION

988.	Christianization of Russia by Vladimir the Saint.
1237.	Russia conquered by the Tartars.
1240.	Alexander Nevsky defeats the Swedes.
1242.	Alexander Nevsky defeats the Germans.
1380.	Dimitry Donskoy, Prince of Moscow, defeats the Tartars at Kulikovo Pole.
1480.	Tartar yoke terminated.
1533–84.	Ivan the Terrible.
1605–13.	Time of Trouble.
1682–1725.	Tsar, then Emperor, Peter the Great.
1709.	Peter the Great defeats the Swedes at Poltava.
1762–96.	Catherine the Great.
1796–1801.	Paul I.
1799.	Suvorov's Italian campaign.
1801–25.	Alexander I.
1810.	State Council created.
1812.	First Patriotic War; Napoleon defeated by Kutuzov.
1813–4.	War for the liberation of Europe.
1820.	First Draft Constitution for the Russian Empire.
1825–56.	Nicholas I.
1853–6.	Crimean War.
1856–81.	Alexander II.
1861.	Emancipation of serfs.
1864.	Judicial reform. *Zemstvos* created.
1870.	Municipal self-government granted.
1877–8.	Russo-Turkish War.
1881.	Alexander II murdered by revolutionists.
1881–93.	Alexander III.
1894–1917.	Nicholas II.
1899.	The Hague conference of peace convoked by Russia.

1904–5. Russo-Japanese War.
1904–6. Preliminary (or dress-rehearsal) revolution.
1905–6. Constitutional reform.
1906. Stolypin's agrarian reform started.
1908. Law on universal education.
1912. Judicial system improved.
1914–17. Russia's participation in the First World War.
1917. February 28 (March 12) Imperial regime overthrown, provisional government formed.
October 25 (November 7) Provisional government overthrown by the Communists.

WAR COMMUNISM

1917. November 8. Land decree.
November 11. Decree on the eight-hour working day.
November 27. Workers' control of industry introduced.
December 1. Supreme Council of National Economy established.
December 18-19. Freedom of divorce granted.
1918. January 4. Finland's independence recognized.
January 17-18. Constituent Assembly convenes and is disbanded.
January 20. Decree on the separation of State and Church.
February 10. Annulment of loans of the Imperial government.
February 14. Gregorian calendar introduced.
February 19. Decree on the socialization of land.
March 10. Brest-Litovsk peace treaty with Germany ratified.
April 22. Foreign trade nationalized.
May 1. Abolition of inheritance.
May 17. Civil war begins in the south.
June 28. Decree on the nationalization of industry.
July 10. Constitution of the RSFSR enacted.
August 30. Lenin wounded by a socialist-revolutionist; Red Terror begins.
August 8. University decree.
September 25. Metric system of measures introduced.
October 16. Education Act.
December 10. Labor code promulgated.
1919. January 2. First decree on universal education.

1919. March 2. Foundation of the Comintern.
November 30. Payment for economic services of the State discontinued.

1920. February 2. Peace treaty with Estonia (first in the series).
November 16. End of civil war in European Russia.
November 20. Freedom of abortion granted.

NEP

1921. March 15. Lenin's speech inaugurates the NEP.
March 18. Riga peace treaty with Poland ratified.
March 21. State corn levies replaced by tax in kind.
August 8. Decree on the denationalization of houses.
August 8. Decree on the reorganization of State industry.
December 10. Decree on the denationalization of small-scale trade and industry.

1922. February 6. Che-ka becomes GPU.
April 16. Rapallo agreement with Germany.
June 1. Penal code promulgated.
October 11. Monetary reform.
October 30. Agrarian code promulgated.
October 31. Civil code promulgated.

1923. February 15. Code of Criminal Procedure promulgated.
April 10. Decree on the reorganization of large-scale industry.
July 6. First Constitution of the USSR enacted.

1924. January 21. Lenin's death.
July 1. Resolution of the Central Committee on literature.
August 8. Trade agreement with England.
November 27. Trotsky dismissed from position of war commissar.

1925. May 9. Stalin's speech on socialism in one country.

1926. February 15. Decree on unrestricted inheritance.
September 28. Pact of nonaggression with Lithuania.

1927. November 12. Stalin gets rid of Zinovyev and Kamenev.

1928. July 17-September 12. Sixth Congress of the Comintern.
August 31. The USSR signs the Briand-Kellogg pact.

1929. January 7. Decree on the seven-hour work day.

SECOND SOCIALIST OFFENSIVE

1929. April 29. First Five-Year-Plan ratified by the Party Congress.
July 22. Bukharin falls in disgrace.
August 22. Decree on uninterrupted work.
December 27. Stalin's speech on the liquidation of the *kulaks.*
December 29. Stalin's fiftieth birthday anniversary used for the official recognition of his leadership.
1930. January 7. Resolution of the Central Committee on the new tasks of Marxist philosophy.
March 2. Stalin's letter on "Dizziness from Success."
March 15. Mitigation of collectivization and religious persecution.
1931. January 15. Resolution of the Central Committee on Dialectical Materialism.
September 5. Resolution of the Central Committee on shortcomings in the school system.
1932. January 26. Nonaggression pact with Finland.
March 26. Decree on "one cow."
August 7. Decree on death penalty for theft of collective property.
September 5. Second Resolution of the Central Committee on shortcomings in the school system.
September 19. Resolution of the Central Committee on shortcomings in Universities.
November 29. Nonaggression pact with France signed.
December 27. Passport system introduced.
December 31. First Five-Year-Plan terminated.
1933. January 30. Rural political sections created.
March 1. Resolution of the Central Committee on socialist realism.
July 2. Skrypnik, Ukrainian commissar for public education, commits suicide.

THE GREAT RETREAT

1934. April 24 and 26. Resolutions of the Central Committee on political education.
June 8. Fatherland reappears in the Soviet press.
June 11. GPU becomes the Commissariat of Internal Affairs.

1934. September 18. The USSR joins the League of Nations.

November 30. Bread rations abolished.

December 1. Kirov assassinated.

1935. February 5. Forthcoming constitutional reform announced.

March 15. New *kolhoz* statute promulgated.

April 7. Death penalty introduced for children over the age of twelve guilty of atrocious offenses.

May 2. Mutual assistance pact with France signed.

July 25. Seventh Congress of the Comintern begins.

September 27. Military ranks restored.

November 6. Stalin applauds a performance of folk songs and dances.

November 17. Three thousand Stakhanovites meet Stalin.

1936. January 28. Attack on formalism in art begins.

June 27. Decree on divorce and abortion.

August 19-23. First Moscow trial.

December 5. Stalin's Constitution promulgated.

1937. January 23-28. Second Moscow trial.

May 27. Pushkin's centennial celebrated.

June 12. Tukhachevski and other Red generals liquidated.

July 9. Electoral law published.

December 12. Elections to the Supreme Soviet held.

December 31. Second Five-Year-Plans terminated.

1938. March 2-8. Third Moscow trial.

November 15. Curb of political education in Universities.

December ? Resolution on New Religious Policy (unpublished).

1939. May 3. Litvinov dismissed.

May 27. Curb of individual lots within the *kolhozes* decreed.

August 23. Pact with Hitler.

September 17. The USSR annexes Eastern Poland.

November 30. Winter war with Finland begins.

December 20. Stalin's prizes instituted.

December 28. *Kolhoz* planning decentralized.

1940. March 15. Peace treaty with Finland.

June 26. Sunday restored as the official rest day.

1940. June 28. Annexation of Bessarabia and Northern Bukovina.

May 7. Ranks of generals and admirals restored.

August 2-6. Annexation of the Baltic States.

August 18. Decree on the compulsory transfer of engineers and technicians.

October 2. Decree on fees in high school and University.

October 2. Decree on Labor Reserves.

November 4. Ranks for noncommissioned officers introduced.

1941. January 9. Decree on the decentralization of industrial planning.

February 5. Commissariat for public security created.

May 6. Stalin becomes chairman of the Council of the People's Commissars.

June 22. Hitler attacks Russia.

August 8. First Slavic Congress held in Moscow.

1942. April 17. Work obligations of *kolhoz* members lifted.

April 25. Second Slavic Congress held in Moscow.

May 21. Order of the Patriotic War created.

June 12. Alliance with England ratified.

June 21. Decree on the improvement of education in schools promulgated.

July 7. Orders of Suvorov, Kutuzov, and Alexander Nevsky created.

November 4. Commission for the investigation of German atrocities created.

1943. January 7. Epaulettes for officers introduced.

May 15. Ranks for diplomatists created.

May 22. Comintern dissolved.

August 8. Conference on public education decrees end of co-education.

August 22. Suvorov schools created.

August 25. Ranks for public prosecutors created.

September 8. The Russian Orthodox Church elects a Patriarch.

October 9. Uniforms for diplomats introduced.

October 12. Order of Bogdan Khmelnitsky created.

November 10. Orders of Victory and of Glory created.

December 19. A new national anthem replaces the International.

1944. February 1. Constitutional reform.

1944. May 15. Death of Patriarch Sergius.
July 8. Second Divorce decree.
1945. January 31-February 2. A National Council of the Russian Orthodox Church convenes in Moscow.
March 11. A new inheritance law is promulgated.
May 9. War against Germany terminated.
June 26. Stalin is granted the title of Generalissimo.

APPENDIX II

STATISTICAL TABLES

TABLE I

Population in Millions

AREA OF THE USSR

Date	Type of Enumerator	Total	Urban	Rural	Per Cent Rural Population
1897, February 8..	Census	106.0	12.2	93.8	88.5
1914, January 1...	Estimate	138.1	25.4	112.7	81.6
1917, January 1...	Estimate	140.2	30.4	109.8	78.3
1920, August 26...	Partial Census	134.2–134.5	19.7	114.5–114.8	85.3
1923, January 1...	Estimate	135.9	21.7	114.2	84.0
1926, December 17	Census	147.0	26.3	120.7	82.6
1932, January 1...	Estimate	163.2	35.6	127.6	78.2
1934, January 1...	Estimate	159.0	NoData	No Data	No Data
1937, January 6...	Census	164.2	49.7	114.5	69.8
1939, January 17..	Census	170.5	55.9	114.6	67.2

TABLE II

SOWING AREA, HARVEST, AND CATTLE

Year	Sowing Area (millions of hectares)	Grain Harvested (millions of metric tons)	Cotton	Flax (millions of quintals)	Sugar Beets (millions of quintals)	Horses (millions)	Horned Cattle (millions)	Sheep (millions)	Pigs (millions)
1913	116.7	81.6	7.4	3.3	109.0	....	....	....	....
1916	106.5	62.3	...	...	.....	35.8	60.6	113.0	20.9
1922	77.7	56.3	...	...	.....	21.5	45.8	84.2	12.1
1928	113.0	73.3	8.2	...	.....	33.5	70.5	146.7	26.0
1932	134.0	69.8	12.7	3.2	101.4	19.6	40.7	52.1	11.6
1933	129.0	80.0†	12.7	5.0	65.6	16.6	38.6	50.6	12.1
1934	131.4	80.0†	11.8	5.3	113.6	15.3	42.4	50.9	14.2
1935	132.8	80.0†	17.2	5.5	162.1	15.5	49.2	60.1	22.2
1936	133.7	74.4†	23.9	5.8	168.3	16.6	56.7	73.7	30.5
1937	135.3	108.0†	25.8	5.7	218.6	16.7	57.0	81.2	22.8
1938	136.9	85.4†	26.9	5.5	166.8	17.5	63.2	102.5	30.6
1940	139.7	94.4†	25.1	4.9	222.0	....	...	.....	....

† Estimates; official data concern crops *in field.*

TABLE III

COLLECTIVIZATION

Date	Number of Kolhozes (thousands)	Total Number of Homesteads (millions)	Number of Collectivized Homesteads (millions)	Per cent of Homesteads Collectivized	Per cent of Sowing Area Collectivized
1929, June 1........	33	24.5	0.4	1.7	4.9
1930, January 30....	59	....	4.4	16.9	....
1930, February 10...	103	....	10.9	42.4	....
1930, March 1......	110	....	14.3	55.0	....
1930, May 15.......	82	....	5.8	24.1	....
1931, June 1........	211	24.7	13.0	52.7	67.8
1932, June 1........	211	....	15.0	61.5	....
1933, June 1........	224	23.6	15.2	64.4	....
1934, June 1........	235	....	15.9	73.0	....
1935, July 1........	246	20.9	17.3	82.8	94.1
1936, April 1.......	246	20.6	18.3	89.0	....
1937, April 1.......	241	19.9	18.5	93.0	....
1938, April 1.......	242	....	18.8	93.5	....
1939, November 1...	242	20.3	18.8	94.0	96.9

TABLE IV

INDUSTRIAL PRODUCTION

	1913	1920	1928	1932	1933	1934	1935	1936	1937	1938	1939	1940*
All producers' goods (1)	....	...	8.2	23.1	25.4	30.5	36.3	42.2	55.3	62.1	....	83.9
All consumers' goods (1)	....	...	10.1	20.2	21.5	23.4	25.3	27.9	40.4	44.0	....	53.6
All goods (1)	....	...	19.3	43.3	46.9	53.9	61.6	70.1	95.7	106.8	....	137.5
Coal (2)	28.9	6.7	35.4	64.7	76.2	93.9	109.0	126.2	127.1	132.0	....	164.7
Pig iron (2)	4.3	0.3	3.3	6.2	7.2	10.4	12.5	14.5	14.5	14.6	....	14.9
Oil (2)	9.4	3.9	11.7	22.3	22.5	25.6	26.8	29.2	30.6	32.3	....	34.2
Electrical power (3)	2.0	...	5.0	13.0	16.4	21.0	26.3	33.0	36.4	39.6	40.1	....
Copper (4)	31.0	...	30.0	46.7	45.4	53.3	76.0	100.7	97.5	103.2	....	166.0
Automobiles and trucks (5)	0.1	...	0.7	23.9	49.7	72.4	96.1	132.8	200.0	211.4	194.9	....
Tractors (5)	....	...	1.3	50.6	78.1	94.4	113.6	111.9	80.3	105.0	....	....
Locomotives (5)	0.6	...	0.5	0.8	1.1	1.2	1.5	1.2	1.6	1.6	1.6	....
Freight cars (5)	11.8	0.5	10.6	20.2	21.6	33.5	90.8	75.9	59.0	49.1	....	51.0
Cotton fabrics (6)	2,227	151	2,742	2,417	2,586	2,732	2,632	3,299	3,450	3,491	....	3,800
Woolen fabrics (6)	95	...	93.2	88.7	83.0	73.7	80.0	97.5	108.3	114.0	....	123.0
Leather shoes (7)	8.3	...	29.6	84.7	80.2	75.7	84.8	104.5	164.2	213.0	148.3	....
Sugar (4)	1,360	150	1,283	1,403	995	1,402	2,200	2,100	2,431	2,520	....	1,622
Paper (4)	205	41	165	479	506	566	641	702	833	834	....	....

(1) Billion rubles, in prices of 1926–7. (2) Million metric tons. (3) Billion kw/h. (4) Thousands metric tons. (5) Thousands. (6) Billion meters. (7) Million pairs. *Including the areas annexed in 1939–40,

TABLE V

RAILWAYS

Years	Length of the network (*thous. klm.*)	No. of locomotives (*thousands*)	No. of freight cars (*thousands*)	Freight (*billion ton/klm.*)
Area of the Empire				
1882................	21.5	....	...	....
1901................	51.9	....	...	....
1913................	59.4	16	535	65.7
1917................	70.0	....	...	....
Area of the USSR				
1917................	59.0	....	...	.....
1920................	....	7.5	...	.....
1928................	76.5	17.8	510	93.4
1932................	83.4	19.5	538	169.3
1937................	86.4	25.2	684	416.0
1939................	....	....	...	392.0
New Area (after the annexations)				
1940................	100.0	....	...	409.0

TABLE VI

ELEMENTARY EDUCATION

Years	Total Population (in millions)	Number of Pupils in Elementary Schools (in thousands)	Index of Education (in percentages)
Area of the Empire			
1880..................	98	1,141	1.16
1891..................	115	2,559	2.22
1894..................	121	3,275	2.80
1898..................	129	4,203	3.26
1903..................	139	5,237	3.76
1911..................	157	6,981	4.32
1915..................	165	8,147	4.93
Area of the USSR			
1914–5..............	140	7,236	5.1
1920..................	134	9,207	6.9
1922..................	137	6,808	5.0
1928–9..............	154	10,468	6.8
1930–1..............	161	15,609	9.9
1933–4..............	159	17,873	11.2
1938–9..............	170	21,288	12.5

TABLE VII

LITERACY

In percentages of the population over 10 years of age

	Total Population	Urban Population	Rural Population	Men	Women
1897. Census.........	27	38	23	38	17
1914. Estimate.......	40	..	..	..	..
1926. Census.........	51	66	45	66	37
1939. Census.........	81	90	76	91	73

APPENDIX III

SELECTED BIBLIOGRAPHY

Only books available in English are listed.

Brief but good surveys of Russia's past, in chronological order, are offered by George Vernadsky, *History of Russia* (1936), and Sir Bernard Pares, *A History of Russia* (1944). A valuable addition is Benedict H. Sumner, *A Short History of Russia* (1943) presenting the facts by topics.

Russia's economic history is treated in Chapters 14, 29, and 38 of W. H. Bowden, Michael Karpovich, and Abbott Usher, *An Economic History of Europe since 1750* (1937). More details on the prerevolutionary period may be found in James Mavor, *An Economic History of Russia* (1925), and Margaret S. Miller, *Economic Development of Russia* (1926). For the historical development of Russian culture, the standard work is Paul N. Miliukoff, *Outlines of Russian Culture* (English translation edited by Michael Karpovich, 3 vols., 1942), treating religion, literature, the figurative arts, and music. On religious developments in the early twentieth century, see also John Shelton Curtiss, *Church and State in Russia, 1900–17* (1940). On literature after 1880 see also Dmitri S. Mirsky, *Contemporary Russian Literature* (1926), and Ernest J. Simmons, *An Outline of Modern Russian Literature* (1943).

The state of Russia on the eve of the revolutionary breakdown is described in Sir John Maynard, *Russia in Flux; Before October* (1943) and in numerous volumes of the *Economic and Social History of the World War, Russian Series*, 12 vols. (1928–32); especially important are the volumes on agriculture (by Alexis N. Antsiferoff and others) and on education (by Paul I. Novgorodtseff and others). The particular standpoint of the Eurasians (a group emphasizing the Asiatic influence on Russia) somewhat impairs the otherwise excellent symposium, *Russia, the USSR* (ed. by Peter A. Malevsky-Malevich, 1933), with data on Russia before and after the Revolution. Also very good is Manya Gordon, *Workers Before and After Lenin* (1941), which gives much more information than announced by the title, namely, a detailed survey of numerous phases of Russian life before and after the Revolution. On conditions in rural areas, Gregory A. Pavlovsky, *Agricultural Russia on the Eve of the Revolution* (1930), and Geroid T. Robinson, *Rural Russia Under the Old Regime* (1932), give detailed and reliable information.

The philosophy of Marxism is best presented by Waldemar Gurian, *Bolshevism: Theory and Practice* (1932), and Charles J. MacFadden, *The Philosophy of Communism* (1939). Harold Laski's *Communism*, and Sidney Hook's *Toward the Understanding of K. Marx* (1933) give to Marxism an interpretation quite at variance with that of Lenin. For the latter's interpretation, the best source is naturally his *Collected Works* (no complete English translation available). The official doctrine as taught in the earlier years after the revolution is reproduced in Nikolai I. Bukharin, *Historical Materialism* (1925). The modern version of the Doctrine is to be found in Joseph Stalin's *Foundations of Leninism* (1941).

The events which were directly leading to the Revolution are described in Michael T. Florinsky, *The End of the Russian Empire* (1931), and Sir Bernard Pares, *The Fall of the Russian Monarchy* (1939), a book full of insight and understanding.

Among the numerous narrations of the revolutionary events, the most reliable is William H. Chamberlin, *The Russian Revolution* (2 vols. 1935) whereas Leo Trotsky's *The Russian Revolution* (1932) is a brilliantly told story, but by one of the actors from an entirely personal point of view.

General works on Russia under Soviet rule differ widely according to the time of their writing and the point of view of the author. The official standpoint, in addition to the numerous but usually short statements of the leaders, is best expressed in Eugene Varga, *Two Systems, Socialist Economy and Capitalist Economy* (1939). The standpoint of Russian liberals and moderate socialists is represented by Nikolai Bazily, *Russia Under Soviet Rule* (1939), and Manya Gordon, *Workers Before and After Lenin* (1941), with some qualification, also by the symposium, *Russia, the USSR* (ed. by Peter A. Malevsky-Malevich, 1933). The standpoint of Socialists rather in sympathy with the Communist Experiment is represented by Sidney and Beatrice Webb, *Soviet Communism* (2 vols., 1935), and Margaret Cole (editor), *Twelve Studies in Soviet Russia* (1933), whereas the disappointment of Radicals, Socialists, and Communists by the turn of events after 1934 is the central theme of Leo Trotsky, *Revolution Betrayed* (1937), Max Eastman, *Stalin's Russia and the Crisis of Socialism* (1940), and E. Strauss, Soviet Russia (1941). What can be classified as attempts at impartial presentation are Michael T. Florinsky, *Toward an Understanding of the USSR*

(1939), where The Great Retreat is not yet grasped as a new period in the development; Harry Best, *The Soviet Experiment* (1941), impaired by an erroneous interpretation of pre-Revolutionary Russia and the presentation of the Communist Experiment as a straight line process; William H. Chamberlin, *The Russian Enigma* (1943), clear and mostly correct (not quite so in chapters on pre-Revolutionary Russia), and G. R. Treviranus, *The Russian Revolutions* (1944), combining the history of the revolutions of 1905 and 1917, a sketchy survey of the transformation of Russia under the Communists and a few "lessons" to the Western World. The June, 1944, issue of the *American Sociological Review* is a symposium on contemporary Russia written mostly by persons with inadequate knowledge of Russian conditions, and with no understanding of the historical perspective. Pitirim A. Sorokin's *Russia and the United States* (1944) emphasizes the similarity of the development of the two countries and the convergence of their contemporary trends. The thesis is brilliantly presented, but very important differences have not received adequate treatment.

Works reproducing the author's personal experience in Russia may be divided into three main groups: (1) works of Russians having lived under Soviet rule; (2) tales of foreigners who were able to write as participant observers; and (3) tales of occasional visitors.

Among the works of the first group, two books written by husband and wife deserve the greatest attention. These are Tatiana Tchernavin, *Escape from the Soviets* (1934), and Vladimir Tchernavin, *I Speak for the Silent* (1935).

Among the works of the second group, three look at Russia through the eyes of an engineer; these are George A. Burrell, *An American Engineer Looks at Russia* (1932), Allan Monkhouse, *Moscow, 1911–1913* (1934), and Walter A. Rukeyser, *Working for the Soviets* (1932).

John Scott's *Behind the Urals* (1942) reproduces the experience of a foreigner who became a Soviet worker and gives a most vivid picture of Russia in the course of the Second Socialist Offensive and The Great Retreat. The experience of disillusioned radicals is revealed in Eugene Lyons, *Assignment in Utopia* (1937), Freda Utley, *The Dream We Lost* (1940), Anton Ciliga, *The Russian Enigma* (1940), Markoosha Fischer, *My Lives in Russia* (1944) and Alexander Barmin, *One Who Survived* (1945). Joseph E. Davis, *Mission to Moscow* (1941), is the summary of observations and reflections of an ambassador; this is one of the most important documents about Russia in the course of The Great Retreat, but contains quite a few groundless generalizations and wrong interpretations.

Between the second and third groups are the numerous works of Maurice G. Hindus, especially *The Broken Earth* (1926), *Humanity Uprooted* (1933), *The Great Offensive* (1933) and *Mother Russia* (1943). The author was born in Russia and, after having emigrated to America, paid numerous visits to his mother country. The books contain good descriptions of everyday life in Russia at different stages of the Communist Experiment and The Great Retreat, but uncritically endorse many official theories. To the same intermediary category belongs Albert Rhys Williams, *The Russians: The Land, the People and Why They Fight* (1943). The author is a former Congregational Minister who was able to observe the Great Experiment in its different phases and has interpreted it as a straight line progressive movement. Also belonging to the intermediary category are books written by foreign correspondents having spent many years in Russia and having achieved real understanding of her problems. Among them the most important are: Paul Scheffer, *Seven Years in Soviet Russia* (1932), William H. Chamberlin, *Russia's Iron Age* (1935), Walter Duranty, *Duranty Reports Russia* (1934), and *The Kremlin and the People* (1941).

Among works of occasional visitors, up to the outbreak of the war, these deserve attention because of the importance of the facts reported or the personality of the author: Theodore Dreiser, *Dreiser Looks at Russia* (1928), John Dewey, *Impressions of Russia* (1929), Malcolm Muggeridge, *Winter in Russia* (1934), Edouard Herriot, *Eastward from Paris* (1934), Sir Walter Citrine, *I Search for Truth in Russia* (1936), Lion Feuchtwanger, *Moscow* (1937), and André Gide, *Return from the USSR* (1937).

Experience in Russia at war is reproduced in Erskine Caldwell, *All-out on the Road to Smolensk* (1942), Margaret Bourke-White, *Shooting the Russian War* (1942), Ralph M. Ingersoll, *Action on All Fronts* (1942), Alexander Werth, *Moscow War Diary* (1942), Wallace Carroll, *We're in This with Russia* (1942), Eve Curie, *Journey Among Warriors* (1943), Alice Moats, *Blind Date with Mars* (1945), Walter Graebner, *Round Trip to Russia* (1943), Wendell Willkie, *One World* (1943), Henry C. Cassidy, *Moscow Dateline* (1943), James E. Brown, *Russia Fights* (1943), Edgar Snow, *People on Our Side* (1944), W. L. White, *Report on the Russians* (1945), Edmund Stevens, *Russia is no Riddle* (1945), Edgar Snow, *The Pattern of Soviet Power* (1945), and Richard E. Lauterbach, *These are the Russians* (1945).

There is no adequate description in English of the political organization of the Soviet State piercing through the crust of official verbal behavior. The best approximations are Roger N. Baldwin,

Liberty Under the Soviets (1928). Walter R. Batsell, *Soviet Rule in Russia* (1929), Bertram W. Maxwell, *The Soviet State* (1934), and Samuel N. Harper, *The Government of the Soviet Union* (1938), whereas Sidney and Beatrice Webb, *The Truth About Russia* (1934), is a condensed restatement of their famous thesis according to which, under Soviet rule, the Russians enjoy a much more democratic regime than the British or Americans. On the organization of inter-ethnic relations, see Hans Kohn, *Nationalism in Soviet Russia* (1932). Because of the personal character of the regime, the biographies of the leaders are of importance; among them, these may be recommended: George Vernadsky, *Lenin* (1931), and, with qualifications, Boris Souvarine, *Stalin; Critical Study of Bolshevism* (1939). The official version appears in *Vladimir Lenin, A Political Biography* (prepared by the Marx-Engels Institute, 1943). The famous Moscow trials are reported in *The Case of the Anti-Soviet Trotskyite Center* (1937); for a criticism see John Dewey (chairman) *Report of the Hearing of the Case by the Preliminary Commission of Inquiry* (1937). Some methods of the secret service are disclosed in Essad-Bey, *OGPU* (1933), and Walter S. Krivitsky, *In Stalin's Secret Service* (1939), but the books cannot be considered absolutely reliable.

The social and economic transformation of Russia under Communist rule has always been in the center of interest. The earlier phases and achievements have been described in Maurice H. Dobb and H. S. Stevens, *Russian Economic Development Since the Revolution* (1928), Aron Yugov, *Economic Trends in Russia* (1931), Calvin B. Hoover, *The Economic Life of Soviet Russia* (1931), and Lancelot Lawton, *Economic History of Soviet Russia* (1932). On the recent phase the most important is Aron Yugov, *Russia's Economic Front for War and Peace* (1942). Four books by Leonard E. Hubbard, *Soviet Money and Finance* (1936), *Economics of Soviet Agriculture* (1939), *Soviet Trade and Distribution* (1938) and *Soviet Labor and Industry* (1942), give detailed accounts of the individual phases of the economic life of the past few years. On agriculture, see also Sir John Maynard, *Collective Farming in the USSR* (1936); on industry and labor, Manya Gordon, *Workers Before and After Lenin* (1941). The official view on planning is expressed in V. V. Obolenski-Ossinsky, *Socialist Planned Economy in the Soviet Union* (1932); an abridged translation of the First Five-Year-Plan is available in G. T. Grinko, *The Five-Year-Plan of the Soviet Union* (1930). The best picture of the embodiment of the plan in reality is Boris Brutskus, *Economic Planning in Soviet Russia* (1935). For later years, see Gregory Bienstock, Solomon Schwarz, and Aron

Yugov, *Management in Russian Industry and Agriculture* (1944). For the understanding of the difficulty to judge correctly about the economic achievements of the Soviets, see Colin Clark, *Critique of Russian Statistics* (1939).

The transformation of the family and the sexual mores has been treated many times with more enthusiasm than real understanding; the individual books are Jessica Smith, *Women in Soviet Russia* (1927), Alice W. Field, *Protection of Women and Children in Soviet Russia* (1932), Fannina W. Halle, *Women in Soviet Russia* (1933), Ella Winter, *Red Virtue* (1933), Susan Kingsbury and Mildred Fairchild, *Factory, Family and Women in the Soviet Union* (1935), and Vera M. Fediaevsky and P. S. Hill, *Nursery Schools and Parent Education in Soviet Russia* (1937).

On the school experiment up to 1930, the standard work is Nikolaus Hans and Serge Hessen, *Educational Policy in Soviet Russia* (1930). For the later years, the best presentation available is contained in Manya Gordon, *Workers Before and After Lenin* (1941). On the political phase of education see Samuel N. Harper, *Civil Training in Soviet Russia* (1929), and *Making Bolshevists* (1931).

On religion up to 1942, see N. S. Timasheff, *Religion in Soviet Russia* (1942), and Serge Bolshakoff, *The Christian Church and the Soviet State* (1942). Paul B. Anderson, *People, Church and State in Modern Russia* (1944), is an attempt to understand the situation using the dialectical method of the Communist leaders.

On the position of science under Communism, no adequate work exists. Albert P. Pinkevich, *Science and Education in the USSR* (1935), Joseph Needham and J. S. Davis, *Science in Soviet Russia* (1942), and James Crowther, *Soviet Science* (1942), express the official view. On the development of literature under the Soviets, see Dimitri S. Mirsky, *Contemporary Russian Literature* (1926), Ernest S. Simmons, *An Outline of Modern Russian Literature* (1943), and Gleb B. Struve, *Twenty-Five Years of Soviet Russian Literature* (1944). On art, for the earlier period, René Fülöp-Miller, *The Mind and Face of Bolshevism* (1927), contains all the essentials; for the later period, Kurt London, *The Seven Soviet Arts* (1937), gives abundant information; the author accepts the principle of managed culture, but dislikes the actual choice of trends. On the theater, see Paul A. Markov, *The Soviet Theater* (1934), and Henry W. L. Dana, *Handbook of Soviet Drama* (1938). Chapters on literature, the arts, and music under the Soviets in Paul N. Miliukoff's *Outlines of Russian Culture* (made up to date by Michael Karpovich) must also be consulted.

The population trends in Russia are discussed in Frank W. Notestein and others, *The Future Population of Europe and the Soviet Union* (1944). On the first famine (1921–22), Harold H. Fisher, *Famine in Soviet Russia* (1935), is the standard work. No similar work exists in English on the second famine (1932–33). The most complete account of the present-day class structure of Russia is given by David J. Dallin, *The Real Soviet Russia* (1944). On socialized medicine, Nicholas A. Semashko, *Health Protection in the Soviet Union* (1934), reproduces the official standpoint, while Henry E. Sigerist, *Socialized Medicine in the Soviet Union* (1938), is an attempt at impartial presentation, with due recognition of the pre-Revolutionary background. On the punitive system of the Soviet Union, see Judah Zelich, *Soviet Administration of Criminal Law* (1931), Mary S. Callcott, *Russian Justice* (1935), and Lenka von Koerber, *Soviet Russia Fights Crime* (1934).

On the creation of the Comintern and the internationalist tendency in Soviet foreign policy, the best works available are: Michael T. Florinsky, *World Revolution and the USSR* (1933), Franz Borkenau, *World Communism: A History of the Communist International* (1939), Olga H. Gankin and Harold H. Fisher, *The Bolshevists and the World Revolution* (1940), and Timothy A. Taracouzio, *War and Peace in Soviet Diplomacy* (1940). The fluctuations of Soviet foreign policy are followed by Louis Fisher (editor), *The Soviets in World Affairs* (2 vols., 1930), David J. Dallin, *Soviet Russia's Foreign Policy, 1939–42* (1942), and *Russia in Post-War Europe* (1943). The author exaggerates the persistence of the internationalist tendency in the course of the past few years. A more optimistic view appears in Sir Bernard Pares, *Russia and the Peace* (1944).

The interest in the Russian Army aroused by the Finnish war and especially by Hitler's aggression resulted in the publication of numerous books on the subject. They are: Erich Wollenberg, *The Red Army* (1941), Serge N. Kournakoff, *Russia's Fighting Forces* (1942), Michel Berchin and Eliahu Ben-Horin, *The Red Army* (1942), Nikolaus Basseches, *The Unknown Army* (1943), and D. Fedotoff-White, *The Growth of the Red Army* (1944). The last is a monumental work on the organization of the army and its class and party structure, but does not discuss its spirit.

For an understanding of the interaction between the USSR and the United States, in addition to Pitirim A. Sorokin's *Russia and the United States* (1944), these books are of importance: Eugene Lyons, *The Red Decade* (1941), Meno Lovenstein, *American Opinion of Soviet Russia* (1941), and John L. Childs and others, *America, Russia and the Communist Party in the Post-War World* (1943).

INDEX

I. Persons

Aladov, composer, 273
Alexander I, Emperor, 27, 169, 404
Alexander II, Emperor, 27, 34, 39, 47, 57, 404
Alexander Nevsky, prince, 168, 171, 173, 180, 310, 350
Alexandrov, film producer, 270
Alexei, Metropolitan, then Patriarch, 231, 234-5
Alexeiev, N., professor, 428
Antokolsky, sculptor, 174
Antsiferoff, A., professor, 420
Arkhangelski, member of the Academy of Sciences, 432
Aseff, revolutionist, 423
Asseyev, author, 278

Bagration, prince, general, 170, 175
Bakunin, anarchist, 49
Balzac, author, 280
Bazhenov, architect, 175
Bebel, socialist leader, 422
Bedny, Demyan, poet, 269
Benjamin, Metropolitan, 434
Berdyayev, N., philosopher, 420
Berman, N., author, 432
Best, H., professor, 420
Bezymenski, author, 263, 270
Bienstock, G., author, 428, 438
Blanqui, revolutionist, 49
Block, A., poet, 36
Bogdanoff, painter, 439
Brinton, C., professor, 439
Brutzkus, B., author, 422, 428
Bubnov, people's commissar, 433
Budenny, general, 218, 220, 405
Bukharin, Communist leader, 62-3, 156, 172, 241, 251, 424, 432, 439
Bussygin, worker, 136, 138

Catherine the Great, Empress, 26, 169, 174
Calcott, M., author, 439

Chamberlain, Sir Austin, statesman, 151
Chamberlin, W., author, 426
Chekhov, author, 280-1, 422
Chukovsky, author, 177
Citrine, Sir Walter, labor leader, author, 441
Clausewitz, general, 169

Dallin, D., author, 423, 427, 438
De-Man, socialist leader, 396
Derzhavin, author, 178
Deterding, Sir Henry, industrialist, 157
Dickens, C., author, 278, 323
Dimitrov, Communist leader, 156
Dmitri Donskoy, prince, 168, 175, 180, 232
Dostoevski, author, 424
Dunayevski, composer, 270
Duncan, I., dancer, 289

Ehrenburg, author, 426, 431
Eisenstein, film producer, 430
Engels, F., social philosopher, 25, 49, 51, 245, 250, 256, 258-9, 420
Essenin, poet, 263

Feder, G., Nazi theoretician, 65
Fedotoff-White, author, 423, 440-1
Fenomenov, author, 441
Ferrero, G., author, 442
Fet, poet, 280
Florinsky, M., professor, 422-3

Galpin, C., professor, 420, 428
Gertenson, author, 439
Gillin, J., professor, 439
Ginsberg, M., professor, 437
Glinka, composer, 173, 280
Gogol, author, 277-8, 281
Goichbarg, professor, 247
Goncharov, author, 172

II. Subjects

going to lose her after all – he ran to the north window, and then smiled. For far below, with Grenville frisking round her, was Sienna, parting the ferns and filling up her glass with ice-cold water from the spring. Glancing up, she waved and smiled at him, her orange towel slipping as, very carefully, she carried the glass back into the house.

EPILOGUE

The ancient warder in charge of the Old Masters Gallery at the Abraham Lincoln Museum was taking the weight off his legs during a hot crowded Sunday afternoon. As the sun poured in through the half-open window, a young girl student joined him on the bench and introduced herself.

'My name's Zelda. You are just so lucky to work here and see these pictures every day.'

The ancient warder agreed that he never got tired of them, adding that the gallery had never been so busy before the Raphael *Pandora* arrived.

'It's that little picture over there, Zelda, glows like a jewel even on the darkest day, always got folk round it. There was a big court case over it years ago.'

'Isn't that portrait next to it by Raphael too?' asked Zelda.

'Sure is. That's *Pandora*'s companion picture,' explained the old man enthusiastically. 'Sitter was a feisty young beauty called Caterina, who evidently gave Raphael the run-around. He nicknamed her "The Proud One", but at the big ceremony here when the two pictures were reunited after more than three hundred years, folk swear there were tears in The Proud One's eyes. Probably just a trick of the light.'

'That's really cool,' sighed Zelda.

As she climbed onto the bench to have a better look, a family walked in through a side door and the room fell silent. From the back, the tall guy, who had thick grey hair, looked oldish. He must have brought along his daughter, Zelda decided, and her two teenage kids, a boy and a girl.

But as he glanced round, waving and smiling at the warder, Zelda said 'Wow!' because he had such an extraordinarily alive, young face and was probably only in his late forties. The family all looked so excited and because of their beauty – like visiting angels – the crowd round the Raphael dispersed to let them through. The grey-haired guy had his arm round the woman as they both pointed out aspects of the picture to the kids.

'They come here two or three times a year,' said the old warder, offering Zelda a toffee. 'Seem such a happy family, and they're always so pleased to see the picture.'

'She looks kinda familiar,' said Zelda.

'Sure – she's Sienna Belvedon.'

'Oh wow! Isn't she British? I've heard of her.'

'Should have done,' reproved the old warder. 'Stirred up enough controversy around the Millennium. Churchmen and public figures in an uproar over some picture she painted, all threatening to withdraw public money in the UK.'

'I've heard of that picture.' Zelda wrinkled her freckled forehead. 'Wasn't it called *Visitor's List*?'

'That's the one. Made a helluva difference,' conceded the old warder. 'Drew attention to terrible things we once did to animals. What upset folk most was to have all the poor critters arriving in heaven and being welcomed by God portrayed as a big yellow dog. But the fuss died down. Now it's regarded as one of the finest pictures of the twenty-first century. Always thought Visitor was a funny name for a dog.'

A furry tail ending.

THE END

ACKNOWLEDGEMENTS

Life may be brief, but art, and consequently *Pandora*, my novel about the art world, is long. Which means a huge number of people to thank.

Nobody, for a start, could have been more helpful than Sotheby's and I'm particularly grateful to Diana Keith-Neal, a senior director, for introducing me not only to the Chairman, Henry Wyndham, but also to Richard Charlton-Jones, Lucian Simmons, Natacha Chiaramonte, Patti Wong, Chris Proudlove and Tatiana von Waldersee. All experts in their fields, they were unstinting with both their time and their advice.

I had fantastic help from many art dealers, who allowed me to infiltrate their private views, took me to auctions, showed me marvellous pictures and beguiled me with outrageous anecdotes. They include Johnny and Sarah Van Haeften and their assistant Camilla Clayton, Tim Bathurst, Christopher Burness, Francis Kyle, Jay Jopling, William Darby, Peyton Skipwith, Edward Horswell, James Colman and Maurice Howard.

Excellent technical advice or more outrageous tales were supplied by ace picture framer Mark Wallington; by Rungwe Kingdon and Claude Koenig, whose Pangolin Gallery and Foundry is one of the splendours of Gloucestershire; and on the insurance front by Aaron

Shapiro, Michael St Aubyn, William Marler and Andrew Colvin.

There are many sculptors and painters in *Pandora*, so I am deeply indebted to my dear neighbour Anthony Abrahams, and other fine artists including David Backhouse, Daniel Chadwick, Paul Day, Paul Grellier, Christopher Dean, Hamish Mackay, Caroline Wallace, Tory Lawrence, Charlotte Bathurst, Anna Gibbs-Kennet, Michael and Sybil Edwards and the mighty Maggie Hambling for either allowing me to invade their studios or sharing their secrets with me.

During my research, my portrait was painted for Yorkshire Television by Alan Hydes and my head sculpted by Frances Segelman. Both artists gave me invaluable insight into the creative process as well as an end product of great beauty.

In earlier books I have been accused of making my young heroines too attractive, but anyone meeting Emma Sergeant, Tanya Brett or Georgie Taylor, all three of whom helped me hugely, will vouch that where the art world is concerned I have not exaggerated.

Most of all I must thank artist extraordinaire, Sargi Mann, who heroically continues to paint despite failing sight. His extraordinarily beautiful oil of a pale blue canal idling through golden autumn fields, which hangs in our bedroom, constantly revealing fresh enchantments when viewed from different angles and at different times of the day, was the initial inspiration for *Pandora*.

I never fail to be touched and astonished by the magnanimity of intellectuals prepared to enter into the fun and adventure of producing popular fiction. The Pandora of the title is an invented picture by Raphael of the opening of Pandora's Box. In her creation and historical background I was enormously privileged to be given advice by Dr Nicholas Penny, Keeper of the National Gallery and one of the greatest experts on Raphael in the world. David Jenkins, a brilliant classics master at Monmouth, threw light on the myths of Pandora and the Seven Deadly Sins. Peter Clarkson, Associate Lecturer in Art History at the Open University, specializing in the Renaissance, lent me endless arcane art books and allowed me to pester him with questions. Denis Napier corrected my Latin. Caterina Krucker, Lecturer in Modern Languages, brushed up my French and Italian.

On the art establishment side, I am grateful to Robert and Kate Gavron, John Cooper, ex-Head of Education at the National Portrait Gallery, Maggie Guillebaud, formerly of the Arts Council, Christopher and Angela Dowling of the Imperial War Museum, and Francis Corner of Cheltenham and Gloucester College of Higher Education.

As *Pandora* is also a novel about art that belonged to the Jews being looted by the Nazis, I was unbelievably lucky just before I started writing to lunch with the mercurial, perennially innovative Tom Rosenthal, who was not only illuminating on the contemporary art scene but also dreamed up the way in which my picture could be looted. For further illumination I must thank Karen Pollock and Rosie Barton of the Holocaust Trust; Constance Lowenthal, Commission for Art Recovery, New York, and Eva Kurz, a solicitor specializing in looted art.

I am especially indebted to Ruth Redmond Cooper, Director of the Institute of Art and Law, and her team. On my way to their conference on Art, Law and the Holocaust at the Courtauld Institute in October 1999, I was involved in the Paddington train crash. Arriving at the conference, I couldn't have been treated with more kindness and sympathy; and as the speakers in turn described how the Nazis had tried to eradicate not only a people but their art and culture as well, they put any horrors I had experienced earlier in the day into perspective.

I am extremely grateful too to British Transport

Police for later retrieving early chapters of *Pandora* from the wreckage of the train.

The law surrounding the restitution of looted art is extremely complex, often involving the legal systems of several countries. I would never have been able to tackle a big court case had it not been for the advice of my dear friends, the Right Hon. Dame Elizabeth Butler-Sloss, President of the Family Division, and the Right Hon. the Lord Hoffman, Lord of Appeal in Ordinary, who also lent me a brilliant and famous judgement on a looted art case by the Hon. Mr Justice Moses, presiding judge at the Royal Courts of Justice. Lawyers John Davies, Elizabeth Jupp, Hetty Cleave, Martyn Daldorph, Graham Ogilvy, Gillian Geddes and Michael Flint also helped me.

In my travels, I was incredibly lucky to meet Jamie Tabor, QC, who, while wrestling with a long and gruelling case in Norwich, nobly spent his evenings reading my court case chapters for howlers. But as in every aspect of *Pandora*, I took his, or anyone else's, specialist advice only in so far as it suited my plot. Any mistakes are mine and in no way reflect on their expertise.

I am also indebted to Stephen Burrows, Chief Security Officer at the Royal Courts of Justice, to Emma Macdonald, Bob Parry and the staff at the County and Crown Courts at Gloucester, and to Gil Martin, ex-Gloucestershire CID, for his encyclopedic knowledge of matters criminal.

Writers need geographical locations on which to anchor their stories. Since moving to Gloucestershire, I have been haunted and captivated by two beautiful, historic and adjoining houses flanking our local church. On them I have based Foxes Court and the Old Rectory in *Pandora*. I should therefore like to thank Simon and Mindy Reading and John and Elizabeth Cowan for allowing me to range freely round their glorious gardens, but would emphasize that they and their sweet families bear absolutely no resemblance to the Belvedons and the Pulboroughs in my story.

I must equally thank our former High Sheriff of Gloucestershire, Major John Eyre, for explaining the duties of and historical background to the appointment, but would again stress that as a man of great charm and integrity he bears no resemblance to my frightful High Sheriff in *Pandora*.

Everyone, in fact, in *Pandora*, unless they are so eminent, like Joanna Lumley or Sotheby's Chairman Henry Wyndham, as to appear as themselves, is made up and in no way based on any living person.

My characters sometimes fall ill and make miraculous recoveries. It was invaluable to be able to seek medical information from Joe Cobbe, Sarah Morris, Pat Pearson, Graham Hall, Tim Crouch and Martin Joyce.

On a Ritzy front, interior designer Nina Campbell dreamed up a beautiful bedroom for my heroine's glamorous mother, while Lindka Cierach, Mariska Kay and David Shilling were a constant inspiration for lovely clothes and hats. Aspreys, Tiffany's, Alfred Dunhill and Robert Young the florists in Stroud were also a great help, and I must especially thank Denise Dean and David Risley of Zwemmers and Stephen Simpson of Hatchards for so tenaciously tracking down books I needed.

Writers do not always expect kindness from their own profession. Few, however, could have been more welcoming and helpful than Lesley Garner, Nigel Reynolds, Will Bennett, David Lee, Bevis Hillier, Lucinda Bredin, Peter Harclerode, Matthew Collings, the sublime Brian Sewell, Esther Oxford, John Hawkins of Gloucestershire News Service, Robert Pearson of UK Law News, Peter Davies, Philip Jones and Maria Prendergast. I am also grateful that the *Art Newspaper*, *Art Review* and the *Jackdaw* kept me up to date with events.

I should like to thank Chris Wood of Decca Records for permission to quote five lines from his translation of

Richard Strauss's *Arabella*, and also William Mann for permission to quote four lines of Hermann Hesse's poem 'Going to Sleep', which form part of the lyrics for Richard Strauss's *Four Last Songs*.

The press offices at Middlesex County Cricket Club, the British Show Jumping Association, the All-England Tennis Club, Wimbledon, Conservative Central Office, the Lord Chancellor's Office, and the staff at the Public Records Office at the Angel, Islington, were wonderful, always stopping whatever they were doing to provide crucial helpful information.

Another theme in *Pandora* is an adopted child's quest for her natural parents. I am eternally grateful to Marjorie Dent, who formerly ran the Phyllis Holman Richards Adoption Society, for her wisdom and constant support; to social workers Clodagh Howe, Sue Jacobs and June Sellars, and to Felicity Collier, Chief Executive of the British Agencies for Adoption and Fostering, for their advice and ideas and for providing helpful literature on the subject.

I am also much beholden to the authors of the following books, which provided illumination or factual background on looted art, the art world and adoption. They include *The Lost Masters* by Peter Harclerode and Brendan Pittaway, *The Faustian Bargain* by Jonathan Petropoulis, *Portrait of Doctor Gachet* by Cynthia Saltzman, *Raphael* by Roger Jones and Nicholas Penny, *Blimey* by Matthew Collings, *Boogey Woogey* by Danny Moynihan, *Duchess of Cork Street* by Lillian Browse, *Sotheby's* by Robert Lacey, *Groovey Bob* by Harriet Vyner, *The Sorcerer's Apprentice* by John Richardson, *Birth Records Counselling* by Pam Hodgkins, *Adopters on Adoption* by David Howe and *Ithaka* by Sarah Saffian.

My friends as usual came up with endless ideas. They include Dominique Bagley, Pussy Baird-Murray, Francis Burne, Ailsa Chapman, Sarah Collett, Mike Coppen-Gardner, Fran Cook, my stepdaughter Laura Cooper, Michael Cordy, Susan Daniel, Pam Dhenin, John

Ferguson, Dorry Friesen, Glyn and Vanessa Hendy, Bill Holland, Ute Howard, Tidl Jefferies, James Johnstone, David Laurie, Bruce and Janetta Lee, Ava Myers, John Parry, Patrick Scrivenor and Heather Ross.

On my way home from the courts a couple of years ago I met a delightful and elated woman who told me about her daughter's boyfriend who had longed to be married before he was forty and how the relevant families effected this. Leaping out at Stroud, I asked her if I could use the story in *Pandora* but failed to catch her name. Wherever she is now, I would like to thank her, and anyone else I may have forgotten.

Transworld, my publishers, have all been marvellous in every way, but I would particularly like to thank Mark Barty-King, their Chairman, to whom *Pandora* is dedicated, and my editor Linda Evans, who is simply a darling, who has constantly supplied me with comfort, joy, support and good advice. Richenda Todd has also been a terrific copy editor. Henry Steadman designed the wonderful hardback jacket, on the front of which is a beautiful painting of the myth of Pandora by Chris Brown. Henry has also designed the equally wonderful new cover for this edition. Neil Gower also drew a beautiful map.

I am extremely grateful to Steve Rubin, president and publisher of Doubleday, Broadway Publishing Group, and Jane Gelfman my agent in New York, for so kindly reading the chapters set in America.

I cannot thank my agent in London Vivienne Schuster enough for her kindness, enthusiasm and sympathetic encouragement in the many dark days when I thought *Pandora* would never be finished. Her colleagues at Curtis Brown, Paul Scherer and Jonathan Lloyd, and Euan Thorneycroft, her trusty lieutenant, were also always there when I needed them.

On the home front I am singularly blessed. My PA Pippa Birch is owed a huge debt of gratitude for typing the lion's share of the synopsis and the penultimate draft, and for checking and seeking out endless facts and figures. Pippa came up with many ideas, as did Annette Xuereb-Brennan, Mandy Williams and Caterina Krucker, who heroically typed the rest of the manuscript and refused to go crackers over the endless corrections. To them all I am truly obligated – and also to dear Ann Mills, our housekeeper, for her sweetness and patience in keeping us all sane and comparatively tidy. Phil Bradley, of Cornerstones, drove me to endless places while I was writing the book and always got me there on time.

Most of all I want to thank my darling family, for putting up with shameless neglect for months on end. My husband Leo, who was encyclopedic on military matters, our son Felix and his wife Edwina, our daughter Emily, Bessie the Labrador, Hero the lurcher and our four cats, all provided their essential mix of good copy and endless cheer.

WICKED!
by Jilly Cooper

'Wicked pleasures'
Observer

Two schools: **Bagley Hall**, wild, ultra-smart independent, crammed
with the children of the famous, and **Larkminster Comprehensive**,
demoralised, cash-strapped and fast sinking.

Janna Curtis, the young, feisty and highly attractive new head,
drafted in to save the failing Larkminster comp, faces a daunting
task. Her pupils are out of control, her teachers bolshy, and
Larks's prime site has made it the target for greedy developers.
She detests private education, but to rescue Larks she will go to
any lengths – even forming a partnership with Bagley Hall and its
arrogant but utterly gorgeous headmaster, Hengist Brett-Taylor.

Hengist, in turn, knows that sharing his school's magnificent
facilities with Larkminster Comp will not only bring him vast tax
concessions, it will also ensure frequent meetings with the
tempestuous but captivating Janna. Teachers and parents are
horrified by such a bonding, but for the pupils, the scheme
provides joyous opportunity for scandalous behaviour.

Will our heroine emerge with her heart and her school intact?

'Can there be any other beach book this summer?'
Tatler

'I devoured it with as much joy as I would a bucket of pistachio
ice cream. It's vintage stuff'
Tanya Gold, *Daily Mail*

9780552151566

CORGI BOOKS